The Fall of the 1977 Phillies

The past is never dead. It's not even past.
— William Faulkner

Half this game is ninety percent mental.
— Philadelphia Phillies manager Danny Ozark

The Fall of the 1977 Phillies

*How a Baseball Team's Collapse
Sank a City's Spirit*

MITCHELL NATHANSON

McFarland & Company, Inc., Publishers
Jefferson, North Carolina, and London

Library of Congress Cataloguing-in-Publication Data

Nathanson, Mitchell, 1966–
    The fall of the 1977 Phillies : how a baseball team's collapse sank
a city's spirit / Mitchell Nathanson.
        p.   cm.
    Includes bibliographical references and index.

    ISBN-13: 978-0-7864-3217-2
    softcover : 50# alkaline paper

    1. Philadelphia Phillies (Baseball team)— History.   I. Title.
GV875.P45N38   2008
796.357'640974811— dc22   2007043491

British Library cataloguing data are available

On the cover: (inset) Manager Danny Ozark, Garry Maddox and Larry
Bowa in the rain during game four of the 1977 NLCS (Temple University Library); background ©2007 Shutterstock

Manufactured in the United States of America

McFarland & Company, Inc., Publishers
    Box 611, Jefferson, North Carolina 28640
    www.mcfarlandpub.com

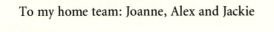
To my home team: Joanne, Alex and Jackie

Table of Contents

Prologue   1

1. The Fall of Philadelphia   7
2. Professional Baseball in the Quaker City   25
3. Baseball's Pre-Expansion Power Structure: New York's
   Boon, Philadelphia's Doom   52
4. The Fall of the A's, the Rise of the Phillies   74
5. The Phillies and Philadelphia: Into the Abyss   104
6. The Structural Renaissance of a City and Its Team   128
7. Social Rebirth on the Streets and on the Field   154
8. Breaking from the Past   171
9. History's Ultimate Triumph   190
10. Results, Repercussions and Reassessments   209

Chapter Notes   237
Bibliography   257
Index   261

Prologue

From the start, Wednesday October 22, 1980, promised to be the sort of day that makes liars out of everybody. Bright and crisp yet still with the warm sweater of summer hovering in the air, it beckoned people out of their cubicles, away from their desks, cajoling them to think up something quick as an excuse. Even those with no routine to break would consider their lot more fortunate than common sense would otherwise dictate after inhaling the brilliant morning air. For the hundreds of thousands of people who lined Broad Street and filled creaky JFK stadium that morning, the feeling was only amplified. Only hours earlier, Tug McGraw threw a pitch, Kansas City's Willie Wilson missed it and a 97-year-old black cloud lifted over the sorriest franchise in American professional sports history. Standing there, jammed together, the congregants basked in the incandescence that engulfed them after decades of nothing but darkness. At last, they were now converted. They were finally believers.

Such transformations oftentimes come at a cost, however, as perspective becomes skewed through the kaleidoscope of the conversion, truth fades and is eventually replaced by gilt-edged, sepia-colored memories. Such was the case with the masses gathered in South Philly the day of the historic victory parade, along with the multitudes who were there in spirit across the region. For on that day, there wasn't anybody south of New York or north of Baltimore who wasn't living and dying with the Phillies through each gut-wrenching moment of the glorious 1980 championship season. From that day forward, the Vet was filled to the last yellow seat all through the season with loyal and supportive fans—from opening day through the last home game of the year and especially for the dramatic, unbelievable, 15-inning season-saving come-from-behind win against the Chicago Cubs only a few weeks earlier. Everyone was there. And everyone was with them. Every step of the way. "We Win!" proclaimed the *Daily News* headline trumpeting the Phillies' inaugural World Series championship, the paper held high by McGraw that morning to a thunderous ovation.[1] We win. All of us. Together. That's what it said and on this morning, nobody was going to question its veracity.

In truth, there was nothing communal about it. In truth, the Phils played many of the key games down the stretch of that taut 1980 season before brutally hostile fans. In truth, many of the fans present for that 15-inning game on September 29th viciously booed the home team even though it was a mere half game out of first with just a week remaining in the season.[2] In truth, this game was similar to the one the day before — the one against the Montreal Expos, the team the Phils had been battling for the NL East lead. That game was repeatedly interrupted by angry partisans showing their support for the Phils by tossing so many paper airplanes on the field that it took six grounds crewmen just to clean up the resurgent mess following each inning.[3] In truth, the Phillies faced two different types of opponents throughout the 1980 season: the players in the other dugout and the fans in their own home stands.

The divisional crown provided not a hint of détente between the team and its city. During the postseason, the Vet was filled with enmity, replete with fans salivating for an opportunity to vent their rage. In the midst of the pomp and merriment that typically accompanies the pregame festivities before the start of a League Championship Series, boos thundered down on four of the nine announced Phillies starters.[4] Victory over the Houston Astros in a playoff series many still believe to be the single most exciting postseason series of professional baseball ever played quelled this rage only to a degree. Game one of the World Series contained its share of boos directed toward the first Phillies team to deliver a pennant to Philadelphia in 30 years.[5]

More than a quarter century after that championship season, after the darkness quickly returned, dissipating only briefly in the mirages of aberrant pennants won in 1983 and '93, the wistfulness for a return to the communal joys experienced throughout the 1980 season has only intensified. To spend another summer so engaged with the daily machinations of the Phillies, many believe, would be truly exhilarating. However, while many Philadelphians may remember the details of those thrilling games, the warm feelings of attachment they so long for stem not from that season but, rather, from the parade the day after. Truth fades. Sepia-colored memories take its place.

Rather, the 1980 season, from its fitful start to its glorious end, was a surprisingly typical one in the team's historical relationship with its fans. Only the parade was out of the ordinary. Philadelphians, as they had done for decades, expressed their hostility toward the Phillies loudly and demonstrably all season long. Although Philadelphia fans have been known to boo all of their professional sports teams, few would deny that there's usually more than a little extra gusto reserved for the Phillies. The Eagles, Sixers and Flyers may hear it from the rafters when they're not playing well but only the Phils will hear it when they are. The 1980 pennant race was merely another chapter in the uniquely uneasy relationship between the city of Philadelphia and the Phillies. Although the Phils were consistent winners for the first time in their forgettable history, loaded with All Stars and two future Hall of Famers; although they spent their money as freely as the Yankees, snaring, in Pete Rose, the most coveted free agent ever up to that point; and although they played in a stadium that was considered state of the art (criticism of it would not come until many years later), a fan transported from 1959 or '69 would be eminently familiar with the friction rising from the stands. Save for the earthtone plastic seats, it was as if nothing had changed. Six consecutive winning seasons had had little effect.

A little more than a month after the season, Mike Schmidt, the Hall of Fame third baseman who was just named league MVP, reflected on the unique relationship between the Phillies and the city of Philadelphia. Although his comments centered on the media, they would apply just as accurately to the fans themselves:

> I think the writers that cover the Eagles probably as a whole want to see the Eagles succeed more than anything in the world. I'm not so sure that's true with ... the Phillies. I may be wrong, but my opinion is (that) not everyone is totally, 100 percent happy for the guys on the Phillies.... I think in the end, some writers were hurt that they had to put "world champions" behind the Phillies name. It would have been a much more Philadelphia-type story had we lost.[6]

Despite the drama of the season, despite the glorious seasons of Schmidt, McGraw and Cy Young award-winner Steve Carlton, and despite the first world championship in the history of the franchise, resentment remained. Schmidt's frustration with the writers—the conduit to the city of Philadelphia and the face of the pulse of the city—highlighted a dark yet unmistakable reality: the city of Philadelphia is a baseball town that passionately hates its baseball team. To dismiss Schmidt's comments as nothing more than a recognition that a century-old baseball town had morphed into a football town would be to ignore the obvious and unrelenting passion, negative as it is, that has been directed toward the Phillies from the days of the Whiz Kids of the 1950s to the present. No, the city of Philadelphia cares about its Phillies. That much is obvious. Exactly why it hates them so vehemently is much less so.

The story of the relationship between the Phillies and the city of Philadelphia is ultimately one of an unhealthy marriage. Born out of contempt, in 1954, after a seven-decade engagement that inflamed passions on neither side, and consummated only because the city's true love, Connie Mack's mythical and magisterial Athletics, were whisked away that year to serve the greater interests of the New York baseball establishment, the wedding of the Phillies to the city has, more often than not, only served to confirm the inferiority complex Philadelphians have historically maintained with regard to their neighbor to the north. Due to the circumstances surrounding the departure of the Athletics as well as the Phillies' perennially blundering teams, the Phils have become to many Philadelphians a symbol of all the many ways their city comes up short and the embodiment of the perceived second-class status of Philadelphia, the eternally poor relation to New York City. As the face of a city's discontent, the Phillies have suffered continual abuse for a half century and counting.

This book provides a social history of Philadelphia through the lens of its professional baseball teams. It examines the roots of the city's inferiority complex and how, over time, it manifested itself in the negativism that has so characterized the city for decades— a negativism that eventually found in the Phillies a perpetual whipping boy. It likewise charts the rise and fall of the Athletics and shows how the seeds of their demise were planted very early on in their existence. As such, when the early 1950s saw a remarkable confluence of events surrounding the Athletics, the Phillies, Major League Baseball, and the U.S. Congress, it was the Athletics, and not the largely ignored Phillies, who packed up and left town. Because of this cruel hand of fate, only Philadelphia — unlike its sister cities Boston and St. Louis, which were likewise stripped during that time of the status that went with being two-team cities— suffered the additional indignity of seeing the wrong team leave town.

However, the social forces that undermined the relationship between the city and the Phillies ironically worked to repair the rift along with the city's image of itself, so that, for a brief time during the 1970s, the city shed its inferiority complex and truly embraced the Phillies— who now became the face of a city reborn —for the first time. The chapters that follow examine the effect of urban renewal during the 1950s and '60s on the city and how, surprisingly, Philadelphia was seen as one of the few success stories amid the failure of urban renewal in virtually every other major American city, most notably New York. By the early 1970s, urban renewal had sparked in Philadelphia a cultural, social and gastronomical renaissance that, particularly when compared with the troubles then ensnaring the city of New York, made Philadelphians feel good about themselves on a national level. The Phillies, through a change of management, relocation to Veterans Stadium, and an influx of infectious new talent, caught this wave and put a red pinstriped face on this new feeling of optimism. It would be the first and, to date, the last time the Phillies would be so embraced in their history.

The good feelings swelled during the 1970s and reached their peak during the summer of 1977, when Philadelphia thrived while New York teetered, occasionally in the dark, on the brink of bankruptcy. On the field, the Phillies— division winners in 1976 — put together what many believe to be the best team in their history, 1980 included. The team excelled not merely in pitching, hitting and defense; it boasted perhaps one of the deepest benches and bullpens in the history of baseball. The team not only won 101 games but brushed off the demons of past Phillies teams, having survived a near catastrophic collapse that recalled the horrors of 1964, and the tempestuous return and ultimate departure of Dick Allen in 1976.

By the start of the 1977 League Championship Series against the Los Angeles Dodgers, it seemed clear to everyone that this Phillies team, much like the city of Philadelphia, bore no resemblance to its inglorious, hard-luck past. Rather, a new era was in bloom, one in which Philadelphia took a back seat to no one. The past was past; the Phillies, along with their city, were looking forward to a glorious future. After splitting the first two games of the five-game series in Los Angeles, there was no reason to question this optimistic view. The Phils were coming home for the final three games, their fans were demonstrably raucous but wholeheartedly behind them (in ways that would become apparent to the nation very soon), the demons had been exorcised. Black Friday (as game three of the 1977 League Championship Series came to be known in Philadelphia) would change everything.

The events that unfolded during the afternoon of Friday, October 7th, 1977, would forever change how Philadelphians viewed the Phillies, recast old events in a harsher, more critical light, and lead to a collective change of mind-set, which would result in the end of Philadelphia's urban renaissance of the 1970s. After Black Friday, Philadelphians would question whether things really were as different with their team and, ultimately, their city, as they had been led to believe. By game's end, it would become clear that these Phillies had much in common with the bumbling teams that came before them and, by opening day of 1978, the team would once again become the image of a city whose identity was less than favorable. In the succeeding months, events would unfold in the city that would demonstrate that, in fact, Philadelphia had not, as many assumed, escaped the racial and economic problems suffered by New York and other large northeastern cities. Rather, it had at most done a better job of hiding them through the redevelopment policies of Ed Bacon and his Philadelphia Planning Commission and the bluster of Mayor Frank Rizzo. As the 1970s came to an end and the social and economic woes of the city crept back to the forefront, it was plain that the new Philadelphia wasn't much different from the old one. Very quickly, the old insecurities and inferiority complex returned. And very quickly, the Phillies returned to their familiar role as the face of all these.

In the pages that follow, Black Friday, the histories of both the A's and the Phillies, and the roots, rise and fall of Philadelphia's urban renaissance unfold together as the connection between the city's perception of itself and its relationship with its professional baseball teams are shown to be inexorably intertwined. Because this is a book that examines the divergence of feelings from fact, events are organized in an effort to re-create the mood of the time. Although the reader has the benefit of hindsight and is witness to the triumph of reality over perception, those living in the moment oftentimes do not have readily available to them as many tools, or, if they do, may be less willing to make use of them out of fear of what they may reveal, subject as they are to the consequences of such knowledge. As the pages, chapters and years turn, however, truth inevitably redefines itself, casting new light on old events and ideas, exposing folly for what it is and inevitably repainting the landscape in retrospect. Today we see only that which has been retouched through time; this book utilizes the tools of history, sociology, psychology and linguistics in an attempt to scrape away this layer, to unearth an earlier era to reveal its original hue.

Through this process, it becomes clear that the city of Philadelphia has seen its reflection in the Phillies more than in any other team or institution, finding in them support — or blame — for its opinion of itself. That it is the Phillies and not the NFL's Eagles who have been the public face of Philadelphia ever since the Athletics left town in 1954 says much about the city itself. It says foremost that, despite chatter to the contrary, Philadelphia always has been and always will be a baseball town first. It says that, with the notable exception of the mid–1970s, given the hostility reserved for the Phils even during their brief good times, the circumstances surrounding the departure of the Athletics have left significant and telling scars on the city that remain to this day. And it says that, while Philadelphians may love the Eagles, they identify with the Phillies.

This, then, is the story of one city's identity.

1

The Fall of Philadelphia

The anticipation at Lou's Crab Pad was palpable. The tiny waterfront shack on the corner of Delaware and Washington avenues thrummed with energy, offering customers lobster, shrimp and Phillies fever, all at affordable prices. "We've got it this year! We've got it in four," the proprietor's father bellowed to anyone happening by, regardless of whether they were in the mood for lobster or shrimp.[7] For today, an oversized helping of Phillies fever was on the house and samples were being passed around for all to try. Judging by the responses, most found at least the fever to be to their liking.

At the time, Lou wasn't around so his father Tony had free rein. He literally beamed as he stood before his son's shop, plastered as it was with red and white slogans and placards urging the Phils onward, toward their destiny. As the 1977 regular season wound down and the Phils had once again secured the National League East title, there were many in the region who had signed on, who had decided to join the ride before it was too late. Tony, however, was different. He had been on board all along: for all of the years of hopelessness, for all of the years of vanished expectations, for 1964 for crying out loud. And he knew that 1977 was unlike all of the others. That 1977 was theirs. All that remained was for it to play itself out.

The next day would be particularly special, not merely because it was a Friday portending brisk business but because it was a coronation of sorts. The Phillies were returning from Los Angeles, where, in Tony's deep-set, knowing eyes, they had done what no Phillies team before them had done: put their foot on an opponent's neck with such force that, although they might be breathing, there was no real hope of recovery. True, the Phils left LA technically tied with the Dodgers at one game apiece in their five-game National League Championship Series, but to anyone who took the time to watch the games—*really* watch the games—the outcome had already been decided. Friday's third game would see Philadelphia cut off LA's wind just a little bit more.

Game one of the series played out exactly according to script, with just one minor improvisation that, in the end, only ingrained the belief more deeply that the Dodgers had absolutely no chance. For starters, the Phils had their ace on the hill, Steve Carlton, whereas the best LA could counter with was Tommy John — a solid starter, in fact a 20-game winner that year, but suspect nonetheless given his recently bionicized arm. All year, everybody had been waiting for him finally to give in to reality and break down and all year he hadn't. But this was the playoffs, he'd already pitched an excess of innings (220 in 1977 and 427 in the two years since his return from an elbow reconstruction so radical that no one, not even his doctors, knew what to expect from one day to the next) and was due for a setback. Very quickly, it became apparent that it was going to occur that night. Left fielder Greg Luzinski torched him for a two-run blast in the first, super-sub Davey Johnson knocked in two more in the fifth and John was gone. Meanwhile, Carlton was cruising, as he had all through the season (he'd won 23 games and would pick up his second Cy Young Award a month later). Given these circumstances, the Philadelphia faithful were able to relax as destiny marched relentlessly on.

In the seventh, however, the Dodgers loaded the bases and then Carlton veered off script, serving up a mistake to Dodgers third baseman Ron Cey. Cey pounced on his good fortune with alarming ferocity. His shot was a screamer, hurtling toward the pavilion in left as if on a mission, and one certainly had to give Cey credit. But that, by itself, could not have changed things in Tony's mind even though his grand slam had tied things up at five, for if anything, the inning only confirmed that the only team capable of beating the Phillies was the Phillies themselves. Carlton, pitching perhaps with less focus given his 5–1 lead, lost his edge. He walked pinch hitter Jerry Grote, gave up a single to Davey Lopes and then walked Reggie Smith to load the bases. So when Cey hit his homer, it was an impressive blast but one that would have meant nothing had not Carlton allowed the Dodgers back into the game. What was more, by this point, the Phils were already deep into the Dodgers' bullpen — it would not take much to get those runs back.

To be sure, after Carlton was relieved after giving up a single to Steve Garvey, the Dodgers were into the Phillies bullpen as well. But here things differed from what they had ever been in Philadelphia before. For here, the Phillies were deep — historically deep. Gene Garber, Tug McGraw, Warren Brusstar and Ron Reed — all with earned run averages of 2.75 or better (compiled while pitching a wearying 378 innings in all), all who would have been considered "closers" by later day standards, all who had pitched out of countless jams all season — were available for the Phils. This year, unlike in years past (such as in 1964, for example, when, in the course of losing 10 straight in the midst of perhaps the most infamous September collapse of all time, the Phils surrendered a lead in the sixth inning or later a heartbreaking four times), there would be no late inning collapses. That was all in the past. And the past, as people who watched these Phillies would say, the people *who knew*, was history.

The Dodgers, on the other hand, had Charlie Hough, a knuckleballer who was prone to squirting one through his catcher's legs at the most inopportune time, and journeyman Elias Sosa, working on his fourth team in the last four years. So when Sosa gave the game away in the ninth by allowing consecutive singles to Bake McBride, Larry Bowa and Mike Schmidt, giving the Phils the lead once again, and then balked in an insurance run for good measure, it was not at all unexpected. After McGraw set LA down in the ninth to preserve the Phils' 7–5 victory, the faithful were happy although not relieved. To be relieved would be to acknowledge some reservation over the outcome. Here, however, the series was a mismatch. Throughout game one, the Dodgers had done nothing other than confirm that suspicion.

Perhaps in retrospect, game two should have shaken the city's collective confidence, but at the time few thought much of it. It was a 7–1 Dodger blowout — punctuated by yet another grand slam, this one by left fielder Dusty Baker. But there was really nothing to get all worked up about — no reason to recall the horrors of 1964 or anything else that had gone on in years past because it was just one game. And it was of no matter. The Phils did what they needed to do, split in LA, and now they were coming home to the Vet, where they'd played .750 ball all season. What's more, center fielder Garry Maddox, who'd missed the first two games with a knee injury, pronounced himself fit to play on Friday, which meant that McBride could move back to his natural position in right. With Hebner returning to first and Davey Johnson returning to the bench, that would mean that the Phils would be at full strength for the first time in the playoffs. Given all this, two out of three at the Vet seemed only slightly less certain than Friday itself.

For game three, the Phils were sending 23-year-old Larry Christenson to the mound, a tall, powerful righthander who was coming off a 19-win season. The Dodgers would counter with Burt Hooton, a dour-looking man who went by the ironic nickname "Happy."[8] Until recently, he had owned the Phils, beating them in seven straight starts over a two-year period until Philadelphia finally broke the streak in late July 1976. In 1972, while with the Cubs, he even no-hit them. Over the past season, however, the tide had turned and the Phils finally had some success against him. More important, at least in the eyes of many of the Phillies' faithful, Hooton's success against them had clearly waned as the Phils steadily improved through the mid–1970s. In 1972, he no-hit what was, except for the days in which Carlton was pitching, one of the worst teams in baseball history — a team that won only 32 games all season (for a wretched .269 winning percentage) on the days between Carlton's starts. Back in 1974 and '75, during the height of his more recent dominance over the Phils, he was beating an improved but middling team at best. Once the team became a powerhouse in '76, however, his dominance disappeared. As such, the best that could be said about him was that he was adept at beating a team he should have beaten. Ever since he started facing a Phillies team that was better than he was, he had pitched accordingly. With that in mind, many Philadelphians found yet another reason to throw the past out the window.[9]

Black Friday: First Inning

Divine providence, through the vessel of the commissioner's Office of Major League Baseball, smiled down on the Quaker City this day through its designated 3:15 P.M. start time. The more glamorous American League playoff series featuring Reggie Jackson, Billy Martin, Catfish Hunter and the New York Yankees (against the Kansas City Royals, as if that even mattered) was chosen to be the prime time game, thereby sparing those in attendance at the Vet the sharp chilling winds and steady rain making their way up the Atlantic coast. Instead, game three would see brisk, cloudy, but comfortable conditions. And if it was being played largely in national anonymity, this would not be the case forever. Soon the World Series would start, forcing the entire country to sit back and take notice of the transformation of what was once the sorriest franchise in American team sports—a team that had lost more games than any other in any major professional league. But that was an issue for another day. First, the formalities had to be completed and these were finally at hand. The mammoth auxiliary scoreboard in right center announced the lineups in twinkling yellow with black relief: Davey Lopes, Bill Russell, Reggie Smith, Ron Cey, Steve Garvey, Dusty Baker, Rick Monday, Steve Yeager and Burt Hooton for LA; Bake McBride, Larry Bowa, Mike Schmidt, Greg Luzinski, Richie Hebner, Garry Maddox, Bob Boone, Ted Sizemore and Larry Christenson for the Phillies. Soon, the stands were filled beyond capacity: 63,719 in a stadium officially listed as holding only 58,651, the players were neatly in order along the first and third base lines, the city was present and accounted for. All that remained was for the game to be played.

A few moments later, things got underway. Lopes dug in and, almost as quickly, popped out to Maddox. Watching Maddox close in gracefully, swiftly, until he practically had to wait for a ball that otherwise might have found the gap between the second baseman and center fielder engendered an immediate sense of calm, as perhaps those in attendance realized in that one, simple act, just how much peril the Phils had been in back in LA, when McBride was filling in for him. Not that McBride was a bad fielder, he just wasn't Maddox. As the saying went: two-thirds of the earth's surface was covered by water, the rest by Maddox. With leaden Greg Luzinski in left and an often confused Jay Johnstone occasionally in right, that was a requirement for any Phillie center fielder. Shortstop Russell was up next and he was just as easily retired: two pitches and then a soft liner to Sizemore. Reggie Smith, the right fielder, was next and he too went down without much of a fight. He was often overlooked in the Dodger lineup, relegated to the background behind the marquee of Cey, Garvey and Baker, but Smith could scare an opposing pitcher more than any of them. He had a vicious swing and the ball seemed to come off his bat with more sizzle than with any of the others; here, however, he was unable to do much against Christenson, who fooled him early with his change and then blew his fastball right by him.

McBride led off the bottom of the first, faring no better than did Lopes, beating a knuckle-curve (Hooton's signature pitch) right into the ground, where it then bounced harmlessly to Hooton, for an easy out on one pitch. Bowa followed McBride and did the same, grounding out to Russell, this time in two pitches.

Up then came Schmidt. Not surprisingly, the thinking-man's hitter had thought himself into another slump: one for nine up to now in the playoffs. For a man as remarkably consistent as he was over the long haul (this was his third consecutive season with 38 home runs) he was maddeningly streaky from one week to the next. At times, it appeared as if he knew what was going to be thrown to him even before the pitcher did, so aggressively would he pounce on the ball; other times the game itself seemed to be foreign to him, played in another language altogether. With each at-bat, it looked as if this playoff series was going to be another one of those times. He was a hard man to love, so often would he disappoint. His intervening hot streaks only made him more of a frustrating figure, but the folks in the stands were giving him their best support. "Little bingo, baby," "Let 'er rip, Michael Jack!" and other shouts of encouragement followed the announcement of his name from the loudspeakers. When he was going well, he made everything look so easy, as if the game were as natural as breathing. It was because of Schmidt, perhaps more than any other player, that so many young Delaware Valley boys harbored notions of playing baseball for a living themselves. Watching him snare rockets at third and effortlessly toss them across the diamond, he provided a false sense of security with regard to their own, comparatively limited, abilities. It just looked so laughably basic, unlike science or algebra, which were abstract and forced. How could it be possible that one's talents lay anywhere other than on the baseball field? Despite their own struggles at the plate in Little League, they'd no doubt go home, watch him hit and *know* the simplicity of it all.

Of course, then came the cold streaks. The seemingly interminable winters when he'd swing at balls in the dirt, grab the barrel of his bat in disgust and look to the heavens for an explanation. No doubt the younger children would try to block those out or, better yet, ignore them altogether. Eventually, however, as the realities of their own athletic abilities would set in, even the most starry-eyed couldn't help but relate to Schmidt more closely during these baffling times than during the others. For, paradoxically, Schmidt was also the conduit of the distressing reality that the game was impossibly complex, indecipherable to even the most accomplished. Through Schmidt, an entire generation of Delaware Valley baseball fans came to learn that, ultimately, nothing was capable of complete mastery, regardless of natural affinity or the amount of work put into it. Because lessons highlighting our limitations rather than our potential are ones more begrudgingly received, he often bore the brunt of a city's collective disdain in its attempt to kill the messenger in hopes that the message would never get through. But despite their efforts, it always did. This afternoon would see it reinforced once again. Schmidt popped weakly to Lopes, ending the inning. As the Dodgers trotted off the field for the top of the second, Schmidt lingered at the plate for a moment, searching the skies, grabbing his bat in bewilderment. He was now one for ten.

Philadelphia: The Preeminent American City

To understand the Phillies, or more specifically, their relationship with their fans, one must first understand the city in which they reside. Although it is nigh impossible for any American youngster to pass to middle school without a rudimentary knowledge of the city's colonial high points—home of the Founding Fathers, birthplace of the Declaration of Independence and Constitution, the dubious legend of Betsy Ross—the story of the Philadelphia that evolved afterward is telling when it comes to appreciating what makes Philadelphia fans do the things they're famous for doing and why, of all the professional sports teams in the city, they harbor a particular animosity toward their baseball team.

No other American city ever soared as high as Philadelphia in its heyday and no other city fell as far, as fast, or as forcefully at the hands of outsiders looking to bring it to its collective knees. The scars left by this fall from prominence remain to this day, and they have shaped the character of the city. Philadelphia has spent two centuries attempting to recover and right itself, neither forgiving nor forgetting anything along the way. The Phillies—more so than any other team or organization in the city—have felt the sting from these scars, some of this as a result of their own doing but much of it outside of their control, ever since they set up shop over a century ago and then had the temerity to stick around after the Athletics left town in 1954. But this is getting somewhat ahead of the story. In order to understand just how it came to be that the Phillies would stand for all that is wrong with the City of Brotherly Love, it is necessary to start at the beginning — when America was young and Philadelphia mattered.

Before there was New York, there was Philadelphia. During the eighteenth century, Philadelphia was the epicenter of colonial America, not merely the largest city on the continent, but home to the "wealthiest, most successful, gayest, and most brilliant elite in the land."[10] Geography had much to do with this as Philadelphia benefited from being the most centrally located city within the colonies. As such, it was a natural gathering place for those who hoped to shape the future of the country. Pennsylvania's abundance of natural resources also played an important role. Rich farmland and vast open spaces suitable for cultivation helped to steer settlers to the area and allowed them to farm on a scale much greater than in many of the other colonies. Philadelphia reaped the benefits of this bounty in becoming the commercial hub of the colonies, its port being the largest by far.[11]

Perhaps most important, however, religion played a crucial role in the early preeminence of Philadelphia. The city's Quaker majority was openly tolerant of dissent and opposing views, themselves having been persecuted at the hands of the Anglicans in England.[12] Unlike the Puritans, Philadelphia's Quakers took the hard lessons learned back in Britain to heart and, as a result, Philadelphia became, in the words of one historian, a "liberal gem, a bastion of religious freedom in a world of religious chains."[13] This liberalism attracted the best and the brightest minds of the time to the city, where they could exchange ideas freely without fear of censure or oppression. Theories and ideas could be discussed in Philadelphia that could not even be raised in various other colonial cities. For all of these reasons, Philadelphia's population boomed, increasing more than 200 percent between 1740 and 1776 when it grew to become one of the largest cities in the vast British Empire.

New York City, by contrast, played a soft second fiddle. Although certainly a major city by colonial standards, its influence and prestige were no greater than that of any of the other cities that took a clear back seat to Philadelphia during this time, including Boston, Charleston and Baltimore. As a port, colonial New York ranked fourth, behind Philadelphia, Boston and Charleston.[14] During the Revolutionary War, New York suffered a crippling blow to its development when it was captured by the British during the summer of 1776. Much of the city was torched during this time and New York remained an occupied territory for the next seven years until liberated at the conclusion of peace when the Treaty of Paris was signed in 1783.[15] Philadelphia, by contrast, remained free throughout much of this period,[16] and it continued to develop in trade and prominence, solidifying its position as the newly formed country's center of commerce. By 1800, Philadelphia's exports constituted a quarter of the burgeoning nation's total, amounting to nearly $7 million a year.[17] As such, it was the natural epicenter of the fledgling nation's mercantile information. The most important and widely circulated business periodicals were published within the city — documents that quoted current prices and reported news relevant to the state of the economy.[18] These sheets were required reading for merchants throughout the country and were often republished in local newspapers. When it came to the economy, in the words of one financial historian: "everyone in trade wanted to know 'What's happening in Philadelphia?'"[19] Accordingly, just as it played host to the great minds of colonial America such as Benjamin Franklin, Thomas Jefferson and Alexander Hamilton before the Revolution, it naturally became *the* destination city for statesmen and leading people of influence throughout Europe who hoped to get rich or otherwise gain the good graces of the new government afterward. During the Revolutionary postwar period, access to the newly formed United States of America came through one city and one city only: Philadelphia.

As the eighteenth century grew to a close, there was no question that Philadelphia was the "first city" of America.[20] It was not merely the financial capital — a title that proved self-perpetuating as its growing financial sophistication allowed for the expansion of even more industries, such as the marine, fire and life insurance trades, that could not have developed as quickly in climates that were less economically advanced[21] — it was also the country's political capital, with the official proclamation of the city as the nation's capital (at least temporarily) in 1790 merely confirming the reality that Philadelphia had been, for as long as anyone could remember, the hub of American political activity. Likewise, was the de facto intellectual capital of the nation, with the publishing, literary and artistic world centered in the city[22] — each of these an outgrowth of the freedom that drew the liberal intelligentsia to this city in droves. The Quaker City was, as an American contemporary stated at the time, "our London,"[23] and it would be the only time in the history of the United States when the financial, political and intellectual centers would be located within a single city. In Philadelphia, much like the greater United States at the time, optimism ran rampant — the future was wide open and the possibilities seemed endless.

Philadelphia's Decline

Political Decline

At least as far as Philadelphia was concerned, this optimism was short-lived. By the turn of the nineteenth century, Philadelphia's gentle — and, at times, not so gentle — decline had already begun, leaving scars that would shape the attitudes and outlook of Philadelphians for the next 200 years and which remain to this day. The first blow came in 1800 when it ceded its stature as the country's political capital following the relocation of the federal government to the newly formed District of Columbia. Although the designation of Philadelphia as the nation's capital was only temporary — the result of a compromise that called for the seat of the nation to be housed in Philadelphia only until the new federal city was created — many Philadelphians had hoped that, once ensconced, the federal government would remain.[24] To these people, it was only natural that Philadelphia should be officially designated the capital, a status that it had held in practice for much of the previous century. Besides, once "completed," Washington was not really finished at all. Rather, it was a muddy, desolate burg that was largely uninhabited except when Congress met there a few months out of the year. The new capital was a far cry from the culture and civilization of Philadelphia and that fact led some to believe that, when the time came, the government would remain — at least for a little while longer — where it was and where it rightly belonged. Much to their dismay, however, the federal government packed up and moved south as planned, leaving Philadelphia behind. It would be the first, but by no means the last, time the nation would turn its back on the city.

Economic Decline

At the same time, Philadelphia's position of prominence in the financial world was beginning to erode. During the colonial and early postcolonial eras, Philadelphia thrived as America's financial epicenter mainly because of the advantages (many of them either artificial or only temporary as it would turn out) of its port. Because it was the busiest seaport, it only made sense that the nation's commercial center be located in the Quaker City. This status, in turn, attracted still more financial institutions to the city and further ingrained its status. One of the most significant of these institutions was the First National Bank of the United States. Chartered in 1791, the bank operated much as the Federal Reserve does today, acting to fight inflation, quell financial panics and serve as institutional the backbone for the American economy. Given its power, it is no stretch to say that the control room of the fledgling United States was housed in the bank, which itself was housed in the nation's preeminent city, much as it should have been. However, within a few years, the economic advantages of Philadelphia's port would diminish, with disastrous results for both the bank and the city of Philadelphia, thus signaling the latter's decline as the nation's financial capital.

By 1803, New York's port had been free from British occupation for 20 years. Its huge harbor had not only recovered from its seven-year isolation, it was also thriving, having overtaken Philadelphia as the leading exporter and importer in the nation.[25] By this point, the geographic advantages of New York's port were plain for all to see. Unlike the shallow, freshwater Delaware River, the Hudson was both a deep and a saltwater river.[26] As a result, while the Delaware was prone to extended freezing during the cold winters, the Hudson remained passable.[27] Thus, while Philadelphia would virtually shut down during these deep freezes, New York's economy felt fewer ill effects from the weather. Accordingly, New York boomed. From 1800 to 1810 its population increased by more than 40 percent, causing it to leap past Philadelphia in numbers of residents.[28]

The economic shift in favor of New York's harbor might have been seen as temporary at the time, the result of a natural ebb and flow between one region and another. All things being equal, it is possible that Philadelphia might have regained its status as the nation's premier city over time, or, at least, it might have shared this status with its neighbor to the north. After all, while its port may not have been the equal of New York's, it was nevertheless large and busy, despite the occasional navigational problems. But things were not equal because up in the Hudson Valley, work soon began on the Erie Canal, which, when completed in 1825, would connect New York City to the vast interior of the country. From that point on, Philadelphia's secondary status was assured.

THE ERIE CANAL

The impact of the Erie Canal on the history of Philadelphia (not to mention the nation as a whole) cannot be understated. Without it, the United States would likely look very different today, perhaps expanding no farther west than the Appalachian Mountains.[29] With it, the nation expanded west, became unified and, as it grew into an international power, New York emerged as the world's capital city. Philadelphia, by contrast, continued to shrink. In short, while the decline of Philadelphia began prior to the completion of the canal, it was reversible until that point. Afterward, there was no turning back for either New York or Philadelphia. The course of these two cities for the next two centuries was charted at the ceremonial "Wedding of the Waters" in 1825, with each city traveling in opposite directions ever since.

Demographically speaking, the impact of the Erie Canal was swift and extreme. New York City, which was already thriving, quadrupled its population between 1825 and 1850. This population was not only large but also, at least comparatively, wealthy. Due in large part to the volume of commerce passing through New York's harbor, the city thrived economically. Property values tripled in the first 11 years after the canal's completion. By 1830, the exports out of New York quadrupled those out of Philadelphia. By 1860, exports grew by an additional 160 percent. Philadelphia experienced relatively little growth during this same period. As such, it fell further and further behind as New York established itself as the port of choice in the United States.[30]

It should be noted that Philadelphia did not sit idly by while the Erie Canal was first being debated and later built. In fact, some of the earliest proponents of canals proposed a link between the Great Lakes and Philadelphia, not New York. Had their vision been realized at the time, Philadelphia, not to mention New York, would undoubtedly not merely look far different today, but the worldview of their populaces would most likely be radically different as well.

In 1791, the Pennsylvania legislature incorporated two canal companies, one to connect the Schuylkill with the Susquehanna River and the other to connect the Delaware to the upper Schuylkill.[31] However, engineering and financial difficulties abounded and these projects were slow to get off the ground. Financing proved particularly difficult given the mood of the times — most investors were simply more interested in the financial certainties associated with direct international trade than with the uncertainties associated with trade expansion inward, to a less-developed interior. In 1811, by the time the canal question had crystallized into a race to connect the Atlantic with the Great Lakes, these two companies merged to form the Union Canal Company of Pennsylvania. The company's officers contended that the ocean-to-lakes connection could be achieved more quickly and more cheaply through Philadelphia than any other port city, but their claims failed to excite investors as their proposal by now lagged well behind the Erie Canal project.

Once the success of the Erie Canal was demonstrated, however, Philadelphia was able to finance its projects and step up efforts to complete its own canals. In fact, by the Civil War, Pennsylvania spent lavishly — sums amounted to $41.6 million — on internal transportation improvements, much of this canal-related. Once completed, these canals brought financial benefits to Philadelphia although it was far too late to catch New York City, which by then had become the new economic hub of the nation. There were several reasons why Pennsylvania's canals were not the boon to Philadelphia that the Erie Canal was to New York City but perhaps the most significant was the simple fact that Philadelphia failed to reap most of the benefits of these new Pennsylvania canals. Much of the trade of the central and western parts of the state ended up in the ports of Baltimore and New Orleans, not Philadelphia. Philadelphia *was* able to import, among other things, the raw materials such as wood, marble and iron that would enable it to become a manufacturing hub — the "workshop of the world"— later in the century, but this was not enough to prevent the nation's financial capital from shifting north to New York. Moreover, once the Erie Canal became established, it was impossible for any other canal, or system of canals, to compete with it simply because the

Erie Canal effectively drained the Great Lakes basin economically. So much commerce was flowing through the Erie Canal that little remained to travel elsewhere. By losing the race to the nation's interior, Philadelphia had put itself in a position in which, for ever after, it would be unable to catch up.

Having lost the great canal race, Philadelphia and Pennsylvania would then turn to the railroad in an effort to compete with New York. Here, they were ahead of the curve rather than behind it but this would not be enough to offset the economic losses caused by the Erie Canal. Initially, the railroads provided weak competition due to problems associated with early railroad technology. Unlike the barges floating down the canals, railroads were difficult to operate and required specialized skills—skills that comparatively few people possessed. For this reason alone, canals were the preferred choice for many merchants. The cost of running a railroad was also high. The expense ate into profits and made railroads undesirable. Finally, although some goods, particularly perishable items, could be shipped more profitably via the quicker railroads, for nonperishables, particularly those with "high bulk to value" ratios, the canals were much more efficient. Thus, although Pennsylvania outpaced New York in miles of tracks— by 1859 it would trail only Ohio in this regard—this would not be enough to stave off the inevitable. It should also be noted that, just as with its canals, Pennsylvania's railroads did not accrue solely to the benefit of Philadelphia. Much of the rail traffic led to Baltimore or New Orleans (via Pittsburgh), which also diminished the railroad's overall impact on Philadelphia.

The impact of the Erie Canal on Philadelphia was more than merely economic. True, the Delaware Valley suffered economically because of the canal but, as noted above, because the area eventually did build canals, and later railroads, of its own, it did survive and, in becoming the "workshop of the world," it eventually thrived. However, losing the race to the nation's interior changed the makeup of the city because, as its international preeminence waned, its character changed. Although the goods produced in its factories ensured that the city would remain a significant international player for decades to come, its decline was nevertheless underway, slow but sure as it receded behind the brightening glare of New York. As mills and factories popped up, processing the raw materials that were now streaming into the city, a different type of worker was required, one who excelled with his hands rather than his mind. In time, Philadelphia—once the gathering place for the nation's great thinkers—would become the blue-collar city it is still regarded as today.[32]

THE DEMISE OF THE FIRST AND BATTLE OVER THE SECOND BANK OF THE UNITED STATES

In due course, the economic shift from Philadelphia to New York became inevitable, causing much of the financial world to follow the money that was pouring into the Empire State. And as New Yorkers gained financial strength, they were not opposed to flexing their bulging political muscles in a further attempt to knock Philadelphia from its perch. In 1812, after a tie vote in the Senate, Congress voted against rechartering the First National Bank, with Vice President DeWitt Clinton — who, at various junctures in his life would be a senator, lieutenant governor and governor of New York, as well as mayor of New York City for six years—casting the deciding "no" vote.[33] At the time, Clinton was also championing his vision of the Erie Canal to potential investors, certainly aware of the impact the canal would have on the fortunes of his home state.[34] His desire to knock Philadelphia off its economic pedestal had disastrous national effects, however. In 1812, the United States was at war with England once again and without a national bank, the country was unable to borrow the money it needed to fund the effort.[35] As the war dragged on, the nation realized the importance of a national bank. Therefore, in 1816, the Second Bank of the United States was chartered and once again housed in Philadelphia. The battle over its failed recharter in 1836 would leave Philadelphia with scars that remain to this day.

In the first decades of the nineteenth century, New York became an able copier of many Philadelphia institutions. After Philadelphia founded its stock exchange, New York followed suit. After Philadelphia established the Philadelphia Savings Fund Society (PSFS), New York founded its Bank for Savings. Soon after Philadelphia founded the first marine, fire and life insurance companies, similar incarnations arose in Gotham. With New York gaining economic strength via the Erie Canal and surpassing Philadelphia in many ways, and with many financial services now available in New York as well as in Philadelphia, many New Yorkers wondered why New York still took a back seat to Philadelphia. The answer lay in the Second Bank of the United States. As long as it was headquartered in Philadelphia, the nation's financial heart would always beat in the Quaker City. It would not be long before some New Yorkers would try to change all that.

Given the hard lessons learned after the failure to recharter the First Bank of the United States, it would have been too much to simply expect the federal government to make this mistake again with regard to the Second Bank. As such, the bank, along with Philadelphia's position in the financial world, appeared secure. However, New Yorker Martin Van Buren, along with other New York financiers, devised an alternative to the Second Bank — a disastrous one as it turned out — that provided the impetus for the demise of the Second Bank and the transfer of financial supremacy to Manhattan. As governor during the 1820s, Van Buren introduced a set of banking reforms intended to stabilize New York's fledgling banking system that included something known as the "Safety Fund." Pursuant to the Safety Fund, banks were required to pay a tax of 3 percent on their capital to the fund, which would reimburse investors should any particular bank fail. Through this mechanism, the stability of New York's banking system was seemingly guaranteed (although this was not true in reality, as the nation would soon discover). When Andrew Jackson assumed the presidency in 1828, Van Buren found the perfect opportunity to use the Safety Fund to New York's advantage.

Jackson himself was an opponent of the Second Bank, and of all banks in general, for that matter. He had teetered near bankruptcy twice in his lifetime and blamed "voracious bankers" for his situation. He had also borne witness to the less than stellar early years of the Second Bank, which, due to mismanagement, led to the Panic of 1819. Although the bank had stabilized since then and was now run by Philadelphian Nicholas Biddle, called "the most storied banker in U.S. history to that time" by one financial historian, Jackson's attitude had not changed. When, during his 1832 reelection campaign, he chose Van Buren as his vice presidential candidate rather than his current vice president, the pieces were in place for New York to topple Philadelphia once and for all.

During Jackson's campaign for reelection, Biddle campaigned hard against him, realizing full well that the election of Jackson and Van Buren would likely spell trouble for the Second Bank. He lobbied to have the bank rechartered in 1832, forcing a bill through both the House and the Senate that approved the action. Jackson not only vetoed it but, in doing so, alleged that the bank was "a tool of evil aristocrats and leechlike financiers." He claimed that the bank did little more than make "the rich richer and the potent more powerful." Biddle responded by alleging that Jackson's words were "a manifesto of anarchy." The Second Bank — and elitist, aristocratic Philadelphia as a whole (at least in Jackson's opinion) — thereby became *the* campaign issue. Jackson, with prodding from Van Buren, forced Americans to make a choice in 1832: either him or the Second Bank. On election day, the American people spoke: they wanted him. They rejected Philadelphia, electing, in addition, many other legislators who rode Jackson's antibank, anti–Philadelphia coattails.

Once ensconced, Van Buren was able to convince Jackson that the Safety Fund would be able to provide the financial protection necessary to allow the Second Bank to fade away. Over the next few years, Jackson tested Van Buren's theory out. In 1833, he ordered his treasury secretary to start depositing the government's tax receipts in state banks, particularly those of New York, with its seemingly protective Safety Fund, and not Philadelphia's Second Bank. Eventually, the federal government would remove all of its money from the Second Bank. In 1836, the Second Bank's charter was not renewed. Although it would remain in existence for five more years, it would no longer serve as the financial heartbeat of the nation. As a result, that heart would almost stop altogether. As the money left the Second Bank, the economy deteriorated and, by 1837, despite the Safety Fund, which was clearly providing no safety at all, the country again would be in the throes of a panic. Regardless, the reign of the Second Bank had ended. The economy would eventually recover and, when it did, it would call Manhattan home, not Philadelphia.

New Yorkers cherished their victory over Philadelphia, demonizing and belittling the city in the process. New York newspapers regularly assailed prominent Philadelphians as having little "capacity" or brains when it came to finances, and they were portrayed as being slave to special interests rather than to the nation as a whole. Philadelphia took a public flogging from its neighbor to the north, which must have been difficult to swallow. On top for as long as anyone could remember, it had now been rejected by New York and the nation in the span of a few short years, ridiculed by both as being aristocratic, out of touch and plain old stupid. Without Philadelphia, New York could have never existed and now, having copied it incessantly and taken what it needed, the new money center was now doing all it could to beat the old into obsolescence. With the demise of the Second Bank in 1836, Philadelphia's reign of financial supremacy was over. Van Buren and his cohorts had gotten just what they wanted.

In truth, even without the considerable effort exerted by New Yorkers, Philadelphia's status as the economic epicenter of the country would eventually have come to an end. The superiority of New York's harbor and the presence of the Erie Canal made this inevitable. Still, if there was a single event that gave birth to modern Philadelphia's outlook and personality, it was the failure of the Second National Bank because it was at this point that Philadelphians themselves realized that they had been surpassed and, in essence, rejected by the rest of the country. This realization would have a profound effect on the attitudes of Philadelphians and it reverberates to this day. As one historian noted:

> When the Bank broke ... Philadelphia closed its doors against the nation as a whole. The nation had rejected the leadership of Old Philadelphia; very well, Old Philadelphia rejected the nation.... Old Philadelphia retired into itself. Henceforth, let vulgar Washington take over politics and vulgar New York take over finance. Philadelphia gentlemen would at least remain Philadelphian and gentlemen.[36]

Philadelphia would never be the same.

Intellectual Decline and the Rise of Cynicism and Negativity

Having been burned by the nation on several fronts, Philadelphia soon became a city hesitant to stick its neck out for fear of it being chopped off once again. Content to withdraw into itself, where it was shielded from further attack on its status and character, gentlemanly Philadelphia soon became an intellectually stifling place; a place where progressive thought and national leadership were immediately suspect.[37] This atmosphere, in turn, led to the exodus of many of the great minds who once roamed its streets as Quaker liberalism was gradually replaced with cynicism and derision. Soon, the era of Philadelphia as the intellectual capital of the nation was over as well.

Philadelphia's unique religious heritage played a significant role in this intellectual exodus for the simple reason that it created, in Philadelphia, an atmosphere that would eventually ensure that, as time went on, the city would become less central and thus less necessary as an intellectual gathering place. The most important document produced as a result of the open, tolerant atmosphere provided by Quaker liberalism — the Constitution — assured that Philadelphia would no longer stand alone as it once had. The individual freedoms assured in the Bill of Rights gave the same rights to all Americans (at least all white males), including freedom of speech and of assembly, regardless of whether they lived in Boston, Baltimore or Philadelphia. To the intelligentsia, Philadelphia was no longer a destination city because they could now gather and speak their minds wherever they lived. Any town could now be the intellectual capital of the nation. Philadelphia no longer stood out.

Moreover, once the United States was formed, Philadelphia became, if anything, a less tolerant place than it once had been. After the Revolution, the Quakers no longer controlled state government; thus, their official influence on the temperament of the city began to wane.[38] As the nineteenth century progressed, Quakerism likewise declined overall from a population standpoint as a wide range of people poured into the city, drawn to the mills and factories sprouting all over the burgeoning "workshop of the world." Over time, Philadelphia itself no longer appeared to be the "liberal gem" it had been lauded for during colonial times. As such, it became less desirable than some other cities. As the great minds abandoned the city, Philadelphia was left rudderless. Those of superior ability who remained chose to pull up shop and withdraw from the public spotlight rather than assume command of the listing city out of fear of future recriminations.[39] As a result, Philadelphia was left in less able hands with grave results. Liberalism, the hallmark of colonial Philadelphia, disappeared and was replaced with cold, skeptical conservatism.

In time, Philadelphia became a cynical, suspicious place. One resident of Philadelphia in the late nineteenth century highlighted this communal mind-set when he wrote:

> When in Boston any fellow-citizen paints a picture or writes a book, he is approached and fostered for Boston's sake and in Boston's name. We of Philadelphia steer quite wide of this amiable if hasty encouragement. We seem to dis-

trust our own power to do anything out of the common; and when a young man tries to, our minds close against him with a civic instinct of disparagement. A Boston failure in art surprises Boston; it is success that surprises Philadelphia.[40]

It is no wonder that, amid such an atmosphere, ever more intellectuals soon found themselves more comfortable in places such as Boston and New York, with populaces more apt to embrace than criticize them. Cynicism and negativity, however, found an increasingly welcoming home in Philadelphia. In 1896, one historian of Pennsylvania made note of the numerous "bright and able men" who, if not lucky enough to have been "neglected and forgotten," saw their reputations "deliberately attacked or ruined."[41] This narrative concludes: "It is really extraordinary the vindictiveness with which the Pennsylvanians have assailed any one of their own people who has shown striking or supreme ability." By the close of the nineteenth century, much of Philadelphia no longer desired to compete with New York for supremacy of any kind. By then the battle was long over. Philadelphia, which began the century as the nation's first city, would end it as something else entirely: a city with a chip on its shoulder.

While it was the process of the usurpation of national leadership that contributed in large part to the cynicism and negativity that survives and thrives in the city to the present, this does not mean that Philadelphians had nothing to take pride in at the dawn of the twentieth century. On the contrary, gentlemanly Philadelphia, embodied in person and in spirit by those who had withdrawn from public life, could now sit comfortably on the national sidelines, leaving the ugly battles of politics, finance and culture to other, less refined locales. Instead of worrying itself with these matters of current interest, Philadelphians were now free to do what they would soon do better than any other major city in the nation: focus on their past.

In the twentieth century, no other major American city would take as much pride in its history as would Philadelphia.[42] Although Philadelphia could no longer compete on a national level in many areas, there could be no challengers to its numerous "firsts." This, perhaps, provided a comfort level for Philadelphians that was missing in the daily scrum, where, as they experienced first hand, what is yours today might be someone else's tomorrow if you weren't careful. Thus, rather than being a city of "mosts" or "bests," Philadelphia became a city of "firsts": first zoo, first medical school, first hospital, first mental institution, first penitentiary; the list goes on. This inclination to look back rather than forward soon seeped into other areas of local life as well. As Mark Twain once noted: "In Boston, they ask: 'what does he know?' In New York, 'How much is he worth?' In Philadelphia, 'who were his parents?'"[43] Philadelphians soon became accustomed to looking backwards rather than forward in all aspects of life.[44] And while this intense focus on the past, fostered by ever increasing conservatism, hindered the development of new ideas, hastened the city's decline as an intellectual center of the United States, and resulted in the cynicism that is the city's calling card to this day, it would serve it uniquely well in one area of national life that through the late nineteenth and early twentieth centuries was taking the country by storm: baseball.

2

Professional Baseball
in the Quaker City

Black Friday: Second Inning

The brevity of the first inning would contrast with the elongated drama of the second. Ron Cey waddled to the plate and quickly fell behind 0–2. Christenson had fooled him with two straight sliders, a pitch that he, under tutelage from the master of the pitch, Steve Carlton, had come to rely on but one that he hadn't often thrown recently due to a blister problem. Apparently, that had resolved itself because, today, he was throwing it with regularity and getting a sharp bite on it as well. His next pitch looked like a strike to the 63,000 umpires in the stands, but the umpire, Wendlestadt, called it a ball. The crowd groaned in disapproval. But no matter. Cey grounded the next pitch to Schmidt for out number one.

After Garvey singled to center for the first hit of the game, Dusty Baker stepped up to the plate and was welcomed to the Vet with a chorus of droning boos. Because victory is a salve and defeat an open wound, nobody thought to do the same to Cey, perhaps because *his* slam in game one didn't beat the Phils. Baker quickly fell behind 0–2, the third straight hitter this inning to do so, but then Christenson made a mistake. After blowing two straight fastballs by him, he went back to his slider, which may have been an effective tactic with Cey, or most other hitters for that matter, but which was a colossal blunder with Baker up there — one of the few hitters in the game who could drive sliders with regularity. He walloped it, sending it to the wall in left center where Maddox, rusty after his time off, bobbled it momentarily before firing it to Larry Bowa. That bobble was all Garvey — who was having troubles of his own — needed. He stumbled over second base as he rounded it, his eyes on Maddox in the outfield. Regardless, he was determined to score on the play and would have if Bowa hadn't thrown an absolute laser to the plate — a strike to Boone, who had the plate blocked and who

Boone blocks both the plate and the view of the umpire, Wendlestadt, in the second. Garvey was called safe despite the tag (Temple University Libraries, Urban Archives, Philadelphia, PA).

tagged Garvey out as he stumbled past, never getting within six inches of the plate.

The only problem was that Boone had done such a good job of blocking the plate that he blocked home plate umpire Wendlestadt as well, who was out of position behind Boone and as such unable to see the play clearly. Wendlestadt called him safe, and the stadium erupted. All around, arms went up, first in disgust, then in anger. Boos rattled the stadium to such a degree that some would later claim they actually felt the mammoth concrete structure shake.[1] Manager Ozark came out to argue. He followed Wendlestadt around the home plate cut-out as if trying to scold a petulant child who refused to listen. Wendlestadt never showed Ozark anything other than his back — a sure sign that he knew he blew the call. After a few seconds, Ozark gave up and returned to the dugout. His point was made, however, as would become apparent very quickly.

The fans found their seats and waited for centerfielder Rick Monday to dig in. Sanity was restored as he flied out to Maddox. Baker stayed at second. With catcher Steve Yeager coming up with two out, and with Hooton on deck, Ozark found himself in a quandary. On the one hand, there was really no reason to pitch to Yeager. First base was open, the pitcher was up next, and it would have made perfect sense to either pitch around him or intentionally walk him in order to get out of the inning without further damage. But Yeager presented a complication: he was such a poor hitter that it was almost as if there were two pitchers in the LA lineup. True, he was coming off what was, at least for him, a career year: .256 with 16 home runs. But the year before he'd hit all of .214, which was more typical of his prowess at the plate. He was a walking contradiction: a hulking presence physically, his musculature bubbled and popped as he moved, threatening to burst out of its fleshy casing like a bratwurst on the fire. Anyone who saw him in uniform and knew nothing more about him would no doubt have concluded that he was one of the top power hitters in the game. Yet, one swing of the bat would smash all such assumptions. His swing was without purpose and balls would come off his bat heavy, lacking zip. So Ozark tried to get away with something. He decided to pitch to Yeager in the hopes of getting him here and then force Hooton to lead off the third. His gamble backfired. Yeager slapped a Christenson slider to right (maybe it wasn't breaking as sharply as it had earlier appeared), scoring Baker. It was now 2–0 Dodgers.

Discontent rattled through the stands as fans were left to wonder why on earth Yeager was given a pitch to hit. In his five-year tenure at the helm of the Phillies, Ozark had become infamous for stupefying decisions followed by even more stupefying explanations of them afterwards—taking pitchers out, leaving them in, pinch hitting, deciding not to pinch hit. All of his decisions seemed to come from somewhere other than the areas of logic and common sense. And what was worse, he often had no suitable explanation for why he had just gone against the "baseball book" yet again. Instead, his postgame comments would often center on a flawed recollection of the situation in question or a misunderstanding of the context of the play or game at issue. (Perhaps most famously, he began one post-game interview after the Phils had just been eliminated from the 1975 division race by insisting that the season was not lost. When informed that, in fact, it was, he replied, "that's disheartening."[2]) This season, however, he seemed to have been touched from above. All of the moves that had backfired on him in years past were somehow working out. So he got a pass on this one—for now. And he received vindication with the very next batter when Hooton whistled a shot to the left field corner that was hit twice as hard as Yeager's. Luzinski played it off the wall and relayed to Schmidt, who was way up the line in left in recognition of the Bull's weak arm. He then wheeled and, seeing Yeager round third heading for home, fired yet another strike to Boone, who was braced for the second play at the plate this inning. Again he blocked the plate, but, this time, it appeared as if Yeager had slid under the tag. Wendlestadt called him out, however, and this time it was LA's turn to gripe. Yeager leaped up and lunged for the umpire, stomping his feet in righteous indignation. Comic relief was provided when little Davey Lopes stepped in and attempted a bear hug on the big catcher in an effort to restrain him. Again, Wendlestadt didn't argue but, instead, let Yeager make his point. In Wendlestadt's book, justice had been served. There had been two plays at the plate this inning, one in which the runner was safe, one in which he was out. This too was how he called them. That he called the safe runner out and the out runner safe was of little matter in the big picture. The score was 2–0 as it should have been. Although Ozark was hidden within the dugout, there was more than likely at least a hint of a smile somewhere on that craggy face.

Which led to the bottom of the second. Immediately after it had ended, it would have been reasonable enough to believe that this half inning would be the one that would be remembered forever. At the time, it seemed to be the defining moment for both the city and its team. Actually, separating the two like this would be inappropriate. It became a defining moment precisely because, afterward, there was no delineation between them — no way to tell where one ended and the other began. That afternoon, 63,719 people had not merely attended a baseball game, they became a part of it — they were responsible for its outcome, or at least that's how it appeared at the time. Perhaps because such moments are so infrequent, when one occurs, not only is it recognized immediately but also it is assumed that, once it has passed, everything else thereafter could be nothing other than denouement. Little did those in attendance at the Vet that day know that, in retrospect, this half inning would merely provide a contrast for what was later to transpire.

Although he was a control pitcher, Burt Hooton was a guy who could be gotten to. Everything about him suggested as much. For one thing, his nickname, "Happy," a moniker that Dodger manager Tommy Lasorda allegedly tagged him with a few years earlier while watching this sad man play solitaire one New Year's Eve in the midst of seemingly inescapable merriment.[3] He was a man who appeared to have demons and who was not afraid to let the world know it, as he did not hide the fact that he saw a hypnotherapist.[4] Perhaps he did so simply to improve his focus on the mound but, given the ironic nickname, his doing so was seen as indicative of deeper troubles gurgling within.[5] However, perhaps most damning, at least in Philadelphia, was the fact that he could be demonstrative on the mound — a direct counterpoint to the stoic majesty of Steve Carlton, who appeared to be unmovable even in a hurricane and who once claimed (back when he was still talking to the press) that he never even noticed the batter in the box when he pitched. Instead, in Carlton's mind, once on the mound, all he was doing was playing an elevated game of pitch and catch with his catcher. The batter, the umpire, and everyone else for that matter, were irrelevant and invisible. Carlton's poise rubbed off on the rest of the staff, with the obvious exception of Tug McGraw, and, as such, Phillies fans came to expect unshakable pitchers on the hill; pitchers who were immune to their barbs as well as their cheers. Thus, the typical Philadelphia fan didn't waste his time on them. Instead, he would save his lungs for the everyday players, the ones who slid in the dirt and ran and sweated and laughed and grimaced and sometimes even cried. These he could relate to. Pitchers, on the other hand, were inhuman. It wasn't worth the effort to try to rile them. They were impenetrable. Except Hooton.

Things started out innocently enough. True, Luzinski singled sharply to left to lead off the inning, but this could just as well have been considered a break as far as Hooton was concerned. For the Bull stepped to the plate amid a buzz that accompanied few other players in the game. Word of his tape measure shots during batting practice rippled through the press box and, although few in the crowd were around early enough to have actually seen them, by the time he stepped to the plate, it was as if the entire stadium had been in attendance for all of it: the drives into the 500 or, if you chose to believe it, the 600 level in left, the soaring rainbows into the press level. He had come off a sure-fire MVP season if only George Foster of the Reds hadn't done the unthinkable and hit 52 home runs. As such, his 39 home runs, his 130 runs batted in and, most impressively, his .309 average (incredible for a man who lumbered as he did and who appeared to have trouble even making it to first) would have to take a back seat, but only a little ways back. He was inarguably one of the best all around power hitters in the game, perhaps second only to Foster this particular year, and a smoked single — compared to what might have been — should have comforted LA. Very quickly, it was clear that it had no such effect.

"The Hacker," Rich Hebner, followed the Bull. He'd done nothing but look bad against Hooton all season: 0 for seven with three K's. And when the Hacker looked bad, he really looked bad: pulling off, losing balance, lifting his head. This time, however, Hebner smacked a hard grounder, unfortunately right to Lopes at second — a perfect double play ball. Lopes fielded it cleanly, pivoted sharply and flipped the ball to Russell — who dropped it. He dropped it even though it hit him chest high, just like they taught you back in Little League. For an instant, it appeared as if the Phillies had really been blessed and that there would be runners on first and second with no outs, but then the second base umpire called Luzinski out and claimed that Russell somehow caught the ball but dropped it only when taking it out of his glove to fire to first. It all happened so fast and without the benefit of instant replay that it was difficult to tell exactly when Russell lost control of it, but the crowd began to boo with a sense of rage and injustice anyway, in tacit recognition that the ump had blown the call. Thus, although the Phils had received a gift from the Dodgers, all anyone could focus on was that they'd been hoodwinked by the umps again. By the end of the inning, that wouldn't even matter.

Garry Maddox was next up. He straddled the batter's box as he always did with that wide, St. Louis Arch of a stance of his. It looked to be quite painful, as if one could almost pull a groin muscle simply by watching him take his turn at the plate. Perhaps not coincidentally, he was an anxious hitter — hoping to get out of there as quickly as possible — rarely taking anything within shouting distance of the strike zone. This at-bat was typical. The knuckle-curve is not a pitch for the less-than-patient, teasing and tantalizing as it does before dropping out of sight. Maddox looked bad, whiffing on a steady diet of them, missing the last one by about a foot. This brought Boone to the plate, who proceeded to single to left center, sending the heavy-legged Hebner no farther than second. With two out and tiny Ted Sizemore coming to the plate, things didn't look all that ominous for Hooton and the Dodgers who found themselves in a position much like the Phils were in at the top of the inning: facing a weak eighth-place hitter with a man on second and the pitcher on deck. There were a few differences that would prove to be crucial, however: the Phils, unlike the Dodgers, had a man on first, so Hooton could not walk Sizemore without moving the runner on second to third. More importantly, however, Ozark bluffed by getting Ron Reed up in the bullpen, raising the possibility (however remote) that he would hit for Christenson should Sizemore reach base. Lasorda called Ozark's bluff, decided to pitch around Sizemore, and then could do nothing more than pace the dugout while his pitcher unraveled.

It's always a risky proposition to have your pitcher pitch around a hitter without intentionally walking him. For one thing, he could miss, fire a fat one right down the plate and watch it leave the park. This was a possibility even with Sizemore at the plate, as he did have four home runs that season. So he was capable of capitalizing on a mistake and blowing the game open. For another, he could throw a ball in the dirt, allow the runners to advance and so negate the very reason you decided to pitch to him in the first place. And finally, even if all went well otherwise, you could alter the strike zone of the home plate umpire, who, knowing that you're pitching around the hitter, starts looking to call balls rather than strikes. This is the last thing a pitcher wants. And this is exactly what happened here. Hooton walked Sizemore on four pitches, never giving him anything to hit, thereby loading the bases, and then he waited to see if Ozark was going to make good on his threat and pull his starter after only two innings. It was a completely wasted at-bat from Hooton's perspective because he never even gave Sizemore the opportunity to swing the bat. As such, he might as well have intentionally put him on base. He did, however, succeed in shrinking Wendlestadt's strike zone, to disastrous effect.

Christenson was no slouch at the plate. He'd hit three home runs during the season, including one grand slam, and seven in his career up to that point. So when he strode to the plate, the crowd rose in anticipation. Good things to come were not out of the question. Hooton started him off as he should have: with two straight knuckle-curves for two quick strikes. The crowd moaned. Hooton's next knuckle-curve missed and then Christenson fouled off the next one as the tide began to shift. After four straight knuckle-curves, Christenson was starting to catch on to it. Hooton would have to go to something else. He tried a fastball. It caught the corner. However, with Wendlestadt's redefined strike zone, he called this one a ball. Hooton took visible exception as he became demonstrably incensed. Even so, things could have ended right then and there with another strike to end the inning; after all, it was a bad call, but, in a game replete with them by now, and with the pitcher at bat, it really was not that big a deal. But this was Hooton on the mound, not Steve Carlton. And Hooton being Hooton, he began to pace around the mound, squinting into the batter's box seemingly in an attempt to get a glimpse inside Wendlestadt's head. Too late. Having seen all this, the crowd was already inside of his. Once again they rose and began to roar. Hooton acknowledged them by stepping off the mound, refusing to throw another pitch. Once again, Lopes came in to play the peacemaker. He said a few words to no obvious effect and then returned to his position. Finally, Hooton returned to the mound and went with old reliable — his knuckle curve. This one just missed again. Perhaps last inning it would have been a strike but no more. Again he took umbrage at the call and again he made no attempt to hide his anger. He scowled, shook his head and began grumbling to himself on the mound. Smelling blood, the multitude ratcheted it up just a little more — yelling, stomping and generally injecting themselves into the game on the field. By the time Hooton went into his windup on the 3–2 pitch, the torrent of energy emanating from the stands had apparently frazzled him beyond redemption.[6] His fastball was low and away. Not even close. Ball four. He'd walked the pitcher with the bases loaded, sending Hebner home with the Phillies' first run of the game. From that moment on, the Vet Stadium crowd was secure in the knowledge that he was theirs.

At this point, Lasorda had no other choice but to trudge out to the mound in an effort to calm his pitcher and defuse the situation. However, he only heated things up even more when he made a detour on his way to Hooton and chewed out Wendlestadt. A few moments later, after Lasorda stood on the mound waiting for Wendlestadt to come and get him, another confrontation ensued as Lasorda jawed at him some more. By now, some in the stands were confused as to what to do next. Some booed, others cheered. Still others tried to do a little of each. The cacophony of sound built as Lasorda grew closer to them, on his way back to the LA dugout. They derived energy from it and turned it up even louder. Soon, individual voices became indistinguishable, muted even, drowned out even between neighbors in the raucous moment.

McBride was next. Although it was highly unlikely that he would swing the bat until Hooton proved that he could throw a strike, Hooton still was unable to find the plate. His first pitch was low. This time, it was Yeager's turn to spar with Wendlestadt. It would not have taken much to rile him as he was most likely still fuming over the call that went against him at the top of the inning. Ball one was as good an excuse as any. For his next pitch, Hooton threw a knuckle-curve. Low again. By this point, Hooton had lost it completely, pacing like a caged animal from one side of the mound to the other between pitches.[7] A fastball came next and, surprisingly, McBride almost swung out of his shoes. Perhaps he knew not only that it was coming but also that it was coming right down the heart of the plate so he might as well take advantage of his good fortune. He fouled it straight back, an indication that he had just missed it — another fraction of an inch and it would have been driven good and far to dead center. Regardless of how mightily he was struggling, Hooton could not afford to make that mistake again. He returned to his knuckle-curve and missed again for ball three.

As soon as Wendlestadt made his call, the crowd ratcheted it up even more. This time, along with the deafening roar, so loud as to cause one's ears to register it in waves, contracting in self-defense, there was a rumble as well.[8] Some fans on the third base side, in the lower stands that contracted during football season, had started to jump up and down on the temporary metal risers, causing them to rattle and shake, giving rise to a pounding, rhythmic stomping noise. McBride fouled the next pitch, a fastball, straight back again. By this point, it was clear that Hooton had only two options, either throw another knuckle-curve for an almost certain ball four or throw the fastball — the only pitch he was even relatively certain he could get over the plate — allowing McBride to wallop it and hope for the best. He chose the knuckle-curve. It wasn't even close. Boone trotted home and the game was tied.

By this point, Hooton was completely unhinged. He was upset with Wendlestadt, true, but he found no solace anywhere else either.[9] As a result, the negative energy directed at him caused him to redirect his displeasure toward the crowd, focusing on the avalanche of sound cascading in his direction, taunting and threatening him.[10] Given his makeup, he was unable to

Hooton melts down on the mound in the bottom of the second (Temple University Libraries, Urban Archives, Philadelphia, PA).

do the prudent thing and simply stand there and take it. Had he done so, it was likely that he would have eventually shaken off the bad calls, rediscovered the strike zone and gotten out of the inning, with some damage, yes, but with certainly nothing catastrophic. Instead, he allowed the crowd to drive him deeper and deeper into the maelstrom within his head until he was unable to climb out.[11] As soon as McBride reached first, Cey waddled in from third to try his hand at the impossible. He spoke briefly and then returned to his position.

Next it was Bowa's turn. At first, Hooton didn't acknowledge him, choosing instead to look up at the sky, and then down at the ground — anywhere but toward the plate. Finally, he toed the rubber and delivered once more. The result was inevitable: fastball high, ball one. The roar that accompanied Wendlestadt's call was as one might imagine the sound in the middle of a tornado — gusts of violent noise swirling all around in an ever-rising vortex. It was enough to knock anyone unsuspecting backwards. Hooton could do nothing now but stare at Wendlestadt after every pitiful pitch. His next pitch was no different and no better than his first: fastball for ball two. By his third try it had become almost pathetic, like watching a frustrated puppy try to catch its own tail. Fastball again (he had completely given up on the knuckle-curve) outside for ball three. Finally, Wendlestadt presented him with a gift: a called strike on a fastball that appeared to have been outside. Bowa, being

Bowa, complained, but, really, even he had to know by now that it was not going to make any difference in the long run. He dug in again and waited for fate, disguised as a fastball, to take care of Hooton once and for all. On the next pitch, it did. Outside, ball four. Sizemore trotted home with Philadelphia's— the team and the city's— third run of the inning, all three walked in by Hooton.

In the delirium that accompanied Sizemore's stroll to the plate, Hooton wandered the infield between the mound and the second base cutout as if lost. By this point, he presented a much different picture from the one in which he first demonstrated his righteous indignation to Wendlestadt, seemingly eons ago. Now he looked bewildered, not angry, but simply confused and overwhelmed. As the inning wore on, he began muttering to himself, shrugging his shoulders, apparently at a loss to explain what had just transpired.[12] When Lasorda finally did the honorable thing and came out to get him, putting him out of his misery (replacing him with Rick Rhoden who got out of the inning by inducing Schmidt to pop out to Yeager on his first pitch), he raised his arms to his dual tormentors, Wendlestadt and the crowd, not in fury but in resignation.[13] He walked onto the mound that inning expecting to face the Phillies and walked off having battled the entire city of

Hooton leaves the game to the taunts of the Philadelphia faithful (Temple University Libraries, Urban Archives, Philadelphia, PA).

Philadelphia. The undertaking had clearly taken its toll on him, for as he shuffled to the LA dugout, he squinted into it, focusing on a target against the dugout wall. He then tore off his glove and hurled it angrily, hitting his mark.[14] At long last, he had thrown a strike.

Baseball Takes Root in Philadelphia

From its earliest days, baseball was immensely popular in Philadelphia, more so than in any other city. Although, depending on whom one chooses to believe, modern baseball was born in either New York or northern New Jersey, by the 1860s there were five times as many teams in Philadelphia as in New York.[15] By 1884, as the professional leagues became more established, Philadelphia could boast of having more professional teams (6) than any other city. Moreover, it was the only city that fielded a team in each of the three professional leagues (the National League, the American Association and the Union Association) that existed at the time. It was also the home of *Sporting Life,* a weekly baseball paper that, by the 1880s, had the largest circulation of any baseball or sports-themed paper in the country. As the nineteenth century turned into the twentieth, the city's enthusiasm for the game remained. With development of the Negro Leagues, Philadelphia became a hub of black baseball as well.[16] For decades, it could be relied on as the city that most consistently and fervently supported baseball, regardless of who was playing it.

There are several reasons why baseball took such firm root in Philadelphia. Initially, having a professional team was considered a point of civic pride, as it was in many major cities.[17] Nearly from the game's inception, and certainly by the time baseball morphed from an amateur to a professional game, the connection between the sport and contemporary society was a strong one, with baseball acting as a window into the character and status of the towns in which it was being played.[18] Therefore, it was important (at least to those who considered such things important) that a city's teams accurately reflect the city's position (or desired position) in the nation's hierarchy. As such, the largest cities naturally demanded not merely the most teams but, just as importantly, participation in the most prestigious leagues. The battle for financial, political and intellectual supremacy may have been long over but, through baseball, there were still battles between cities to be fought. The stakes were far lower but, nevertheless, fought with similar passion.

As such, many major cities took pride in their teams, Philadelphia being no exception. By the twentieth century, when the dust settled and only two major professional leagues remained — the National and the American — Philadelphia could take pride in the fact that it, like Boston, Chicago and St. Louis, boasted not one but two teams in the highest professional leagues in all the land. This separated it from the likes of lesser weights such as Pittsburgh, Cincinnati, Cleveland, Washington, D.C., and Detroit, all of which only housed one. New York, however, validating its status as the nation's premier city, claimed three.

Simply judging by the sheer number of teams, the Philadelphia of the early twentieth century would appear to be both a major city and an avid supporter of professional baseball. This does not, in and of itself, separate it from the myriad other cities that likewise called themselves home to one or more Major League Baseball teams during this time. Philadelphia *was* different, however, from every other major American city in one important way and, because of this difference, baseball grabbed hold of the local populace more tightly in that city than it would in many others.

Quite simply, Philadelphia, as a result of all of its trials and tribulations during the nineteenth century, was uniquely primed to appreciate and embrace the nuances of the game as no other city could. Just as no other sport looks to its past more than baseball so no other city learned to look to its past more than Philadelphia. The marriage between the two could not have been more perfect. As has been noted by many writers, the past is recalled with regularity when it comes to baseball while it is routinely ignored in most other sports. One author remarks: "(no) other sport so assiduously cultivate(s) its history and make(s) it a part of the continuing life of the game."[19] He continues, "you can still find twelve-year-olds who will exclaim 'Willie Mays!' if you make a basket catch while tossing the ball around in the backyard." By contrast, the names of Paul Hourning, Johnny Unitas, Bill Russell and even Wilt Chamberlain are relegated more often than not to the classic sports channel. Baseball historian Harold Seymour observed: "Americans have frequently been criticized for a lack of historical sense, but this generalization does not hold when it comes to baseball. The mass of statistics on players' performances allow ... comparison of the current titans with former heroes, however much these comparisons become warped by changed conditions and rosy memories."[20]

As such, baseball was uniquely designed for a city that, by the dawn of the twentieth century, had become comfortable in its ability and propensity to look backward rather than forward. Many cities appreciated and loved the game of baseball and took pride in their teams. Many Philadelphians, however, developed deeper attachments to the game simply because they came to it already equipped to do so. Throughout its early years, the baseball moguls had significant work to do, selling the game to the rest of the country as a synonym for America, developing what has become known as the "baseball creed"—the idea that baseball was not merely a game but "contributed to individual and public welfare" by "building manliness, character and an ethic of success"—and claiming that it instilled the proper values in America's children as well as acculturated immigrants to the American way of life.[21] Much of this fiction worked its way into the minds of Americans to the extent that they equated devotion to their teams with devotion to their country. Such devotion, however, due to its faulty premise, runs only so deep. When the winds blew in different directions, so did the allegiances of fans—these to football, basketball, boxing, horse racing, whatever else captured their imagination, much as baseball once did. In Philadelphia, things were different. It did not take the syrupy philosophy of the baseball creed to cause Philadelphians to embrace the game. Therefore, when things would go bad, as they soon would—for years and years to come—Philadelphians would not abandon the game to which they had an undying and natural affinity.

The Birth and Rise of the Philadelphia Athletics

On December 11, 1900, Ban Johnson, a former sportswriter, and Charles W. Somers, his financial bag man, arrived in Philadelphia and announced that the Phillies, Philadelphia's National League representative since 1883, were about to have company.[22] Johnson's fledgling league, the former Western minor league, would be coming to Philadelphia, New York, Boston and Chicago, among other cities, to challenge the supremacy of the National League, which, after the demise of the American Association in 1891, had had the stage all to itself. In order to prove that it would not accept subservience to the Nationals, Johnson further announced that while his league, now renamed the American, would respect the contracts of players currently under contract to a National League club, it would not honor the reserve clause that thereafter bound these players to their teams for all eternity. In effect, Johnson had just declared war—with the stars of the National League his primary targets.

In Philadelphia, the Phillies were ill-equipped for battle. In the glare of the Major League spotlight in the late 1800s, they withered greatly, becoming a middling team at best and a poor one more often, despite a disproportionate number of stars. From 1891 to 1895, the Phils boasted what is arguably the greatest outfield of all time with Ed Delahanty, Big Sam Thompson and Sliding Billy Hamilton—all future Hall of Famers—but still they managed to finish no higher than third place in 1895.[23] The previous four years they finished fourth. In 1895, Hamilton was traded but the very next year the Phils acquired Napolean "Larry" Lajoie who would become the finest second baseman of his era and one of the finest of any to come. Nevertheless, the Phils continued to struggle. In 1896, they slipped to eighth place in the 12-team league and the next year they plummeted all the way to tenth. The year 1898 saw some gradual improvement as they rose to sixth, and then to third the following two seasons. However, by the time Johnson and Somers rode into town after the 1900 season, Philadelphia baseball fans had seen in the Phillies nearly two decades of mediocre baseball.

Johnson appointed Connie Mack, a former manager of the Milwaukee club in the old Western League, to be his point man in Philadelphia. Mack had recently assisted Johnson in putting together the fledgling Red Sox in Boston[24] and he was now called upon to do the same once again. However, this time Johnson wanted Mack to stick around once the pieces were in place. As incentive, Johnson offered Mack 25 percent of the new franchise, now called the Athletics—a nickname that harkened back to the old Philadelphia Athletics of the now defunct American Association[25]—and thereby set in place even before it was born a management structure that was to be the ruin of the franchise a half century later. Mack then called upon a couple of sports writers for the *Philadelphia Inquirer* to work with him in securing a playing field. They did and were rewarded with their own 25 percent share in the club. This too was to have grave repercussions in the years to come. For the final 50 percent share, Mack turned to Benjamin Shibe, a partner of Phillies owner Al Reach in Reach's sporting goods business. In order to entice the wealthy Shibe to sign on, Mack promised that Reach's baseball would be chosen as the official ball of the American League. After consulting with Al Reach, who not only did not mind that his business partner would be owning a team in direct competition with his Phillies but actively *encouraged* it, Shibe accepted Mack's offer. The Philadelphia Athletics were in business.

From the very beginning, in 1901, the Phillies never had a chance. Given the strong ties between the American League teams and the writers who covered them (starting, but by no means ending, with the former sportswriter Ban Johnson himself), the fledgling league was guaranteed to receive copious attention in the media. The Athletics, with their *Inquirer* connection, were no exception. Even before they had played their initial game, there was no question that they would not become buried in the sports pages irrespective of the plight of the Phillies or their own ineptitude. Philadelphians were going to read about the Athletics regardless of the quality of the team they put on the field. Right away, however, it was clear that the Athletics were not going to need any help in attracting the attention of Philadelphia baseball fans.

Before even taking the field for their initial opening day, the Athletics stole the spotlight from the Phillies by convincing Napolean Lajoie to bolt to the A's. With that move, Philadelphia's marquis player now played for the upstarts and the established Phillies were relegated to the background, where they would remain for the next half century. Led by Lajoie, who led the American League in batting with a .422 average, home runs with 14 and RBIs with 125, the A's posted a winning record, finished fourth in the eight team league, and nearly matched the Phils in attendance, trailing them by a mere 28,000 fans. The next year, they would improve on all fronts despite losing Lajoie in a protracted court battle. (Although it would not be to the Phillies. Lajoie, after much drama and speculation, would be sold to the Cleveland Indians by Connie Mack, who remained adamant about protecting the interests of his fellow league members as against the hated Nationals.) To compensate, the Athletics signed even more players away from the Phils, won the 1902 American League pennant and became the highest drawing club in all of organized baseball, outdrawing the Phils by nearly a 4–1 margin. They also added a nickname that season when John McGraw, manager of the New York Giants in the rival National League, derisively announced that, in the Athletics, Ben Shibe had a "white elephant" on his hands. Mack soon made the symbol his own, going so far as to stitch it on his players' uniforms in later years[26] and using it for motivation.[27] By season's end, Mack surely had to be satisfied on all counts: his Athletics not only finished on top in their league, McGraw's Giants finished in the basement in theirs, 53.5 games out of first. In 1903, the Athletics slipped to second place but, due in large part to the last place finish by the Phillies, they outdrew their intracity rivals once again nearly 4 to 1.

The city quickly became enamored of the Athletics in part because of their success but also in part because of the aura of Mack himself. Initially, he drew praise in an era in which success was determined as much by the skills of the manager in the dugout as by the players on the field. Because the Athletics won, attention was directed toward Mack, and he was soon viewed as a unique baseball visionary. In this early era of "disorganized" organized baseball, when the concept of an organizational farm system was still decades in the future (to say nothing of long-term contracts), teams were able, if not expected, to reshuffle and remake themselves from year to year. If a particular player underperformed, it was up to the manager to call upon his informal network of "scouts" (often his cadre of baseball friends) to unearth for him a suitable replacement from out in the bushes. Mack was particularly adept at this and this skill was on grand display during the 1902 season when, due to the Lajoie contract imbroglio that also involved four other players who jumped from the Phils to the A's, he was forced to reconstitute his team after the season had already begun. In late April of that year, after Lajoie had in fact suited up for opening day and taken his place at second base for the A's, an injunction was issued (with service being perfected just before the ninth inning of that game, to be precise) preventing these players from suiting up for the A's. As a result, Mack pulled Lajoie from the field and thereafter lost not only his Hall of Fame second baseman from then on but also Elmer Flick, a Hall of Fame outfielder, plus his top pitchers in Bill Duggleby, Bill Bernhard and Chick Fraser. Undaunted, Mack retooled on the run and

Gentlemanly Connie Mack, left, studies pitching prospect Stew Bolen during spring training, in 1929. Regardless of the occasion, Mack was rarely seen in anything other than formal attire (Temple University Libraries, Urban Archives, Philadelphia, PA).

won the American League pennant anyway. It was this performance that cemented the idea in many Philadelphia fans' minds that Mack was more important to the success of the franchise than any of the players on the field. The legend of Mack was born during the 1902 season and grew more pronounced as the decade unfolded with the A's perennial contenders.

Philadelphia fans may have been drawn to Mack at first simply because his teams won, but, over time, there was another aspect of the man that drew their attention. Mack personified the gentlemanly image of postcolonial Philadelphia unlike any public figure who came before him. Described by one historian as "tall, handsome and soft spoken,"[28] he was "lace curtain Irish," and he appealed to many as much as for what he represented as for who he was. He was the polar opposite of his managerial rival John McGraw, another Irishman, but one who was short, rough and profane. Mack, by contrast, exuded the standard of manliness of Teddy Roosevelt's Progressive Era in that he was tough yet gentlemanly. He was, in short, Philadelphia — or at least what Philadelphia longed to be.

In reality, Mack had something of the maverick spirit in him (as did anyone who agreed to cast their lot with the upstart American League) and was in many ways a forward thinker, as his managerial prowess in 1902 demonstrated. Regardless, his image nevertheless fit the image of staid Philadelphia. A teetotaler and a man who never swore, Mack, dressed impeccably in suit and tie in the dugout, discreetly waving his players into position with a flick of his scorecard, presented a familiar and comfortable image of his city — the genteel, refined, gentlemanly neighbor of rough and crude New York.[29] Because of this, Philadelphians identified with Mack and his Athletics much more so than the Phillies, who were perpetually in disarray and had no image at all, let alone one that meshed so perfectly with their city.

As the A's continued to win during the first decade of the twentieth century, their popularity soared. They would win another pennant in 1905 and, even when they lost, because they were at least in contention, they would set attendance records. In 1907, for example, they set a club attendance record of 625,581 despite finishing second. They would backslide the next couple of years, both in the standings and at the gate, but they rebounded in 1910 to win not only the pennant but also the World Series. The following year would be even sweeter for the city of Philadelphia as the A's not only repeated as world champs but, this time, they defeated McGraw and the hated New York Giants, providing the city with a rare opportunity to throw out its chest at the expense of its rival to the north. As the more substantive battles for political, financial and intellectual supremacy had been ceded long ago, battles on the ball field were, if not the only venue that remained where local honor could be defended, the most visible. Mack's victory may not have changed anything on a grand scale but, at least in some respects, Philadelphians could feel as if their city still mattered. A victory by gentlemanly Mack over the rough and crude McGraw was a victory for the city of Philadelphia, and all that it represented, over New York.[30] To Philadelphians, this was not an insignificant thing.

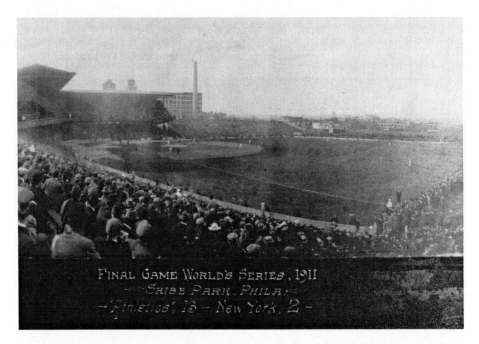

FINAL GAME WORLD'S SERIES, 1911
SHIBE PARK, PHILA.
Athletics 13 – New York, 2 –

A packed Shibe Park on October 26, 1911, the day the A's defeated McGraw and the Giants to win their second consecutive World Series (Temple University Libraries, Urban Archives, Philadelphia, PA).

These swelled feelings of Philadelphians continued for the next few seasons. After winning 90 games and finishing third in 1912, the A's, with their famous "$100,000 infield" of Stuffy McInnis, Eddie Collins, Jack Barry and Frank "Home Run" Baker, beat the Giants again in 1913 to recapture the world championship. They won the pennant the next year, ultimately losing to the "Miracle" Braves in the World Series. The appellation "miracle" was an apt one, for, in the eyes of the nation, no professional baseball team would be able to beat the Athletics without the aid of one. By the end of the 1914 season, the A's, with their six pennants to date and three World Series victories in the previous four seasons, were a source of pride for a city that had largely abandoned much of it a century earlier. The city did not merely enjoy the play of the Athletics, it was indebted to them.

After several "down" seasons in the late teens and early 1920s, Mack would again prove his managerial mettle by resurrecting his Athletics once more. In the process, he would further ingratiate himself and his team with the city of Philadelphia by providing it with yet another opportunity to strut at New York's expense. After selling off many of his star players after the 1914 season (and finishing last for seven consecutive seasons between 1915 and

1921), Mack began reacquiring talent in the early 1920s. As a result, beginning in 1922, the Athletics steadily rose in the American League standings, from seventh in 1922 to sixth in 1923 to fifth in 1924 and then to second in 1925. At this point, his Athletics were the clear cut challengers to the New York Yankees and their famed "murderer's row" lineup of Babe Ruth, Lou Gehrig, Tony Lazzeri and the like. The excitement generated by the 1925 A's resulted in a team record attendance of 869,703 — a mark that would stand until after World War II. By the late 1920s, Mack had assembled a formidable murderer's row of his own, with Hall of Famers Mickey Cochrane, Al Simmons and Jimmy Foxx in the lineup and Lefty Grove on the mound, and he was prepared to dethrone what legend declares to be the greatest team of all time — the 1927 Yankees. After finishing second in both 1927 and 1928, the A's finally toppled the Yanks in 1929.

In fact, a sound argument can be made that it was Mack's 1929 Athletics, rather than the 1927 Yankees, that was the greatest ever to take the field. Although the 1927 Yanks defeated the A's by 19 games, the 1928 team, which was essentially unchanged, won by merely two and a half. In 1929, the A's completed their reversal of fortune by crushing the Yanks by 18 games. In the World Series, they dismantled the Cubs in five games. The next year saw a continuation of the same as the A's cruised to the pennant and then crushed a legendary team in its own right — the "Gas House Gang" of the St. Louis Cardinals—four games to two in the World Series. Testament to the greatness of these Athletics teams comes from the simple fact that they managed to limit the reign of the legendary 1920s Yankees to two short years. Ruth, Gehrig, and the rest of this famed bunch would continue to post impressive numbers for years to come; they could not, however, compete with the Athletics when both teams were at their peak.[31] The A's would continue their assault on the American League in 1931. They won the pennant easily, by 13 and a half games over the Yanks, winning a franchise record 107 games that remains to this day. This time, however, they fell to the Cardinals in the World Series in seven games.

When discussing the greatest teams ever, perhaps the more accurate debate lies in the comparison between the 1929 and 1930 versions of the Athletics rather than any analysis involving the Yankees. Critics and baseball historians may take sides on this one but many agree that, on the whole, the Athletics of the late 1920s and early '30s were superior to the Yanks of that era for the simple reason that they maintained their greatness longer.[32] Moreover, their roster was legendary in that it contained not only Hall of Famers such as Foxx, Simmons, Cochrane and Grove — all in the prime of their careers— but also, at one time or another, players who were already legends, and future Hall of Famers themselves, such as Tris Speaker, Ty Cobb, Zack

Wheat, Eddie Collins and Waite Hoyt.[33] As a result, a fan going out to see the Athletics in the late 1920s was likely to see as many as six future Hall of Famers on the field playing for his A's alone. A collection of talent of this magnitude on one team was, and remains, unprecedented.

By the close of the 1931 season, the Athletics had won nearly one-third (nine of 31) of all the American League pennants to date and five world championships. By contrast, the Yankees had only three pennants and three world titles to boast. The Athletics were the class of the league and were thought of much like the Yankees are today: as far and away the dominant team in Major League Baseball. That their two dynasty teams won at the primary expense of two New York teams, which were accomplished in their own rights but clearly no match head to head with the Mackmen, only added to the pride Philadelphians had in their Athletics. Connie Mack was not merely the greatest manager in the game but the dignified symbol of the city, a city that, at least in one respect, had the measure of their uncivilized rivals up the road.

The Perpetually Befuddled Phillies

The Phillies, to the contrary, could not have provided a greater contrast to the majestic portrait painted by Connie Mack and his Athletics. In fact, the Phillies projected no image at all. For most of the first three decades of the twentieth century, the Phillies were invisible to all but their small cadre of supporters. From 1901 through 1910, while Mack was building his first dynasty, the Phillies countered by finishing last once, seventh twice and in the middle of the pack the rest of the time. During the next decade they would improve, and actually reach the World Series in 1915, losing to the Red Sox in five games. However, even this accomplishment was a Pyrrhic victory in that the Major Leagues had been severely weakened during the 1914 and 1915 seasons due to the loss of many players to the upstart Federal League.[34] The Phils, who had assembled a decent roster by 1913, spearheaded by Hall of Fame pitcher Grover Cleveland Alexander and slugger Gavvy Cravath, managed to maintain more of it than most other contending teams. As a result, they won the National League pennant. They would remain competitive during the next two seasons, finishing second both times, before crashing to the basement in 1919. They would not escape the second division thereafter until 1932.

Far from being a point of pride to their city, the Phils seemed to arouse its citizens' ire, thus erasing whatever goodwill their 1915 pennant created. In 1923, the team made national news and legal history when it chose to prosecute a child for refusing to return a foul ball caught in the grandstand during a game.[35] On orders from team owner William Baker, the 11-year-old child was charged by the Philadelphia police with larceny after he put the ball in his pocket. He was taken to a house of detention where he spent the night. In the ensuing squabble over the Phils' right to take such action (a judge ruled the following day that the boy was not a felon and lectured the Phillies on their actions), a new rule was created. Henceforth, any fan fortunate enough to catch a foul ball was entitled to keep it. That the Phillies played no small role in the creation of this baseball tradition would be laudable if only they had not found themselves on the wrong side of the argument. That they were says much about their connection to the city of Philadelphia during this time. Connie Mack may have dismantled his dynasty in 1915 and presided over seven consecutive last-place finishes, but eventually he rearmed and gave the city something to be proud of. The Phils, by contrast, followed up their singular World Series appearance with a very public tiff with their fans and, more importantly, decades upon decades of miserable baseball. Unlike the Athletics, the Phils would not rebuild for a long time. In fact, after 1917, the Phils would remain in the second division for 30 of the next 31 seasons, reaching a high-water mark of fourth place in 1932. They would finish last or next to last in 24 of those seasons.

Shibe Park and the Seed of the Athletics' Demise

Although the Athletics achieved unrivaled success throughout the first decades of the 1900s, the seeds of their eventual undoing would be planted during these heady times. In fact, those seeds were a direct by-product of their prowess on the field, such that one could make the ironic argument that if they had only been a bit more pedestrian during their infancy, they would have survived in Philadelphia and very likely would have given its citizens baseball of a much higher quality than they were destined to endure throughout the century. In the end, it would be the very edifice erected to celebrate their success that would eventually doom them to failure.

From the very beginning of the National League in 1876, stadiums were integral in creating and showcasing the aura of both the teams playing on the field and the owners sitting in their private boxes. More than utilitarian places to play, stadiums were designed to be luxurious symbols of success. As far back as the early 1880s, owners boasted of stadiums replete with private boxes furnished with elaborate drapery and "comfortable armchairs."[36] The message these stadiums conveyed was clear: herein plays a successful, well-run team overseen by intelligent, philanthropic management. It was a message no rival owner could ignore, and it was only natural for each to want such a palace, and all that it represented, for himself.

In Philadelphia, Ben Shibe was no different. He had invested in an upstart team in an upstart league and, very quickly, things had paid off handsomely. By 1906, with both attendance in suddenly cramped Columbia Park (capacity 13,600) and his chest swelling, he decided that his Athletics deserved a palace of their own. Financially, the time seemed right: The A's were not only stable, they were thriving, with Shibe having earned approximately $350,000 from the Athletics alone by that point and Mack earning not only his $15,000 yearly salary but also an additional several thousand dollars annually as a result of the team's profits, which very quickly made him a rich man.[37] It seemed as if the Athletics were printing money and, with the migration of thousands of potentially new fans streaming into Philadelphia and cities across the Northeast, things looked to be only getting better. Between 1900 and 1920, the population shift from rural to urban areas exploded, with 25 percent of the nation relocating to the cities during this time.[38] It did not take long for Shibe to attempt to capitalize on his good fortune.

He decided to build a new ballpark as a testament not only to his team but also to himself. Appropriately, he named it Shibe Park. (Such was the tradition of the time. Soon, among others, Ebbets Field — after Dodgers owner Charles Ebbets— and Comiskey Park — after White Sox owner Charlie Comiskey — would be similarly christened.) Given that the ballpark needed to make a statement and not merely provide his Athletics with a suitable field on which to play, he spared little expense, building the world's first concrete and steel stadium. In keeping with the grandiose stadium tradition, Shibe's stadium was replete with "an ornate façade in what was called the French Renaissance style, with rusticated bases, composite columns, arched windows and vaultings, and a domed tower."[39] There were also "Ionic pilasters flanking recessed arches on either side of the building," which was composed of brick with terra-cotta ornamentation.[40] The stadium itself dwarfed old Columbia Park, seating, when it opened in 1909, 20,500 fans. All of this luxury, all of this style, and all of this ornamentation came at a steep price for its time: $301,000.[41] Every penny of it was privately financed.[42]

Suddenly, Shibe had much more at stake in the Athletics than ever before. Now, for the first time, he had significant debt to service and needed to keep interest in his team high. Although attendance in 1909 soared, jumping to 674,915 from 455,062 the previous year, the numbers would not be sustainable without perennially competitive clubs. And, in the catch-as-catch-can atmosphere of the early 1900s, where farm clubs were nonexistent and teams remade from year to year, the key to sustainable success appeared to be tied to the team's manager more than to anyone or anything else. So naturally, in order to protect his investment in Shibe Park, Shibe strove to ensure that his manager wouldn't be going anywhere anytime soon. In time, Shibe's success in doing so would prove to be the undoing of the entire franchise.

1908 Groundbreaking ceremonies for the construction of Shibe Park. Tom Shibe at left, Ben Shibe third from left, Connie Mack seventh from left and John Shibe fourth from right (Temple University Libraries, Urban Archives, Philadelphia, PA).

Soon after Shibe Park was completed, with the Athletics the toast of the American League in the early teens, potential suitors for Mack came calling. Most significantly, the New York Highlanders (soon to be renamed the Yankees), a heretofore struggling franchise that had come off a last place season in 1912 in winning all of 50 games, made overtures to Mack. They envisioned him as their answer to the Giants' John McGraw in their quest to take at least some of the spotlight away from his juggernaut, which had relegated the Highlanders to also-ran status— the New York equivalent of the Phillies.[43] In order to keep him away from his New York rivals, Shibe enticed Mack to remain with the Athletics by offering him a 50 percent share in the team, thereby making him an equal partner. In the short term, Shibe's move proved brilliant. Mack spurned the Highlanders, and Shibe, by in essence forcing potential suitors to come up not only with cash but with an equal stake in their franchise, succeeded in scaring off any other teams looking to pluck Mack from his Athletics in the future. He had succeeded in what he set out to do: protect his investment by ensuring that Mack would never leave. However, in the long run, he also positioned his manager so firmly within the organization that Shibe and his successors would be unable to remove him, regardless of how long he stuck to antiquated ideas regarding the running of a Major League Baseball franchise. Those ideas would turn the once mighty Athletics into the laughingstock of baseball.

The Enduring Images of the Athletics and Phillies

All of that would be many years in the future, however, when a much less glamorous portrait of Mack would emerge as the Athletics disintegrated in the 1940s and '50s and the city was left to wonder just what had happened to this once magnificent franchise. For a long time, however, and even as the A's began to lose with both regularity and stunning force, the city remained charmed by his gentlemanly persona — the Grand Old Man of Baseball. By 1934, the Athletics would join the Phils in the second division and remain there for much of the next two decades. Between 1934 and 1954, when they packed up and relocated to Kansas City, the Athletics would finish in the first division only twice, 1948 and 1952, and then only barely, finishing fourth both times. Fourteen times they would finish last or next to last. By this point, however, it was of little matter. Philadelphia had firmly become an A's town and no amount of losing (provided that the Phils complied and lost as well) would change the allegiances of the vast majority of Philadelphians. The city had grown to love the A's and revere Mack such that their shortcomings on the field made little difference. Regardless of how bad they became, they still meant more, because perhaps they symbolized more, than the Phillies ever could.

Mack himself had grown to become a mythical figure who both defined and transcended the game. He and his 1911 team were the subjects of a famous Ring Lardner short story, "Horseshoes."[44] Ernest Hemingway likewise took literary notice of the Mackmen in his short story, "The Three Day Blow," remarking that it seemed as if one had to have had the good fortune of living in either Philadelphia or New York if one wished to see a World Series game.[45] In 1929, Mack was honored with the Bok award, "presented annually to the individual who rendered the greatest service to Philadelphia," becoming its first recipient not associated with either the art or business community.[46] The selection of Mack for this award signified the city's acknowledgment that his gentlemanly persona had become the desired image of Philadelphia. More than any other individual living at the time, Mack *was* Philadelphia. Or, at least the image Philadelphians wished outsiders to associate with their city.

This image would serve both Mack and the Athletics well when times became so bad that they and the hapless Phils were largely indistinguishable on the field. In 1937, for instance, both teams finished seventh. Nevertheless, the Athletics doubled the Phils in attendance. The year 1941 was a similarly horrendous one for both clubs, as each finished in the basement. However, 528,000 fans came out to see the A's as compared to 230,000 for the Phils. Throughout the late 1930s and 1940s, as both teams fielded one bad team after another, fans stuck with the A's. Commenting on the city's undying allegiance to the moribund Athletics, Sam Breadon, owner of the St. Louis Cardinals, remarked, "If I finished last twice in succession in my town, I would be through. Mack can finish last season after season and still have the fans piling up in front of his turnstiles."[47] As late as 1948, despite nearly two decades during which mediocrity was the high-water mark, the Athletics were still outdrawing the Phils more often than not.

There were two main reasons why most Philadelphians remained loyal to Mack and the A's during this time: the history and tradition of the A's and the continued ineptitude of the Phils. Given the realities of the professional baseball scene in Philadelphia in the 1930s and '40s, fans had a choice: either root for a terrible team with a great tradition or root for a terrible team without one. Given these parameters, the choice was not all that difficult. Moreover, Philadelphians by now were adept at looking beyond the present and focusing on the past. And when they blocked out the team on the field, the A's were magnificent. Fans could watch the A's and recall their dismantling of the Giants in the teens and Yankees in the late twenties and early thirties. They could tell stories about Eddie Plank, Rube Waddell, "Home Run" Baker, Jimmie Foxx, Mickey Cochrane and Al Simmons and feel good about their team and their city. The Phils offered no such comfort. Without such tradition, fans had little choice but to focus on the product on the field. And no one could take pride in that. In short, even during the 1940s it was possible for Philadelphians to watch the Athletics and feel a sense of pride. It was impossible for them to watch the Phils and feel anything other than contempt and misery. This sentiment was echoed by a sportswriter after the Phils moved into Shibe Park in 1938. To this writer, the Phils simply did not belong on such historically sacred ground. He wrote: "There ... where the ghosts of Bender and Plank and Baker and Collins and Cochrane still cavort in their brilliance, where every retrospect is pleasing, there you see the Phillies."[48] Despite the ugly reality of the late '30s A's, history still mattered. In Philadelphia, it always has.

Of course, history did not have to be all there was. The Phils, as they would demonstrate late in the early 1950s, could have trumped the A's with an extended run of glory or even a few years of passable baseball. Instead, they remained mired at the bottom of the heap, the "laughing stock" of baseball.[49] They were so bad so often that even their natural geographic rivals, the A's, were hardly rivals at all. In Chicago, which too has borne witness to decades of ineptitude by both of their Major League franchises, one could be either a Cubs fan or a Sox fan but never both. In Philadelphia, however, one could safely root for the Phils (not that too many people did) without feeling disloyal to the A's. It was not so much that Philadelphians disliked the Phils as much as it was that they did not care about them one way or the other.

If any one attribute was to be considered the calling card of the pre–World War II Phillies, it would be their failure to inflame the passions of their city either way. Fans might become upset over the persistent struggles of Mack's later A's teams, but at least they cared. The Phils, by contrast, would endure one losing season after another in relative anonymity.

Aside from losing, it appears that the Phillies' greatest sin was their failure to carve out a niche for themselves in the Philadelphia baseball marketplace. Perhaps the city would have developed some allegiance to them if the Phillies had possessed familiar and exciting players who fans could root for. However, as far back as the early teens, the Phils maintained a practice of regularly selling their better players to rival teams. This provided ownership with a steady cash flow and allowed the Phils to be at least minimally profitable, despite their poor attendance and poorly performing teams. This had the residual effect of creating a revolving door in the clubhouse and a faceless team year after year. Thus a vicious cycle began with the team selling players in order to replace the cash flow missing due to poor attendance, which itself was caused, at least in part, by a lack of identifiable players. With no one to root for, it was no wonder fans stayed away. The Athletics also engaged in the practice of regularly selling players, but at least they had their tradition and the near-mythical figure of Mack to fall back on. The Phils had neither of these advantages.

Hindsight being what it is, it is difficult to reflect on the 1940s and '50s without recognizing the enormous opportunity presented to the Phils to carve out a niche in another way. As the pressure intensified for the integration of Major League Baseball, the Phils were uniquely situated to take advantage of the large black baseball fan base in Philadelphia by breaking the color barrier themselves. However, they were not only unwilling to do so, they remained one of the final holdouts in the integration process. In the 1940s, there were nearly 400,000 black citizens in Philadelphia. According to a 1951 study prepared by the Wharton School of the University of Pennsylvania (interestingly, with the assistance of the Phillies), many of these residents were inclined to spend their discretionary income on activities such as professional baseball.[50] The study concluded that "it would be economically advantageous for Philadelphia teams to hire black players and cultivate blacks as fans."[51] The Phillies ignored this advice.

Mack himself was an opponent of integration. After Jackie Robinson broke the color barrier, Mack told reporters, in comments that he was later persuaded to take off the record, that he had no respect for Branch Rickey for doing what he had done.[52] Later, he made a token effort as he hired Judy Johnson, a former Negro League legend, to scout black talent, but then he refused to sign the players brought to him by Johnson, most notably Larry

Doby, Minnie Minoso and Hank Aaron.[53] The Phillies could have stepped into this void and finally emerged from the shadow of the Athletics. Given the decades of futility that had preceded this moment, it would have taken a step of this magnitude for the Phils to grab the attention of a city, which up to then had largely ignored them. However, they failed to act. In this regard they were certainly not alone but, given their inability to create an identity up to then, they perhaps should have raised their antennae higher than some other clubs. Instead, in 1942, they dissuaded Philadelphia native Roy Campanella from even trying out for their club by indicating that if they were to sign him, they would have no choice but to assign him to a Southern minor league team.[54] Satchel Paige and Josh Gibson were other names that failed to stir the competitive juices of Phillies owner Gerry Nugent.[55] Later, when Bob Carpenter bought the club, he was at best indifferent to the issue of integration. The Phillies would remain an all-white outfit until 1957 when an undistinguished talent named John Kennedy finally made the roster and appeared in a handful of games. But by then it was too late. By that point, the Phils were the last National League club to integrate and the next-to-last in all of baseball, with only the Boston Red Sox remaining a holdout.

Having failed to distinguish themselves either on or off the field, the Phils remained in the shadow of the Athletics for the entire first half of the twentieth century. Because of everything the Athletics stood for, and all that Connie Mack represented, Philadelphia remained an A's town through the late 1940s, even though their play was often indistinguishable from that of the Phillies. The Athletics were the face of the city. The Phillies were an afterthought — if they were even thought of at all.

3

Baseball's Pre-Expansion Power Structure: New York's Boon, Philadelphia's Doom

Black Friday: Third Inning

As the Dodgers retreated to their dugout, the entire stadium stopped to catch its breath. In a way, Hooton had it easy: he may have been spent but at least he was able to take the rest of the afternoon off. The crowd, on the other hand, had seven more innings to go with no hope of anyone coming out to relieve them. They'd just have to make do with what they had left. The top of the third inning gave them a much needed respite. Lopes led off and grounded out to Hebner on one pitch. Russell waited until the second pitch to pop out to Schmidt for out number two and Smith doubled Russell again, lasting all of four pitches before striking out on a Christenson fastball. Three outs in seven pitches. The wind, having been sucked out of the stadium during the riotous second inning, slowly returned as everyone was finally permitted to exhale.

Almost as soon as Luzinski dug into the box for the bottom of the third, Rhoden got in front of him 1–2; even this, however, provided no boost to LA's shattered confidence. For the Bull just missed sending one clear out of the stadium with a vicious swing at a fastball that missed by only a fraction of an inch. The ticked ball went straight back, slamming against the protective screen behind home plate and saving someone thousands of dollars in reconstructive surgery. The crowd gasped at the force of his swing, registering a level of collective disappointment in what they had just missed witnessing. Luzinski had once planted one on the replica of the Liberty Bell in left centerfield (off of Hooton, coincidentally), just below the 500 level in the

Luzinski (left) and Schmidt compare lumber during the 1976 playoffs (Temple University Libraries, Urban Archives, Philadelphia, PA).

upper deck, and this swing promised an even greater spectacle. Even when replays of that historic shot were played (without sound, as was the technology of the time), it was a blast of such magnitude that one could have sworn to have heard a clang when it made contact. It seemed as if only millimeters had prevented a reoccurrence of this event.

Before the Phillies made their ascension to the ranks of respectability in the mid–1970s, Luzinski was just about all they had. The Phils of the early '70s were little more than an assemblage of drifters, has-beens and never-weres, punctuated by this dollop of legitimacy situated out in left field (or, occasionally, at first base). In fact, if anything, the Billy Grabarkowitzes, Joe Hoerners, Dick Selmas, and Roger Freeds who would be foisted upon the fandom in the name of professional baseball looked even more fraudulent when compared with the raw talent batting cleanup. Later, when the talent level rose above sea level and players such as Boone, Maddox and Dave Cash arrived, Luzinski stood out less and became less of an icon, even though his production increased. However, to many, he was always more of a Phillie than the rest — even more so than Schmidt, who quickly outshone him in the talent department. Perhaps it was *because* Schmidt was so obviously gifted that many fans didn't take to him; everybody knew people like Schmidt, that is, people to whom everything came so easily, and very few people liked them. Nobody ever likes the smartest kid in the room. With Luzinski, on the other hand, his grimaces at the plate were something people could relate to, as were his troubles in the field and his never-ending weight problem (in later years, he would start wearing glasses, further endearing him to his less than perfect public). Watching Luzinski, one couldn't help but recognize the effort and this perhaps led many fans to better appreciate it.

Rhoden's next two pitches missed, first low and then high, causing the crowd to reengage. Rhoden looked pained on the mound, as if he saw the events of the second inning being recreated beyond the grasp of his control. Like Hooton before him, there was a sense that the location of his pitches was not wholly his determination. After what had happened in the second, the fans legitimately believed that they had a say in this as well. As he wound up once again, the whistling and taunting reached their apex. There were few in the ballpark who believed that the next pitch had even the slightest chance of ending up within the strike zone and, of course, it did not. It was low and away and the Bull took first.

Hebner followed, and he ended up doing what the Dodgers seemed utterly incapable of on their own: taking the Phils right out of the inning. Going against convention by swinging on the first pitch after Luzinski's walk and the events of the inning before, he succeeded only in lofting a lazy fly to shallow center field. In retrospect, his confounding swing may have turned out to be the most critical moment of the afternoon. In a game that contained as many big moments as this one, it might at first seem surprising that a simple decision to swing rather than take in an otherwise nondescript third inning could have had such an impact, but given what had happened beforehand, as well as what was to come later, this decision may in fact have changed the entire game. If only he had taken and allowed Rhoden to prove to all 63,000 in attendance that he had the ability to do what Hooton could not, it was possible that he would have disintegrated as well, and the Dodgers would have been crushed for good, not only in this game but in the series. Rhoden entered the game on less than steady legs and appeared primed to have the stool kicked out from under him. He had been a starter throughout the season, so coming in during the heat of the action was foreign to him. It was clear from the moment he took the ball from Lasorda that all he wanted out of his outing was to get through it. He looked tentative, unsure, and Luzinski's 1–2 swing may very well have reinforced his doubts as he never threw a pitch anywhere near the strike zone after that. Still, Hebner swung, thereby loosening the noose around Rhoden's neck.

The result was not without a drama of its own, however. What on most days was a simple fly ball, particularly with the Gold Glover Monday on the receiving end of it, was today clearly a different sort of ball altogether. The sun, sitting low in the sky, resting just over the lip of the stadium, met the ball on its way down and swallowed it whole. Monday, charging toward second, slowed and tried to pick it up, for a moment to no avail. He applied the brakes and it seemed as if he was bracing to trap it on the bounce, hoping to stop it before it hopped cartoonishly on the Astroturf over his head. Hebner, it appeared, may have been saved from his mental lapse. However, just as quickly, Monday recovered, picked up the ball just before it reached his mitt, and made the catch.

Up then stepped Maddox. The very fact that Maddox was able to step anywhere this afternoon would have been considered nothing short of a miracle just days earlier. The previous Sunday, the final day of the season, in a meaningless game against the Expos, Maddox fouled a Steve Rogers sinker into his left kneecap, causing what was termed by Phillies doctor Phillip Marone a "flake" fracture. The injury itself was a mystery to everyone involved, as nobody on the team could ever remember a player fouling a ball off of his own knee to such an extent as to cause a fracture. Broken toes, mashed shins and corrupted ankles were to be expected. Fractured knees were something entirely new, however. Regardless, no one informed Maddox's knee of that fact as the center fielder collapsed to the ground and had to be helped off the field.

After the game, with the LA series looming only two days hence, it would have been natural to expect the collective finger to be pointed in Danny Ozark's direction for suddenly diminishing the city's chances of bearing personal witness to its first World Series game in 27 years. After all, there was no reason for any of the regular players to be playing in such a meaningless game. Accordingly, Schmidt and Luzinski, among others, took the day off.

But Maddox wanted to play (he was in the midst of a 14-game hitting streak and was just a few points shy of finishing the season at .300). Given how hot he was, a three-hit day — with his last couple of at-bats most likely coming against minor league call-ups — was not out of the question, and Ozark refused to stand in his way. Besides, with the turnabout in Ozark's decision-making fortunes throughout the 1977 season, whereby the man who for years could do no right suddenly could do no wrong, there was nobody on the team or in the media who was going to challenge him. So the collective finger remained holstered, for the moment at least. By game's end, however, it would become clear that Ozark's decision to play Maddox was one of the early signs that his fortuitous streak was about to come to a crashing and punishing end.

Initially, Marone announced that the injury would take seven to 10 days to heal, thereby putting Maddox out of the entire League Championship Series. Ozark, however, still cresting the wave of good fortune he'd been riding all season, blithely announced that he'd probably be back much, much sooner. Referring to an earlier shoulder injury as proof of his point, he said, "Garry wasn't supposed to play for a long time after that shoulder separation but he came back. I'm optimistic that he can possibly come out here and play."[1] Besides, Ozark continued, even if he couldn't, he had options.

Essentially, his options boiled down to one man: Jerry Martin. Although Bake McBride could move from right field to center without much difficulty, finding a replacement for McBride in right was the key. Although Jay Johnstone was also available, the trio of the poor-fielding Luzinski and Johnstone, centered by McBride playing out of position, was a defensive nightmare of expansion-team proportions. Simply, there was little chance for the Phils to defeat the Dodgers with such a porous outfield playing together for potentially all five games. Instead, Jerry Martin, typically Luzinski's late inning replacement in left, would have to replace McBride, at least against lefties. This was the opportunity Martin had been waiting for all season.

For the better part of the previous two seasons, Martin played the role of Luzinski's disgruntled understudy, a role that allowed him to make cameo appearances in most games but little beyond that. He'd officially appeared in 246 games during that span but came to bat a mere 336 times. He grumbled about his fate, quietly at first, but then more loudly once McBride was acquired in June 1977, taking away the few at-bats he had as part of a platoon with Johnstone in right. "If they play him (McBride) every day, I don't think that's fair to me. And I'll have a lot to say. If I don't play against lefties, somebody's going to hear about it."[2] People did, but nothing was done. Martin continued to sit for seven or eight innings at a time on most nights, strutting out to left to replace the Bull as a defensive replacement in the ninth — the Phils' hedge against Luzinski's defensive limitations. With Maddox seemingly out for the Dodger series, however, Martin would finally get what he wanted. The downside was that Luzinski would be exposed for a full nine innings in left. Although Luzinski also disliked the replacement system Ozark had implemented (he felt that he had sufficiently recovered from a horrific 1974 knee injury and thus was a better fielder than he was given credit for),[3] the system had allowed Ozark to take advantage of what was generally considered the best bench in all of baseball. With Maddox out, his bench strength would be somewhat less; saving Ozark in the long run, but weakening the team in the crucial late innings, when games, series and seasons are often won and lost.

By the start of the playoffs, Maddox's knee had actually gotten worse. It appeared as if he'd be gone the entire series, leaving Martin in right and Luzinski exposed for the duration. However, between games two and three, he improved significantly enough to work his way back into the lineup. Ozark, it appeared, had been delivered from the brink of the abyss. The team survived without Maddox in LA, the centerfielder was back on the field in Philadelphia, his bench had been restored and Luzinski could thankfully be protected. Once again, fortune seemed to have smiled upon Ozark, pardoning him for the sin he had committed, appropriately enough, the previous Sunday. The hard part appeared to be over. All that was required of him now was to manage the game and his players (including, most importantly, Luzinski and his caddie Martin) as he had done all season long. Even for those who still doubted Ozark's decision-making abilities, this did not seem to be too much to ask of the man.

With Maddox now at the plate, Rhoden could see his way clear of the third. Like Hebner before him, Maddox wouldn't test him, wouldn't let the fans do what they had done so well just a short time before, wouldn't let Rhoden repeat Hooton's performance in the second. He walked all of 24 times the entire season. Rhoden knew this as well. As such, he could relax. Maddox was going to help him out. True to form, Maddox bit on the first pitch (as would Boone after him, flying out to end the inning), a nasty fastball that sawed his bat in half, causing the bat head to whirligig all the way down the third base line and into left field while Maddox was left impotently at home plate with the splintered handle. The ball itself trickled down the line where Cey grabbed it and fired to Lopes who forced Luzinski at second. Although the Bull nearly slammed the little second baseman into left field himself with his take-out slide, Lopes managed to fire a bullet to first where umpire Bruce Froemming ruled Maddox (who appeared to be running quite well despite the injury) safe on a close play. It would not be the last close call Froemming would make that afternoon.

Ownership's Quest for Status and the Foundation for the Athletics' Departure

The Phils' historical indifference to putting a winning team on the field was hardly unusual in the pre-expansion world of Major League Baseball. However, because of the progression of events through the early 1950s, Philadelphia would suffer unlike any other Major League city because, as the decades of the first half of the twentieth century passed from one to the next, an entire league full of teams subservient to one — the New York Yankees — emerged. They were run by owners who desired little more than to remain associated with the game and who were determined to do whatever it took to serve the interests of the Yankees in order to avoid their wrath and likely expulsion from the league. In due time, this required the sacrifice of several teams, the Athletics among them, in ownership's service to the Yankee brass, a service that most owners considered to be a far greater and necessary one than anything owed to the fans of their respective teams. Although Boston and St. Louis would also see teams leave town for similar reasons, Philadelphia was unique because here, unlike in Boston and St. Louis, the wrong team left town. The loss of Philadelphia's beloved Athletics would make the price paid by Philadelphia baseball fans far greater than the price fans paid anywhere else and would result in hostility and resentment toward the Phillies for decades to come.

Outsiders Looking In — And Getting There
Through Major League Baseball

From the very beginning of the National League in 1876, team owners have had, for the most part, agendas for their teams very different from those of many within their fan base. While fans in every city want nothing more than to see a winner representing them on the field, many of the myriad owners of Major League teams during this time wanted little more out of the game than to remain associated with it. The perks they derived from ownership came simply from their association with America's National Pastime. Winning added very little to the appeal. This indifference to successful competition would weaken the game, resulting in a competitively unhealthy Major League that was "major" in name only and vulnerable to the abuse eventually inflicted upon the city of Philadelphia in 1954 when the A's left town.

In order to understand just why it was that team owners cared so little about putting a successful team on the field, it is necessary to first understand the nature of these men themselves. For the most part, the original baseball "magnates"— as the men who formed the National League were fondly and optimistically referred to— were not from old, established money.

Instead, they were the nouveau riche: men who worked their way up through the ranks and who had attained wealth but not the status and respect that ordinarily came with it.[4] In part this was due to the simple fact that they were new money, but, in larger part, this was because they were clearly identifiable outsiders in America's upper-crust WASP society — a society into which they desperately wanted admittance — given that many of them were either new or recent immigrants (in many cases, Irish or German Jews).[5] As such, these were not men in search of money. They had that in abundance. What they were looking for was respect, something that branded them as not only rich but also American, just like their WASP counterparts. They found what they were looking for in baseball.

By the late 1850s, baseball's popularity was mushrooming both as an activity and as a spectator sport. Part of this was due to the joys presented by the game itself but part of it was likely due to the notion of the game as being something uniquely American. As the country careened toward civil war, nationalism ran high and the idea of an American game, as opposed to cricket with its obvious English roots, held great appeal. The emergence of baseball during this time, along with the fact that there were few other native sports established enough to challenge its claim as the national game, proved fortuitous.[6] As a result, Americans embraced baseball for both its aesthetic and its civic appeal.

Baseball, however, was not without its problems. The precursor to the National League, the National Association, was rife with gambling and rumors of thrown games. Moreover, players would "revolve" — jump from team to team with regularity, thereby reducing fans' connections with the players. By the mid 1870s, things were so bad that attendance was dwindling and calls for reform could be heard from all corners.[7] With "America's game" under attack, it was up to someone to step up and save it.

The magnates knew an opportunity when they saw one and quickly attached themselves to "America's game" in an attempt to gain the social standing they desired through the back door that they had been denied at the front. They formed a new league, the National League, and attempted to rid the game of the unseemly influences that had previously corrupted it. And they were not shy about trumpeting their good deeds. They brayed unabashedly about their role in creating the National League in an effort "to rescue the game from its slough of corruption and disgrace."[8] They took public stands whenever possible to protect the "respectful and honorable" American game by outlawing Sunday baseball (seen as sacrilegious by the dominant WASP culture), by banning alcohol, and by limiting access to the game by the lower echelons of society — people much like themselves before they attained their wealth — through increasing ticket prices, thereby making the game more appealing to the "respectable classes," the people they so desperately wanted to become.[9] All of these acts were undertaken, in large measure, to announce their presence at the forefront of America's game, to demonstrate to the American public that it was they who were the face of America's national pastime.

Later owners found much the same appeal in a connection with Major League Baseball as did their forebearers. Although owners came from all walks of life, including some, such as Red Sox owner Tom Yawkey, Phils owner Bob Carpenter and, to a lesser degree, Reds owner Powel Crosley, having been born into money and status,[10] many followed the blueprints of the original magnates, working their way up on their own and searching for societal acceptance through baseball once they got there. Others, such as Giants owner Charles Stoneham, looked to connect with the game in an effort to shake the taint of an unsavory reputation garnered in the process of earning their money.[11] For many, owning a team was a cry for acceptance, an announcement that they had arrived and at long last deserved respect.

Over the course of the first several decades of the twentieth century, these owners would build on the foundation that had already been laid regarding America's game in an effort to entrench themselves into American upper-crust society even further — to portray themselves as not merely Americans but as the gatekeepers of the American way of life. They sought to position themselves as the closest thing to royalty this country would ever see. In order to do this, they promoted the game as not only American in origin but as the embodiment of all those values which were believed to exemplify the superiority of the American way of life. In time, this came to be known as the "baseball creed."[12] Essentially, the creed held that baseball contributed to individual and public welfare by "building manliness, character and an ethic of success."[13] The crowds at games were touted (largely disingenuously given the rationale behind the increased ticket prices) as exemplifying American equality in that, at the games, people mingled with others from all walks of life, from each and every class. The owners, moreover, were "benevolent citizens who operated their franchises out of concern for the public interest";[14] and the American dream was alive and well in that anyone at all could become a professional baseball player provided they had the "talent and perseverance."[15] Pursuant to this creed, the virtues of the game were not limited to the ballpark. More broadly, the virtues embodied in baseball could be used to instill the proper values in America's children as well as educate immigrants as to the American way of life. By owning a professional baseball team, the owners — largely a collection of societal outsiders — therefore positioned themselves as the gatekeepers of the American way of life. If this didn't deserve respect and status, what would?

Of course, the owners were not able to spread their message on their own. They would need a mouthpiece, and they found a ready and willing one in the journalists who covered the games. Beginning in the late nineteenth century, owners and journalists banded together to spread the baseball creed to anyone who would listen.[16] There were two primary reasons why so many journalists were such willing accomplices. First, many writers depended on the owners for their livelihoods. Owners oftentimes paid their expenses and hired them for additional promotional work.[17] As such, they were not about to bite the hand that fed them. Second, the relationship between the media and baseball ownership was occasionally incestuous — many team executives were former journalists, not the least of whom was Ban Johnson, the founder of the American League.[18] Johnson's connections with his media friends helped him establish some of his fledgling franchises. In Philadelphia, as discussed in chapter 2, for example, two sportswriters partnered with Connie Mack and put up a substantial percentage of the money necessary to get the Athletics off the ground.[19] They continued to hold a 25 percent stake in the A's through the 1912 season.[20] In St. Louis, the Spink family not only ran *The Sporting News*, which regularly served as the mouthpiece of the owners, but were intermittently involved in ownership of local teams throughout the late nineteenth century.[21] Al Spink was later influential in the placement of the American League's Browns in St. Louis in 1902.[22]

Through the media, the owners' message of the virtues of the baseball creed was spread quickly and thickly. According to an article written in 1907, "A tonic, an exercise, a safety valve, baseball is second only to death as a leveler. So long as it remains our national game, America will abide no monarchy, and anarchy will be slow."[23] Twelve years later, another journalist wrote: "Baseball, to my way of thinking, is the greatest single force working for Americanization. No other game appeals so much to the foreign-born youngsters and nothing, not even the schools, teaches the American spirit so quickly, or inculcates the idea of sportsmanship or fair play as thoroughly."[24] Hundreds, if not thousands, of articles in newspapers and magazines across the country would repeat these themes for decades to come.

It was against this backdrop that many owners sought association with Major League baseball. The desire for status, the urge to promote themselves simply by being connected with the game, trumped everything else. Making money was a secondary consideration, as owners throughout the years have repeated over and over. Rather, they preferred to use their affiliation with the game to position themselves as "sportsmen," much like Britain's landed gentry. In Philadelphia, Ben Shibe's son Jack prided himself as such, as did Phillies owner Bob Carpenter, who considered owning the team his civic duty and a public service to the city of Philadelphia.[25] As recently as the mid–1960s, this

attitude held sway. M. Donald Grant of the Mets described his fellow owners thusly: "We're sportsmen. We're not in this for the money."[26] Of course,
they weren't crazy, either. While making money may not have been a primary
concern of theirs, neither did they want to lose it. Rather, the philosophy of
many of them can be best described as something akin to that of Cubs owner
Phil Wrigley, who said that while "he didn't care much about profits," he "just
didn't care to subsidize losses."[27] The bar for many of them, therefore, was
set exceedingly low. So long as they didn't lose money, or at least so much
money that they would have to part with their indulgence, they were satisfied.
Winning was not what mattered; membership in their exclusive club — the
closest thing to royalty within the United States— was all they were looking
for. It was this that repaid them for their investment in a franchise. And they
treated it as such from the very beginning. Charles Comiskey's private box
in his newly built ballpark was designed to resemble a miniature Roman Col-
iseum[28]; Walter O'Malley often refused to be seen anywhere within Ebbets
Field outside of his private box, so badly did he want to disassociate himself
with the common folk who attended his team's games.[29] To these men, along
with their brethren in ownership, status was everything.

Swimming in Place in a Shallow Pool

Accordingly, their yearly goal was to tread above the surface of the water,
financially speaking. And, given the simple economics of the times, this was
not difficult to accomplish. Prior to the 1950s, baseball revenue consisted
almost solely of ticket sales, from an average of 87 percent of all revenue in
the 1920s to approximately 80 percent as late as 1946.[30] Very little revenue
was brought in through things like concessions, parking and broadcast rights.
Instead, maintaining a positive balance between costs and ticket sales was all
that was needed to guarantee admission in the club from year to year. There
were two different ways to maintain such a balance: by either focusing on
revenue by increasing attendance through winning or by focusing on costs
by keeping expenses to an absolute minimum. Given the perils involved in
the first option, most owners chose the surer route to financial security
by steadfastly forgoing the costs involved in putting a winning team on the
field.

There has never been any question that winning teams bring with them
increased revenues through the uptick in ticket sales. Teams that win draw
crowds; teams that lose do not. However, for most owners, this was not the
end of the analysis. Winning involved risks that many owners were unwilling to take, out of fear that at some point, despite winning, costs would spiral out of control and they would be forced to sell their franchises regardless.
For one thing, a commitment to winning typically involved an outlay of a

significant amount of money up front in the hopes that more would be made on the back end, once the winning commenced. Depending on the state of the art at the time, top minor league prospects would need to be signed at prices even higher than their ever-increasing draft prices in order to secure them; scouts would need to be signed and paid; minor league operations would need to be updated and fed with substantial amounts of cash just to keep them running. Making a profit from these teams was typically out of the question. They were going to lose money — the only question was how much. There was no end to the potential costs.

Worse, once you started to win, the costs only seemed to increase even more dramatically as the players for whom you paid so much initially now needed to be rewarded for their productivity, along with the team's success, at increasingly higher salaries from one year to the next (the reserve clause may have held salaries down but the top players still received greater increases from year to year than everyone else — as the salaries of Mack's powerhouse teams of the late 1920s and early 1930s demonstrate).[31] And then there was the fear, articulated by Mack himself, that at some point, even winning teams would fail to excite fans, leading to a reduction in attendance despite (or, in Mack's belief, precisely because of) an extended period of success on the field.[32] Once this occurred, financial panic would ensue as an owner would be left with enormous costs against ever-shrinking revenue. And all of this would occur even if everything went as planned. If, somehow, all this money were laid out up front and winning did not ensue, the situation would be even worse for the owner. With a commitment to winning, one of two outcomes was likely and each was fraught with the potential for disaster.

By focusing on costs rather than revenue, however, the risks were reduced, solvency was more certain, and membership within the club was all but assured. By placing the emphasis on keeping costs down rather than increasing revenue, the owners needed to spend relatively little money on frivolities such as scouting and player development. What's more, a team with a frugal approach could make money, or at least not lose it, even if it lost repeatedly as the Phillies of the 1920s and '30s showed.[33] And most importantly, by keeping costs down, team owners were less dependent on the fickleness of their fan base. Through this approach, winning provided an unexpected — although welcome — bonus. The uptick in attendance and interest would allow the team to reap even greater rewards than anticipated. If, however, a middling finish or worse was in the cards, it was of little matter since the bottom line was covered nevertheless. Given the choice, it is little wonder that most owners chose to focus on their bottom lines rather than on their turnstiles.

As a result, teams remained small, comparatively bare-bones affairs for decades. In the 1920s, it was noted that only a few employees apart from the players themselves were absolutely necessary to keep a team running. For instance, a team might employ a treasurer, a road secretary, a business manager (responsible for concessions and all forms of advertising), a field manager, a few ticket-takers and ushers and perhaps a scout or two.[34] That was the extent of it. By the early 1960s, things hadn't changed all that much, at least relatively speaking. When judged against the increasingly sophisticated American economy, Major League Baseball remained a comparatively simple enterprise (although on a dollar-by-dollar basis, as discussed in chapter 4, the minimum costs required to run even a bad team rose significantly). Despite the fact that minor league operations were now folded into the mix and the level of scouting had increased, most teams still operated on a surprisingly small scale. In fact, a prominent sports economist studying the structure of the game during this time noted that "even the most successful ball team's revenues were no more than 'those of a department store or large supermarket.'"[35] This surely was not the image in the heads of most fans of "America's game." Their beloved Pirates could not possibly have only the economic swagger of the Acme down the street, could they? In fact, they did.

By keeping their operations small, teams could get by from year to year on the meager attendances that were their annual staple. In 1916, it took approximately all of $250,000 to run a team profitably, a figure that was comfortably surpassed through the average attendance at the time of approximately 5,000 fans per game (indeed, Charles Ebbets once crowed that he needed only 4,000 fans per game to make his Dodgers a profitable enterprise).[36] During the 1930s, this number hadn't increased all that much as Phillies owner Gerry Nugent estimated that he needed approximately $350,000 to run his team.[37] By the early 1950s, despite the additional costs incurred through minor league and other expenses, the revenue provided by the few hundred thousand fans per year that passed through a team's turnstiles were all that were needed in order to remain financially stable.[38] Although it is unclear precisely what each team's financial breaking point was, it is important to remember that up through the end of World War II, many teams such as the Boston Braves, St. Louis Browns, the Phillies and Athletics and others suffered through multiple seasons of horrendous attendance — the 1938 Phillies drew all of 166,111 and many others hovered consistently at the half million mark or below — and not a single team folded. Perhaps they lost money during some of these years, perhaps some owners finally had had enough and decided to sell, giving up their seat in the club, but there never was a situation so dire that a team ever actually folded altogether. The tight rein on expenses and the simple economics of the time made this a virtual impossibility.

A Major League in Name Only

By keeping expenses down, team owners knew they could survive practically anything. In their quest for survival, winning or even maintaining a competitive balance became a secondary concern, if that. As a result, for much of the first half of the twentieth century, the Major Leagues were major in name only as many top-quality players, for one reason or another, played elsewhere. Initially, this is not too difficult to understand. In the catch-as-catch-can world of baseball at the turn of the twentieth century, scouting was informal at best, with a disproportionate share of players hailing from the cities or states within which their teams played.[39] The formalization of the farm system model, initiated by Branch Rickey's Cardinals in the 1920s, changed these habits,[40] increasing the likelihood that a Major League team (or a minor league team that would one day deal with one) would take notice of a player off the beaten track, but still, there remained significant obstacles for many players in reaching the Majors, particularly when many owners were not interested in engaging in the expense involved in signing and developing them anyway. For one thing, despite the initial and obvious effects of Rickey's farm system (four pennants, two world championships won by the legendary Gas House Gang between 1928 and 1934), other teams did not exactly rush to copy it. Connie Mack, for one, repeatedly refused to undertake this expense and made little more than token gestures in the name of player development, content to lose year after year throughout the 1930s and early '40s until finally putting together something crudely resembling a farm "system" in 1946.[41]

Teams— Mack's Athletics and others— were likewise hesitant to offer the salaries necessary to lure top-shelf minor league talent, with the result that many players simply wallowed in the minors for years when their talent would otherwise dictate a promotion to the Majors.[42] Moreover, some players actually preferred to remain in the minors because, surprisingly enough, the pay was better. The Pacific Coast League, for instance, with its long seasons and balmy weather, remained a particularly strong rival to the Majors up through the early 1950s (not nearly as strong from top to bottom but replete with high-quality players) simply because its teams paid their top talent more than they could get in the "bigs."[43] While top PCL talent such as Ted Williams and Joe DiMaggio could expect large enough enticements to be lured away, many less talented (but still Major League quality) players did not. After the 1914 season, in fact, Harry Heilman decided to return to San Francisco of the PCL because his new team, the Detroit Tigers, refused to match what his hometown team, the San Francisco Seals, was promising to pay him for the 1915 season.[44] As late as the 1940s, this practice continued from time to time.

San Francisco manager Lefty O'Doul, generally regarded as one of the top managers in the game, repeatedly spurned overtures in the 1940s to manage in the Majors; his $30,000 annual salary dwarfed many of those of his counterparts east of the Mississippi.[45]

Still other Major League quality players were barred from entry into the game's top rung due to the vagaries of the various minor league draft rules in place during the time.[46] In 1921, the draft rules were altered, raising the price tags associated with players drafted at all levels—from $1,000 for Class D players to $5,000 for top level, Class AA players. However, limitations were placed on the number of players who could be drafted from the upper level (Class AA and A) teams (one from each). More importantly, the top leagues had the option of exempting themselves altogether from the draft if they too agreed not to draft players from lower leagues. As a result, the top minor leagues—the PCL, American Association and the International League—along with two others did just this, meaning that these players could rise to the Majors only through purchase at prices most Major League teams were unwilling to pay. As such, much Major League talent was logjammed at the minor league level. Although eventually the draft rules would be revised and a universal minor league draft accepted (in 1931), Major League quality players were still stuck in the minors for years due to the requirement that top minor league talent was not eligible for the draft until the player had completed four seasons of minor league ball. That requirement, along with the option rule that allowed Major League teams to stash these players in the minors for an additional three seasons, meant that otherwise qualified players could be held back for seven years from their otherwise rightful Major League debuts. Of course, Major League teams were never prohibited from purchasing players from the minors and circumventing these restrictions but, given their concern for the bottom line, many teams balked at the price tags, choosing instead to sell the players they had in order to keep their bottom lines in balance rather than take on this additional expense. The Phillies, for many years (as noted in chapter 2), were a prime example of this. Although the Majors certainly drew heavily from the PCL and other minor leagues during this time, the reality is that there were still Major League quality players and managers plying their trades elsewhere, causing Major League Baseball to be somewhat less "major" than it touted itself to be.

Competitive Imbalance and an Ever-Weakening Structure

These realities had obvious ramifications on the field as competitive balance was a thing of fantasy. Prior to 1920, despite the "wild west" nature of Major League Baseball at the time, it was hardly one that matched Connie Mack's perception of a league in which any team could win the pennant any year. In the National League, 75 percent of the 20 pennants won between 1901 and 1920 were won by three teams.[47] In the American League, this percentage was only slightly less — 70 percent.[48] By comparison, the next four decades would make those first two seem like absolute parity. Between 1921 and 1964, the Yankees would win 29 pennants and 20 world championships in a 43-year span. They would lose only two of the World Series that they were in — 1926 and 1942 — both to the Cardinals, who were themselves a slightly less menacing version of the Yankees in the National League, dominating the league by winning six world championships and nine pennants between 1926 and 1946. On the other end of the spectrum were teams such as the Phillies, St. Louis Browns and Boston Braves — teams that perpetually wallowed in something considerably less than mediocrity for much of the first half of the twentieth century and whose only pennants were made possible by extraordinary circumstances (with the 1914 "Miracle" Braves and 1915 Phils taking advantage of the reduced talent pool caused by the upstart Federal League and the wartime 1944 Browns managing to win largely due to an assist from Uncle Sam — of the 340 players enlisted in military service that season, only one was a Brown. The Yankees, by contrast, were decimated).[49] If league owners cared about this imbalance, they certainly had a funny way of showing it — repeatedly selling their top players to the "have's" such as the Yankees year after year, thereby perpetuating their misery.

Rather, the perpetual competitive imbalance of the Majors did not seem to disturb the owners one bit. The Braves of the mid–1930s were a prime example of the indifference of Major League baseball toward competitive balance. In 1935 they fielded one of the worst teams ever — producing a 38-115 record that at the time was the worst in the modern era. They finished 61.5 games out of first and drew all of 232,754 fans — averaging a mere 3,043 people per game. Yet somehow, their performance, and the yearly performances of several teams like them, did not cause league owners to reassess how they went about their business. Perhaps the largest indictment of the nature of the Majors during that time comes from the realization that the Braves, as bad as they were, were not even the saddest story in the league that year. The Phillies, who managed 64 wins that season, drew only 205,470.

Although baseball, as a concept, may have been a popular sport during the first half of the twentieth century, that popularity could not be gauged through the turnstiles of the Major Leagues. From 1900 through the end of World War II, many teams averaged between 5,000 and 7,000 fans per game.[50] Although this number might not have been bad for the first part of the century, it remained relatively flat in relation to increases in population (with the notable exception of the three New York teams) over four decades[51] — inching up somewhat through the years but still allowing for numerous games to be played in front of virtually empty stadiums. In fact, as metropolitan areas grew, particularly from the 1930s onward, together with the growth of the suburbs and improved access to and from cities through highway construction, it may be said that baseball attendance lagged significantly behind population growth from the 1930s through the 1950s.[52] It should also be noted that the "official" attendance figures of the time were hardly scientifically calculated and were largely inflated.[53] Many owners typically refused to release information regarding ticket sales (either due to limitations of the accounting technology of the time or perhaps because the numbers potentially tarnished their images) so the task of estimating the day's crowd was left to the sportswriters who covered the teams — the same sportswriters who were oftentimes beholden to the owners. Thus, the attendance figures reported in the newspapers were not only small, they were also very likely to have been optimistic figures. Even as late as the 1940s, fan interest in many teams was sporadic at best. As Marty Marion recalled when reflecting upon his early days with the Cardinals: "Baseball wasn't popular at the time. We had a little ballpark. Only 32,000 people could sit out there in Sportsman's Park. But boy, we sure didn't fill that up much either. What did we draw, 300,000 people?"[54] (The 1940, third place Cardinals "officially" drew 324,078 during Marion's rookie year.) In the 1950s, there were still games played in which the "announced" crowd was less than 1,000.[55]

It is important to note that, for the most part, the owners were not ignorant of the business world. They had the wherewithal to gain a competitive advantage over their fellow owners if, in fact, this is what they desired. As noted earlier, many of them were self-made men who worked their way up to the top of their fields, getting there through guile and not a small amount of competitive fire.[56] Several were, in short, financial success stories, achieving their station in life through aggressive risk taking. However, when it came to their baseball teams, they turned their engines off, allowing themselves the luxury of coasting through their experience without much attention paid to the nature of the product they were putting out for public consumption. These men, largely innovators in their chosen fields, instead chose to sit back and enjoy their affiliation with Major League Baseball, seeking nothing more than to continue to do so long into the future. As a result, they either failed to see or chose not to see (most likely due to cost — either financial or social) many innovations that would have spurred interest in their teams and which might have otherwise made them competitive.

Competitive Malaise and the Rise of the Yankees

One innovation ignored by many of them for years was nighttime baseball. As early as 1930, Sacramento of the Pacific Coast League demonstrated nighttime games' impact on attendance, and nighttime ball playing was quickly instituted by other PCL teams as well as other minor leagues.[57] However, Major League owners were content with the smaller daytime crowds for several years. Night baseball finally came to Cincinnati in 1935 but even then, after five years of demonstrated financial success, Connie Mack called it a "passing fad" that "will never make a hit with 'real fans,'"[58] despite mounting evidence to the contrary. By 1939, only five Major League teams had installed lights and it took until 1940 for one of the poorest drawing teams, the St. Louis Browns, to finally accept the money that St. Louis fans had been willing to give them all along by being able to attend a game after work; the 1940 Browns wound up with their highest attendance in over a decade. Perhaps most interestingly, William Wrigley, Jr., owner of the Los Angeles Angels of the PCL, took instant note of the uptick in attendance evident in Sacramento by promising to erect "the best incandescent lighting money can buy" at Wrigley Field in LA.[59] He refused to do the same at his hallowed Major League field in Chicago. Even when the reward was obvious, Major League owners were hesitant to innovate, either out of reluctance to shell out money upfront or because of fears as to what these innovations might possibly do to the status of the game and, therefore, themselves.

Nowhere was this more evident than in Major League Baseball's perennial refusal to acknowledge the largest talent pool it was ignoring: the Negro Leagues.[60] By the 1930s, no one who followed baseball could deny that there existed numerous players in the Negro Leagues who could have held their own at the Major League level. After all, by this time, many Negro League teams played at least some of their games in Major League stadiums and, in the off-season, many Major League players such as Bob Feller, Lefty Grove and others often barnstormed with Negro League stars.[61] So one did not have to look far to see evidence of this unpicked bounty. Moreover, once Jackie Robinson broke the color barrier, the Dodgers demonstrated that not only was this talent genuine, but it was also about as cheap as it could come. Branch Rickey refused to compensate Robinson's Negro League team at all for purchasing his contract, a practice he continued after signing several other players shortly afterward. Thus, unlike the minor leagues where teams may have been hesitant to pay either the draft price or the higher purchase price of a player, here the talent was free outside of the contract itself. Still, there were relatively few takers at even these bargain prices for the first few seasons after Robinson's signing. Owners of teams such as the Phillies, Senators and others preferred losing to potentially sullying their images by stooping to sign Negro League players. To these men, and several others, losses on the field were less important than a loss of status.

And why should they suffer such a loss when the game, as designed and played through the first half of the twentieth century, allowed them perennial membership and all the perks that went with it by simply doing nothing more than putting a team on the field? No matter what they did, owners knew that if they kept their costs down, there would always be two sources of revenue available to them that would see them through whatever financial crisis may befall them: Sunday baseball and the New York Yankees. And neither of these sources was dependant at all on putting quality on the field.

SUNDAY BASEBALL

Upon its founding, the National League frowned on Sunday baseball, alleging that it did not attract the "respectable classes" of fans to their games—the very same classes the original owner-magnates hoped to join one day. However, on May 4, 1919, Sunday baseball came to New York and was an instant success, providing the hometown Giants and Dodgers with their biggest crowds ever (37,000 and 25,000, respectively).[62] While teams may have been hesitant to embrace change in other areas, here they were not. They quickly realized that without having to lay out any up-front money at all, they could go a long way toward meeting their meager attendance requirements through Sunday games alone, regardless of how bad their teams played or how poorly they otherwise drew. The 1920 Giants, for example, drew 40 percent of their total attendance with the season's 13 Sunday games. Other teams likewise saw rapid increases in attendance due to Sunday games, with many of them more than doubling their weekday attendance and making up for all those empty seats that otherwise filled the stands. This trend continued through the 1950s as teams comfortably banked on their Sunday gates to pull them through season after season.[63] And the best part of Sunday baseball was that the crowds came out no matter how wretched the team was.

THE EMERGENCE OF THE PATERNALISTIC NEW YORK YANKEES

The Yankees were another source of bankable revenue for many teams. As the twentieth century progressed, the Yankees asserted their dominance in more ways than simply on the field. Eventually, they would provide a life support system for many other team owners who, because they wanted nothing more than to perpetuate their association with the game, soon developed a vested interest in keeping them happy and maintaining their dominance. In fact, the anticompetitive nature of team owners manifested itself most damagingly when it came to the rest of Major League Baseball's relationship with the Yankees; eventually, in 1954 and the years beyond, the city of Philadelphia would pay a heavy price for this.

Most obviously, American League teams benefited directly from the aura of the Yankees (they of the "great DiMaggio" of Hemingway fame) on the 11 days or so each season when the Bronx Bombers rolled into their towns. For many teams, their gates from Yankee games were even better than during Sunday games, providing that much more of the necessary yearly attendance requirements. The 1953 Browns, for example, drew nearly half of their entire season's attendance on their 19 Sunday/Yankee games. It took another 46 games to make up the other half.[64] The 1954 Athletics drew similarly, drawing on these 18 dates nearly what it would take them another 49 to equal the rest of the season.[65] These examples are not unique. For many years, the Yankees were far and away the leading road attraction in the Majors.

American League teams also benefited from the large crowds that came out to see their Yankees play at Yankee Stadium. Unlike the National League, which for years offered a meager slice of the gate to road teams (47 cents per ticket for many years), American League rules provided for an 80–20 split, allowing road teams to profit from the particularly lucrative gates at what was America's largest drawing stadium.[66] In the 39 years between 1921 and 1960, the Yankees led the American League in attendance for 33 seasons and accounted for more than 20 percent of total league attendance 25 times.[67] Accordingly, the large crowds at Yankee Stadium and the nation's fascination with the mythic team benefited everyone, not just the Yankees themselves.

National League teams similarly benefited from the existence of a dominant team, although here, due to the meager split of the gates, the direct gain was somewhat less. For much of the 1940s and '50s, the Giants needed the Dodgers to survive, sometimes drawing as much as one-third to one-half their annual attendance in their games against their rivals from Brooklyn.[68] Other teams were likewise dependant on their Sunday/dominant team draws. The 1934 Reds, for instance, drew 70 percent of their total attendance on these 15 dates.[69] Just as in the American League, National League teams could survive merely by scheduling Sunday games and the 11 or so dates with whatever team happened to be the top draw at the time. However, neither of these factors depended on the quality of the hometown team, thus minimizing the incentive of team owners to spend much in the way of improving their product on the field, resulting in the imbalance that persisted for much of this time. But in many ways National League teams benefited from the dominance of the Yankees just like their American League counterparts. This led to an unhealthy reliance on them, which allowed the Yankees to perpetuate their dominance for decades and cause team owners to act in ways that appeared to be contrary to their competitive best interests, to the detriment of both the game and the fans in the cities affected by their decisions, none more so than in Philadelphia.

To begin with, given the stature most owners were seeking, merely being affiliated with the legendary Yankees of Ruth, Gehrig, DiMaggio and others provided these owners the glory they were seeking. Owning a team that competed in the same league as the country's premier team allowed them to bask in their reflected glow. As such, every other team owner had a vested interest in maintaining this glow. In addition, the mythic Yankees helped to spur interest in Major League Baseball more successfully across the country than the local affiliates could ever hope to do. Given the perpetually sorry nature of many teams, they would have been hard pressed on their own to stimulate the minds and open the wallets of the local fandom to even a meager degree.[70] The Yankees, however, brought attention to the game, giving it prestige and creating whatever national buzz existed toward the Major Leagues at the time. Many fans in Cincinnati, for example, might never have cared at all for the local Reds were it not for the aura about the game created largely by the legendary Yankees. As such, even if they never faced a particular team, the Yankees still sold tickets to their games.

More directly, the Yankees, because of their success both on the field and in the box office, were always available to keep other teams afloat by purchasing their top players from them, thus providing them the cash these teams needed to operate from one day to the next. Of course, a natural by-product of this was the perpetuation of the Yankee dynasty and the creation of a two-tiered Major League, with the Yankees on top and everybody else struggling merely to survive. In this sense, many Major League teams operated not unlike their minor league counterparts in that they balanced their books through the sales of tickets to their games along with the sale of their top players. Viewed from this perspective, it is difficult to see a difference between the two systems. For many teams, while they were Major League in name they were minor league in business mentality.

In fact, the Yankees would very likely never have achieved their legendary status without the generous support of their fellow owners through the years. The first great Yankee teams of the 1920s were built largely upon the purchase of several players (most notably Babe Ruth) from the great Boston Red Sox teams of the late teens and early twenties.[71] Because Red Sox owner Harry Frazee required a constant stream of cash to support his investments in Broadway shows, he sought out and found a willing partner in Yankees owner Jacob Ruppert. Within a few short years, more than a dozen players were sent from the Sox to the Yanks; the largest purchase was that of Ruth but other notables such as Carl Mays and Waite Hoyt also were sent packing. Later, Ruppert advanced Frazee a $350,000 loan and took a mortgage on Fenway Park as security. In order to pay this off, Frazee sent even more players to the Yanks over the next several years. Other teams likewise aided the Yankees cause: Connie Mack gladly surrendered future Hall of Famer Frank "Home Run" Baker's contract to the Yanks prior to the 1916 season, Wally

Pipp was purchased from the Detroit Tigers in 1915, the list goes on and on. As the Yankees improved, they only became more financially able to purchase the cream of the rest of the league's crop, which was a practice they continued through the 1940s and '50s when their dynasty was fueled largely through their acquisition of players such as Johnny Mize, Bob Turley, Roger Maris, Clete Boyer, Bobby Shantz, Ryne Duren, Ralph Terry, Hector Lopez, Johnny Sain, Enos Slaughter, Don Larsen and others in either flat out purchases or thinly veiled, one-sided trades with teams looking to dump salary and add revenue.[72] Despite the presence of the reserve clause, the free market nevertheless reined in Major League Baseball in that the team with the deepest pockets found a way to secure the top talent.[73]

As this practice continued, the rest of the league became subservient to the Yankees since there was little question that many team owners needed them in order to survive, given their chosen business plans. If they were not willing to invest much money in their teams upfront, the presence of a financial reservoir such as the Yankees was necessary in order for them to equalize any shortfall they may have realized at the end of the season. In short, the Yankees permitted many of the other team owners to remain the collective face of "America's game." As this was all most of them wanted, they were indebted to them. Between 1920 and 1964, owners worked overtime to perpetuate the imbalance of power that existed, outdoing each other by making deals that crippled them competitively. As a result, during this period, a typical season would result in 95 wins for the Bronx Bombers and a staggering 13 game advantage over whoever happened to finish second — a pennant "race" in name only. Of course, these team owners would likely argue, they needed to make these deals in order to survive. However, there were other ways to bring in revenue — ways that would have improved their teams on the field as well — and these were men who had been successful in ferreting them out in other walks of life. But here they simply did not care. Prior to expansion in the early 1960s and free agency in the 1970s, when the economics of the game would begin to change drastically, Major League Baseball was unhealthy from both a financial and a competitive aspect. And many of the team owners were committed to keeping it this way. As such, certainly by the late 1940s (and probably well before this), the Yankees *were* Major League Baseball — virtually every other team owed their existence to them. Soon, the Yankees, with the willing approval of their fellow team owners, would wield this power in an attempt to ward off Congress and solidify their dynasty even more. And the city of Philadelphia would pay the price.

4

The Fall of the A's,
the Rise of the Phillies

Black Friday: Fourth Inning

The sun, which had nearly shone to the Phils' benefit in the bottom of the third, wreaked havoc once again in the top of the fourth, with the Dodgers the beneficiaries of the assist this time around. Ron Cey stepped up in the darkened infield, the reverse of the brilliance in center, and awaited his opportunity. He surely could not have believed that he needed anything beyond what was there for him on the mound—a pitcher he owned during the season, going four for seven with three home runs—but he would get something anyway. After working the count full, Cey lined a fastball into center field. It sank quickly as it reached Maddox, finally hitting the ground inches before reaching his glove. On other days, without the sun glaring at him at eye level, and without the accumulated rust caused by a week of inactivity, that would have been the end of it, a simple single to center. Today, however, was not like other days. The ball kicked off the heel of Maddox's usually golden glove, bounding in one direction while his momentum continued to propel him frustratingly for several steps in another, allowing Cey to waddle into second with a fortuitous double. Right off the bat, the Phils were in trouble.

Garvey was next and as soon as Christenson fell behind him 1–0, Ozark got Warren Brusstar up in the bullpen. Christenson had danced around trouble all afternoon and it was becoming apparent that he was headed for more; still, it was only the fourth inning and Ozark tried to squeeze just a little more out of what was quickly becoming a dry dishrag. Christenson succeeded in inducing Garvey to ground out softly to Bowa at short but that allowed Cey to move to third and, with the tying run now breathing down Boone's neck, Ozark realized that he had to act preemptively to keep the game in check. With Dusty Baker strolling to the plate, he ordered his infield in, hoping to cut off the run and protect his lead. On the first pitch, his move succeeded, at least for the moment, although in a way he could not have hoped to predict. Baker hit a lazy pop in foul territory between Hebner and McBride in right. Normally, the ball would have been Sizemore's, the second baseman, who would have had to make a run for it, but who most likely would have caught it with his back to the infield. However, Cey would have scored easily on the play because Sizemore, without a particularly strong arm to begin with, would have been unlikely to reorient himself and fire to the plate in time to get a runner, even one as slow as Cey. Regardless, because he was drawn in under Ozark's orders, he was unable to catch up to it. The ball bounced harmlessly away in foul territory. An out had not been recorded, but neither had a run. The Phils could live with that trade-off.

All of this became academic very quickly, however, as, after smoking a liner foul down the third base line, Baker went the other way, dropping a looper into shallow right, just short of McBride's range. The single scored Cey and the sixth RBI for Baker in the series tied the game at three apiece.

Brusstar was now throwing with more purpose in the bullpen, the hollow pop of his catcher's mitt echoing off of the plexiglass divider that separated rightfield from the Phillies bullpen ever more loudly with each pitch. Christenson was not long for the game; everybody was aware of this by now. After Monday sliced a line drive foul in left and then, as Baker did before him, adjusting and then ripping a single to right, Ozark had had enough. He trudged his baggy self to the mound like a salesman late for an appointment, right finger in the air, calling for his rookie righthander. Although he had struggled, Christenson departed to mild applause, perhaps more due to the season he'd just completed than to his performance that afternoon. And in any event, there were more pressing matters to consider: men on first and second, one out, and the game possibly hanging in the balance. As soon as Brusstar emerged from the motorized Phillies-capped baseball that escorted him from the bullpen to the edge of the infield, he bore the weight of all this. And as he had done all season long, he responded.

Once again Steve Yeager was at the plate and, very quickly, once again Ozark was presented with a dilemma. Brusstar's first pitch sailed high and tight, barely missing Yeager and skipping past Boone for a passed ball, allowing Monday and Baker to advance to second and third. Just as in the second, first base was open. Just as in the second, Yeager was at bat. Just as in the second, the pitcher was on deck. Unlike in the second, however, Ozark decided to walk Yeager intentionally, loading the bases for the pitcher, in this instance Rick Rhoden. Given his decision to pitch to Yeager with the weak-hitting Hooten on deck in the second, it seemed curious that he would walk him now to get to Rhoden, one of the best hitting pitchers in baseball. In 1976, he batted .308 with 20 hits. In 1977, he cooled off to .231 but still managed 18 hits, including 3 home runs and 12 RBIs. Of course, walking Yeager would set up the double play, and with the sinker-ball specialist Brusstar on the mound, a ground ball was more likely than not, but with Rhoden, that certainly was not a guarantee.

Brusstar started him off with a fastball that he clearly could not catch up with. He swung weakly for strike one. After missing low with his next pitch, he followed up with a sinker that did not sink. Rhoden jumped on the flat pitch and lofted a fly ball to shallow right. McBride charged and caught it on the run. Despite this, Baker tagged and headed for home. And so, the third play at home plate in LA's four at-bats thus far was imminent. McBride's throw was as one imagines all such throws in the dusty trunks of one's baseball memories; however, here it was fact, not fiction. It buzzed toward the plate seemingly on a line until it bounced just before the home plate cut-out, hopping true right into Boone's awaiting mitt. Boone squeezed it and braced for the onrushing Baker who, realizing he had been beaten by the throw by several feet, sought to dislodge the ball by barreling the catcher over. He led with his elbow, aiming it at Boone's sternum and hitting it but failing to do anything else. Boone hung on, tagged the now stumbling Baker out and completed the double play. The game remained tied and the crowd found their voice, roaring in aggressive approval. It seemed as though no matter what LA did — no matter how many hits they got, no matter how poorly the Phillies' pitchers pitched — in the end, when it counted, they were never going to be able to do enough. The Phillies, despite themselves, were going to prevail. The teams headed to the bottom of the fourth technically tied but with the feeling that LA was well behind.

The Phils were unable to do anything off of Rhoden in the home half of the inning. Sizemore attempted to bunt his way on and, in the process, demonstrated precisely why the bunt had become an endangered species ever since the advent of Astroturf in the mid '60s. His form was textbook, his aim (past the pitcher's mound, between the first and second basemen) was true, and the play never had a chance. The ball sped along the surface, appearing, if anything, to actually pick up speed if that were physically possible, as it made its way toward Lopes, who easily grabbed it with his bare hand and flipped to Garvey for out number one. Tommy Hutton then came out to pinch hit for Brusstar and popped weakly to Russell for the second out; and Bake McBride kept Russell busy by grounding out to him on the first pitch for the final out. That quickly, the teams switched sides as the game neared the halfway point. Ron Reed strolled in from the bullpen to keep a lid on things. He would be near unhittable — baseball's best bullpen appeared to have things well in hand once more.

Darkening Skies and the Gathering of Philadelphia's "Perfect Storm"

The Fall of the "House of Mack"

As Major League Baseball entered the decade of the '40s, the game was not all that different an economic model from what it had previously been. Teams could survive, although not thrive, by keeping a tight rein on their bottom lines and limiting expenses up front in order to compensate for the limited revenue they would no doubt receive by season's end given the product they were putting on the field. As they had done before, most teams chose this route in order to ensure their survival from one season to the next. What *had* changed, however, was the bottom line itself. Slowly, as the game modernized, the bar had risen to the point where the minimum input (the amount needed merely to subsist) in the 1940s was substantially more than it had been a mere 15 or 20 years earlier. Now, even if the economic goals of a particular owner were the same as they had been previously (not to make money but rather simply not to lose any) significantly more revenue was required merely to achieve this modest result. This reality would doom the Athletics in Philadelphia as they entered the decade less able to adjust than any other Major League team.

There were two main areas that exemplified these changes. One was the proliferation of night baseball. Despite most owners' initial reluctance, as the 1940s, progressed (most notably after World War II), night games finally became more common, although not nearly to the extent they would be in the 1960s and '70s. Still, some teams recognized this increased revenue stream early on — in 1946, the Boston Braves played nearly a third (24 games) of their home schedule under the lights.[1] Although these games brought in additional revenue through increased ticket sales (the Braves, for example, drew 568,083 fans for these games that season), there were significant expenses involved. For one thing, there was the cost of erecting the light towers: the 1939 installation of lights at the Polo Grounds, for example, cost approximately $135,000.[2] For another, there were the increased electricity costs that went with them once they were up. Although these costs were not significant enough in and of themselves to doom a team to bankruptcy, they did have the effect of causing the bottom line to inch up ever so gradually. During this time, some teams also began to pay a bit more attention to marketing in conjunction with night baseball, adding just that much more to their expense ledgers. Turning to the Braves once again, they invested in neon foul poles (under the theory that they would be more easily seen at night) and sateen uniforms (which were hailed to "shimmer" under the incandescence). In addition, night baseball necessitated installation of electronic scoreboards (the traditional manual ones could not be seen as easily once the sun set), costing $50,000 or more to install. And once they were installed, someone had to be hired to run them. Each of these expenses, on their own, was not significant. Together, they had a cumulative impact.

However, these costs were small compared to the expenses associated with supporting a full-fledged farm system, which, by the 1940s, had become the rule rather than the exception that it had been previously. Only three decades earlier, in 1914, Branch Rickey's attempt to purchase a minor league team to be run as a farm team for the St. Louis Browns was stopped by the National Commission, which officially outlawed the practice.[3] Now, Rickey's farm system was a staple of most teams. Where once all minor league teams were independent entities, by 1952, 55 percent of them would be under the control of one Major League team or another.[4] And these teams cost substantial amounts of money to run — oftentimes, unlike their Major League brethren, without hope of ever seeing a profit from them in return no matter how tightly the financial reins were held. Where once it cost a mere $250,000 to run an entire Major League organization, now it cost more than that simply to purchase a single *minor league* team to add to a team's growing farm system. In 1946, the Braves purchased Milwaukee's AA team for $270,000 alone. And once acquired, there were additional yearly expenses. Players needed to be paid, coaches needed to be hired, and both of these needed to be supervised by the Major League organization, which operated them if the system (and the teams' investment) was to have any chance of success. Young players needed not only to be taught how to play the game, but also to be taught the "Braves" way or the "Yankee" way, assuming that a given team cared about such things. Several, such as the Athletics and, until the late 1940s, the Phillies, clearly did not. All of this cost money. In short, by the late 1940s, it cost more just to break even than it ever had before.

In Philadelphia, it had long become clear that Connie Mack was not up to this task. Initially, this was due to his sheer stubbornness and his slavish devotion to the bottom line more than anything else. Perhaps because of his fantastic success during the first decades of the 1900s, Mack defiantly stuck to the method of selecting players for his team that worked so well for him, at least in the early years, eschewing the benefits of a farm system even as that system began to change the nature of the game. Instead, Mack preferred to rely on his cadre of unofficial "scouts" (mostly friends and former players) to unearth talent for him even as this approach became passé.[5] He preferred this method to the more structured farm system approach because, in his mind, his method allowed for more players to be up for grabs, which, in turn, would mean that in any given year, any team had a chance to win the pennant if only it could sign enough of the top players.[6] He believed that this approach gave hope to fans of even the poorest teams, because, in increasing competitiveness within the league, it would increase attendance. For a man with no outside income who made his livelihood solely from baseball, he was one of the few owners who needed to see a profit from his team every year and thus he frowned on any system that seemingly infringed on his ability to do so. In his opinion, a farm system would make it more difficult for poor teams to improve and would perpetuate the success of good ones. Thus, Mack believed this system to be hazardous to his financial health. In his mind, even perpetually good teams such as his Athletics were problematic because eventually, or so he was convinced, fans would tire of dynasties and stop coming out to the ballpark. Regardless of how wrong-headed he was, there was nothing either Shibe or the fans of Philadelphia could do. By now a well-entrenched owner, he could remain in control of the franchise for as long as he pleased.

Mack's stubbornness and penny-pinching showed up in other ways as well. In 1914 and '15, with the upstart Federal League now on the scene and threatening to engage the American and National Leagues in bidding wars for top players, Mack stuck firm to his bottom line and refused to compromise his salary structure. Instead, he dealt the core of his first dynasty away to American League rivals, breaking up his famed "$100,000 infield" by selling star second baseman Eddie Collins, in the prime of his career, to the Chicago White Sox for a reported $50,000.[7] He also refused to renegotiate slugging third baseman Frank "Home Run" Baker's contract, allowing him to sit out the entire 1915 season. He likewise waived star pitchers Eddie Plank, Chief Bender and Jack Coombs, choosing instead to take the field with lesser known, and lesser salaried, players. When 1915 proved to be a failure both in the standings (the once mighty A's finished last, winning only 43 games) and in the stands (finishing at the bottom here too, drawing all of 146,223 fans for the entire season), he sold off even more players, including his last remaining star pitcher — Herb Pennock — to the Red Sox, choosing a meager profit (or an acceptably small loss) over achievement on the field. In 1916, Mack fielded what some believe to have been the worst team ever assembled, a team of no-names who managed to lose a whopping 117 games for a .235 winning percentage, virtually assuring A's fans that if they dared come out to the park, they'd go home having witnessed another miserable defeat.

For seven years, from 1915 until 1922, Mack continued along this path, eking out a small profit on his horrendous teams. Rather than pay for quality minor league players who might actually improve his club, Mack preferred to regularly audition local sandlot players in the hope of eventually finding someone who could actually play at the Major League level. In 1914, he was offered the opportunity to sign a bright prospect who went by the curious nickname of "Babe" Ruth. Ruth was creating quite a buzz for the

Baltimore Orioles in the minor leagues. The financially strapped owner of the Orioles offered Ruth and two other prospects to the A's for $23,000, but Mack refused, suggesting that the owner contact the Red Sox and try to make a deal with them. Instead, Mack continued to suit up dozens upon dozens of sand-lotters and recent high school graduates in the hope of finding his own Babe Ruth without the accompanying price tag. He never did.

As the teens grew to a close, fans began to grumble about what had become of their once proud franchise, but nothing could be done about it. Mack was entrenched and he was not going anywhere soon. Although he would hold on for another three decades, even now fans were starting to realize that Ben Shibe may have made a mistake back in 1913 by making him an equal partner, as they knew that no one without Mack's job security could have (or, more importantly, should have) survived the seven-year run of futility Mack foisted upon the city of Philadelphia.[8]

Although finally, in 1922, Mack would change course and begin to restock his club with talented minor leaguers,[9] eventually putting together his second and greatest dynasty in the late 1920s and early 1930s, this too would prove to be little more than a temporary blip on the horizon of the Philadelphia Athletics. For once again, due to stubbornness and economics, Mack would break this team up as well, returning the Athletics to competitive slumber, this time for good. By the late 1920s, Mack was a supremely wealthy man, having invested heavily in the stock market. When it crashed in 1929, he suffered greatly, more so than many others in baseball who were not as deeply invested. Now, however, due to the success of his Athletics, he was saddled with superstars such as Jimmie Foxx, Al Simmons and Mickey Cochrane, who carried with them not only legendary reputations but salaries to match. Simmons alone earned $33,000 in 1932, more than half of Mack's $50,000 salary. Other players earned upward of $16,000 apiece. Added to Mack's troubles were the costs associated with a recent renovation of Shibe Park. Altogether, combined with attendance figures that had decreased steadily from 839,176 in 1929 to 721,663 in 1930 to 627,464 in 1931 to 405,500 in 1932, Mack decided to protect his bottom line by selling off his star players once again. He ignored the fact that American League attendance due to the Great Depression had similarly decreased since 1929 (from 4,662,470 in 1929 to 3,133,232 in 1932) and that, comparatively, the Athletics were still among the top drawing teams — ranking third in 1932 behind only the Yankees and Cleveland Indians. Mack focused instead on the money coming in and going out the door. And here, things were not balanced. Players would have to go in order to rectify the situation.

As time wore on, Mack's words and deeds grew more and more curious, with the other investors in the team impotent to do anything about what he was saying and doing. For instance, Mack initially blamed his inability to retain his high-salaried players on Pennsylvania's archaic blue laws, which, among other things, forbade Sunday baseball, thus forcing Mack to forgo the gate receipts for what were typically the most well-attended games of the week. Sunday doubleheaders drew well across the league, so well that Sunday attendance alone offset the typical meager weekday crowds that, by themselves, would have sent many teams into insolvency. Without the benefit of Sunday baseball, Mack argued, he had no choice but to send his best players packing. However, when, in November 1933, the blue laws were finally lifted, Mack celebrated by selling off even more players, including future Hall of Famers Mickey Cochrane and Lefty Grove, for cash.

He also attempted to manipulate the competitive structure of the American League in the hope that his Athletics would be able to compete with their lower payroll and lesser talent. Rather than sell his players off all at once, as he did in the teens, now he chose to sell them off in stages, figuring that by doing so, he'd be able to maintain at least a competitive club for a while, thus spurring increased attendance.[10] In addition, when he did sell off his players, he attempted to sell them to the weaker clubs as part of a strategy to improve them enough to increase the competitive quality of the league as a whole.[11] Neither of his mad scientist schemes worked. Attendance continued to fall off— to 297,138 in 1933, up slightly to 305,847 in 1934 but then plummeting to 233,173 in 1935. On the field, his teams lost 72 games in 1933, 82 in 1934, 91 in 1935 and 100 in 1936. They would go on to lose 100 or more games five more times before they would relocate after the 1954 season. Regardless, no one had the power to remove him and he was free to dabble in his unique baseball theories for as long as he pleased, to the detriment of both his franchise and the city of Philadelphia.

To add insult to injury, Mack proceeded to bleed the coffers dry during the 1920s and early '30s, draining the franchise of the excess capital it would need to right itself and prevent the hostile takeover that was to come later. Although frugal when times were bad, Mack, along with his co-owners, was hardly cautious with the team's money when times were good. Rather than store up the team's vast reserves built up during their 1920s dynasty, Mack and the Shibes took huge dividends for themselves. Of the $1.1 million in profit generated by the club between 1925 and 1931, they claimed $400,000 of this as dividends for themselves.[12] In 1931 alone they declared $250,000 in dividends even as they pleaded poverty and began dismantling what was perhaps the greatest club of all time.[13] As a result, when times really went bad later on, there was no money left to save the franchise. All of it was gone, having disappeared long ago into the pockets of Mack and his partners.

As the 1930s rolled on, leaving the Athletics far behind, Mack reverted to his old ways, auditioning sandlotters and high school grads once again. One well-known rumor has it that Mack kept one player on his squad during the 1940s merely because his father ran the best butcher shop in the neighborhood and Mack used the player in order to secure the best cuts for himself.[14] Regardless of the veracity of this tale, it became clear during the 1930s and afterward that the talent on the field in what was once Ben Shibe's grand palace was not nearly on a par with the magnificence of the structure. And, rather than things getting better over time, as even the worst things tend to do, when it came to the Athletics, there seemed to be no bottom in sight. In the midst of several successive 90-loss seasons, Mack was able to increase his stake in the club even more, buying out the shares of the widow of Ben Shibe's son in 1937.[15] Now, despite everything else, Mack had a controlling interest in the A's for the first time. Unlike in 1913, however, very few Philadelphians took comfort in this news.

As the costs associated with operating even a minimally solvent team rose throughout the 1930s and '40s, Connie Mack dug an increasingly deeper financial hole into which his Athletics would descend until, finally, they would be unable to crawl out. In 1935, Mack was the first American League owner to install lights, despite his aforementioned opinion that "real fans" would never take to night baseball. In addition, by 1946, he had finally abandoned his informal band of scouting friends and put together a 12-team minor league organization. These expenses, among others, would require additional revenue (mainly through ticket sales) in order to balance the team's ledger from one year to the next. However, unfortunately, by this time, Mack was in no shape to put a team on the field competitive enough to bring in the additional fans needed. By the early 1950s, it became clear that the A's had become a hopeless cause, at least so long as the Macks were involved with them.

Quite simply, after nearly a half century in the Majors, Connie Mack's skills had finally deserted him. By this time, stubbornness and profiteering were no longer the issue, mental capacity was. Where once he was the keenest talent evaluator on the scene (rivaled only perhaps by John McGraw), deftly making and remaking his team from year to year and presenting championship-caliber teams to the Philadelphia faithful, now, when these skills were needed most, they were no longer at his disposal. In May 1946, he traded future Hall of Famer George Kell to the Tigers for outfielder Barney McCoskey, an outfielder hitting .198 at the time. Although McCoskey was a solid player (he'd retire with a .312 batting average, although his best days were behind him, due to a troublesome back, by the time of the trade), Kell was a special one and Philadelphia fans could not help but make the comparison between the two as the years went on. Both Mack and Kell claimed that Mack knew what he was giving up but Wish Egan, Detroit's general manager, had a different take: "I was a little ashamed of myself for taking advantage of the old man," he said.[16] Three years later, after the 1949 season, Mack let another future Hall of Famer go when he traded Nellie Fox to the Chicago White Sox for Joe Tipton, a weak-hitting backup catcher coming off a .204 season. For some reason, Mack considered Fox lackadaisical and did not see much of a future for him. The young Connie Mack would probably have seen things a bit differently. Moreover, in 1952, Mack rejected an opportunity to sign Hank Aaron out of the Negro Leagues for a mere $3,500, stating that the price was too high "for a man like that."[17] Whether Mack's decision here was prompted by racism or the loss of his keen eye for talent (or by the fact that he was aroused out of his bed at 1 A.M. by his scout, Judy Johnson, urging him to sign Aaron right away) is unknown but an analysis of Mack's player moves during this time leads to the inescapable conclusion that his judgment was clouded for one reason or another. He was no longer able to compete in this area even to the extent needed just to keep his team above water.

Sadly, the "Grand Old Man of Baseball" was losing his faculties. What was worse, at least for Philadelphia fans, due to the extraordinary efforts made by Ben Shibe several decades earlier to ensure that Mack would never leave, he was now entrenched to such an extent that no one had the power to remove him regardless of how much his skills had eroded. He could stay on as manager, de facto general manager and owner for as long as he wished, regardless of the damage he was doing to the franchise. And, despite the increasing frequency of calls for him to step down, Mack was insistent that he never would. In June 1946, in the midst of what would be another 100-loss season (105 to be exact), Mack announced that not only was he not stepping down, he would continue to manage the A's "as long as I live."[18] This sort of proclamation led to celebration and sighs of relief in 1913 when Shibe had beaten back the advances of the Highlanders to hijack perhaps the most valuable commodity in the American League at the time. In 1946, it was viewed as a death sentence. The execution would be carried out a mere eight years later.

By 1951, it was an open secret that Mack was in the throes of dementia. He would provide incoherent statements to the press, who would then straighten them out in print in order to save him from embarrassment; "he would call out the names of stars of bygone days— Baker! Foxx!— to pinch hit"[19]; he would attempt to run the game from his position in the dugout, waving players around with his signature scorecard in hand, but he would frequently make mistakes, causing his coaches (who were by now effectively running the team for him) to scramble to correct them. Eventually, his players learned to ignore the "Grand Old Man" altogether. Worse, he would occasionally break down and sob, and at other times would be prone to outbursts of anger: during one game in June 1948 he became so upset at pitcher Nelson Potter that he released him *on the field* during the middle of a game in progress. As the cries for Mack to step down increased, Mack steadfastly refused to do so. For him, abandoning his perch atop the Athletics mantel was more than simply a baseball decision. It was one of personal survival. "If I did," he once replied to one such question concerning the possibility of his retirement, "I'd die in two weeks."[20] Regardless, and despite the protection he was receiving from sportswriters, fans began to realize that he was, in the words of one writer, "off the beam" and wanted him out. They were growing increasingly impatient with his moves both on and off the field that seemed to make little sense, baseball or otherwise. They wanted change and had little sympathy for a failing old man.

Mack's image took another hit during this time when his personal life became exposed for all to see.[21] This caused even greater instability in both himself and his franchise. By the late 1940s, Mack's family life was, to be kind, complicated. He had married twice: first in 1887 to a woman who bore him three children (Roy, Earle and a daughter who would later die) before she died in 1892. In 1910, he remarried and had five more children, including Connie Mack, Jr. When, during the 1930s, Mack sat down to decide who would take over the Athletics when he passed, he had several options. He could split the shares equally among his seven surviving children and the heirs of the eighth, or he could attempt to assert greater control over his beloved A's. Not surprisingly, he chose the latter. He split his shares among himself and his male heirs — Roy, Earle and Connie, Jr. — leaving nothing for his four surviving daughters or the heirs of the fifth. In his mind, this simplified the issue of succession. There would be no women involved in ownership (Shibe's heirs included women in the ownership group and there is speculation that Mack believed that this arrangement "muddled" things on that end). The A's would be a male enterprise only such that "the name of Mack, the House of Mack," would continue.

Mack's wife understood the implications of this arrangement. As drawn up, the franchise would be controlled by the children of Mack's first wife and not the children of his second (Roy and Earle would always have a 2–1 advantage over her son Connie, Jr.). She demanded that the shares be split equally among herself and all of the children (along with the heirs of Mack's deceased daughter) so as to give her family a controlling interest in the Athletics. Under this scenario, not only would her family gain control over Mack's first family (6 shares to 3), but, if it came to it, to the women over the men (6–3 once again). Mack refused. What ensued was a very messy and very public spat in the winter of 1946, with the 84-year-old Mack separating from his wife and being evicted from his home. Although the couple would eventually reconcile, it was nevertheless a humiliating experience for Mack, and one that, in his increasingly infirm condition, he was in no shape to handle. However, he held firm in his allocation of shares to what would become, very soon, disastrous effect.

With Roy and Earle now firmly in line to succeed him in controlling the Athletics, the stage was set for the final chapter in the demise of the franchise in Philadelphia. From this point on until the team would relocate after the 1954 season, it would be enmeshed in chaos until it would appear that nothing could salvage its hopes of remaining in the city. Roy and Earle were both undistinguished, unmotivated individuals, incapable of rescuing a team that was already in the midst of a free-fall.[22] They fought among themselves, uniting only whenever necessary to combat their stepmother and half-brother, Connie, Jr. These battles only dragged the team down further because, if any of the family members had the ability to save the team, it was Connie, Jr. Connie, Jr. took note of the post–World War II boom in Major League Baseball — a boom that rubbed off on the Athletics along with virtually everybody else — and sought to improve decaying Shibe Park much the same way the Braves had done up in Boston. He proposed spending $2.5 million to modernize and expand it, increasing seating from 31,500 to nearly 50,000. However, ultimately, he was rebuffed. In the end, minimal improvements were made, costing a fraction of what was proposed, a mere $300,000.

As time went on, the split between Roy and Earle on one side, and Connie, Jr. and his mother on the other, deepened. Eventually, Connie, Jr. approached the Shibe heirs and formed an alliance with them, using their 40 percent share in the club as additional heft to battle Roy and Earle. All the while, Connie, Sr. was either unwilling or unable to step in and play peacemaker. Finally, in 1950, Connie, Jr. attempted an end-around move when he tried to convince his father to retire before the season. He failed, but he did succeed in removing Earle from his position as assistant manager (and, presumably, his role of "manager in-waiting"). In what appeared to be yet another in a succession of questionable moves made by Mack during this time, he had primed his son for a job he seemed incapable of handling. A's players reacted by ignoring Earle, who commanded, and received, little respect. In order to oust his half-brother, Connie, Jr. voted against his father for the first time, aligning with the Shibe faction and forcing Earle out as assistant manager and into the position of "chief scout." Jimmie Dykes, a more capable baseball man, replaced Earle, and Mickey Cochrane was named general manager. Dykes would now run the club on a daily basis as Mack would remain on the bench but as a figurehead only. Connie, Jr. had won this battle but the war — yet another one — was now out in the open. Moreover, Roy and Earle were now more determined than ever to remove Connie, Jr. from the picture.

Later that season, things came to a head. With the Athletics once again in the cellar, and with the "Whiz Kids" of the Phillies capturing the hearts and minds of Philadelphia on their way to the pennant, the three brothers agreed to a plan that would give either Roy and Earle or Connie, Jr. an opportunity to buy out the other, provided they could come up with the requisite amount of cash. Whoever raised the money first would succeed in ousting the other. This set off at least one race (as opposed to the pennant) that Roy and Earle were determined not to lose. Unable to come up with enough money on their own, they approached Connecticut General Life Insurance Company and took out a $1,750,000 mortgage on Shibe Park, borrowing the rest from a local builder. Technically, they won the race and, on August 28, ousted Connie, Jr., their stepmother, the Shibes and the McFarlands (who also owned a portion of the club). Connie, Sr. remained, at least as a figure-head, but he was now joined by a member of Connecticut General who took a seat on the A's board of directors, overseeing his company's new invest-ment.

For the next 10 years, Roy and Earle would have to come up with approx-imately $250,000 in interest payments on this loan or effectively lose the club.[23] Very quickly, it became apparent that Roy and Earle's business acumen was not the sharpest and there was little chance of their meeting this obligation. Their 1950 budget depended on the club drawing 800,000 fans. This figure in itself was not an unreasonable number — the Athletics drew 816,514 in 1949 and had drawn over 900,000 fans each of the two seasons prior to that one — but with the A's hopelessly out of it in 1950, paired with the excitement over the first-place Phillies, there was no way they were going to draw anywhere near that number this time. Their final gate was a meager 309,805, a whopping 500,000 fans below what was needed for the brothers to make their payment to Connecticut General. In their zeal to remove their rivals from the picture, Roy and Earle had only succeeded in slitting their own throats.

The Athletics descended even farther into the abyss in the early 1950s. Saddled with an infirm leader who could not be removed by any means (and with Roy and Earle now in charge, it was clear that they did not want to remove him), an executive staff incapable of running things, and a mortgage hanging over their head like a guillotine, the team became a focal point for derision. Where once fans came to cheer some of the greatest teams ever assembled, they now came, when they came at all, mainly to boo and mock. The city had finally lost patience in "the name of Mack, the house of Mack" and wanted them, each and every one of them, gone. Connie Mack, once the city's greatest sports asset, had now become a liability.

The Carpenters, the "Whiz Kids" and the Rise of the Phillies

Perhaps more surprising than the descent of the Athletics was the con-current ascent of the Phillies if only because, like snow in the summer, such an occurrence was virtually unthinkable. By the end of the 1943 season, the Phillies were in their typical shambles, coming off a 90-loss season (a marked improvement given that it was the first year in the last six in which they had not lost at least 100). Commissioner Kenesaw Mountain Landis threw Phils owner William Cox out of baseball for betting on his own team (if he had bet on them to win, then he could have been booted for sheer stupidity as well) and the team was in search of a new owner. Robert R. M. Carpenter, vice president of E. I. DuPont de Nemours, Inc., who had married into the DuPont family, was interested in the team for his son, Robert R. M. Carpenter, Jr., a college dropout who fancied himself a "sportsman" and who was looking for something to do.[24] For a time, the younger Carpenter worked as a business associate of Connie Mack as part owner and president of the Wilmington Blue Rocks minor league baseball team, which Mack eventually brought into his minor league organization once he finally gave into, at least in theory, the farm system approach to player development. On Mack's assurance that Carpenter would be a capable owner, able to stabilize the franchise, Landis approved the sale and the 28-year-old Carpenter took over the Phillies. Ironically, it would be Carpenter who would eventually destabilize the Athletics once and for all, greasing the skids for their departure from the city a mere 11 years later.

For the first time in their history, the Phillies had money to burn. And, unlike most other clubs who were content to tighten the reins financially in order to ensure solvency from year to year, Carpenter seemingly embraced the Yankees' business plan of spending up front in the hopes of reaping even more (both on the field as well as financially) in the end. One of his first moves was to hire a legitimate baseball man as his general manager. He set-tled on Herb Pennock, the Hall of Fame pitcher sold off by Mack during the 1915 season and a friend of the Carpenter family, who quickly demonstrated his keen eye for talent and organizational management. Under Pennock's direction, the club upgraded and modernized its farm system. Then, once World War II ended, he realized an opportunity to change the direction of the Phillies more immediately by capitalizing on the surplus of players return-ing from service (and who no longer had teams to play for due to suddenly overflowing rosters) by offering many of them contracts for the 1946 season. In this way, the Phils were able to improve quickly, discarding the "talent" that contributed to the team's 108 losses in 1945 and replacing them with legitimate Major League-caliber players. The effect was swift and sure: the team improved by 23 games, finishing fifth, but, more important, hope had been restored to the Philadelphia faithful, particularly in comparison to the deteriorating situation in the Athletics' camp. No fewer than 1,061,807 fans turned out for Phillies games that season as compared with only 621,793 for A's games. The Phillies were aggressively courting the city's fans and were sending the message that they would spare no expense in doing so. And the city responded.

The aggressive spending continued. In 1947, the Phillies outbid several other teams and signed pitcher Curt Simmons for a $60,000 bonus. In 1948 they did the same with regard to another highly touted pitching phenom: Robin Roberts, snaring him with a $25,000 bonus. Like the Yankees in the American League, the Phillies had sent a message to both the league and the public that they were not about to be outspent by anyone for talent. Given that so few other teams took this approach, by simply opening their checkbook they had little competition in acquiring whomever they desired. By 1950, when several seeds of their newly fertile farm system had reached fruition — players such as Richie Ashburn, Del Ennis and Granny Hamner — the Phillies had stolen the Athletics' thunder once and for all, marching toward the pennant and spoiling Connie Mack's "Golden Jubilee" season in the process. In what Roy and Earle Mack assumed would be a triumphant year for their Athletics, celebrating their father's 50 years at the helm of the club, it was the Phillies who celebrated instead, crushing the A's at the gate by drawing 1,217,035 — nearly four times as many fans. By the end of the 1950 season, Philadelphia fans would not have been mistaken for seeing these new Phillies as Philadelphia's answer to the Yankees, outspending everyone, signing top talent, and winning year after year. Perhaps initially it was hard to believe that it was the Phillies of all teams who had adopted this approach, but after considering the organizational framework that had been set into place, their rapid rise from the dustbin of professional baseball, along with the financial backing of the Carpenter family, it was not such a crazy notion after all.

The fans' newfound faith in the Phillies was at no time more evident than during the 1952 season, one in which both the Phils and the Athletics finished fourth. In previous years, all things being relatively equal, fans would turn out to see their A's in greater numbers than the Phils. The sartorially dressed Connie Mack — the Grand Old Man of Baseball — waving his players into position with a flick of his scorecard, the ghosts of Eddie Plank, "Home Run" Baker, Jimmie Foxx, Mickey Cochrane, Al Simmons and others conjuring up memories of past glory was enough to trump the reality of confronting the connective void that was the Phillies. But no more. In a season in which both teams finished above .500, it was the Phils who had the measure of their American League counterparts this time: 775,417 to 627,100. The present had overcome the past. After half a century, the tide had finally turned. For Connie Mack's Athletics, the timing could not have been worse.

Relocation, Relocation, Relocation

Before the relocations of the Boston Braves, St. Louis Browns and the Athletics prior to the 1953, '54 and '55 seasons, respectively, Major League Baseball enjoyed half a century of rock-solid stability. After the relocation of the original Milwaukee Brewers to St. Louis in 1902, there was not a single franchise shift or addition for the next five decades.[25] Beginning in March 1953, however, three teams would relocate within 19 months. Although each individual relocation can be explained away (and has been, historically) simply as instances in which these particular franchises found themselves struggling and losing the battle for supremacy in two-team markets that couldn't support two teams[26] (indeed, the Red Sox, Cardinals and Phillies were all stronger franchises at the time of their cross-town rival's departure), this does not explain why all three franchises moved in brisk succession in the early 1950s. After all, Boston, St. Louis and Philadelphia had long since proven that they could not support two franchises, and the Braves, Browns and Phillies spent the vast majority of Major League Baseball's half century of stability struggling mightily, eking out their meager profits or sustainable losses while wallowing in virtual anonymity.[27] The possibility of relocation was occasionally discussed during this time but always dismissed as the protection of the integrity of the owners' cabal always trumped individual profit (as, here again, team owners demonstrated their ambivalence to actually *making* money out of their investments rather than merely not losing any). Apart from the near move of the St. Louis Browns to Los Angeles in 1941, which was spurred by an owner acting to stanch the bleeding of a seemingly failing franchise and which was called off due to the United States' intervention into World War II,[28] relocation was simply something that was not seriously considered by Major League Baseball despite relatively flat attendance in several cities—particularly two-team cities—for decades.

Now, however, in the early 1950s, relocation was suddenly not merely acceptable to the owners, it was in fact pushed on these franchises—in the case of the Athletics, and to a lesser extent the Braves who found themselves backed into a corner, against their will. Although this drastic change in mind-set may seem odd at first glance, an analysis of the events that immediately preceded these relocations brings clarity. It was the fear of congressional intervention and the possible loss; as a result; of their antitrust exemption leading to the possible unwanted enlargement of their cherished, elite club that spurred team owners to accept what had been unacceptable to them for the previous half century. And all of this had its origins in a place thousands of miles from the nearest Major League city, namely the Pacific Coast League.

Ever since its inception, the Pacific Coast League (PCL) toyed with the idea of competing with the American and National Leagues and becoming a third major league. In fact, the PCL has its roots as an outlaw league that refused to sign the National Agreement recognizing the reserve rights of the National League in 1899.[29] Eventually, in 1904, it joined the National Association and accepted its status as a minor league. However, the outlaw spirit of the PCL was never far away and on several occasions throughout the first half of the twentieth century, it contemplated a promotion to major league status. After the end of World War II, it believed that it finally had its chance.

Spurred by the manufacturing boom created by the war, the West Coast grew rapidly during the 1940s. Between 1940 and 1950, California saw a 53 percent increase in population and became the second-largest state in the nation.[30] Still, it lacked major league baseball. Once the war ended, the PCL owners decided that they were going to do something about this. In March 1946, Major League Baseball entertained a request by the PCL owners to meet with them to discuss the possibility of the PCL becoming a third major league.[31] Although Commissioner Happy Chandler gave appropriate lip service to the possibility, it was clear that this was the only service team owners were prepared to provide the PCL.[32] Indeed, the PCL's official request to Major League Baseball for promotion to major league status in July 1947 was met with deafening silence. The league never even prepared a response.

This kept the wolf at bay, but only for a while. In June 1951, the PCL owners voted to give Major League Baseball one more chance to consider their proposal.[33] This time, they came prepared with ammunition, publicly entertaining the possibility that the PCL would return to its roots, renounce the National Agreement and become an outlaw league once again, setting off a bidding war for players with Major League Baseball if MLB refused to even consider their request.[34] Although the PCL owners subsequently agreed to drop their threat to become an outlaw league,[35] it was clear that now they meant business. Major League owners would have to deal with them, regardless of how repugnant they found this possibility. And in order to ensure that they did, the PCL brought out an even more powerful weapon: the intervention of the House Monopoly Subcommittee.

Chaired by Emanuel Celler of New York, the subcommittee initially took an interest in the PCL's charge that MLB failed to respond to its 1947 request.[36] National League president Ford Frick testified in July 1951 that in fact a request had never been made and that the PCL, after being given data on the costs and problems associated with major league status, had changed its mind. "It became obvious to us that the Pacific Coast League had no desire to become a major league," said Frick before the subcommittee.[37] Clearly, Frick's recounting of events did not sit well with the subcommittee's members as his testimony was met with a warning that MLB's antitrust exemption would be removed if it did not act to expand west of the Mississippi River.[38] Frick responded by stating that the PCL would join the majors "if and when" its (the PCL's) clubs felt they were "ready."[39] With this apparent concession, Congress then acted on Frick's words.

In order to set firm guidelines for determining if and when they were "ready," California congressman Patrick Hillings challenged MLB to come up with a comprehensive plan for the promotion of the PCL to major league level or risk being found in "bad faith" by Congress.[40] Hillings made this challenge on the eve of the resumption of the subcommittee's hearings in October 1951, which put even more pressure on the league to act before the heavy hand of Congress came down and acted for it, prying open its cherished club to unwanted outsiders. This motivation was echoed by a subcommittee member who stated that it wasn't the preference of the subcommittee to act at all. Rather, it was their hope "that the owners will correct these evils and abuses and not force Congress to do it."[41] In order to get the congressional monkey off their back, the owners had to come up with something.

On November 14, 1951, they responded. In an effort to appease the PCL and, consequently, Congress, they unveiled the first step of a two-step program that initially appeared to give the PCL everything it wanted. It was only after step two was unveiled two weeks later (conveniently after the heat had been turned down when the PCL and Congress publicly lauded the owners for their swift and decisive action) that it became clear that, in fact, nothing had been accomplished and, if anything, the PCL now faced an even more daunting and all but impossible task of achieving major league status.

First, however, there was good news. Among other things, step one proposed an "open" classification (above the current highest AAA) for those qualified minor leagues wishing to join the Majors, a move that brought with it the ability of the qualifying league's players to opt out of the annual Major League draft, thereby allowing the league's teams to build up their rosters to major league quality "within a reasonable time." Rejecting as "unsound" the possibility of individual teams or cities moving up to major league status, MLB announced that only entire eight-team leagues could advance to major league status. Happily for the PCL, it easily met all six conditions set forth by MLB on November 14 for promotion to "open" classification.[42]

Not surprisingly, PCL officials were overwhelmed by step one. Pacific Coast League president Clarence Rowland stated:

Commissioner Frick's proposed legislation favoring the Coast League is most encouraging. While he has been in office less than a month, this is the first recognition by the majors that the Coast League is faced by unusual and special problems. This gives us renewed confidence and shows that our requests were not out of line. Commissioner Frick is to be commended for his insight into our problems.[43]

The reaction to step two would be markedly different.

On November 28, MLB announced the specific requirements for those "open" classification leagues seeking to make the final step up to major league status. Among the requirements were population and league attendance requirements that were impossible for the PCL, or any other minor league for that matter, to meet.[44] Moreover, the possibility of one or two strong cities, such as Los Angeles or San Francisco, applying for a promotion to major league status was forever quashed with the previously agreed-upon requirement that any expansion be done in eight-team units. In its enthusiastic acceptance of step one of MLB's "expansion" plan, the PCL had unwittingly tied its own hands. Now, not only was there no chance for the league as a whole to earn a promotion but it was also impossible for Los Angeles, the second-largest city in the nation, to do so on its own. If ever any doubt existed as to the disinclination of MLB to expand — opening up their cherished club to outsiders who by their sheer presence would dilute the exclusive prestige of their cabal (for what good is an exclusive club if it cannot keep the riff raff out?) — this underhanded two-step "plan" surely disabused anyone of the notion.

Once again, however, the owners had only managed to keep the wolf from their door temporarily. In May 1952, the subcommittee issued its report and again suggested the possibility of removing MLB's antitrust exemption as a way to force the owners to commit to expansion.[45] In its report, the subcommittee sympathized with the plight of Los Angeles and singled out Boston, St. Louis and Philadelphia as two-team cities that clearly could not support both teams.[46] It noted that St. Louis was smaller in size than either Los Angeles or San Francisco but enjoyed two teams, one of which, the Browns, that continually lagged in attendance. Philadelphia's attendance problems were also noted. The report openly questioned the validity of such an arrangement and wondered aloud whether an antitrust exemption was warranted given these circumstances. The continued presence of these weak two-team cities amid the repeated reluctance of MLB to expand to the rapidly growing West Coast was becoming an increasingly large albatross around its neck.

With the House subcommittee's hearings as a backdrop, the owners actively encouraged the series of franchise relocations that took place shortly thereafter in an effort to relieve some of the pressure applied by Congress and to protect the sanctity of their cabal. Concurrent with these hearings were the ramblings of St. Louis Browns owner Bill Veeck. Not one to quarrel with the findings of the subcommittee's report, Veeck, a maverick at heart who proved again and again to be the exception to the rule among his fellow owners, announced that his plight left him no alternative but to relocate to Milwaukee — a city that was presently building a stadium in the hopes of landing a Major League team.[47] In order to do so, however, Veeck needed to purchase the territorial rights to the city from Boston Braves owner Lou Perini.[48] When Perini refused to relinquish the rights,[49] a skirmish ensued that left the other owners in a bind.

For here was Milwaukee, yet another city without Major League baseball, with a brand new stadium larger than any in the PCL,[50] being denied a Major League franchise by an owner (Perini) who sought to keep it as a minor league jewel and a safety net should *he* ever decide to move his Braves, which was unlikely to occur, given a half century of not having done so. With the subcommittee's hearings hanging over their heads, MLB no doubt understood that to prevent Milwaukee from becoming a major league city would most likely result in the end of its exemption, potentially opening the floodgates to large-scale, uncontrollable expansion. This was particularly true after Perini had previously stated in public that he never would stand in the way of Milwaukee obtaining a Major League team, and then went out and did precisely that.[51] They knew all too well that they could not sit back, allow Perini to refuse Veeck's substantial offer for the Milwaukee territorial rights[52] to move a team identified by the subcommittee as a perennial weak sister, and expect Congress to turn a blind eye. Therefore, on March 9, 1953, after a series of maneuvers that compelled Perini to act on his refusal and move his Braves to Milwaukee immediately, the National League voted unanimously to allow the Braves (one of the two-city weak sisters noted within the subcommittee's 1952 report) to relocate to Milwaukee.[53] The vote marked the first approved relocation in Major League Baseball in half a century.

All of this left Bill Veeck and his St. Louis Browns in limbo. But not for long. If there was ever any doubt as to who ran Major League Baseball before, the sequence of events surrounding the eventual relocation of the Browns made it clear that it was the New York Yankees who called the shots for everyone, and anyone who failed to toe the line would receive the harshest penalty possible — excommunication from the "club." This was a sanction that the Yankees, as a result of the power they had amassed over the previous decades, had the muscle to mete out seemingly on their own, despite league rules that technically required a super-majority for any such action to be taken. The Browns drama demonstrated that mere technicalities were irrelevant in the face of raw power and an ownership group that wanted little more than to remain connected to "America's game" and all of its attendant benefits. This reality would play out with ramifications for Philadelphia just a short time later when it was the Athletics who were up for grabs.

To understand the Browns of the early 1950s is to understand their owner, Bill Veeck. On July 15, 1951, Veeck purchased the club from Bill DeWitt.[54] Veeck's father had been the general manager of the Chicago Cubs under William Wrigley, and Bill, Jr. had hoped to one day follow in his father's footsteps. However, from a young age, Bill, Jr. demonstrated his nonconformist approach such that Wrigley refused to entrust him with his franchise. This led Veeck to forge his own path, which he did to great success. He first bought a minor league team and then sold it, using the profits to buy his way into Major League Baseball, getting in at least partly on the grease of his father's good name. He bought the Cleveland Indians, won the 1948 pennant, sold them at a profit as well and used the proceeds to buy the sorriest team in the land, the St. Louis Browns, an outpost considered "the Siberia of baseball" for decades.[55]

Almost immediately, Veeck drew the ire of his fellow owners. For starters, he had always been a fan of gimmicks to draw fans to the games (indeed, he was one of the few owners who seemed to care at all about such things). He once stuck thousands of S&H green stamps under certain seats of Cleveland's Municipal Stadium and then "at a given signal, everyone jumped up and closed their seats to see if they'd won."[56] He took things, perhaps out of necessity given the pitiful state of his new franchise, to a new level at the helm of the Browns. To be sure, other owners did not care for his wacky promotions, including such gimmicks as using a midget to pinch hit; "Grandstand Managers Day," when fans took on the role of manager (in the midst of yet another last place, 100-loss season, probably doing no worse than official manager Zack Taylor); and voting on whether Browns players should "hit away" or "bunt." However, his fellow owners were annoyed with Veeck for many other seemingly innocuous things he did, as well as for the image he portrayed, believing that Veeck's sheer nature sullied the image of all of them. Since it was their image that meant more to them than anything else, they simply were unable to tolerate him. At his core, Veeck fancied himself a man of the people and went out of his way to connect with those paying to watch his team play baseball. Whereas Charlie Comiskey famously sat in his royally appointed owner's box and Walter O'Malley abhorred mingling with mere commoners, Veeck was known as "Shirtsleeve Bill," wearing open-collared shirts and moving freely and easily among the fans. In reality, Veeck was every bit the savvy businessman as his fellow owners. It was just that with Veeck, like Mack, his business *was* baseball. It was not a sideline to him. The image he portrayed brought fans out to see an otherwise forgettable product. He needed the approval of the fans in order for him to continue to make his living. Quite simply, unlike many of the other owners, Veeck could not afford to merely break even and expect to survive. He stood out in that he needed his team to turn a significant annual profit. Because most of his brethren were not in such a position, they saw him only as a misfit, a "carney and a hustler,"[57] who had somehow gotten himself mixed in with royalty. If left unchecked, the fear was that he would eventually bring all of them down to his level. As such, they were soon going to check him. Hard.

In practically any other business, an owner like Bill Veeck would have been a welcome addition as he did the one thing anybody with business sense would appreciate: he put money in their pockets. After the moribund 1951 season, Veeck signed many legendary former Cardinals to be the new face of the Browns, such as Rogers Hornsby as manager, Marty Marion as a player/manager, Dizzy Dean as announcer, and Harry Brecheen on the active roster. By any measure, the results were impressive. The Browns improved by 12 games in the win column (although still losing 90 games for the season) but, more importantly, attendance nearly doubled. Given the 80–20 gate split in the American League, every other league owner benefited from the improvement of the Browns. But money was not what it was all about. Image was everything and the other owners believed that Veeck was debasing everybody else's. The Cardinals went out of their way to distance themselves from their stadium mates by adopting as their new slogan: "The Cardinals, A Dignified St. Louis Institution." Other owners felt similarly.

In so many ways, Veeck just did not fit in with them. A liberal, he stood out like a sore left thumb in their conservative, tight-fisted ownership cabal, and he was not shy about speaking and acting out against his brethren. At one point in his younger days, he wrote a letter to Commissioner Landis, decrying ownership's beloved reserve clause as "morally and legally indefensible." Later, one of his first moves after purchasing the Browns was to vote against Ford Frick for commissioner. Although he would later rethink this approach in voting for Frick when the final ballot was tallied, the damage had already been done. However, what ultimately sealed his fate was his particular disdain for the Yankees. Rather than choosing to avoid the behemoth that held the power to crush him and banish him to the real Siberia if it so chose, Veeck enjoyed picking fights with them, arousing their ire until finally they acted upon it. Veeck liked to disparage the Yankees in print, repeatedly calling them cheap. Once, when Joe DiMaggio was holding out for more money, Veeck took the opportunity to humiliate Yankees general manager George Weiss (who he once referred to as "a fugitive from the human race") at a baseball dinner by publicly offering to take DiMaggio off of the Yankees' hands for a mere $200,000. Weiss, who was on the dais with Veeck, stormed off.[58]

Beginning in December 1952, Veeck would need the assistance of Frick and the Yankees and should not have been surprised when he found that it was not forthcoming. That month, Gussie Busch of the Anheuser-Busch Brewing Company bought the Cardinals. At that moment, Veeck realized that with their enormously deep pockets, he would never be able to drive the Cardinals out of town — a necessity if he was going to ever be able to attract enough fans to allow him to remain in charge of his Browns.[59] Following the sale of the Cardinals, Veeck announced his intention to move. In response, at the 1952 baseball winter meetings, Yankees co-owner Del Webb convened a meeting, which Veeck declined to attend. During that meeting, Webb and the other owners agreed to essentially starve Veeck out of their club by refusing to schedule any lucrative night games against the Browns. After the winter meetings, and after the Braves blocked Veeck's proposed move to Milwaukee by moving there themselves, they continued their assault on Shirtsleeve Bill. After Veeck identified Baltimore as his next intended destination (a city similar to Milwaukee in that it was likewise in the process of building a Major League–caliber stadium in the hopes of eventually luring a Major League team), the owners conspired to block his move there as well. The succession of moves in this dance would prove illuminating, particularly to the other owners when it would come time to deal with the Athletics the following year.

By spring training in 1953, Veeck was itching to move. Once Milwaukee was out of the picture — that deal was finalized on March 13, 1953, with the Braves relocating immediately to Milwaukee for the opener just a few weeks away — his fellow owners assured Veeck that he too would be free to move wherever he wished for the 1953 season. Veeck took them at their word. He announced his intention to relocate to Baltimore (so sure was he that he had already lined up Baltimore's National Brewing Company to be the team's local sponsor), asked for a league vote on the matter and was promptly rejected 6–2. Officially, he was told that it was "too close to the start of the season" to even consider such a move. However, a mere two days earlier, National League owners approved the relocation of the Braves, a move that would necessitate drawing up the very same television, radio and concession contracts that were cited as so burdensome when it came to Veeck's proposal. The real reason Veeck was voted down was because his brethren, led by the Yankees, wanted him gone. He was then offered what turned out to be a retractable lifeline: he was told that once the 1953 season was complete (and after he had absorbed another season of crushing losses) his proposal would be accepted and he would be allowed to relocate before the 1954 season. Veeck had no choice but to accept it. He surely had to know what was coming next.

In late September, after an earlier attempt to schedule a meeting to consider the matter was cancelled when the American League's Relocation Committee members, led by Yankee co-owner Dan Topping, failed to show up,[60] another vote was taken. This time Veeck's proposal included a local buyer, Clarence W. Miles, who intended to purchase half of Veeck's 79 percent interest in the team and allow Veeck to remain as general manager. Once again, Veeck's bid was denied. Dan Topping then made explicit what had been implicit earlier. He told one of Veeck's major stockholders, "we're going to keep you in St. Louis and bankrupt you. Then we'll decide where the franchise will go."[61] To add insult to injury, Topping's partner, Del Webb, announced that he had found a mythical buyer who wanted to purchase the Browns and move them to Los Angeles. When Webb's proposal was put before the same group of owners who had just rebuffed Veeck, it passed unanimously.[62] This vote made it clear: as long as Veeck was involved in the process, the other owners (led by Topping and Webb of the Yankees) were not going to permit it. Realizing that he was beaten, Veeck stepped out of the picture, allowing Miles to purchase the team himself. Yet another vote was taken and this one approved both the sale and the relocation.

In the end, the Browns were permitted to relocate and, indeed, would thrive as the rechristened Baltimore Orioles. Nevertheless, the message conveyed by Topping and Webb to their fellow league owners in the process was clear: buck the establishment and prepare to be excommunicated from the club. As this was the last thing these owners wanted, they were prepared to do whatever the establishment commanded. And since the establishment was, essentially, the Yankees, league owners were fully prepared to act in ways that would further the business and competitive interests of the New York Yankees even if it meant perpetuating their own competitive misery. This was precisely what would happen when the fate of Connie Mack's once mighty Athletics came into their hands.

After the relocations of the Braves and Browns were finalized, speculation arose that the Athletics would be next. Although the A's were similar to these clubs in that they too were struggling financially, the situation in Philadelphia differed greatly from that of either Boston or St. Louis. Ever since the birth of the American League in 1901, Boston had always been betrothed to the Red Sox. In the 52 seasons that the Braves and Sox competed in Boston, the Braves managed to outdraw the Red Sox a mere seven times, and not at all after 1933. Similarly, the Cardinals had owned St. Louis for decades prior to the departure of the Browns. St. Louis fans turned out in greater numbers to see the Browns only 17 times in the 52 years both teams competed within the city and only once since 1925. Philadelphia, on the contrary, was an A's town through and through with the tide having turned only very recently and, most likely, temporarily, toward the Phillies. In their 54 years together in Philadelphia, the Athletics outdrew the Phils 40 times. Although the Phillies outdrew the A's six times in their final 10 years in

Philadelphia (1945–1954), it should be noted that this 10-year span marked the *only* ten-year period in which the Phillies held such an advantage. Moreover, it was a slight advantage (6–4) at that. Looking at things from a wider lens, the differences between, on the one hand, Boston and St. Louis and, on the other, Philadelphia become even starker. From 1940 until the departure of the Braves, Browns and Athletics from their birth cities, the Braves failed to outdraw the Sox even once; the Browns managed a lone Pyrrhic victory (in 1944 when it took a devalued American League pennant to accomplish the trick); while the A's outdrew the Phils seven out of 15 years. Only very recently — since the Whiz Kids of 1950 — had allegiances shifted in the Quaker City. As a result, relocating the Athletics would not be the equivalent of relocating those earlier, second-banana clubs. If the Athletics were to move, it would be something quite different indeed — for these A's had roots in the city that ran deep, regardless of their recent downturns. If they were to move, more than a few people in Philadelphia would care. And years later, after they did, many Philadelphians were left to wonder why it was their city, unlike Boston or St. Louis, where the wrong team left town.

In short, it happened because of the convergence of events that was just now sweeping over both the city of Philadelphia and the landscape of Major League Baseball: the Athletics were weak, the Phillies were strong, and team owners wanted Congress off their backs. Given this climate, the A's were ripe for the picking. Little attention was paid to allegiances of the fans or the propriety of moving one team versus another. Somebody simply had to move if the owners were ever going to have a chance to keep Congress's nose out of their club and, God forbid, opening it up to others against their will. And so it was the A's.

In analyzing the specifics of the A's relocation to Kansas City, it becomes clear that, in the end, they did not have to move. Regardless, the Yankees wanted them in Kansas City to use them as fuel for their ongoing dynasty. Their fellow owners, having learned where they stood from the Veeck affair, were not about to step in and prevent this from happening despite the likelihood that the move would serve to perpetuate only their own competitive misery, which by the mid 1950s was in its third decade with no end in sight. So the move was approved and the Athletics were used, as everybody knew they would at the time the deal was consummated, as a pawn to serve the greater interests of New York, thereby cementing Philadelphia's image once again as a second-class city, particularly in relation to Gotham. The Phillies, having seemingly won the battle, would bear the brunt of this weight for decades to come, indicating that, in the end, they clearly lost the war.

In 1953, the A's were certainly in trouble, having drawn only 362,133 fans, not nearly enough to pay the interest on their mortgage to Connecticut

From left: Roy Mack, Arnold Johnson, Connie Mack (Temple University Libraries, Urban Archives, Philadelphia, PA).

General. The following year was no better. The A's finished last in 1954, drawing 304,666 fans. They could not even afford to pay for their new uniforms that season, let alone their mortgage.[63] Roy and Earle Mack were drowning in debt and the sharks were circling. Foremost among them was real estate magnate Arnold Johnson, a man with significant ties to the New York Yankees, who, in July of 1954; made an offer to buy the A's and relocate them in Kansas City.[64] At the time of the offer, Johnson was mired in real and potential conflicts of interest with the Yankees as he was not only the owner of Yankee Stadium, but he also owned the Yankees' Kansas City farm team's stadium.[65] While an initial "Save the A's" campaign drew sporadic interest from Philadelphia's business leaders, a late offer arrived in October of 1954 when a Philadelphia syndicate made up of eight prominent businessmen matched Johnson's offer and promised to keep the team in Philadelphia.[66] This offer was deemed acceptable to Roy, who, like his father, preferred that the team remain in Philadelphia,[67] and he promptly accepted the offer.[68]

Unfortunately, the offer was not deemed acceptable to the Yankees, who stood to gain significantly if Johnson were to purchase the team. With Johnson, a business partner of Topping and Webb, in charge of the Athletics, his team could be used as a thinly disguised Yankee farm team, shuffling players to the powerful Yankees whenever they needed some extra punch. In this sense, they could serve much the same purpose as did the Red Sox (albeit as the result of different circumstances) in the late teens and early twenties to fuel the front end of the Yankee dynasty. Beyond this, Webb stood to personally gain as the Del E. Webb Construction Company could then be tapped for the multimillion dollar renovation of Kansas City's stadium that would be necessary once the A's relocated.[69] As such, they had a lot riding on Johnson's eventual acquisition of the club. On October 28, the American League owners convened and, on the urging of Topping and Webb, blocked the sale to the Philadelphia syndicate, leaving the Macks no choice but to sell to Johnson and see the team uprooted to Kansas City.[70] After one more comic (or tragic,

From left: Roy, Connie, Sr., Earle, and Connie III (Roy's son) await their fate on October 28, 1954, at New York's Waldorf Astoria while the other AL owners meet to determine whether to accept the proposed sale of the A's to a Philadelphia syndicate (Temple University Libraries, Urban Archives, Philadelphia, PA).

depending upon one's viewpoint) turn, in which members of the rejected Philadelphia syndicate literally raced Johnson through the streets of Philadelphia to Connie Mack's house with the failed hope of convincing Mack to sell his shares of the team directly to them (thereby blocking Johnson's purchase), the deal was finalized.[71]

Although the sale of the Athletics to Johnson was officially justified by the owners on the ground that no sufficient offer was received by anyone seeking to keep the team in Philadelphia, it is important to note that in fact there were three such offers: the one described above and two earlier ones, dismissed by American League commissioner Will Harridge as being without "substance."[72] Only Johnson's offer was, according to Harridge, "really sound."[73] Apparently, the substance of Johnson's offer came from the notion that it was a cash offer whereas the others were not.[74] However, an analysis of the sale of the franchise to Johnson shows that it was a cash deal in name only. While cash may have technically crossed the negotiating table, most, if not all of the money for the $3.5 million sale of the Athletics came from outside sources with a significant amount coming directly from Topping and Webb's fellow owners. In fact, it is very likely that the sale went through without a single dollar of new money being laid on the table by Johnson. The specifics of the deal bear this out.[75] In order to finance his purchase of the Athletics — and Connie Mack Stadium, which was part of the deal — Johnson promptly sold the stadium to Phillies owner Bob Carpenter for $1,675,000, sold his stadium in Kansas City to the city for $650,000, and got an extension for the roughly $800,000 he owed the Jacob Brothers concessionaires (who worked the stands at Connie Mack Stadium and who often went without payment in the team's dwindling days in Philadelphia), who agreed to take repayments out of future profits with the Athletics in Kansas City. This brought in roughly $3,125,000 of the $3.5 million purchase price. He then raised the remaining $400,000 through sales of minority stock, specifically to Roy Mack himself, who invested a large portion of the $450,000 he received through the sale back into the Athletics. On top of this, there were additional investors from Chicago who gobbled up any remaining crumbs. In the end, the entire purchase price (or, at a minimum, the very great majority of it), came from sources other than Johnson. A cash deal from a buyer without cash in hand. While the substance of the three Philadelphia offers are unknown in their entirety, it is safe to say that at least the Johnson offer was not nearly as sound as Harridge, the Yankees and the other owners led the public to believe.

In truth, the Yankees wanted the Athletics in Kansas City and there was nothing anyone, neither their fellow owners nor, most certainly, Roy and Earle Mack, could do to stop them. The futility of any attempted resistance to the relocation was best summed up by Mack's wife who said, "New York wants this club to go to Kansas City. When New York's in the back, pushing it, well, there's your answer."[76] In Johnson, Topping and Webb hand-picked a trusted colleague, one who had served them well in the past and who could be trusted to continue to serve them well into the future. Johnson, Webb and Topping had worked together since 1951, purchasing real estate in both New York and Kansas City and operating as landlord (Johnson) and tenant (Webb and Topping) in multiple ventures that netted the three of them capital gains into the millions.[77] The competitive damage that could potentially be done with Johnson's purchase of the Athletics was well known before the deal was finalized but, ultimately, of little concern to these owners, who were more concerned with protecting their own seat at the table.

Once in Kansas City, the anticompetitive nature of the move quickly became apparent as Kansas City became little more than a way station for players on their way to the Bronx. Between 1955 and 1960, 29 players were exchanged between the two clubs, with the Yankees getting the better end of these deals almost exclusively: Roger Maris, Bobby Shantz, Clete Boyer, Ryne Duren and Ralph Terry were just a few of the stars who made their way to New York via Kansas City in these one-way deals as the Yankees retooled to continue their dominance through the early 1960s.[78] Between 1955 and 1964, the Yankees won every American League pennant except one and added four more world championship trophies to their already overcrowded shelf. On the flip side, the Athletics remained dreadful, as any bright spots were quickly shuffled off to Johnson's friends in New York and replaced with untested rookies or retreads. In their 13 seasons in Kansas City (1955–67), the A's lost 90 or more games nine times and 100 or more four times. These consequences were not unexpected. Yet the move was approved.

In retrospect, none of the three relocations benefited Major League Baseball from either a competitive or a financial aspect. The Braves moved to a city that had demonstrably failed to support minor league baseball, drawing only 195,000 people in 1952 despite winning the American Association championship.[79] Although they would draw exceedingly well in their initial years in Milwaukee (due in large part to the excitement over a new team in town, the fact that the team was very good and would win the 1957 World Series and, not insignificantly, their decision not to televise home games),[80] they severely dented the fan bases in Detroit and Chicago to do so, with the Cubs, White Sox and Tigers attendance declining by 8 percent in 1953.[81] The Cubs were hit particularly hard, suffering a 21 percent drop in attendance that season, a drop that would remain a constant for years afterward. In 1950, the Cubs lost 89 games and drew 1,165,944 fans to Wrigley Field. In 1953, after the Braves moved nearby, they would lose 89 games again but this time would only draw 763,658 fans. The Orioles would similarly leach fans away from an already struggling Washington Senators franchise, further weakening them as well.[82] All three of these moves weakened an already unhealthy game in one way or another. And this was precisely what the owners had set out to do.

Each of these clubs was used as a pawn to protect the integrity of the closed club that was Major League Baseball ever since the formation of the National League back in 1876. As the New York Yankees grew stronger during the first half of the twentieth century, they became more and more able to determine the parameters of membership within this club, and, in the early 1950s, they saw an opportunity to use their power to both strengthen and enrich themselves at everyone else's expense. Not surprisingly, particularly after the Bill Veeck affair, their fellow owners were content to fall in line behind them, sacrificing their competitive best interests to their desire to remain affiliated with "America's game" and all of its attendant perks. While every other Major League city was harmed by this collective effort, none was devastated nearly as much as Philadelphia, which saw its treasured Athletics uprooted in the name of New York's dominance. In the process, Philadelphia was left with the Phillies, a second-rate team — they quickly descended from the "Whiz Kids" to the "Was Kids" within a few short years—for what was considered by many to be a second-rate city. Because of the convergence of events that unfolded during the early 1950s, the wrong team packed up and deserted Philadelphia at the close of the 1954 season. And once the storm had ended, a black cloud would remain over both the city and the Phillies for decades, further entrenching the image of Philadelphia as little more than a poor relation to New York City. The events that would grab headlines in the city over the course of the next two decades would only further ingrain this image.

5

The Phillies and Philadelphia:
Into the Abyss

Ron Reed was the anti Tug McGraw. Where McGraw was exuberant, Reed was dour, where McGraw was loose, Reed was wound as tight as an alarm clock before the first day of school. Unlike the alarm clock, however, no one ever knew when Reed was about to go off (albeit in the clubhouse, never on the mound; in 1980 Reed would stew through much of the stretch drive, ultimately choosing to sit alone in Philadelphia International Airport waiting for a plane to take him home rather than join his teammates for the victory parade down Broad Street. He was the only one not to show up at the celebration).[1] On the mound he was all business: he would never slap his glove on his thigh, pat his heart after a close call or chat with invisible leprechauns between pitches, all quirks that made McGraw lovable the moment he arrived from the Mets two years earlier. Reed was supremely efficient and effective. In these final years before the era of the closer as superstar would dawn, Reed oftentimes finished the game; his 15 saves led the team in 1977. In this era, however, who finished the game was less important than who came in when things got tough, regardless of the inning. And for the Phillies, Reed was, more often than not, *the man,* in a bullpen replete with them, when it came to such things.

Black Friday: Fifth Inning

This day was no different; the game was tied, the series was tied, and the Dodgers would be sending up the heart of their lineup over the course of the next two innings. So naturally, the call went to Reed even though it was "only" the fifth inning. As Reed, a former forward for the NBA's Detroit Pistons, finished his warmup tosses, Lopes strode to the plate, taking measure of his unusually long, deliberate delivery made necessary in order to clear the sprawl of his body, which created a traffic jam of arms and legs as he delivered each pitch. If Lopes got on base he would be able to run on him. Reed set about making sure that would not happen. After tantalizing him with a couple of fastballs, Reed induced a grounder to Bowa who threw across the diamond to Hebner for out number one.

Russell was next. After blowing a fastball by him (which was particularly strong this afternoon; a hitter like Russell had little hope of catching up with it) he left his next pitch over the plate, allowing Russell to make contact. He lofted a lazy fly ball that appeared to hang in the air forever above left field. Luzinski, who had been shading him slightly to left-center, stampeded back toward the line but could not reach it before it hit the ground, fielding it with his bare hand after an interminably high bounce off the turf and firing it into second, too late to catch Russell who strolled in with a double. It was precisely doubles like this one that made Jerry Martin invaluable, regardless of his complaints about being Luzinski's understudy: the ball was all but begging to be caught, seemingly suspending itself in mid-air for no other purpose than to allow for even the most out-of-position outfielder to outrun his mistake and catch it. But the Bull was unable to outrun pretty much anything. The play was not even close and Russell had himself what would read like a line drive double in the next day's box score but which was, in reality, nothing more than a dying quail fortuitously directed toward a three-legged retriever. Despite his protestations, this was why Luzinski often found himself on the bench in the ninth inning of most games. Ozark, for all of his curious in-game decisions, at least knew enough to protect himself in this regard.

With the tie-breaking run now on second, Reggie Smith, LA's most dangerous hitter, stepped up. Accordingly, Reed did as well. Reed's sneer, which was omnipresent even when things were going well, became just a little bit tighter now as he peered in to Boone for his sign. After running the count full, he unleashed a bullet, a fastball that Smith failed to recognize until too late. He checked his swing, helpless as the ball popped into Boone's mitt for strike three, the dirt from his mitt dissipating into the air in a puffy beige cloud as Wendlestadt rung him up, the third strikeout of the day for Smith. Realizing now that on this day no one would be able to catch up with his heat, Reed went with it exclusively against Cey, blowing him away as well for the final out of the inning. As Boone flipped the ball back toward the mound amid the percolating din of the crowd, Reed headed toward the dugout, walking the walk of a man in complete recognition of the fact that at least on this day, he could not be touched.

In the bottom of the inning, the Phils were anxious to get something going. Larry Bowa led off and crouched down even more than usual, hoping to work a walk out of Rhoden. After working the count to 2 and 2, he realized that this was not going to happen so now he shifted modes, this time choking up in the hope of slapping something somewhere. He fouled off a couple of pitches with his chopping swing and appeared to be getting the better of Rhoden, who was unable to get anything by him to finish him off. With each pitch, the crowd sensed the shift in momentum, whistling and roaring, producing an ambience that felt half Wimbledon, half Super Bowl. Finally, Bowa smacked a low liner that appeared to be headed for the hole between short and third. Russell, however, caught up to it, backhanding it no more than six inches off the ground for out number one.

Schmidt then dragged his silent bat, one-for-eleven this series, to the plate. As he dug in, his body language reeked of defeat and confusion, of the notion that he was the prey and not the predator. He settled himself in tentatively and got a break as Rhoden missed with three straight fastballs. Now up 3–0, he stepped out and took a long look toward third-base coach Billy DeMars: take or swing? When he was going well, such a look would have been perfunctory; only Schmidt could tell Schmidt to take on such a favorable hitter's count. But he was not, so the look, as well as the response, was a break from the norm; the next pitch came right down the middle and Schmidt's bat never left his shoulder. Again he stepped out and searched for the sign. What it was is anybody's guess as Rhoden's next pitch was inside for ball four. Schmidt took first.

The connection between Schmidt and the game, at least from an offensive standpoint (defensively he was consistently brilliant regardless), varied depending on how well he was hitting at the time. When he was hitting well, he was engaged; when he was not, he could be off by himself in a place only he seemed to know even while the action unfolded all around him. Taking his lead off of first base, Yeager noticed that this appeared to be one of those times. After the first pitch to Luzinski, he fired to first and nearly picked him off. A good throw would have had him easily. This appeared to have had the effect of bringing Schmidt back from wherever he was; thereafter, he danced off the bag with each pitch, tempting Rhoden and causing distraction in someone else for a change. After running the count to 2–2 to the Bull, Rhoden became drawn to the suddenly kinetic Schmidt, staring over at him repeatedly until finally stepping off the mound to a reception of boos. The boos were replaced with ascending hoots and whistles that reached a crescendo just as he delivered his next pitch. Luzinski popped it to Cey in foul territory and the whistles ceased. Thereafter, Hebner took all of one pitch to fly out to Smith in right for the final out of the inning.

Second Rate and Second Division — Again

The hijacking of the Athletics at the hands of calculating New Yorkers was just the latest example of a practice that had been repeated numerous times ever since New Yorker Martin Van Buren schemed to bring down the Second National Bank over a century earlier. As a result, many Philadelphians could be forgiven for the inferiority complex they harbored that by now had become ingrained with regard to New York. The need to justify themselves, to prove themselves the equal of their neighbors to the north was ever present,[2] but it was becoming more and more difficult to accomplish given the recent rapid spate of humiliations foisted upon their city by New York. The Athletics debacle came on the heels of another public flogging only a few years earlier, this one on an even grander, international scale.

At the close of World War II, a replacement for the failed League of Nations was proposed and then established. The newly created United Nations would wield more power, have more influence and hopefully do a better job of preventing world war than had its predecessor. One of the most important initial concerns was finding a home for its headquarters. It had been agreed that it would be somewhere in the United States, but it couldn't be just anywhere. It had to be in a city with influence, a city with power, an international city — or at least a city with the potential to become all of these things. In April 1945, Philadelphia threw its name into the hat.[3] Mayor Bernard Samuel and Governor Edward Martin initiated the push while numerous other city leaders formed a committee, headed by Robert L. Johnson, president of Temple University, to promote the city and all it had to offer the world if it were so chosen.[4] Initially, not much was made of the Philadelphia delegation, as other cites such as Boston, San Francisco and, of course, New York, were seen as being more appropriate locations. Australia's minister of external affairs even brushed off Philadelphia by taking note of the city's reputation as a loser. "How can you put the capital of the world in a town that has both clubs in last place?" he asked[5] (the last place, 108-loss, 1945 Phillies were so bad that they actually changed their name temporarily to the Blue Jays, perhaps in an effort to make it through the season incognito; the A's joined them in the cellar, losing 98 games themselves). Later, the delegate from the Philippines piled on by calling Philadelphia, "'a ghost city' with a rich historical past, but with no present and a dubious future." Present-day Philadelphia, he believed, reminded him "of a man in a cutaway coat, but with soiled underwear ... three hours ahead of San Francisco in time, but three centuries behind otherwise."[6]

Undaunted, the Philadelphia committee persisted, hoping to draw the world's attention to Philadelphia as the most symbolic of all American cities. Unexpectedly, its work started to pay off. By December 1946, the United Nations Site Committee had rejected Boston's application and San Francisco's was staunchly opposed by Britain, the Soviet Union and (under pressure, after being accused of improperly advocating for it) the United States, leaving Philadelphia as the surprising frontrunner with New York still in the picture, although lagging far behind.[7]

The city mobilized its forces, coming up with the money and, most importantly, an array of choice locations within the city for the UN to choose from, including the area surrounding Independence Hall[8] and a two-square-mile section of the Belmont Plateau in Fairmount Park. Ten square miles in the Roxborough–Chestnut Hill area[9] were likewise put on offer after the UN made it known that it preferred a location replete with open air, preferably in the countryside.[10] The city was prepared to condemn whatever land was necessary and give it to individual countries to be used as embassies or to the United Nations as a whole for the erection of the headquarters building, all of it free of charge — a gift valued at approximately $20,000,000.[11] New York, on the other hand, was scuffling, unable to match Philadelphia's offer either in funds or in location: the best it could offer was a site outside of Manhattan in Flushing Meadows Park, on the decaying grounds of the 1939 World's Fair.[12] In fact, the United Nation's temporary headquarters were housed at this location but it was no secret that many delegates did not like the site and preferred the permanent home to be elsewhere.[13] Moreover, the UN's site inspection subcommittee toured it and declared it "unsuitable."[14] When New York continued to push this unfavorable site — it was unable to find a suitable vacant location on Manhattan and acquiring one would require extraordinary expenses, which could not thereafter be recouped through real estate taxes given that the UN insisted on a permanent exemption from these[15] — it appeared as if Philadelphia had finally gotten the measure of its bigger brother. By December 6, with a decision imminent and New York appearing to be hopelessly out of the picture, the city of Philadelphia, confident of the UN's ultimate decision, jumped the gun, commencing condemnation procedures for the erection of the headquarters building.[16] The official proclamation of Philadelphia as the home of the United Nations was scheduled four days hence — 96 hours; why wait to get started?

Those 96 hours proved to be Philadelphia's undoing. In that time, Robert Moses, New York's transportation, construction and planning czar, in the tradition of DeWitt Clinton and Martin Van Buren before him, set about redirecting the stream of momentum away from Philadelphia and toward New York. He called on his good friend, John D. Rockefeller, Jr., to come up with both the money and the land where, until then, there had been none: Rockefeller would donate $8.5 million to the UN, enough to buy up all the necessary property to erect the headquarters.[17] The city chipped in its share (on Rockefeller's insistence), the state legislature quickly convened and approved the required alterations to the city's infrastructure in order to accommodate the UN, and the deal was done.[18] When the UN Headquarters Committee convened its scheduled meeting, it announced its recommendation that New York, not Philadelphia, be its new home. Three days later, the UN's General Assembly voted 46–7 to approve this recommendation.[19] Just like that, New York had swept in and snatched another prize out of the hands of Philadelphia.

After it was done, many United Nations delegates, the same ones who previously crowed about the virtues of Philadelphia, deserted the city and announced that New York was where they felt the world's permanent capital deserved to be all along.[20] After months of deliberation, after approximately 20,000 miles traveled by various UN committee members in order to survey numerous proposed sites, after hundreds of thousands of dollars spent researching the issue, the UN decided on a site that it had spent no time or money surveying, studying or deliberating over.[21] Moses and Rockefeller literally swooped in at the absolute last minute and soared off with the bounty.

In Philadelphia, of course, condemnation procedures ceased, the committee disbanded and everybody was left with egg on their faces. After months of planning and posturing, after giving the United Nations everything it had asked for, and more, it was rejected. In the end, power won out. The United Nations wound up in New York because powerful people — powerful New Yorkers such as Moses and Rockefeller — wanted it there. There was nothing Philadelphia, a second-rate city by comparison, could do about it. Faced with another stinging defeat, Philadelphia retreated to its comfortable position on the sidelines, seeking shelter, much as it had done for the past century, behind its dignified, gentlemanly façade. The *Philadelphia Inquirer* reacted to the news by distancing its city from the "dead end kids ... and unsavory drinking places" that haunted New York. "The atmosphere of Manhattan's gin and jazz would probably be to the liking of international lobbyists, parasites and camp followers," it wrote, "but it is far from that of quiet and dignity in which the United Nations should properly work."[22] The city hid behind the safety of its history, calling attention to "the cultural background, the historic traditions, the true American spirit" of Philadelphia that contrasted with the "blatant commercialism" of modern New York. Philadelphia may have lost yet again, but at least it had its dignity. Or so Philadelphians were urged to believe.

In truth, the United Nations saga demonstrated that Philadelphia could get what it wanted only so long as New York did not object. If it did, however, then Philadelphia would have to settle for something else. The relocation of the Athletics eight years later sent the same message to Philadelphians. They could control their destiny only to an extent. Whenever it came into conflict with the desires of New Yorkers, Philadelphians had no choice but to yield. Inferiority was stamped on their foreheads once again.

If any doubt remained that Philly had been had by New York yet again a few years later, at the time of the relocation of the Athletics, the shuttle between Kansas City and the Yankees between 1955 and 1960 erased whatever may have been left. Just as was the case with the United Nations, power dictated circumstances and Philadelphia was but a pawn in the wielding of it. As one player after another moved from Arnold Johnson's Midwestern, Major League farm team to his friends Topping and Webb's, what had been hinted at earlier was being openly discussed now; soon, in baseball circles, KC came to stand not for Kansas City but "Kissing Cousins," so close, obvious and unsavory was the relationship between the Athletics and the Yankees.

Unlike the battle over the United Nations, much less was at stake here, at least on the surface. The relocation of the Athletics had a minimal impact on Philadelphia's economy, particularly when compared with the boon that would have occurred with the construction of the numerous United Nations buildings along with the attention and acclaim that would have accompanied the city's reemergence onto the international stage. However, given all that the Athletics meant to the city — and all that professional sports had come to mean to any city during the twentieth century — the psychological scars left by the move were significant. As cities grew during the industrial and postindustrial age, sports teams, particularly baseball teams, came to stand for much more than simply the game on the field. They became status symbols, providing the most visible indication of where a particular city stood in relation to other cities.[23] As a result, a considerable amount of psychological baggage has always been heaped on a city's sports teams. "Big league" towns had, and have, big league teams, or so that grew to become the perception — they brought respectability and status even if their impact on their local economies proved negligible.[24] Losing a team, or worse, losing one at the hands of one's arch nemesis, had the opposite effect, namely, damaging morale and causing the local populace to question their city's place in the national hierarchy despite the economic realities of the loss. The relocation of the Athletics was such a loss, particularly coming as it did so close on the heels of another heist at the hands of New York. The message to any Philadelphian could not be missed: here lies a city on the decline, a city ill-equipped to compete with the major players on the national stage. And when these people turned inward to contemplate what they had been left with, the bitter taste left by this message would be even more difficult to rinse clean.

The Phillies' Return to the Basement

The contrast between what had been taken from them and what they had been left with could not have been made more clear as the 1950s and early

'60s progressed. Gone was "The House of Mack," with the majestic ghosts of Al Simmons, Eddie Plank, Jimmie Foxx and Mickey Cochrane; left behind was "The House of Muck," a team with a forgettable past to the few who had paid enough attention to even have borne witness of what there was to forget. Once the brief high of the Whiz Kids of the late 1940s and early '50s faded, what remained was a tangible reminder, trudging into what was now called Connie Mack Stadium[25] (yet another reminder of what the city had been stripped of to anybody who bought a ticket thereafter) 77 times each year to let everybody in the Delaware Valley know that theirs was a second-rate city. It was a message nobody liked to hear. And the Phillies would pay the price for its role as the messenger.

Even before the magical 1950 season, the Phillies began to deteriorate. In 1948, General Manager Herb Pennock died. He took with him his eye for talent; it was not replaced. Instead, Bob Carpenter, a man of "ordinary abilities"[26] who had the good fortune — and good sense — to hire a capable baseball man in Pennock when he first took over the team, chose this time to run the baseball side of things himself.[27] Perhaps he saw himself as instrumental in the signings of players such as Simmons and Roberts, the development of the farm system and everything else that finally turned the franchise around. In truth he *was* instrumental, but mostly because he opened up his wallet. The baseball decisions were largely to the credit of Pennock.[28] Regardless, Carpenter believed that he knew enough by now to run the team himself. The results were soon to be disastrous as the Phils, even before they would win the pennant in 1950, were already on their way back down to the basement.

Despite the reality that the Whiz Kids were a mirage — a one-season wonder who experienced a miracle year during which almost everything went their way — Carpenter refused to accept this fact for years. In 1951, the Phils dropped back into the second division, finishing fifth, leading credence to the opinion that the team was more closely akin to a fourth or fifth place team on talent rather than a division winner. Between 1951 and '57, they would win only eight more games than they would lose, a further validation of the talent level of the team, but still Carpenter held out, refusing to believe that the team "he" put together was a middling one at best. He remained devoted to his Whiz Kids, tinkering with them rather than tearing them apart as soon as it became clear that the miracle of 1950 was not about to be repeated any time soon.[29] Any time now, he thought, they would put it together again, just as they did before. He continued signing tall pitching prospects, believing that another Simmons or Roberts was just around the corner.[30] Most of them flamed out, never reaching the majors. As the '50s wore on, it became more and more obvious that, despite the initial optimism, the business model of these Phils in no way resembled that of the Yankees. Whereas the Yankees would retool from one year to the next, rebuilding whenever necessary to remain on top, Carpenter was content to remain devoted to his cadre of Whiz Kids, hoping against hope for lightning to strike them again. It was a failed strategy and one that the Yanks had never been accused of pursuing.

As the Phillies continued their descent, Delaware Valley baseball fans continued to follow them; not because they wanted to but because now, without the A's around, they no longer had any choice in the matter. Very quickly, they began to take out their frustrations on the team they had been left with, the team New York left behind as "good enough" for a city of their caliber. Del Ennis bore the brunt of their wrath the hardest of any Phil during this time. Despite being a solid player, he was booed lustily, the disappointing face of a disappointing team.[31] Heckling, which to some extent had always been a Philadelphia tradition (the *Sporting News* noted the particular viciousness of Philadelphia fans as far back as the late teens[32]), grew worse. On occasion, games were stopped as umpires attempted, often without success, to eject particularly disruptive fans.[33]

In 1954, to his credit, Carpenter realized, at least to a degree, that he needed help on the baseball side of the ledger, so he hired H. Roy Hamey as his new general manager.[34] However, Hamey's eye for talent was not much better than Carpenter's. A series of poor trades marked the now accelerating decline of the club until January 1959, when he was finally let go after his contract expired. When the 1959 season had come to a close, the Phils found themselves in the basement, precisely where they had finished a season earlier as well. When fans looked back on the decade just completed, they saw a team that had managed to work itself from the top of the league to the bottom in rather deliberate fashion, finishing fourth four consecutive seasons from 1952 to 1956, followed by back-to-back fifth place seasons, followed by two in the cellar. But not only were the Phillies bad, they were boring as well.[35] There was no reason to root for them other than the most obvious one, namely, that they were there. And Philadelphia fans were in no mood to do that.

In searching for reasons to feel connected to this team, many fans came up empty. Although the Phils did have a past, it was not only an inglorious one but also one that, unlike that of the Cubs, very few people had ever paid any attention to while it was occurring. These Phils were anything but the cuddly, lovable losers of Chicago's North Side. Rather, they were more akin to an expansion team although given the half century of futility that Philadelphians may not have followed closely but were certainly aware of, without the accompanying feeling of optimism and hope. The depth of most fans' knowledge of the Phillies history extended little further than the running joke attached to the club from its Baker Bowl days when a billboard on its rightfield wall proclaimed that "The Phillies Use Lifebuoy," which brought on the refrain, "yeah, and they still stink."[36]

To be sure, despite their habitual sorry state, the Phils, like every other club in the Majors, had their share of great players over time, players who would have been revered and loved despite the wretchedness of the teams on which they played, players on whose shoulders the affection of the city would have rubbed off on their teams, players like Ernie Banks of the Cubs and Ted Williams of the Red Sox. But unlike in Chicago or Boston, in Philadelphia, because nobody was paying attention, there was very little connection to these players and, hence, to the Phils. No player exemplified this more than Chuck Klein.[37] In his day, he was one of the greatest all-around hitters in the game, hitting for both average and power, batting .320 over his 17-year career with 300 home runs and 1201 RBIs. Until Ichiro Suzuki matched him in 2005, he was the only player ever to get at least 200 hits in his first five full seasons; in 1930 he had one of the greatest single seasons ever, hitting .386 with 40 home runs, 170 RBIs and set a league record with 107 extra base hits. He was awarded the league's Most Valuable Player award in 1932, an "off" year by comparison (he hit .348 with 38 homers and 137 RBIs to go along with 20 stolen bases). Yet, he played the majority of his career in virtual anonymity. Without the efforts of a devoted fan in the 1970s who, year after year, bombarded the electorate with Klein's dazzling statistics until they finally realized what they had been ignoring up to then, Klein may very well have never been elected to the Hall of Fame (he was finally inducted in 1980 by the Veterans Committee).[38] Most Philadelphians never pushed for him simply because they were not aware that such a great player had been performing in their midst. They were too busy rooting for the A's at the time.

In the search for a connection between team and city, the Phillies didn't help matters when, in the late 1950s, they threatened to follow the Athletics out of town, further alienating a fan base that wasn't in their corner to begin with. By the end of the decade, few would disagree that Connie Mack Stadium, once Ben Shibe's palace, was by now something considerably less. It was difficult to get to, located in a rapidly deteriorating neighborhood, unkempt and falling apart. After the Dodgers and Giants vacated New York, Carpenter saw his chance to rid himself of the old relic once and for all. With New York anxious to replace these departed National League teams, Carpenter took advantage of the situation and met with New York's mayor, Robert Wagner, and Bill Shea, the chairman of the mayor's baseball committee, to discuss the possibility of the Phillies relocating to New York, of all places.[39] The talks continued behind closed doors for 18 months until they were made public in April 1959.[40] In truth, Carpenter never harbored any real intention of moving his team to New York; instead, he was just hoping to use the threat to forge a new stadium deal with the city of Philadelphia, which to that point had been reluctant to put forth the funds.[41] In conjunction with Philadelphia's mayor, Richardson Dilworth, who had previously served as Connie Mack's attorney and who also wanted to see a new ballpark erected within the city, he hatched a plan to squeeze money out of city authorities who were reluctant to let it go. They covered their bases further in that they also courted Camden, New Jersey, as part of an effort to turn up the heat on the city.[42] In the end, no stadium deal was forthcoming (at least immediately) because Carpenter and Dilworth overestimated the loyalty of the city's fans to the Phils; *New York Times* columnist John Drebinger remarked that should the Phils leave the city, not only would the city not raise its arms in protest but also "the home-town fans would not mind at the moment if you ... drowned the last-place Phillies in the Delaware."[43] Realizing that the leverage they counted on was nonexistent, they soon dropped their threats and resigned themselves to several more years playing in decrepit Connie Mack Stadium.

In the early 1960s, the Phillies managed to do the seemingly impossible: they actually got worse. The resentment toward the team grew in conjunction with every defeat. On opening day 1960, Eddie Sawyer, the former Whiz Kids manager who had been brought back in 1958 in yet another misguided attempt to recapture past glory, quit after surveying the team he was bringing north with him from spring training. After taking a wallop from the Cincinnati Reds in the opener, Sawyer rationalized his decision to the media, saying "I'm forty-nine years old and I want to live to be fifty."[44] Few could argue with his logic. However, if the 1960 Phils were awful (they lost 95 games), they could not hold a candle to the 1961 edition, which managed to lose 107 games including 23 straight — a record for futility that stands to this day. By the end of the 1961 season, things looked hopeless and now, without the A's in town, there was nowhere anyone could turn for refuge from the stench emanating from Connie Mack Stadium. For better or worse, and Philadelphia fans were still waiting for the "better," the Phils were now the city's team. And the city was not at all happy about it.

The Deepening of the City's Negative Self-Image and the Phillies as Its Public Face

In Philadelphia, where few people felt good about their city beforehand, things turned even more grim after the end of World War II. During and after the war, the city suffered one loss after another as much of its pharmaceutical, metal manufacturing, food processing and electronic industries abandoned their long-time home and relocated elsewhere, either moving south to the emerging Sunbelt states, north or west to the nearer suburbs, or east to

New Jersey, just as the Phillies would threaten to do.[45] Those who did not abandon the region altogether took with them much of the white middle class who followed their employers out to places such as Cherry Hill, King of Prussia, Plymouth Meeting and Fairless Hills.[46] The suburbs were booming, the city was hemorrhaging. As the city's tax base shrank, it became increasingly unable to provide even the most basic services—streetlights went unfixed, water was barely potable.[47] On top of this, poor, rural African Americans streamed into the city from the South under the mistaken impression that work was available for them in the "workshop of the world." However, once they unpacked their bags, many of them realized that their arrival coincided with the final stages of the shuttering of that workshop as most of the manufacturing jobs they had been hearing about were gone. As a result, poor blacks, with no work to sustain them and crowded into substandard housing located in neighborhoods that were already starting to buckle due to the declining tax base, formed a permanent underclass, further weighing down a city that had increasingly fewer resources to combat the myriad problems with which it was now confronted.[48] The stress on the city from so many different sources soon caused the infrastructure to crumble. By 1947, the Philadelphia Housing Authority concluded that 80,000 of the city's approximately 550,000 occupied structures were "substandard."[49] Property values across the city plummeted. The city was a mess.

Watching their city fall apart all around them, many locals soon lost whatever faith they had in it. By the late 1940s, many blamed the city's corrupt Republican machine that controlled much of the city.[50] They viewed its ancient, insular practices, favoring patronage above all else, as an impediment to the social, economic and physical reform that was needed to save their city from even further decline. They viewed their elected officials—as a collective body, Philadelphia itself—as the enemy. That this pessimism soon permeated every aspect of life within the city became evident when the populace reacted lukewarmly to the supposed good news that Philadelphia, despite all of its problems, might possibly be chosen as the permanent home of the United Nations. One resident questioned the UN decisionmakers directly: "We have bad water, a smelly river, dirty streets, no airport, badly run liquor stores, a wage tax, no snow clearance, inadequate police and a very poor climate. What have you got against peace?"[51] Over time, there came to be no harsher critics of the city than the people who lived there, prompting one civic advertising campaign to actually adopt as its slogan the mantra that "Philadelphia isn't as bad as Philadelphians say it is."[52]

Compounding the actual problems of the city were the ones perceived to have been created by a populace streaming out to the suburbs, unwilling to check for verification after abandoning their homes for new ones in the rapidly developing hinterlands. Between 1950 and 1960, Philadelphia's population dipped slightly, losing approximately 69,000 residents (from over 2 million) during that time.[53] However, more telling of the true picture of Philadelphia's woes (along with those of most big northeastern cities) was what was going on in the suburbs during this time. During the early part of the twentieth century, the nation was truly becoming urbanized. Metropolitan areas (defined as cities combined with suburbs) were growing but, at first, the cities experienced most of the growth. In 1910, three times as many people lived in cities as suburbs (21.2 percent versus 7.1 percent).[54] The remainder lived in the rural areas that typified nineteenth-century society.

By 1960 the picture would change drastically. By this time, nearly twice as many people in the nation lived in metropolitan areas as rural ones and, between cities and suburbs, for the first time, the population stood nearly equally divided between the two.[55] Much of this city-to-suburbs shift occurred after 1930 when the rate of suburban living first began to accelerate, but the transformation was completed during the 1950s when suburban growth literally exploded. Here, the numbers, much as they often do in baseball, tell the story. Between 1910 and 1960, the nation's urban population increased by less than 50 percent whereas its suburban population exploded by nearly seven times this amount — 335 percent.[56] In Philadelphia, events played out even more severely: while the city lost those nearly 70,000 residents during the decade of the 1950s, its suburbs saw a population boom of over ten times that number (740,942) during that span of time.[57] Thus was the tale of Philadelphia during the 1950s: white and/or white collar residents, fearful of the changing racial makeup of the city as well as increasingly insufficient government services, streaming out of the city and into the burgeoning suburbs, being replaced by a poor, largely black underclass who arrived to find a city less equipped than ever to serve their needs. The vicious cycle that was created only sped up as time went on: as more African Americans arrived, more whites fled, taking with them the tax base the city so desperately needed more than ever to pay for the services that were seen as lacking even before the demographic shift. And as services deteriorated, increasing numbers of long time residents abandoned the city, causing it to buckle under the weight of its responsibilities. However, just as important as the tax revenues that these people took with them to the suburbs were the impressions they took of their former city — negative ones (the ones that caused them to leave in the first place) and ones that were increasingly prone to manipulation through fear given that they now came to the city less often as they settled into their new lives outside of it. This would further erode the image of the city and cause the Phillies to become the unwitting face of that poor image.

With the migration to the suburbs came a change of identity for many of the newly relocated. As time went on and they settled more firmly into their adopted suburban communities, they began to consider themselves suburbanites rather than Philadelphians. No longer did they wake up in the city, shop in the city, work in the city, dine in the city, relax in the city and go to sleep in the city, day in and day out. Now, ensconced in their new communities, they might do a few of these activities on occasion but, over time, they visited less and less often and of the activities they still did, they did with less frequency than before. Soon, they considered themselves an entity apart from Philadelphia and its inhabitants. Instead, they were from Wynnewood, Springfield, Cherry Hill, Cheltenham or wherever it was that they had chosen to establish their new roots. This change in self-perception would have grave consequences for the city they left behind.

As large numbers of people streamed out of Philadelphia, they left their urban identities behind. Now, city dwellers, once a group they were proud to call their own, comprised the "other," the "them," a group to which they no longer belonged and, consequently — given the basic human urge to denigrate out-groups[58] — a group that could not help but suffer in comparison.[59] Moreover, the image of the city suffered even further given the natural tendency for in-group members to not only draw individual distinctions between other in-group members (the result of a constant, daily contact between these members that causes them to see the true individuals rather than the facade of the group[60]) but to see out-group members (the "other") negatively and as homogeneous, interchangeable representatives of an undesirable whole.[61] Due to less frequent contact with the city, as well as with the people now residing there, the actions of any one urban resident were now more likely to be seen as representative of the city as a whole. A murder occurring in Ardmore could be seen as an isolated incident, unrepresentative of anything beyond the bare facts of the crime; a murder occurring in Philadelphia could be seen, however, as another example of a violent, dangerous city overall — a city full of criminals where anyone was liable to be killed at any time.[62]

As the '50s and '60s progressed, the Delaware Valley's increasingly suburban population's perception of Philadelphia proper stemmed more and more from their less and less frequent encounters with it. Now, many suburbanites would only enter the city for special occasions to do things they otherwise were unable to do in "their" new hometowns — occasions like attending a Phillies game. And when they did venture into the city, rather than looking to build up the image of the city and the people who lived there, these people were looking to tear it down, to denigrate it even further in an effort to make the suburbs, and therefore themselves, look better by comparison. When attending a Phillies game, these people did not have to look hard.

1956: A local youth offers to "watch" the car of a fan headed to Connie Mack Stadium (Temple University Libraries, Urban Archives, Philadelphia, PA).

By the late 1960s, the neighborhood surrounding the stadium had deteriorated and had become a battleground of various turf wars. The decline of the area was both precipitous and steady. In 1954, racial tensions in the area broke out when a black family attempted to move into what was then still a white neighborhood. They were welcomed with broken windows and obscene chants.[63] Within a short period of time, the neighborhood was considered dangerous. Black activism soon migrated into the city, with many black activists concluding that the source of black America's problems lay with white racism.[64] Tensions among the residents living around the stadium ratcheted up even further as the neighborhood became increasingly black but played host several days each summer to the Phillies' largely white, increasingly suburban, fan base. Although fans parking in the area had felt compelled for years to pay local children fees to "watch" their cars for fear that their tires would be slashed if they refused, by now, their fears were being realized and then some. By the early 1960s, local police reported an average of five complaints per game concerning damage done to cars.[65] In August 1964, a difficult situation became even worse when a violent race riot erupted in the neighborhood, compelling the mayor to declare an emergency and cordon off a

125-block section of the city for four days.[66] Looting was uncontrolled and uncontrollable, gunshots could be heard zipping through the air and residents were urged to stay off the streets. In the end, two people died, 339 were wounded and 308 were arrested. The neighborhood was now referred to as "the jungle" by the police and members of the media, with all of the implied ugly racial overtones seemingly intended. Afterward, once the Phillies returned home from their road trip (they were fortunate to have been away from the stadium during the entire riot), fans venturing into the area to see a game were greeted with all of the perceived horridness of the city — bombed out, vandalized buildings, with hundreds of police patrolling the streets in a

August 27, 1964: Riot at 22nd and Columbia, a few blocks from Connie Mack Stadium (Temple University Libraries, Urban Archives, Philadelphia, PA).

desperate effort to maintain order. In later years, gangs took over the neighborhood completely and would harass fans, occasionally mugging them on
their way to the stadium.[67]

Suburbanites could not help but take these images back home with them
and project them upon the entire city. Every negative encounter on their way
to a game was perceived to be merely a microcosm of the city as a whole —
an interchangeable representative of a homogeneous group: the neighborhood
was bombed out so therefore the city was decaying; the heavy police presence surrounding the stadium was indicative of an entire city that required
the suspension of civil liberties, and which needed to be run as a police state
just to maintain order. The city, once a part of them but now something apart
from them, was believed by many suburban fans to be comprised of the exact
same elements they had encountered whenever they attended a Phillies game
at Connie Mack Stadium. With increasingly fewer interactions with the city
to counteract this impression, the Phillies, and the Phillies experience, became
symbolic of the entire city.

August 28, 1964: Philadelphia police, with riot gear and night sticks, patrol the
neighborhood surrounding the stadium. Many photos documenting both the riot
and the heavy police presence in the area appeared for days in local newspapers
(Temple University Libraries, Urban Archives, Philadelphia, PA).

Although suburbanites ventured into the city for reasons other than Phillies games, no other organization served as so frequent and public a symbol of the city at the time as the Phillies. They now not only played 81 games each season in north Philadelphia,[68] but also their games—as well as the harrowing, frightening stories recounting the experience of attending their games—were reported for everyone to read about the next day even if they never set foot in the city themselves. By following the Phillies in their newspapers every day each summer, hundreds of thousands of people were likewise receiving daily updates on the state of the city (or at least what they perceived as the state of the city) as well. The Phillies during the late 1950s and 1960s served as a powerful force in conveying a plethora of distressing news to a populace who had fled the city for the precise reasons they were now reading about. Reading about the Phillies only provided confirmation to these people that they had not abandoned the city foolheartedly. To these people, the Phillies were Philadelphia and Philadelphia was the Phillies. In their eyes, both were losers, both were poorly run, both were crumbling. After a while, it became difficult to tell one from the other.

The Issue of Race

Nowhere was the Phils-as-Philadelphia phenomenon more evident than when it came to the city's racial identity. Like many cities, Philadelphia has struggled with the issue of race for decades; in this it is certainly not unique. The Phillies, however, ever since the debut of Jackie Robinson in 1947, provided what many assumed to be a convenient mirror for many of the issues confronting the city such that the connection between the team and the city is unusually close here, to the point that, once again, the team became the face of the city's discomfort with a troubling issue. Just as they saw the neighborhood decaying all around the stadium, suburbanites could look at the Phillies and consider them merely a microcosm of all of the problems and tensions that confronted the city as a whole during the 1950s and '60s. This resulted in a generally negative perception of both the team and the city in which they played.

Almost immediately after Robinson broke Major League Baseball's color barrier with the Brooklyn Dodgers, the Phillies became a focal point in the integration "experiment." And very quickly, as a result of the treatment by some Phillies toward Robinson, the city became labeled as a segregated, particularly hostile place to blacks. The truth, however, was somewhat different from the reputation. In fact, at least through the early 1950s, Philadelphia was *less* segregated than most major cities—cities such as New York, Chicago, Cleveland and others; cities that likewise had Major League Baseball teams but ones that did not develop racist reputations as did Philadelphia.[69] Although many of Philadelphia's black residents lived on all-black streets, these streets were oftentimes no more than one or two streets away from predominantly white ones. One study done at the time found that the overwhelming majority (two-thirds) of Philadelphia's 404 census tracts contained black residents; this could not be said of many other cities despite the reputation enjoyed by those cities of being less racially hostile than Philadelphia. While Philadelphia may have been segregated block by block, segregation on a macro level was far less prevalent there than in many other cities, with the result that the large, concentrated ghettos that predominated in those other places did not dominate the Philadelphia landscape, at least not initially. After 1950 this would change, but by the late 1940s, the time when Philadelphia's reputation as a racist city flourished, it was anything but, at least comparatively. (Of course, it was not a unique bastion of racial tolerance either, as the 1954 incident in Connie Mack Stadium's Lower North Penn neighborhood attests; as the 1950s progressed, these types of incidents would increase.) And when it came to baseball, Philadelphians were particularly tolerant. As noted in chapter 2, Philadelphia was a hotbed of Negro League baseball, to the extent that, by the mid 1930s, the financial stability of the Negro National League was due, in overwhelming part, to the support provided to the league's Philadelphia Stars.[70] In 1942, the Stars began playing some of their games in Shibe Park, drawing impressive crowds. Soon, they outgrew their former home at Parkside Field in west Philadelphia and played many of their biggest games at Shibe, drawing large, mixed, crowds to what was still a white neighborhood. The games were played without notable incident either on the field or in the neighborhood surrounding the stadium.

The city received its racial identity, however, not from these facts but from the Phillies. Manager Ben Chapman was an overt racist and very early in the 1947 season, he had the opportunity to display his prejudice.[71] On April 22, the Phils went to Brooklyn to take on Robinson and the Dodgers. Chapman, along with some of his players, taunted Robinson relentlessly, to the extent that fans seated near the Phillies dugout complained to Commissioner Happy Chandler. Commentator Walter Winchell picked up on the story and publicly lambasted Chapman on his show, broadcast to the entire nation. Later, when the Dodgers visited Philadelphia, Chapman continued with his taunts, focusing, in the words of a Brooklyn reporter who would later make them national news, on "everything from thick lips to the supposedly extra thick Negro skull ... [and] the repulsive sores and diseases he said Robinson's teammates would become infected with if they touched the towels or combs he used."[72] Phillies pitchers threw at his head, players attempted to spike him and, at one point, several players stood on the steps of their dugout, "pointing their bats at him and making gunshot sounds."[73] To compound matters, General Manager Herb Pennock was likewise unsympathetic to Robinson's plight, to say the least. Prior to the Dodgers' first trip to Philadelphia, he attempted to dissuade Dodgers general manager Branch Rickey from bringing Robinson on the trip, threatening at one point that his Phils would boycott the games should Robinson attempt to take the field, backing down only when Rickey called his bluff. "[You] just can't bring that nigger here with the rest of your team, Branch," he allegedly said. "We're just not ready for that sort of thing yet."[74] In reality, Philadelphia was probably as ready for integration as any other large northeastern city.[75] It was only the Phillies who were not. Regardless, the attention these stories received gave birth to the racially hostile reputation Philadelphia would thereafter become saddled with. And with this reputation came yet another reason for suburbanites to look down their noses at their former home.

Even though Pennock would die in 1948 and Chapman would be fired the same year, the Phillies remained a symbol of Philadelphia racism for nearly another decade, due more to indifference and confusion over how to deal with the race issue than to anything else. The team would remain an all-white outfit until 1957, the last such team in the National League and the last team in all of baseball outside of Boston. Bob Carpenter, wearing both the owner's and general manager's hats for much of this time, was a man troubled and confused by the race issue and unsure how to approach it. Publicly, he stated that he was not opposed to signing black players but he did not consider doing so a priority. At one point, when confronted on the issue directly, he replied that he was not "going to hire a player of any color or nationality just to have him on the team."[76] In his mind, this approach to the gnawing racial questions surrounding the Phillies was appropriate: everybody would be treated equally regardless of race. In practice, however, as each year passed and the Phillies remained an exclusively white ballclub, this approach smacked of something else altogether. Despite Carpenter's public sentiment on the issue and his stated desire to create a racially neutral atmosphere on his team, the absence of a single black face on the Phillies for an entire decade after the debut of Jackie Robinson made just the opposite point in most people's minds.

Carpenter's failure to sign black players throughout the '50s was likely exacerbated by two additional factors: his continuing, misguided devotion to his faded Whiz Kids and his weaknesses when it came to spotting talent. To his credit, however, when he finally realized the folly of his Whiz Kids dreams, he overhauled the entire Phillies organization and signed more black and Latin American players than most other teams. From a pittance of three such players in their entire system in 1958 to 34 (nearly 15 percent of the approximately 200 players on the organization's 10 teams) in 1961 to even more as the '60s progressed, Carpenter and new general manager John Quinn changed the complexion of the organization virtually overnight.[77] More importantly, just as he had done in the 1940s with prospects such as Roberts and Simmons, Carpenter spared no expense in signing future stars, often doling out more money for top black prospects than white ones. Larry Hisle was given a $50,000 bonus, the promising Haines brothers (Richard and Robert) were given $40,000 each, Richie Allen was given $70,000. Top white prospects, by comparison, received far less: Rick Wise got only $12,000 in 1963, Joe Lis managed to wrangle only $3,000 more than that out of Carpenter the next year.[78]

These top prospects, black and white along with Latino players such as Ruben Amaro and Tony Taylor,[79] transformed the team during the early 1960s. By the time they all reached the majors and joined others such as Wes Covington who arrived via trade, the Phils trotted out one of the most racially diverse teams in baseball. Unfortunately, race once again became a focal point of the team when, before long, the local sports media would begin to play up the alleged racial tensions on the team, casting it in a negative light and using it as a mirror for all of the racial problems occurring outside the walls of Connie Mack Stadium. The racial battles that so scarred the city and frightened the suburbs in August 1964 as to cause attendance to plummet even during the heat of the Phils' pennant drive that season were reprised in the media's daily accounts of the goings-on within the team's clubhouse. Once again the Phils were seen by many as a microcosm of the racial discord believed to be crippling the city.

In July 1965, Richie Allen and Frank Thomas fought during batting practice after Thomas (appropriately nicknamed "The Big Donkey" due to his penchant for saying "the wrong things to the wrong people"[80]) hurled both a bat and a collection of racial slurs in Allen's direction. Largely because Allen was a superstar and Thomas a marginal player, Thomas was placed on waivers five hours later and Allen was ordered not to speak about the incident to anyone.[81] Many fans reacted negatively to Thomas's release, blaming it on Allen. Soon they took to jeering and harassing him, with some fans hurling racially charged taunts in his direction. As a result, Allen became a target due to circumstances that initially were hardly his fault. The bulls-eye on his back was only enlarged in subsequent seasons when Carpenter (in yet another example of his confusion when it came to matters involving black players) began covering for Allen, refusing to enforce a succession of fines imposed on him by Manager Gene Mauch, thereby undermining Mauch's authority and singling Allen out as a target for the fans' derision. In time, Allen found it convenient to hide behind the growing taunts and jeers hurled at him, using them as cover for the peccadilloes that were causing his mind to wander from the game and for him to be increasingly absent from it physically as well. He claimed he was a black militant, piggybacking on the fears many suburbanites had over the changing face of the city, and as such became a lightning rod for the root of white fear. Fans took out their frustrations over what they perceived to be happening to their former hometown, with some calling him "nigger" to his face and telling him to "[g]o back to South Street with the monkeys."[82] In Allen, suburbia found the face of its panic.

Allen, however, was hardly such a face. Despite his insistence that he was a black militant, there is no evidence that he ever was. He remained on the sidelines during the civil rights movement as well as the myriad political protests that took place during the '60s. In addition, historians who have searched for other instances of Allen's societal agenda have largely come up empty.[83] Instead, Allen's mind during much of this time was largely taken up with racehorses: he bought a few and spent much time at the track, occasionally showing up late for games as a result.[84] Later, he began drinking heavily, sometimes showing up for games so drunk that he was unable to walk a straight line.[85] Race, however, provided an easy cover for him so he took it, playing up the racial angle in his repeated attempts to get himself traded out of Philadelphia in the late '60s.

The media, knowing quite well what made interesting copy in the increasingly influential suburbs, went along for the ride. To be sure, the Phils were no racial oasis during the turbulent decade (as the Allen-Thomas incident attests), but many members of the media looked for a racial angle even when it wasn't there or, if it was, brought it out from the background to the fore.[86] After the Thomas fight, stories of the supposed racial division within the Phillies clubhouse became more common and provided a neat parallel with the racial strife occurring in the surrounding neighborhood. Whether knowingly or not, the media played on the fears of many suburbanites toward the city and heaped all of them on the Phillies. Allen was only too happy to accommodate this as it both masked his true problems and eventually helped him to escape Philadelphia once and for all. Before he left, however, he took over for Del Ennis as "the most booed man in Philadelphia from April to October,"[87] providing a convenient outlet for the white populace to vent. The negative feelings these people had toward the city and the Phils were one and the same, tied together and inseparable.

The Myth of 1964

As time has marched on and the decades have passed, it has become increasingly popular for those searching for the genesis of the city's hatred toward the Phillies to pin it on the epic collapse of the 1964 team. The team lost a seemingly insurmountable 6-and-a-half-game lead with 12 to play, losing 10 straight games at one point and eventually surrendering the pennant to the Cardinals. In their eyes, this was the turning point, when whatever trust folks had in the team was "shattered," causing a city that had a tenuous relationship with the team to abandon it once and for all.[88] As Phillies general manager Paul Owens would say years later, "I don't think a lot of the fans realized it at the time, but it was something they would never really be able to shake ... like a great big cloud hanging over the city."[89] Certainly, the collapse was memorable and, as a baseball event, deserves its place at the pinnacle of the heap of professional sports disasters; as a sociological event, however, it was far less relevant.

To conclude that the September 1964 meltdown changed the city's relationship with the team is to assume that it was somehow different beforehand. This was not the case. As the 1950s wore on, the ambivalence most fans felt toward the team stemming from its anonymity during much of the first half of the twentieth century turned to anger as they realized what they had been stuck with as a result of the highjacking of their Athletics. By the early 1960s, after the mirage of 1950 had evaporated completely and the Phils were once again among the dregs of all of baseball, the relationship was one of open hostility. There was little in the way of deep abiding affection for the team (such as that found with fans of other perennial losers like the Cubs or Red Sox) given that, for almost any Delaware Valley baseball fan over the age of 25, the love of their youth had been the A's, not the Phillies. Younger fans may have had stronger allegiances to the Phils but here too this was tempered by the reality that they had grown up in an era of deep enmity toward a perpetual loser. There was not much expected of them so there was not that much to lose after the collapse was complete and the team had finished out of the money once again.

In reviewing the seasons that preceded 1964, it is clear that the team that fell apart in September of that season was not one in which too many fans had earlier invested much of their energy and hope: the 1961 team was horrible, losing more games than any Philadelphia team (Phils or A's) since 1942. The 1962 team finished out of the basement in large part because of the presence of the wretched expansion Mets and Houston Colt .45's, two teams whose ineptitude made every other National League team look better on paper than it actually was. The Phils technically were above .500 in 1962 (81-80) but still finished seventh, 20 games out of first. The 1963 team was in last place until mid–July when it got hot and finished fourth, never challenging for the pennant and finishing 12 games out. As such, going into 1964, expectations were muted at best. Only 10 of 232 sportswriters picked them to even be in the race at all, let alone win it, and a preseason poll of

National League managers resulted in a predicted fifth-place finish for the team.[90]

The 1964 season, therefore, was an unexpected, magical ride, much like the one that would occur 29 years later in 1993, where everything went right until the very end when things would go horribly wrong.[91] In the end, however, after the smoke cleared and the Cardinals were in the World Series instead of the Phils, no one could say that the National League's best team was on the sidelines. The loss may have hurt but because so little had been invested in the team beforehand, as a larger, cultural event it was hardly a watershed moment.

After 1964, most fans responded to the Phils much as they had before that glorious summer and heartbreaking fall, viewing them with a combination of skepticism and derision. If 1964 had any effect, it was that it merely served as confirmation of what many had increasingly suspected ever since their Athletics left town 10 years earlier: that in the Phils, they had had forced upon them a second-rate team deemed appropriate by others (namely, New Yorkers) for a second-rate city. Whenever the Phils took the field thereafter, the negative feelings these suburban fans felt toward their former city swelled to the fore, confirming in their minds that their former home was a city without hope, a city full of losers.

6

The Structural Renaissance
of a City and Its Team

Black Friday: Sixth Inning

After the multiple dramas of the early innings, the middle few careened along, speeding for the final turn to come in the ninth, as if everyone involved just wanted to get there already, to see what was going to happen, given what already had. Garvey hauled his muscular body to the plate, chopping short practice swings along the way. Watching him, it seemed as if his build got in his way at times, so compact and dense, he appeared to have been sculpted from granite rather than from flesh and bone, with just about as much flexibility — a full, elongated, fluid stroke like Schmidt's appeared to be out of the question. He dug in against Reed, who pitched in the sixth as a continuation of the man who strolled off the mound in the fifth — a man who knew that today, no one was going to get the better of him. After dazzling Garvey with a broader arsenal of pitches than he had displayed before (his off-speed and breaking pitches appeared to fluster Garvey after the array of heat served up as an appetizer in the fifth), he got the statuary slugger to ground out to Bowa for out number one.

Dusty Baker then brought his hot bat to the plate to see if he could fare any better. He would not. After doubling and singling in his first two at-bats, this time all he could manage was a first-pitch fly ball to Maddox in center. Although shaky in the field up to now, this time Maddox barely had to move, taking three small steps back before putting Baker away for the first time all game.

Which brought up Monday. Taking note of Reed's dominance in the fifth, Monday knew that in order to get to him, he'd need to be two things: quick and aggressive. After a fastball missed low, he guessed fastball again, and guessed right, jumping on it with a vicious swing. The ball, however, reached Boone's mitt unharmed for strike one. Monday then stepped out of the box to regain his composure, staring at Reed the entire time as if to ask how on earth he had managed to do that. Reed's next pitch was yet another fastball, right on the outside corner, a pitch that Monday would have been unable to do anything productive with even had he made contact. Instead, he let it go by for strike two. Now standing on Monday's throat, Reed began to nibble, hoping to induce him to finish the job himself. Monday, however, would not bite. After fouling one more fastball off his bat handle, he took three balls just off the plate for a merciful walk.

Reed seemed disgusted with himself for letting Monday escape. Determined to right his wrong, he threw over to Hebner, repeatedly, hoping to erase him on the bases. The combination of Monday's bad back, which he had injured earlier in the season and which would not heal until the winter, and Reed's habitually poor pickoff move (his elongated body required an uncoiling process in order to allow him to throw over to first, which made success against anyone not in the throes of a sonorous sleep a virtual impossibility) made this unlikely, however. Despite an unusually long lead for somebody in his condition, Monday wasn't going anywhere and was leaning back toward first as soon as Reed went into his stretch; by the time the ball arrived in Hebner's mitt, Monday managed to make it back just ahead of it each time. After the fourth toss, however, Reed had succeeded in shortening Monday's lead a couple of steps for whatever that was worth. It would be worth something very soon.

Finally, Reed turned his attention to the man at the plate, Steve Yeager. Once he did, he made short work of him, inducing on the first pitch a grounder to Schmidt, who, in recognition of the turn of the game toward the stretch drive, was playing him on the line. A likely double down the line earlier in the game, this time Schmidt was right in front of the ball, snaring it and firing to Sizemore at second who stretched like a first baseman, managing to catch the ball for the inning-ending force just ahead of Monday's slide — a slide that came up those same couple of steps short. One way or another, nobody was going to get to Reed on this afternoon.

Rhoden, however, matched Reed and then some. Going into the bottom of the sixth, he had worked three and a third innings of hitless ball after calming LA's waters, disturbed by Hooton's meltdown. And after a Maddox fly-out to Monday to start the bottom of the inning, it looked as if things would continue for some time to come. Boone then stepped up, his right cheek packed tight as a squirrel's nest, spitting tobacco juice in defiance of his Stanford pedigree, determined to break Rhoden's spell. Eventually, Rhoden left a mistake over the corner of the plate and Boone pounced, sending a missile right back to its source, causing Rhoden to duck as the line drive dropped into centerfield for the Phils' first hit off him all day. It was Boone's second hit and, as hard as it seemed to be to believe given the sense of Phillies dominance that permeated the afternoon, only their third hit of the game.

Regardless, for the first time since the second inning, opportunity presented itself. With Boone on first, Sizemore at the plate and the pitcher's spot on deck, Ozark got Gene Garber up in the bullpen; he would hit for Reed despite his mastery of the previous two innings. For Ozark, the issue was really not much of one at all — Reed was simply one of four lockdown relievers available to him. He had three bullets left in his holster and a run now could very well seal things up for the day. His was a luxury Lasorda did not have: he was lucky to have gotten as much out of Rhoden, a converted starter, as he did. He could try to duplicate his luck with one last starter, Doug Rau, but after him, there was no one left. After him was Elias Sosa, Charlie Hough and a host of other middling relievers who tried his patience and raised his blood pressure. A couple of more hits now and he would have no choice but to call on them.

After getting ahead 0–2, Rhoden, like Reed before him, started to nibble, hoping to induce Sizemore to swing at something low and away. Twice in succession he tried to tempt him, but, both times, Sizemore resisted. And each time he did, things got just a little bit louder. Soon, the at-bat took on the feel of a boxing match as Sizemore answered the next three pitches with foul balls, drawing the throaty, aggressive, cheers of the crowd with each deflected blow. Finally, Sizemore landed one of his own, a grounder down the third base line, like Monday's in the top of the inning, only this time it was Cey at third, not Schmidt. Not playing the line, Cey was forced to run full speed toward it just to stop the ball before it rolled past, which he did but which caused him to run 10 feet into foul territory before he could set himself for the throw to first (with his momentum going toward foul territory, a throw to second was out of the question). His throw was a lazy arc, bouncing on the turf before reaching Garvey, allowing even the slow Sizemore to beat it out for what was, for him, a rare infield hit.

With runners on first and second, Tim McCarver was sent up to pinch hit for Reed. Now, for the first time, Rhoden appeared to be on the verge of veering out of control. After throwing a first-pitch strike, he followed with three pitches high and well out of the strike zone. Left with little choice now, he grooved one, which McCarver just missed, fouling it straight back. With the count full, everyone was on their feet; the few who did not rise on their own were prompted out of their seats by several blue-smocked, paper-hatted vendors who had abandoned their beer and hot dogs in the aisles and who were now running through them, yelling and urging everyone to take no notice of the promise of the free food and drink left unescorted on the steps but to focus instead on the possibility of driving yet another Dodger pitcher from the game. Hoping to force the issue, Ozark sent both Boone and Sizemore, setting into motion what, with McCarver at the plate, may have been the slowest hit and run in history (but a smart one given that McCarver struck out relatively infrequently). McCarver slammed Rhoden's pitch deep but foul into the rightfield stands. On the next pitch, with the thunder of the crowd rolling in behind him, McCarver straightened his drive out but lost some of the distance, sending a fly to Reggie Smith for out number two.

The out was of little matter to most folks in attendance, particularly the vendors. Now, several of those who hadn't done so beforehand took note of the others and they too dropped their trays in order to lead a crowd that did not appear to need much assistance. The sale of hot dogs, pretzels and beer was largely and unofficially suspended in many sections, at least until the end of the inning. With McBride at the plate, Lasorda's bullpen was now fully operational. Doug Rau and Mike Garman were up and throwing but Lasorda decided to stick with Rhoden in the hope that he could at least get him out of the sixth. His decision was an apt one. After missing on his first pitch, Rhoden induced a grounder to Lopes at second, who flipped the ball to Russell who caught it this time for out number three. As he trotted off the field, Lopes raised his arms in quick celebration, recognizing that it had been no small task to exit the sixth unharmed.

The Seeds of Rebirth

The city may have presented a disheartening face to the world in the 1950s and '60s but, deep down, its soul was stirring and had been for some time. And the man pushing, urging, forcing the city out of the darkness and into the light was a product of the gentlemanly Philadelphia thought to have been banished to the sidelines decades earlier. A man named Edmund Bacon.

Bacon was Philadelphia through and through. Born in Philadelphia, he "came from a family of 'Quakers unbroken for nine generations back to William Penn.'"[1] As an architectural student, he was fascinated by cities, none more than his own — his 1932 senior thesis at Cornell was entitled "Plans for a Philadelphia Center City."[2] His fascination was considered out of step at the time. To many young architects and urban planners the real action, the future, lay in the suburbs: those wide-open, untamed spaces just waiting to be developed. Their vision involved dreaming up ways to get people out of the cramped, decaying cities and into the greenery. Bacon, however, was different. Contrary to his classmates, Bacon did not see cities as dead; rather, he saw them as moribund places, still capable of resuscitation. After graduating from Cornell he started on his mission, first bicycling through the great old cities of Europe and eventually landing a job as an architectural designer in Shanghai.³ After further study at the Cranbrook Academy of Art in Bloomfield, Michigan, and a stint as a city planner in Flint, Michigan, Bacon returned home, armed with all he had learned along the way and his vision of what Philadelphia was and could be again. And he was determined to see his vision through.

The uniqueness of Bacon's outlook contrasted sharply with those of so many others who spent their lives thinking about and tinkering with cities, most notably, that of New York's master builder Robert Moses. In the middle part of the twentieth century, no two people had a greater effect on the look, the feel, and ultimately the fate of their cities as did Bacon and Moses. And it was their contrast in vision that helps to explain Philadelphia's eventual resurgence during the 1970s amid the failure of urban renewal and reform in so many other cities, none more so than in New York.

Like Bacon, Moses too wrote a thesis while in school (his was submitted for his Oxford Ph.D.) And like Bacon's, Moses' thesis would be telling in retrospect as well. Moses' thesis was entitled, "The Civil Service of Great Britain" and had as its focus an analysis of the noblesse oblige—the rights and duties of England's upper classes to serve their country, to engage in public service as a means toward bestowing on the lower classes some of the privilege that, until now, only they had enjoyed.⁴ It was a subject Moses could relate to, born as he was into the luxury of New York's Fifth Avenue. As a child, Moses was treated to summers either in Europe or in tony resort towns along the New Jersey shore; he became accustomed to relaxing trips throughout the countryside in his chauffeured touring car. It was a life of pleasure that Moses believed made him duty bound to give back to the masses to whatever extent possible. To do so, to engage in public service for this purpose, was, to him, the noblest of callings.

And so, when he entered public life—following in the tradition of DeWitt Clinton over a century earlier—he either assumed or created so many different positions (at the height of his power he would hold 12 separate government jobs simultaneously) that he would eventually become the single most powerful man in New York City. "The Power Broker" in the words of his biographer, Robert Caro, Moses turned his vision into reality. Upon consideration of the urban condition, Moses saw only "the traditional horrors of old age, disease and unemployment." He saw cities not only as presently being but also as always having been unorganized, unplanned messes that were detrimental to so many people in so many different ways. To deny these urban prisoners the delights of the country he so cherished growing up in was a sin; he was going to wield his influence and his power to see to it that they too could enjoy the pleasures of open spaces just as he had. In this he was not unique. The promise of the suburbs had a hold on many others as well. As such, he was determined to answer his noble calling by shaping New York with two goals in mind: facilitating the process in which New Yorkers could leave their city in order to enjoy the fresh air of the open spaces for themselves; and bringing the essence of country life into the city to whatever extent possible. Practically every major project undertaken by Moses in the 44 years (1924–1968) he was in power was in service of one of these goals. This vision crystallized in one of his first projects, the restoration of Riverside Park. In the new park, out went the urban ugliness of railroad tracks, garbage, and rusted fences and in went tennis courts, sail boats, and a beautiful, scenic drive. In his mind, Moses had figured out the "problem" with cities: the problem was that they looked like cities. He was determined to make them look less so wherever possible, to make them look and feel more like the countryside he had always enjoyed so much as a child.

Later, he would draw up "A State Park Plan for New York," which called for the construction of more tennis courts along with golf courses, athletic fields and other activities enjoyed traditionally by the upper classes. There would also be roads—scenic parkways—that could be enjoyed at leisurely speeds, replicating the chauffeured country drives he remembered. He reconfigured the physical coastline of the city to create a bathing beach—Jones Beach—in an effort to reproduce for New Yorkers the pleasures of the New Jersey resort town of his youth. For those who were determined to experience the real thing for themselves, Moses accommodated them through his bridge and arterial highway programs, which were designed to whisk city dwellers into the countryside as quickly as possible. By the 1940s, he believed he had perfected his vision in his superhighway construction program — a program that, in theory at least, could speed New Yorkers away from the choked city into the greenery of the suburbs in mere minutes. For Moses, the city itself offered very little to its inhabitants. It was his job to either transform it into something else or facilitate escape from its clutches.

Ed Bacon also saw a city that shortchanged its citizens when he considered the Philadelphia of the 1930s and '40s. But the similarities between the two men ended here. Bacon was a true Philadelphian and, as a true Philadelphian, he had a propensity to look backward rather than forward. And when he looked backward, he saw the magnificent city that Philadelphia had once been — the preeminent colonial city that only London rivaled in power, beauty and culture.[5] And he was determined to recapture as much of that as possible. Both Bacon and Moses grew up seeing ugliness when they saw the state of the modern city: however, Moses assumed that what he saw had always been there. As such, he believed cities were in desperate need of something "new" in order to rescue them from their natural state. Bacon, however, realized that what he was seeing was not something that had always been there.

Facing east: Broad Street Station in the early twentieth century. Note City Hall in the background with its tower still under construction (Temple University Libraries, Urban Archives, Philadelphia, PA).

He pined for an idealized return to what had once been — a city that would be home to the cultural elite, a city envied for its greatness. Looking backwards rather than forwards, Bacon realized that what was needed was not anything "new" but, rather, a return to the "old." It would be Bacon's uniquely Philadelphian approach to urban renewal that would eventually save the city from the ruinous path many perceived it to be on for decades during the early and mid-twentieth century.

Although a visionary, Bacon was also a realist. Perhaps Philadelphia could never again be the cultural, political and economic capital of the country as it had been nearly two centuries earlier but that did not mean that those elements could not be restored to the city to some extent and with style and glory in their own right. He saw Center City not as a decaying edifice beyond hope but as a commercial opportunity to be gained if only the infrastructure could be remolded.[6] He saw Philadelphia's Broad Street Railroad Station — a behemoth parked inconveniently in the middle of the city creating what was referred to as a "Chinese wall" splitting Center City in half — as an impediment to commercial growth. Remove it and the economic power of the city could once again be unleashed. He saw the blighted neighborhoods that surrounded the University of Pennsylvania and other academic and medical institutions in West Philadelphia as barriers to the explosion of a cultural and intellectual Mecca not unlike Cambridge, Massachusetts—Clear away the blight and watch this area flourish anew.[7] He saw the decrepit houses in the city's historic core suffer through lack of proper zoning and upkeep. Restore them and so many who abandoned the city for the Main Line decades earlier, so many who could return the city to cultural preeminence once more, would be lured back. He saw all of this. Eventually, he would solidify his vision for Philadelphia by calling for the restoration of a "bright, clean city," with restoration being the key to it all.[8] Under Bacon's eye, and in contrast to that of Moses, restoration and preservation of the colonial city would be the order of the day.

Whatever doubts he may have harbored about this approach vanished very quickly when they were put to an early test. As a result of growing fears during World War II that national shrines such as Philadelphia's Independence Hall would be bombed, the city adopted a plan of demolishing the surrounding buildings under the theory that creating a parklike atmosphere would serve as a protective buffer zone.[9] To Bacon and others on the city's Planning Commission, the idea amounted to a travesty because the fabric of the city — the city's grid, its individual storefronts and buildings, historic and otherwise — would be permanently disrupted by the creation of a park that was out of character for an urban center and more in keeping with suburbia. Bacon and his allies fought the plan, but they eventually lost. He then watched as large swaths of houses were bulldozed, one after another, in order to facilitate his opponents' "pastoral vision" of the city — a vision shared by Robert Moses, among others. Afterward, Bacon became even more determined to never to let that vision prevail again.

He became a staunch proponent of "select clearance," a method that recognizes that some buildings are beyond repair but that those that could be saved should.[10] This approach stood in direct contrast to the more popular "bulldozer approach" favored by Moses and others, which called for precisely the type of mass clearance Bacon had witnessed in the Independence Hall neighborhood. In the eyes of Moses the bulldozer approach made perfect sense; why bother to save something that has never been worth saving? The better approach was to clear cut entire areas and start anew. To Bacon, however, who could discern the gleam of a diamond hidden within a heap of trash, who saw what once was and what could be again, attacking blight "with penicillin, not surgery" was the more proper approach.[11] In his mind, the patient could be saved only if the invasion was as minimal as possible. Ultimately, and ironically, by doing what it was accustomed to doing for centuries and looking backward, Philadelphia — largely through the vision of Bacon and his "Young Turk" contemporaries—would become a forward-looking city for the first time since the colonial era.

The Young Turks Take Over Philadelphia

Bacon was not the only one with a vision for the city. Gentlemanly Philadelphia, those among the populace forced into retreat after the demise of the Second National Bank, was stirring for the first time in over a century, preparing to reemerge into the spotlight to right a city that had gone wrong ever since it went into hiding. Eventually, this group would come to be known as the Young Turks. Together they would succeed where countless others failed before them: they would overthrow the bloated and corrupt Republican Party–machine, sweep the city clean and lay the groundwork for the renaissance that would come the city's way during the 1960s and '70s.

To a man, the Young Turks could very well have been direct descendants of the patrician gentry who ruled the city a century earlier, so decorated and deep were their pedigrees.[12] Walter Phillips, of Princeton and Harvard Law School, spearheaded the reform movement by railing against corruption and finally motivating the populace to vote the machine out of office. His main compatriots were Joseph Clark, the son of a prominent Philadelphia lawyer and tennis champion who was born into an old family of Philadelphia investment bankers and himself out of Harvard and the University of Pennsylvania Law School, and Richardson Dilworth, another well-heeled Philadelphian (albeit via Pittsburgh) out of Yale (where he was a member of the football team) and Yale Law School. With Bacon, they worked to revitalize a city many believed to be beyond hope.

Each of them believed that physical planning constituted a vital component to pull the city out of its doldrums and into a new age.[13] However, they needed a forum from which to launch their ideas and insert themselves into the political process. Accordingly, under Phillips's leadership, the Young Turks, which included other crusading lawyers, planners and architects as well, formed the City Policy Committee in 1939. The committee met twice each week to consider ways in which this could be accomplished. Young Ed Bacon, seven years out of Cornell, performed much of the work of the committee and, as a result, in 1941 he was named executive director of the Philadelphia Housing Authority (PHA). Later that year, the City Policy Committee merged with the Junior Board of Commerce and the Lawyers' Council on Civic Affairs to form the Joint Committee on City Planning, which took the Republican machine head on, vowing to overhaul the city's entire 15-member Planning Commission. Using Bacon's vision as a model, and with Bacon doing much of the technical work on the project, the committee drafted a comprehensive city plan and presented it to Philadelphia mayor Robert Lamberton for consideration. Although Lamberton authorized the reorganization of the Planning Commission in response to the committee's plan, his untimely death delayed the progression of the Young Turks' agenda for several months. Finally, in December 1942, the Philadelphia City Council acted on Lamberton's recommendation, approving legislation that established the new Planning Commission. Going one step further, new mayor Bernard Samuel endowed the commission with a generous budget, providing legs to the Young Turks' plans. With the pieces now in place, the City Policy Committee reemerged under the new name of the Citizens' Council on City Planning (CCCP), maintaining its close relationship with Bacon's PHA. Together, they could now set their sights on rebuilding Philadelphia.

They could not do it alone, however. No matter how hard they pushed, their battle against the massive Republican machine would be futile without overwhelming public support. So they went after it by appealing to the public's imagination. In 1947, the CCCP, along with Bacon's PHA, in an exhibit designed by architects Louis Kahn and Oscar Stonorov, unveiled its "Better Philadelphia Exhibit," a project costing more than $400,000.[14] The exhibit provided a glimpse of what Philadelphia could become through organized city planning and allowed Delaware Valley residents to dream of what life in the city could be like without the oppressive machine. Housed in an exhibit space donated by, and within, Gimbels downtown department store, onlookers who paid their dollar to enter saw, among other things, a redesigned Independence Mall, a scale model of a revitalized Center City complete with animated parts, and a full-sized, fully rehabilitated Philadelphia row house. The exhibit ran for over two months and drew more than 400,000 visitors.[15] The "new" Philadelphia, which was, in many respects, an idealized return to the city's glorious past, captivated many who saw it and invigorated the reform movement. Bacon helped to keep the momentum going by appearing at several area public schools, encouraging students to design their own models of how they would like to see their own neighborhoods look.[16]

If the exhibit did nothing else, it focused the public's attention on the contrast between what was and what could be, and caused many to question just why it was that their city bore no resemblance to the magnificent images they had just seen. Now that the Republican machine was vulnerable for the first time in ages, the Young Turks went for the jugular. After yet another fiscal crisis in 1948, the CCCP and the PHA, along with numerous business leaders who were mortified over the decaying state of Center City, were successful in compelling City Council to empanel a "blue ribbon Committee of Fifteen" to investigate city corruption.[17] The committee found "gross governmental mismanagement" and, worse, criminal conduct among city officials. The public response to these findings, particularly as they contrasted with the utopian vision of the city they had just been treated to, was outrage. With reform now on nearly everybody's lips, Walter Phillips formed the Greater Philadelphia Movement (GPM), which was created specifically to circumvent the conservative Chamber of Commerce and rally support from the private sector for the implementation of the planning proposals dramatized in the Gimbels exhibit.[18] Through the GPM, pressure was now being applied to the machine from yet another source — the most powerful business leaders in the city. Left with no choice and fighting for its political life, the machine agreed to draft a new city charter.

The drafting process began in 1949 and was approved by voters on April 1, 1951. The new charter stripped the corrupt City Council's sovereignty and shifted power to a strong "mayor-and-council form of government."[19] It also preserved the City Planning Commission (CPC) as an independent board but gave it a more detailed and narrow focus. Now, the CPC, which as of 1949 had as its executive director Ed Bacon, was required to provide, among other things, an annually updated six-year comprehensive plan for the city — a plan that, under Bacon's control, could finally bring the Better Philadelphia Exhibit out of Gimbels and into reality. Other Young Turks also found themselves with significant power for the first time. Joe Clark, with the backing of the GPM, PHA and CCCP, won the election for city controller in 1949 largely on the promise that, if elected, he'd use his power to appoint Walter Phillips, the "white knight" of the reform movement, to the Housing Authority.[20] In the same election, Richardson Dilworth was elected city treasurer. By late 1951, the Republican machine was dismantled once and for all when Clark was elected mayor, Dilworth was elected district attorney and Phillips was named city representative and director of commerce. The Young Turks were now in charge and prepared to set into motion the most ambitious urban renewal program in the country.[21] For the first time in memory, Philadelphia was ready to be taken off of life support.

Rebirth

Once ensconced in power, the Young Turks sought to bring other members of the area's cultural elite out from hiding, hoping to lure them back from the Main Line where their ancestors fled over a century earlier, abandoning a city that went to pot in large part due to their absence.[22] In an effort to weave these people back into the fabric of the city, the Turks, led by Bacon, sought to appeal to the vision of a city restored rather than a city renewed — to preach rehabilitation and a return to former glory, the glory of the time when the forebearers of the people now burrowed out in the suburbs once dominated it. Before this could be undertaken full bore, however, Bacon's "penicillin approach" would need to be tested to see if it worked anywhere other than on the drawing board. Bacon chose as an early laboratory (in 1948, even before the demise of the machine) a two-block slum located in the city's East Poplar section.[23] His plan was simple: rather than bulldoze the area and rebuild, he would act to "encourage" the residents of the area to either rehabilitate their houses on their own or sell them to people who would. As such, code enforcement would be the prod; a method that resonated not only in theory but also in reality as well, due to the city's financial condition. The city had practically no money to spend on rehabilitation of neighborhoods on any scale. Its tax base was shrinking, resources were dwindling and any large-scale renewal was out of the question. Through code enforcement, the costs of renewal would largely be borne by the landlords and homeowners in the neighborhood, allowing the city, at least in theory, to rehabilitate itself with very little money coming from its own shallow pockets.

The plan was a total failure. The city tried to take action against the 430 housing code violators in the area but it was unsuccessful. Next, another low-cost approach was taken, namely, the "Yardville" approach. Through this plan, landlords, homeowners and tenants were encouraged to clean up their backyards in the hope that the two-block area could be transformed from a trash-strewn ghetto into a "parklike commons." Once this area was transformed, the belief was that the concept would catch on in other areas of the city, with city residents once again bearing much of the costs of rehabilitation. The city announced the creation of "Operation Fix-Up" and expanded the scope of the project to 50 neighborhoods. However, because the plan relied on the cooperation of landlords, who proved to be anything but cooperative, as well as "an outburst of self-help fervor within the community," it too failed miserably as only one neighborhood actually followed through with the program and achieved rehabilitation. By this point, all seemed lost. The visions of the Young Turks appeared to be pie-eyed. Without money to spur the process, rehabilitation was proving to be impossible. And the city of Philadelphia had no money.

In the end, it wouldn't need any. Congress passed the Housing Act of 1949, which came to be better known simply as Title I. Title I of the act would eventually authorize billions of dollars in federal money to "local redevelopment authorities" for the purchase of defined "slum land."[24] Now, with the federal government footing the bill, cities such as Philadelphia could engage in large-scale renewal despite their shrinking tax base and even though they did not have enough money to change even the bulbs in the city streetlights on a regular basis. As the early East Poplar plans proved, without Title I, the vision of urban reform would have gone nowhere given the exodus out of cities across the Northeast. With it, cities such as Philadelphia finally had the financial muscle to clean up and revitalize themselves.

Now, the city could see to it that reform and rehabilitation occurred, and on its terms. Through Title I dollars, the city entered the third phase of reform in East Poplar by simply buying a four-block slum site on its own and rehabilitating it directly under the supervision of Bacon and Stonorov.[25] Without the intrusion of landlords, they were able to dictate the scope of the reform. What they ended up with was something that strongly approximated the vision and ideals of the Better Philadelphia Exhibit; although there were some grassy areas created, the city retained an urban feel. Historic and other significant buildings such as the Edgar Allan Poe House and the St. Nicholas Russian Orthodox Church were preserved and other edifices were either rehabilitated or rebuilt in a style that meshed with the urban landscape. In the end, although significant rebuilding took place in the area, Bacon and Stonorov "reshaped" but did not destroy the neighborhood, creating, in Bacon's mind at least, "harmonious order" where once there had been only chaos.[26]

The response to the East Poplar renewal was swift and strong. Contemporary urban planners and housing reformers praised its respect for history and architectural appropriateness. Visitors arrived from as far away as Japan and Europe to study the merits of the "penicillin approach" and they came away impressed. Although its utopian vision of full racial and economic integration was not realized,[27] this did not dampen the overall enthusiasm for the method used. Nationwide, Bacon's approach was vindicated. The penicillin approach worked. Armed with this success, Bacon moved out of his laboratory and on with his plan to lure people back to the city through planning and architecture. He would do so by maintaining a human scale to his projects, making sure that when completed, rehabilitated neighborhoods recalled the neighborhood "feel" of the old colonial city. As such, high rises were out, at least initially. Between 1949 and 1955, only one project contained such a structure, a break from the national trend at the time, which saw cities such as New York erect one high-rise housing project after another.[28] These high rises would soon become the face of the failure of urban renewal across the country. But not so in Philadelphia. In addition, Bacon insisted on interesting architecture in the design of his projects, regardless of whether they were for the wealthy or public housing. Prominent firms were hired for even the most mundane projects with the mandate that they were "to do their best individual design."[29] Project by project, Bacon was remaking and beautifying the city.

His most ambitious project was yet to come. The city's historic core, nicknamed "Society Hill" for the Society of Free Traders who purchased

Dock Street in Society Hill, during the 1940s (Temple University Libraries, Urban Archives, Philadelphia, PA).

200,000 acres of land directly from William Penn, had long since fallen into disrepair.[30] A disheveled food distribution center, with large, dirty trucks screeching in and out leaving garbage on seemingly every block of pavement, had long since blighted the area and obscured whatever character the area once had. Worse, many of the houses had become victims of neglect and some were literally crumbling day by day, slowly turning into piles of rubble. Factories and storefronts likewise dotted the neighborhood, out of character with the historic nature of the district. In 1956, Bacon was finally in a position to do something about it. Along with real estate magnate Albert M. Greenfield (a Dilworth appointee to the chair of the Philadelphia Planning Commission), Bacon formed the Old Philadelphia Development Corporation, which soon joined forces with the Phillips GPM and focused on the area.[31] Together, under Bacon's leadership, they would jump start the rehabilitation of the neighborhood.

Initially, however, Bacon had a problem. No one was clamoring for rehabilitation of the area. The Main Line residents he was hoping to lure saw the working-class, predominantly Polish neighborhood as an undesirable place. The very real possibility existed that the area could be physically rehabilitated and nobody would care. As such, there was none of the "preexisting gentrification pressure" typically found prior to governmental involvement in a given area.[32] To counter this problem, Bacon embarked on a mission to remake the area not only physically but socially as well, hoping to lure his desired inhabitants to the area on little more than his determination to turn his vision into reality. His social plan was the key to the restoration of Society Hill; only after the neighborhood became populated with people who had both the desire and the bank accounts to rehabilitate their dilapidated properties could his dream of a truly restored historic core be realized. By this method, at least some of Philadelphia's shrinking tax base could be restored. Although the middle class was leaving other parts of the city in droves, some of this loss could be made up through fewer, yet far richer, people — the gentlemen and gentlewomen of the Main Line — he was hoping to lure into Society Hill. However first, he would have to lure them.

He did this by hand picking the people he wanted to buy into the neighborhood. He personally escorted suburban social-register women on trips to the area, explaining to them his vision of a vibrant urban neighborhood in the hope of generating their interest. He scoured the housing applications that came in, searching for people willing to commit to the area not merely financially but also personally. He was not interested in Main Line folks who were looking for additional residences to add to their collections, those who were interested in simply owning a "museum home" in the city. He wanted people who were going to live in the houses, who would move off of the Main Line and back into the city. Through his efforts, he was slowly able to create a demand for housing in Society Hill where previously none had existed. His problem disappeared when, in 1957, Mayor Dilworth bought a colonial revival house in the neighborhood as a show of support. After that, two other prominent families followed suit and then, very quickly, the whole area began to boom. Banks, which initially were hesitant to invest in the area now considered it a good risk and, by 1965, it was a seller's market. In the end, the rehabilitation of Society Hill occurred on a house-by-house basis, not the mass slum clearance that was typical of most urban renewal projects. One-third of the original structures were retained (726 out of 2,197) and those premises that needed to be rebuilt were completed in a style that fit comfortably within the neighborhood. When finished, Bacon succeeded in creating a Society Hill that largely conformed to its idealized image of revived Georgian glory.

Society Hill was a success on far more than a physical level. Through Bacon's efforts, individuals spent considerable amounts of their own money to fix up the area, amounts far greater than those spent by the vast majority of other cities hoping to cash in on the urban renewal craze. Nationwide, private financing outpaced public financing three to one. In Society Hill, the ratio was double that amount, six to one.[33] As such, just as with the East Poplar project, Philadelphia became an enviable case study once again, this time in the area of the public/private financial partnership.

1956: A new Society Hill homeowner restores her fireplace (Temple University Libraries, Urban Archives, Philadelphia, PA).

Bacon also had his eye on the city's central business district, and he was able to put his vision into practice when Title I was modified in 1954.[34] The act, which previously focused on residential properties, was amended that year to promote the rehabilitation of commercial centers as well. For the first time, 10 percent of redeveloped land could be used for nonresidential purposes (this would be increased to 20 percent in 1959). What's more, the definition of "blight" was amended so that now, only 20 percent of an area's buildings needed to be declared "substandard" for the entire area to become eligible for federal funds. In 1956, when newly elected mayor Dilworth appointed William Rafsky as urban development coordinator and charged him with focusing on "the reinvigoration of the city's shrinking economy and the development of a modern central business district," enough money and desire to tackle the enormous problem of Center City head-on finally existed.[35] With that, Bacon went to work.

Bacon realized that the key to the revitalization of Center City was the removal of the physically divisive Broad Street Station. As soon as the Pennsylvania Railroad announced that it had agreed to tear it down, Bacon was ready (at the very same meeting in which the announcement was made) with comprehensive, detailed plans for its replacement that included a "sunken garden concourse three blocks long, lined with shops, bridged by the cross streets and straddled by three 20-story office buildings."[36] Through Bacon's "Penn Center" project, the east and west sides of Center City would be united at last, with glimmering office buildings as enticements to lure business back from the suburbs. In the Penn Center project, as was the case with virtually every one of his projects, functionality was merely a part of the equation. Aesthetics and beautification also played a key role. Whereas most city planners (including his predecessor at the CPC) were more concerned with traffic and flow throughout the city, Bacon had set his sights elsewhere, seeking to improve the look of his city more than anything else.[37] It was why he had no qualms designing the Penn Center complex without a client — a radical approach that earned him censure from both the American Institute of Architects and the American Institute of Planners.[38] Bacon, however, preferred to create the image first and then use it to attract the client later. He was wary of working with short-sighted clients who would pressure him to alter his vision in order to suit their immediate needs.[39] Later, in 1959, the city would codify his approach in its "beautification ordinance" that required that 1 percent of the cost of any public project be set aside "for fine arts to decorate the project."[40] This focus on aesthetics was yet another example of the city moving forward by looking backward. Philadelphia had long held a reputation for combining beauty with functionality; the Philadelphia Water Works, completed on the bank of the Schuylkill River in 1822, was admired as much

1950, from left: Earle N. Barber, chairman of the Philadelphia Redevelopment Authority, Ed Bacon, and architect Vincent G. Kling consider their options once the Chinese Wall on Market Street is removed. Under consideration here is an early model of what would become Penn Center (Temple University Libraries, Urban Archives, Philadelphia, PA).

for its look as for its engineering, quickly drawing the attention of tourists and artists alike and helped to give the city its antebellum nickname as the Athens of America.[41] In his work, Bacon was merely striving to rekindle this feeling.

Bacon waged his share of battles in the design of the Penn Center project, and eventually he was compelled to cede ground in some important areas. His vision of a grand public space surrounding the three towers was sharply modified after concerns arose that the towers needed to be taller in order to be profitable.[42] This additional height required that they be reoriented, which in turn meant that Bacon's open, sunken garden concourse would have to be covered. Nevertheless, when completed, the complex stood as an important symbol of the promise of revival in Center City. This promise was also apparent in the decayed Market East section of Center City when Bacon announced his intention to lure shoppers away from the suburbs by erecting — of all things — a mall right in the heart of the city.[43] Rejecting the popular idea that what city dwellers wanted most were efficient routes out of the city, Bacon focused on reversing the flow of traffic by giving them reasons to stay put.

Of course, in order for the revitalization of Society Hill and Center City truly to work, he would have to deal with the images wary and frightened suburbanites were seeing every evening on television, reading about in their newspapers, and experiencing every time they headed out to Connie Mack Stadium to take in a Phillies game. He decided to tackle this problem by championing a ring of highways that would surround Center City, creating a "safe zone" within, which would act as a buffer from the mayhem that was occurring in North, West and South Philadelphia. Through this highway ring, Bacon's work would be protected along with the moneyed elites he had worked so hard to convince to move back into the city.[44] The idea was first proposed by his predecessor at the City Planning Commission back in 1945 but, under Bacon's watch, it really took off. To the west there was the Schuylkill Expressway, to the north the Vine Street Expressway and to the east Interstate 95 (which, although built on stilts throughout much of the city, dipped underground as it passed Society Hill so as to preserve these residents' view of the Delaware River). The final circuit in the ring, a proposed South Street Expressway, was planned but staunchly opposed by residents. Plans for it were eventually abandoned in 1970 when energies in this area were redirected toward protecting the southern border of Center City through a revitalized South Street instead. Through the creation of the safe zone, the '60s image of an entire city in flames was countered. The highways spoke volumes: here marks the end of the chaos and anarchy widely reported in the media. Under their watchful eyes, suburbanites could feel secure in placing their faith in Bacon's vision.

Although the bulk of Bacon's rehabilitation efforts were contained within the safe zone, he forayed out of it on occasion as well. He turned his attention to the West Philadelphia slums surrounding the University of Pennsylvania and created a new address within the city: "University City," which, he envisioned, would one day become an intellectual headquarters much like Harvard Square.[45] He and his Young Turk compatriots also tapped deep into the bowels of Southwest Philadelphia in an attempt to preserve the tax base by creating a blue collar equivalent of Society Hill in the hope of convincing at least some of the working class bent on relocation to consider moving within the city rather than to the suburbs. The project, which ultimately would become the single largest urban renewal project in the nation at the time (with a $300 million price tag)[46] was centered on an isolated, 3,000 acre area of the city known as Eastwick.[47] Geographically, it was perfectly situated in that it was located within a natural safe zone, bordered as it was by the airport and Interstate 95 on one side and the Schuylkill River and numerous oil refineries on the other. Before the reform movement hit, it was a lightly populated area dominated by crushed automobile husks and heaps of trash, some of them perpetually aflame. The Turks, however, had grandiose plans for the area, hoping to create a "city within a city" that not only would house 60,000 members of the working class but also would provide 20,000 jobs. Perhaps the most idealistic aspect of this project was that, unlike Society Hill, and unlike the vast majority of housing projects that were going up across the nation, Eastwick was going to be racially integrated. In Eastwick, the wildest dreams of the reform-minded Young Turks were going to be realized and in a manner that would far exceed any renewal project anywhere else in the United States (indeed, in keeping with the Turks' focus on aesthetics, Phillips insisted that the renewed Eastwick would even be able to boast a bird sanctuary, the first of its kind in any major American city). If there was ever any question that the corrupt, oppressive, machine was gone and that a new day had dawned in Philadelphia, Eastwick provided the answer. In Eastwick, along with Society Hill, Penn Center and University City, urban renewal was percolating loudly, with a vision and methods radically different from anywhere else. By the mid 1960s, Philadelphia was finally in a position to demonstrate to both the country and the world exactly what urban reform could accomplish, not merely what it could destroy.

Praise for Philadelphia

The response to Philadelphia's urban renewal efforts was the polar opposite of what it was in most cities, most notably New York. By the late 1950s, the shortcomings of renewal in general and Title I in particular were coming to the fore and were on the lips of anyone concerned with the future of cities. In many cities, urban renewal was seen as inherently corrupt and merely a vehicle for pushing the working class and poor out of the way in order to build palaces for the wealthy. And no one took a bigger, more regular beating on these counts than did Robert Moses, to the point where eventually he would become the symbol for all that was wrong with urban renewal. By 1956, New York newspapers were pounding on him, noting how Title I was being used to clear not slums but well-kept, middle-class neighborhoods.[48] Worse, in many cases, nothing was being rebuilt. Instead, much of these "slum clearance" areas were left vacant once the bulldozers had finished, leaving the fabric of many of these neighborhoods irreparably torn. Other articles noted the irony of Title I in that, in the name of slum clearance, it oftentimes produced the opposite. It created slums where previously there had been none, pushing the poor into already overcrowded housing and then either failing to rebuild at all or building luxury housing in its place, thereby reducing the stock of affordable housing even more and causing neighborhoods to buckle under the weight of these displaced low-income families. In response, Moses didn't even pretend to address these concerns, often choosing instead to validate them. In discussing his plans for the construction of Lincoln Center (erected largely through funds generated through Title I), he noted that although 7,000 low-income families would be displaced, 4,400 units of new housing would be erected where their homes once stood. And 4,000 of them would be luxury apartments.

On top of these concerns came the scandals. Phony developers making off with Title I funds, shady, underhanded deals made in the name of urban renewal, became daily fodder in the city's newspapers. By February 1959, the city's dailies actually divvied the juicy stories up between themselves so as to ensure that each would get its moment in the sun, pillorying Moses and Title I in the name of yet another uncovered scam or injustice. As a result, hardly a day went by in New York without another story concerning the horrors of urban renewal. By 1960, the city's verdict was in: urban renewal was a complete and utter failure.

In Philadelphia, the reaction could not have been more different. Although criticism to some degree is unavoidable in a city the size of Philadelphia, particularly given the radical methods employed by Bacon (indeed, protesters rallying against his South Street Expressway plan came armed with placards saying "Fry Bacon"[49]), the nation responded to the city's urban reform approach with praise and envy. By the early 1960s, the same New York papers that were skewering Moses were praising Bacon's efforts, distinguishing New York's urban renewal nightmare from the "Philadelphia Renaissance."[50] Beyond New York, other cities struggling with their own urban renewal dilemmas took note of how well things seemed to be going in Philadelphia, of all places. In the *Los Angeles Times*, Casper Weinberger remarked how Philadelphia "has set the pace in urban renewal redevelopment" and that the Philadelphia method should serve as a lesson for how the issue should be approached in Los Angeles.[51] In 1965, just like the East Poplar project a decade earlier, architects from around the world descended on the city, this time studying Society Hill and Penn Center "to probe the mysteries of good urban design" and then, in a three-day program sponsored by the very same American Institute of Architects that once censured Bacon, "went back to school and learned directly from those involved about the economic, political and social forces that brought about Philadelphia's much touted urban renewal."[52] The next year, Lady Bird Johnson stopped in the city as part of her "national beautification" campaign and found the rehabilitated city a

1959: Mildred Custin, chairman of the Philadelphia More Beautiful Committee (second from left), and Ed Bacon (fourth from left), among others, commemorate the ceremonial planting of the last shrub at the Penn Center Garden Court (Temple University Libraries, Urban Archives, Philadelphia, PA).

symbol of the potential for urban reform.[53] "Beauty was part of Philadelphia's planning from the first," she remarked at a ceremony at Independence Hall. "For any history-minded American — and I am one — a trip to Philadelphia is a pilgrimage into a proud past." She also commended the city on its beautification ordinance, calling it "a milestone of foresight."

Soon, Philadelphia's urban renewal projects were singled out as glittering exceptions to the general rule that urban renewal simply did not work. Society Hill was widely regarded as "the single most successful urban-renewal project in the nation"[54] and the city's attention to housing for the working class in its Eastwick project was contrasted with New York's, which was criticized for ignoring the very same folks. Unlike New York, rehabilitation in Philadelphia was considered an early success because it was able to lure not merely the upper classes back to the city but the middle and working classes as well, and in places other than Eastwick. Neighborhoods in South Philadelphia as well as Bridesburg and Port Richmond experienced the return of some members of the working class, stanching at least some of the fear that they would become abandoned and dilapidated amid the rush to the suburbs.[55]

The city, and Bacon, peaked in national exposure in November 1964 when *Time* magazine selected Bacon for the cover of a special issue devoted to urban renewal — a decision that immediately solidified both Bacon and Philadelphia as the national faces of the movement.[56] The magazine's publisher noted within that the examples provided by both Philadelphia and Bacon made them the appropriate focal points for its study of urban renewal particularly given the timing of the issue — on the eve of the 1964 presidential elections with the future of Lyndon Johnson's Great Society platform hanging in the balance. The magazine noted that of all the cities "under the planner's knife, none has been so deeply and continuously committed to renewing itself" as Philadelphia and that the city was in the midst of carrying out "the most thoughtfully planned, thoroughly rounded, skillfully coordinated of all big-city programs in the U.S."[57] Finally, in a discreet stab at programs such as those of Moses that valued efficient egress out to the suburbs, *Time* praised Bacon for making "the city attractive and stimulating again —creating new neighborhoods, bringing old ones back to life ... [t]o rediscover, in short, the pleasures of urbanity."

By the dawn of the 1970s, with many of the city's urban rehabilitation projects racing toward completion, the true benefits of renewal, the social benefits, could finally come to fruition. As the beneficiaries of reform began to move back into the city, a new attitude would take over, one that would transform the city attitudinally as much as it was being charged physically. After over a century of negativity, Philadelphia's image was about to change, to the point where people would finally start to realize that, contrary to their long-held beliefs, Philadelphia wasn't a city full of losers after all. One major construction project needed to be undertaken, however, in order to shake the city from this deeply entrenched belief once and for all.

The Vet

Throughout the 1960s, a project was underway outside of the official renewal umbrella but which was as important to the resurgence of the city as any other. As far back as 1954, Dilworth had been working with Bob Carpenter in finding the Phillies a new home.[58] After their hollow threats to leave the area for New York failed to motivate the city to provide them financing for a new stadium, the team went to work on finding a suitable location within the city. Eventually, a site located at the largely abandoned nexus of Broad Street and Pattison Avenue in South Philadelphia was selected for several reasons. First, in response to increasing fan complaints about the parking situation at Connie Mack Stadium, there were acres upon acres of available space here. Next, unlike Connie Mack Stadium, which was situated smack dab in the middle of a residential neighborhood that was growing increasingly more volatile and dangerous by the year, here there could be no such fears about the neighborhood given that there hardly was a neighborhood to speak of. Although the new stadium would border 300 houses at the southern edge of a South Philadelphia neighborhood on one side, the other three sides opened up onto largely open space in an area that had become, for the most part, a

The view looking north toward Center City in April 1969. Work continues on the construction of Veterans Stadium. Note the row homes to the northwest and the wide open spaces everywhere else (Temple University Libraries, Urban Archives, Philadelphia, PA).

warehouse district. In fact, "district" was perhaps too generous a term for the area, for that term connotes an image of a carefully thought-out, zoned plan. Here, however, there were mainly abandoned lots and open space, with much of it being used as an unofficial dump for anyone with something large and/or unpleasant to discard.

In all, the tract available for stadium construction totaled 67 acres, with the majority of the land already owned by the city. The rest of it was made up of those vacant lots, although a man with a pet goat resided on one of them.[59] The vast amount of land upon which the new stadium would be built was a far cry from the tight, congested space in which Connie Mack Stadium was located. Coming from a stadium that, by the late 1960s, was noted for having "more arguments per square foot than Belfast"[60] (an appellation that could just as easily be applied to the surrounding neighborhood as well), fans attending Phillies games at Broad and Pattison would forever after be spared the sociological experience of witnessing all that was wrong with the city in which they played 81 times every season. Instead, these now predominantly suburban fans would be whisked to the game by way of the Walt Whitman Bridge from New Jersey, or the safe zone's Schuylkill Expressway from the western suburbs, or Interstate 95 (or, prior to its completion, Delaware Avenue through yet another warehouse district) from the north, bypassing the problems of urban life and parking in a safe, secure parking lot. No more paying off local children to watch their cars for fear of repercussions if they did not; no more muggings on the walk to the stadium; no more militaristic police patrols surrounding the stadium hoping to keep a neighborhood's rage from boiling over; no more racial tension cutting through the heavy summer air. None of that. No longer were the problems of North Philadelphia in the face of every person who wanted nothing more than to attend a baseball game. With the opening of the new stadium in the deep recesses of South Philadelphia, North Philadelphia essentially became invisible. In fact, to these suburbanites, it was as if North Philadelphia no longer existed at all.

Instead, upon its completion in 1971, the newly minted Veterans Stadium offered fans the security and serenity that comes with cleanliness, a stadium that was considered state-of-the-art when it opened and, in fact, superior in many ways to the numerous other "concrete doughnut" multipurpose stadiums that had opened within the previous few years (Three Rivers Stadium in Pittsburgh, Riverfront Stadium in Cincinnati and Busch Stadium in St. Louis).[61] Once again, just as in 1909, Philadelphia fans had a "palace" in which to watch their team play.[62] Although in later years the stadium would be dismissed as being "sterile"[63] and "antiseptic," at the time, these appellations were considered positive traits, not negative ones. For antiseptic not only connotes something "devoid of character" but "cleansing" as well, and if it was one thing the Phillies were in desperate need of by the end of the 1960s, it was a clean break from the past, an opportunity to escape the clutches of history and start fresh. Veterans Stadium offered them this opportunity. No longer would they play in a dirty, unkempt stadium located in a neighborhood reminiscent of all that was wrong with the city as a whole. From now on they would play in a new home, one that was clean and progressive, in keeping with the city's emerging identity as a scrubbed and rehabilitated metropolis.

The absolute necessity of such a break was highlighted even more sharply during the Phillies' last year at Connie Mack Stadium.[64] Initially, the Vet was scheduled to open for the 1970 season but construction delays prevented it from doing so. Finding themselves in the unexpected and unenviable position of having to play one more year at Connie Mack, the Phils, with the city's help, scrambled to prevent catastrophe from sinking the franchise even further. Twenty-five extra police officers were assigned to the area during game days along with numerous plainclothes officers, hoping to protect increasingly frightened fans from the violent gangs that had taken over the area. Additional day games were scheduled to lessen the number of times these wary fans would be asked to spend an evening in the neighborhood. Needless to say, the Phillies, along with their fans, were desperately awaiting the start of the 1971 season.

When it finally arrived, the sense that a new era had dawned in Philadelphia was everywhere. At its unveiling, the Vet was hailed as "a breath of fresh air" after so many seasons in turbulent North Philadelphia.[65] Considered "Nirvana," it was rightly recognized as a vital element in the healing process in the team's relationship with both the city and its fans.[66] After nearly two decades of having the city's baseball spotlight to themselves, the Phils presented an image of a decaying team playing in a decaying stadium located within a decaying city. Starting on April 10, 1971— opening day at the Vet— all of that changed. Now, for the first time in anybody's memory, the team (with emerging young stars such as Greg Luzinski and Larry Bowa), its stadium and the city were clean, fresh and rehabilitated. The Phillies, so long the image of the city's failings, were about to become the image of its triumph.

7

Social Rebirth on the Streets and on the Field

Black Friday: Seventh Inning

The ultimate act of this three-act drama saw Gene Garber take over the leading role from Reed. The two could not have been more different in their approaches. Unlike the tall, fireballing Reed, Garber was listed generously at 5 foot 10 inches, although he was never forced to testify under oath to that measurement. And, in any event, he seemed even shorter on the mound. Far from imposing, he worked out of a perpetual crouch, even when peering in to receive the signs from his catcher. His windup was a continuation of the same: a deep crouch from start to finish, highlighted by a 180 degree turn mid-motion in which he would flash the batter the oversized "26" on his back while he gauged the depth of his centerfielder one last time. Finally, he would whip around, register his catcher's mitt the very last instant before delivering a side-armed offering that would have seemed imposing but for the fact that his best pitch was a changeup. As such, in contrast to Reed, Garber's pitches appeared to have an arc to them, floating softly to their destination before landing silently in their leather pillow. Whereas Reed's pitches would announce themselves in the catcher's mitt with a loud pop and a puff of dust, Garber's arrived in virtual anonymity. Ozark's choice of Garber, who had been both efficient and effective all season in any event with his 2.35 ERA, was brilliant. The Dodger bats, by now reflexively anxious after Reed, would need time to adjust.

The first batter, however, was pinch hitter Ed Goodson. Goodson was in what would be the final year of an eight-year career of mediocrity. In fact, this was his penultimate at bat; he would pinch hit once in the World Series that year and then be released the following spring. Goodson had not faced Reed. His reflexes would not be out of whack as would the others. No matter. He bounced harmlessly to Sizemore, who charged and then flipped the ball underhanded to Hebner for the first out of the inning. Davey Lopes then brought his hitless bat to the plate, 0 for three so far. Quickly, he would be 0 for four as he too bounced softly, this time to Bowa, who tossed it across the diamond for the second out of the inning. Shortstop Bill Russell completed the around-the-horn inning for the groundball pitching Garber when he bounced softly to Schmidt at third. Testament to the fact that despite Garber's lack of sizzle he was difficult to get good wood on came from the third weak chop of the inning, causing Schmidt as well to race in to meet the ball, his hat flying off in the process, and then fire to first to get Russell just in time. As the crowd rose for what was perhaps the most unnecessary seventh-inning stretch all year (few had spent much time in their seats all game), time was running short on both teams. Something would have to give.

The crowd was determined to make this happen sooner rather than later. Rising from their seats, engaging in a boisterous version of "Take Me Out to the Ballgame," they quickly refocused their energies away from the animated scoreboard and back to the field, clapping, chanting and roaring in escalating volume as the teams prepared for the bottom of the seventh. Doug Rau, yet another starting pitcher (in fact, a 14-game winner that season) tossed into the fire in Lasorda's desperate attempt to overcome his bullpen deficiencies, would greet them, hoping to emulate fellow starter Rick Rhoden's on-the-job mastery of relief pitching. He would be just as successful, bailing out Lasorda once again, in what would turn out to be his only inning of work.

Larry Bowa dug in first, accompanied by the now pulsating backbeat of a crowd hoping to inject itself into the game once again. This time it would fail; Bowa popped up to Lopes for the first out of the inning. Schmidt could fare no better; he was completely mystified by now, dragging his .091 playoff average to the plate and wearing an expression that recalled a child hopelessly lost in the mall. After taking Rau's first two pitches, he lunged at one low and out of the strike zone, surprising even himself when he actually made contact. He hesitated in the box for a split second as the ball bounced weakly to Cey, who easily threw him out for out number two.

As Luzinski stepped in the sky darkened noticeably. The lights, which had been on the entire game more as a matter of course than anything else, now flooded the field. It was getting colder too; weather front was beginning to roll in. The Bull tried to hasten things on the scoreboard so as to beat the storm to the punch by putting everything he had into each swing but Rau would give him no satisfaction. With two outs and nobody on base, he gave him nothing but offspeed pitches, not willing to challenge him with a fastball. Luzinski looked fastaball anyway, one pitch after another, on the off chance that Rau would make a mistake. He never did. After swinging through three pitches that fluttered by, practically dying in the dirt before reaching the plate, the inning was over. After all the excitement of the early innings, the game had settled down into a surprising pitchers' duel. Things would change in the eighth, however.

The New Turks and Philadelphia's Restaurant Renaissance

By 1970, the era of the Young Turks was over. That year, Ed Bacon stepped down from the City Planning Commission, bringing the reform era to a presumptive end. His departure from the main stage of Philadelphia reform followed the steady withdrawals of his compatriots during the 1960s: first Joe Clark, who had moved on to the national scene in 1956, winning what would be a two-term seat in the U.S. Senate that, in any event, had come to an end in 1968; next Richardson Dilworth, who quit his mayoral post in 1962 for a failed run for governor, and who was now president of the Philadelphia School Board; and finally Walter Phillips, who receded into the background after failing to unseat Dilworth's successor, James Tate, in the 1963 Democratic mayoral primary. However, by this time, their successors were ready to take their place. These New Turks would differ from their predecessors in a significant way: whereas the Young Turks focused on the physical transformation of the city, the New Turks would draw on these roots and focus on the social changes now possible within the city as a result of the physical transformation. Under their leadership, the Philadelphia renaissance dreamed of by Bacon so long ago at the Better Philadelphia Exhibit would emerge in full bloom.

Due to the efforts of Bacon, Phillips, Clark, Dilworth and others, Philadelphia — or at least the safe zone within Center City — became attractive once again as a residential destination. By the late 1960s, hordes of white-collar people began to return to Society Hill, of course, but to other areas as well. Areas such as Spring Garden, which was on the other side of the safe zone (technically, slightly north of it, at least in part), several blocks west and north of Society Hill, were likewise being revived and bursting with energy for the first time in years.[1] And because businesses were slower to return, many of these new residents were making bold statements by purchasing homes, demonstrating that they were willing to do what would have been inconceivable just a few years earlier, namely, reverse-commute.[2] For the first time in the city's history, hordes of people were living within it even though life would have been more convenient for them in the suburbs. Interest in safe zone real estate boomed throughout the late '60s and into the 1970s such that, by 1977, rents in many of these neighborhoods had increased nearly tenfold in only a few short years.[3] These new residents (8,500 in tony Society

Hill and thousands of others elsewhere) had energy, enthusiasm and, most importantly, money. And they wanted to spend it within the city. By focusing on the needs and desires of the affluent and dynamic people lured back into the city as a result of the physical rehabilitation of the city during the 1950s and '60s, the New Turks who emerged would transform the city even further.

These people were not city planners by trade. Instead, many of them were restaurateurs focusing not so much on the physical space of the city as on the people who now inhabited it. However, because they came of age during the era of urban reform, they were motivated by many of the same ideas people such as Bacon and Phillips had held before them. Together, they carried on the vision of the Young Turks one restaurant at a time.

The pioneering New Turk was a chef named Peter Von Starck, who left his job at the Coventry Forge Inn in Chester County, Pennsylvania, to work in the kitchen at L'Oustau de Baumanière in Paris, becoming in the process the first American ever to be hired by a three-star restaurant in France.[4] After a few years, he returned to Philadelphia, bringing back both a radical vision for what a Philadelphia restaurant could be as well as a fireplug, fire-mouthed, kinetic Lyonnaise chef to bring his vision to life — Georges Perrier. In 1967 Von Starck opened La Panetiere at 1312 Spruce Street and very quickly raised the collective consciousness of the city.

At the time of its opening, Philadelphia's restaurants were as staid and conservative as the image of the city people like Bacon and Phillips had worked so hard to obliterate. Beyond the pedestrian coffee shops and restaurants, fine dining in Philadelphia meant one of two options: steaks at Arthurs or lobster at Bookbinders, with either one a traditional, sober, predictable choice.[5] Regardless of the quality of the restaurant, menus were laminated — a testament to the reality that they never changed, regardless of the season. The possibility that the seasonal availability of ingredients might alter the composition of that evening's menu was never a consideration given the limited cupboard. Restaurateurs stuck with what had worked in the past, what was readily available, what their customers (as well as their customers' parents and grandparents before them) recognized. Meat came frozen, herbs and spices were dried (fresh herbs were unheard of) and oregano was considered exotic. Von Starck and Perrier changed all that. Change would continue when Perrier left La Panetiere in 1970 and opened his own restaurant, Le Bec Fin, at the same 1312 Spruce location after La Panetiere abandoned the tiny space for larger digs due to its overwhelming popularity. Like the Young Turks who preceded them, they used their restaurants to create their own, personalized "Better Philadelphia" exhibits, showing Philadelphians that they were not wed to what they had grown up with, demonstrating potential rather than limitation.

They, particularly Perrier, once ensconced in Le Bec Fin demanded fresh ingredients and, soon, they found them. In time, Perrier had his own fresh herb supplier who brought French tarragon, fresh chives and chervil to the Philadelphia palate for the first time. Soon the supplier would furnish other restaurants as well, helping to spur them out of the doldrums they had been living in for decades. Perrier demanded fresh game birds, hoping to re-create the dishes he loved so much back in France. Soon he found a local supplier from Lancaster County who provided him with fresh pheasant, partridge, quail and pigeon. Perrier even worked with her to develop customized feed for each type of bird so as to bring out the distinctive flavor of each one. Although on the surface, restaurants such as La Panetiere and Le Bec Fin were classically French in concept, catering to people with upscale wallets (the Main Line types who either remained or relocated to Society Hill), they marked a radical departure in practice from anything that had opened before in Philadelphia. In these restaurants, the new, dynamic Philadelphia was taking shape, leaving its stodgy predecessor far behind. Philadelphia was starting to catch up culturally with the physical rehabilitation of the city. Its people were learning how to be as hip as the buildings in which they now lived.

If the epicurean revolution ended there, with the arrival of a few high-end restaurants accessible only to the very rich, it would have been just that — a movement limited in scope and influence. But because it did not, because it soon spread far and wide so as to register an impact on nearly anyone who spent any time within the city, regardless of their budget, it became a social force that altered both the city's image as well as people's feelings toward it. Soon, the city would wear a new face, a progressive, modern, cutting-edge face that would convince both residents and outsiders alike that the new Philadelphia was nothing at all like the one that had preceded it.

By the early 1970s, the city was being bombarded on several fronts by various food revolutionaries. One of them was a young, transplanted New Yorker who had entered the University of Pennsylvania in 1964 at the height of Bacon's popularity hoping to make his mark as an architect.[6] While there, amid the fervor of the rehabilitating city all around him, he struck upon an idea that combined his love of cooking with his interest in continuing the social transformation he found himself in the middle of. After graduating and spending some time in the Peace Corps, Steve Poses returned to Philadelphia on a mission. He first landed in the kitchen of La Panetiere and from there left to open his own restaurant in 1973, Frog, where he would put his ideas into practice. Although now a full-time restaurateur, he retained his architectural and city planning roots. He counted as a primary influence in his mission not a culinary mentor nor cookbook but rather Jane Jacobs's

Death and Life of Great American Cities. Poses was particularly drawn to Jacobs's notion that it was the sense of community that made cities great rather than just architecture or reconstituted physical infrastructure. Jacobs, a Greenwich Village resident and, at the time, the number one enemy of Robert Moses, bemoaned the effects of New York's urban renewal as well as that of several other cities. She believed that while Moses had succeeded in physically remaking the city, he had failed New York in the process by destroying the vibrant neighborhoods that had so defined it.[7] Her discussion of the historical significance of the corner candy store as a means to allow people to define and connect with their neighborhoods struck a chord with Poses, who believed that restaurants could serve the same purpose in 1970s urban America if designed and run properly. Drawing on Jacobs's ideals, Poses embarked on his culinary adventure with his broader social goals in mind. Frog fulfilled those goals with its mismatched chairs and rehabbed furniture. It becoming an affordable dining and community destination that became the focal point of the neighborhood in which it resided. Later, in 1977, he opened another restaurant, the Commissary, that smashed the staid concept of the 1950s fluorescent cafeteria, with its waterlogged vegetables, reheated meats and Formica counters, to bits. Poses's self-serve Commissary enticed people to stay and linger over a glass of one of the 10 different wines by the glass, 15 brands of brandy or 17 of scotch; to save room for a dessert prepared by one of the seven full-time bakers on the premises; to sample a variety of the ever-changing entrées, such as fish pâtés, exotic couscous dishes, seafood strudel or whichever selection of the 150 homemade soups were on the menu at the time; to experience the difference created by homemade mayonnaises, croissants and sherbets; or to just sit down and peruse the restaurant's cookbook library.[8] His restaurants were more than just places to eat. They were, in his words, "personal urban renewal,"[9] part of a cultural revolution of the city — an outgrowth of Bacon's vision several decades earlier.

Other New Turks attacked from different directions. In 1974, Jay Guben, a political activist with a master's degree in conflict management who had been involved in urban renewal in Cincinnati and who had once worked as a potato peeler in the Coventry Forge Inn, opened up the Restaurant School.[10] Unlike other restaurant schools such as New York's Culinary Institute of America, however, Philadelphia's Restaurant School's mission was, like its founder, different and radical. Focusing less on refining the skills necessary to make its students classically trained master chefs, the Restaurant School's primary mission was to train students to learn — in one year — how to open up and run their very own restaurants. As such, it very quickly turned out hordes of ambitious young people intent on emulating visionaries like Poses or Guben who himself ran several restaurants in a style similar to Poses, most

1973: Co-owner Joyce Poses explains the evening's blackboard menu at Frog (Temple University Libraries, Urban Archives, Philadelphia, PA).

notably Friday, Saturday, Sunday, a small restaurant in a previously anonymous West Center City neighborhood that soon became overwhelmed by demand. Unlike Le Bec Fin, however, Friday, Saturday, Sunday's customers were mostly neighborhood residents angling for a seat at their local hot spot that would enable them to choose from the ever-changing blackboard menu that was wiped clean every night and rewritten the next morning depending on whatever ingredients most tickled the fancy of its chef that day.

Soon, the city was awash in "flowerpot" restaurants, so named for the minimalist décor (usually little more than a few daisies in a vase) that so defined these affordable, adventuresome, if often underfunded, start-ups. What defined them more accurately, however, were their blackboard menus that focused on seasonal ingredients, bright, crisp vegetables, exotic preparations (with some restaurants wrapping seemingly everything possible in crusts and others dabbling into what would be the forerunner of fusion cuisine), dishes prepared from scratch right down to the puff pastry and the mayonnaise, and the finishing touch of adding slices of lemon to the water glasses. Very quickly, the influence of the Restaurant School was enormous: by 1978, one-quarter of all Restaurant School graduates were operating their own restaurants while another quarter were working for them.[11] Many Restaurant School grads embraced the spirit in which their institution was founded, helping each other along the way, lending money to get new restaurants off the ground, pitching in to help ones already opened, and spreading the Restaurant School approach wherever they went.[12] As such, its influence spread quickly and exponentially.

Of all the New Turks, perhaps the most radical was a former Restaurant School teacher, Xavier Hussenot, who in 1972 opened up a seemingly innocuous ice cream shop in an undesirable location (Fourth and South Streets), the Black Banana, which turned out to be anything but ordinary.[13] Hussenot hired art students and charged them with designing unique sundaes. It was an instant hit. Later he added a sexually suggestive full menu, served by young and sexy waiters and waitresses, and transformed the restaurant into what one reviewer called "an X-rated bistro." This too was a hit. Soon other restaurants and shops dotted the area and transformed the eastern edge of South Street into a bustling, bohemian mecca. Jane Jacobs and Steve Poses appeared to be right: in the Black Banana, the power of the restaurant to serve as a focal point in the revival of a local community was on display. By 1976, Hussenot relocated the Black Banana to another undesirable neighborhood: Third and Race, a few blocks north of Society Hill (although still within the safe zone), and repeated his success.[14] This time, given the advanced palate of the Philadelphia diner due to the restaurant renaissance over the previous few years, the Black Banana's menu was refined to meet the now heightened expectations.

A first-class wine list was added (many Philadelphia diners no longer found jug Riunite Lambrusco and Gallo Hearty Burgundy acceptable options), full-fledged fusion cuisine was offered, which, although it missed as often as it hit, was a testament to the reality that, by now, steak and lobster would no longer cut it. The sexy waiters and waitresses remained, however: "limber young women floating about like so many Trilbys in sweeping gowns and boas, and lithe young men in tight pants." On top of all this was the newest craze: coed bathrooms (one of which sported a photograph of "interracial gay abandon," as described in a *Philadelphia Inquirer* restaurant review).[15] Bookbinders was nothing like this.

By the late 1970s, Philadelphia was staking its claim as the food capital of the East. A total of 150 restaurants had opened up in the mid '70s alone and most of them were at least surviving if not thriving. Restaurateurs in cities such as Washington, D.C., and New York were now touring the formerly staid city to check out the latest trends, to see what of Philadelphia they could attempt to bring back home with them.[16] They would come away impressed with the Philadelphia chefs' insistence on fresh ingredients, attention to detail and willingness to experiment. On the high end, Philadelphia was leading the way here as well. Craig Claiborne, the *New York Times* restaurant critic, gushed over his visit to Perrier's Le Bec Fin, calling it "one of the finest restaurants in America" in 1974 and adding that "there is not a restaurant in Manhattan with such elegance in its surroundings."[17] After this review, reservations were nearly impossible to get, with the restaurant full every evening with both locals as well as outsiders who traveled hundreds of miles in the hope of sampling a taste of cutting-edge Philadelphia.

As a result of the compactness of the city's safe zone (due to the boundaries imposed by Bacon and others as well as the natural boundaries on the east and west found by the Delaware and Schuylkill rivers), all of this activity had the effect of transforming entire neighborhoods, cleaning up large swaths of the city and making it walkable and, at least comparatively, safe virtually from one end of the zone to the other.[18] The compact nature of the city's core made it different from other cities, which may have experienced similar growth but which was more difficult to discern on a large scale because their renewal was spread out across a larger area, with large patches of blight in between.

Paralleling the case of the Black Banana on South Street, the restaurant renaissance across the safe zone led to other forms of growth. Nightspots popped up, putting to rest at last the age-old joke about visiting the city only to find it closed.[19] In 1976, a real estate magnate and movie buff, Ramon Posel, opened up the Ritz Theater in Society Hill, dedicated to showing not the popcorn hit of the moment but, rather, foreign films that had previously skipped the city altogether and which would have required a trip to Manhattan in order to see them. Now they would play in culturally hip Philadelphia as well.[20] At last, the city had shed its inferiority complex. As the restaurant renaissance demonstrated, success did not have to mean emulating New York. Indeed Jane Jacobs, argued that New York was not a model to be followed. Poses and others, including Guben, Hussenot, Von Starck and Perrier, embraced this seemingly radical notion either explicitly or implicitly in their work, and they remade the city culturally with a consciousness that called attention to the differences between the two cities rather than their similarities. As a result, Philadelphia learned that it could lead; it was not deigned to follow forever.[21] For the first time in memory, Philadelphia had a positive identity to call its own and its citizens, whether they lived physically in the city or in the nearby suburbs, took pride in it.

This pride was enhanced in contrasting what was happening in Philadelphia with what was taking place in mighty New York, which most Philadelphians still kept at least one eye on regardless of how well things were going at home. Throughout the 1970s, New York was literally disintegrating. While Philadelphia seemingly thrived, New York was drowning in debt, chaos and

Young, hip Philadelphians discuss the perils and pleasures of the restoration of their Society Hill row home in this 1973 photograph (Temple University Libraries, Urban Archives, Philadelphia, PA).

destruction.[22] In the fall of 1974, while restaurants and nightclubs couldn't open fast enough in Philadelphia, New York's mayor Abe Beame froze all municipal hiring in an effort to stanch the city's bleeding. When that didn't work, he laid off city employees for the first time since the Great Depression. Later, 38,000 more workers, including firemen, policemen and garbage collectors, were let go. The city's police union reacted to the threat of layoffs by distributing pamphlets to visitors arriving at Kennedy Airport, Grand Central Station and the Port Authority Bus Terminal announcing: "Welcome to Fear City" and providing tourists with a "survival guide" to the city. The guide advised visitors that their safety could not be guaranteed and that they were never to leave their hotels after dark or to ride the subways at all. Regardless of the truth of these pamphlets, millions of visitors left the city thankful that they lived to tell about it. In the summer of 1975, a citywide garbage strike caused the streets literally to stink. Negotiating the city's sidewalks proved impossible in areas due to the piles of garbage rising higher by the day. On top of this, nearly 10 percent of the city's firehouses were closed, and, between 1973 and 1976, the city lost approximately 340,000 jobs. By the mid 1970s, the image of the city had deteriorated to the point where corporate recruiters were reporting an increasing number of résumés requesting employment in any city *other than* New York. In April 1975, New York hit rock bottom when Standard and Poors suspended its rating of the city's securities. Now it was officially a bad investment, no longer able to raise the capital necessary for it to survive. During the administration of President Gerald Ford, the federal government refused to step in and bail the city out (the *New York Daily News* headline ran, "Ford to City: Drop Dead"), and the city appeared doomed. It appeared to be "a failed urban experiment" as the *New York Times* would pointedly suggest a few years later. In Philadelphia, no such questions were being asked.

Nearly a century and a half after the demise of the Second National Bank made Philadelphia the butt of national jokes it was now New York's turn. The city that forcibly wrested the title of financial capital of the nation away from Philadelphia was now itself awash in debt and perceived to be the victim of its own arrogance. And just as no one raced to Philadelphia's rescue in its moment of national crisis, New York now found itself alone as well. In a column that recalled the vicious attacks on Philadelphia in the 1830s, Rowland Evans and Robert Novak wrote: "Americans do not much like, admire, respect, trust, or believe in New York."[23] Political cartoons lampooned the city on a regular basis, portraying it as being ineptly run and deserving of its financial ruin. Johnny Carson picked on the city as well, painting it as dangerous and corrupt, giving credence to the police union's "fear city" portrayal. It may have taken nearly 150 years for it to arrive but, finally, New York was receiving its comeuppance for the actions of Martin Van Buren and his minions. Philadelphia had been there, done that, and was at last out of New York's shadow. Unlike the portrayal of New York at the time, people *wanted* to live in Philadelphia, and they were excited about what the future held for the city. Inferiority was no longer an issue; by the mid 1970s, there appeared to be very little left of New York for Philadelphia to feel inferior about.

Yes We Can

By 1974, however, the optimism that was cascading over the city was receding from the intersection of Broad and Pattison. The Phillies, who cleansed themselves of the aura of North Philadelphia and Connie Mack Stadium through their relocation to the Vet, had spent their first three seasons there sullying themselves anew in their stately home. Three years of bad baseball, interrupted only once every fourth day in 1972 by Steve Carlton's Cy Young season (where he managed to win 27 games for a team that would win all of 59 the entire year), left fans secure in their knowledge that, while their city may have been transformed, the Phillies remained a relic of the past. And even "Super Steve," as he came to be known, was not immune to the (mis)fortunes of the Phils; in 1973 he lost 20 games for a team that managed to finish last, 11.5 games behind, statistically speaking, the weakest division-winning team in Major League history (the Mets, who won 82 games). Coming in to spring training 1974, few people had reason to feel good about the team.

The front office tried its best to spur interest, create hope, but nobody — not the players, not the fans, not the media — was buying it. "I feel right now we have the nucleus and the interest and the dedication (we need)," said General Manager Paul Owens.[24] Doing his best to make lemonade out of the team's lemon of a season in 1973, he continued, "[w]e turned this thing around in my opinion last year." Down in the locker room, the mood was noticeably different. Greg Luzinski described playing for a perennial loser "depressing" and added that while he was looking forward to spring training, "I'm not keyed up about the team."[25] As spring training dragged on, the pessimism surrounding the team became an enveloping cloud. *Philadelphia Inquirer* beat writer Bruce Keidan painted a grim picture of the scene: "The mood of the training camp here is so downbeat that writers covering the Phillies are trying to get Carpenter Complex (the team's spring training home) declared a depressed area. 'This camp is so bad,' said one newsman, 'I've called my wife two nights in a row.'"[26] Soon, gallows humor prevailed, with sarcasm running rampant in reports out of Clearwater. After a particularly ugly spring defeat, Keidan remarked how the Phils were in mid-season form:

"It had been five long months since the Phillies had muffed a routine fly ball, hung a curve or looked at a called third strike in anger. But they are past masters of the art, having lost 273 times in the last three seasons alone."[27] He concluded his rant with a portent of what was likely to come north to Philadelphia in 1974: "So be reassured. Bob Hope still is the king of comedy. Nobody plays poker with Amarillo Slim. And the Phillies still are best at being baseball's worst." After this article and a television report that focused on his weight, Luzinski briefly stopped talking to reporters, citing the negativity of the press as the reason, ignoring the fact that it was he who tossed the first grenade on the season before the inaugural spring game had even been played.[28] The team had not even unpacked their bags in Philadelphia and already the season was over in many people's eyes.

Very quickly, though, the mood began to dissipate. On opening day, the newest Phillie, second baseman Dave Cash — a man who had played on nothing but winning teams in Pittsburgh — announced to all within earshot near his locker before the game that he was proud to be in Philadelphia. "[Y]ou couldn't give me a million dollars to take off this uniform," he said.[29] A few days later, after the team swept a doubleheader from the pennant-winning Mets, Cash raced to the New York dugout shouting "Yes we did! Yes we did!" to the backs of the Mets players as they shuffled into the locker room.[30] Two days after that, in front of a meager 8,107 people at the Vet, Cash saved the game with a diving stop in the ninth and followed that by screaming "Yes we can!" at the top of his lungs. A startled Larry Bowa asked him who he was talking to. "Anybody who wants to listen," was Cash's reply.[31] Soon, everybody was.

From the day he arrived in Philadelphia, Cash realized that the problems on the Phillies ran far deeper than their play on the field. The culture of defeat, the culture of negativity, had infected the organization to the core much as it once had the city in which the team played. On donning his new uniform, he made it his mission to change all this. Not unlike Bacon, not unlike Phillips, not unlike Dilworth, Von Starck, Guben and Poses, Cash was determined to change the mind-set of those around him from one that focused on the limitations to one that focused on the possibilities. Right away, he went about demonstrating that the old Phillies, like the old Philadelphia, were a thing of the past. And the "depressing" vision of Luzinski's Phillies had no place in the exuberant, chattering, bow-legged Better Philadelphia exhibit Cash put on display wherever he went. These Phillies were going to believe in themselves, and this city was going to believe in them too, once they realized what was possible if they committed themselves to change.

He quickly won over his teammates, convincing Mike Schmidt that he was not the .196 hitter he had been in 1973; rather, he was going to be the best third baseman in baseball history. By early May, the usually quiet, introspective Schmidt announced to the media that he was "the best in baseball at my position," adding that "Cash talked me into it. He started telling me I was the best and I started believing him."[32] With his newfound confidence, Schmidt began building up the armor he would need to fend off the attacks that felled his predecessors under the glare of the city's baseball spotlight, Del Ennis and Dick Allen. Cash also told Larry Bowa that he was an All Star shortstop.[33] In July, the diminutive "gnat" (a not altogether flattering nickname in that it connoted little more than a bothersome pest) who had never before hit above .250 in a season, was representing the National League at the game. He even confronted Danny Ozark, imploring the droopy-faced manager to encourage his pitchers to stand up for themselves and their teammates by brushing back hitters after one of their own — most notably Cash, who notoriously hung over the plate — was knocked down.[34] By mid-season, he was the unquestioned leader of the team as well as the caretaker of its newfound image. His personality was so dominant that soon Owens acknowledged that, in the locker room, the team was run more often by its second baseman than its manager. In June, the team acquired an extra outfielder, Ollie Brown, who brought with him a reputation as a good hitter, but a player who was considered to lack motivation. Owens acquired him anyway, believing that Cash would be able to put the necessary finishing touches on him and make the move worthwhile. "I think Cash can handle him. Handle him in that he has to be pushed."[35] Apparently, Ozark was not part of the equation. In Cash, the Phillies received a personality makeover that mirrored the one transforming the city. Within a few months the negativity had disappeared, replaced with an optimism that had eluded the team ever since the early 1950s. "Yes we can" became the mantra in the clubhouse after games, complete with clapping and cheering by grown men, professional athletes — the same ones who found the same physical space depressing just a few months earlier.

Soon the mantra spread. First it infected the journalists who covered the team. Bruce Keidan, who dripped sarcasm in March, was a believer by July, announcing that he had a "hunch" that the "Yes We Can" Phils (by now, the mantra was steamrolling with such force that capitalization was required) would take the division.[36] Next it spread to the city, whose inhabitants started to come out to the games in droves, making the dismal April crowds a thing of the past. Fans who previously sat on their hands or booed indiscriminately now cheered even the smallest moments, standing and roaring whenever Tony Taylor, the last active link to 1964, strode to the plate to pinch hit.[37] They arrived at the stadium early, cheering the pre-game marching bands, the announcement of that night's starting lineups and even, on occasion, the umpires (boos were reserved for the opposing team and, of course, calls that went against their Phils). On July 10, the team passed the one million mark in attendance after 45 games— the earliest any Phillies team had ever reached that mark.[38] Finally, it spread beyond the team itself. "Yes We Can" became adopted by anyone in the Delaware Valley who wanted to let others know that anything was possible, nothing was unattainable.[39] By September, the transformation was complete. Cash had managed to remake the team, as well as its relationship with the city, in his image. "Yes We Can" succinctly embodied the feeling that was sweeping over the city in so many different ways. Baseball was just one part of it. And just as important as the message itself was its messenger: a black man embraced by an organization considered for decades to be racist in a city thought to be the same.[40] In "Yes We Can" the entire package of the city's transformation was apparent. The ugliness of the past was gone. As Keidan, the city's most overt convert, observed: "Times change. Teams change. Towns change."[41] With the transformation of the Phillies, a link barely remained between the modern Philadelphia and the dark decades that had swallowed the city for so long.

That the Delaware Valley had at last connected and bonded with the team was apparent in the mantra itself. For decades, even in the flash of light that was 1964, whenever most people thought of the Phils, it was in terms of how "they" were doing. Did "they" win? Did "they" lose? How have "they" screwed things up this time? Now, however, it was Yes "we" can, and did "we" win tonight, or did "we" lose. The subconscious choice in language indicated that the Phillies at last were no longer the "other."[42] Instead, they were part of the collective "us" that bonded an entire region, which was finally puffing out its chest and feeling good about itself.

The rapid adoption of the slogan by the region was significant. "Yes We Can" was not merely a corporate slogan agreed upon in a board room and then foisted upon the public through

Dave "Yes We Can" Cash (Temple University Libraries, Urban Archives, Philadelphia, PA).

the mass expenditure of advertising dollars. Rather, it was a slogan coined by a player — and a black player at that — who had no idea that it would catch on beyond the locker room. Once it was repeated in the local newspapers as part of a postgame story, it spread of its own volition. The public repeated it so often and enthusiastically because they no doubt identified and connected with it. Mere marketing could never have achieved this effect on its own. In fact, there was practically no marketing whatsoever until very late in the game. The Phillies adopted the "Yes We Can" slogan and emblazoned it on T-shirts and other promotional ideas but not until well after it had already caught fire on its own.

For the first time, fans were including the Phillies as members of "their" group and not as something separate, something different. And, as part of the in-group, the Phils received the benefits that subconsciously flow from group membership. Studies on the effects of language on stereotyping have shown that people have a natural, unconscious, tendency to associate positive traits with people or groups associated with inclusive words such as "we," "us," and "ours," and negative traits with those associated with disjunctive words such as "they," them," and "theirs."[43] As a result, when people thought about the "Yes *We* Can" Phils, they were thinking about members of their own group. And because individuals' definitions of themselves are so intricately intertwined with their perception of those considered to be kindred spirits, they were searching for the good things rather than the bad.[44] It was irrelevant whether the 1974 Phillies were different from any of their predecessors. After all, previous teams had played as well or better than the '74 club did — a team that at no point was ever more than seven games above .500 and spent most of the season hovering around .500, either a few games above or below it. What was more important was that people believed that they were. And once they believed this, the Phils became different as a result of the perception. The subconscious sense of "us" or "them" is based on feelings, not facts[45] and once the feelings were perceived, nothing else mattered.

"Yes We Can" convinced, first, the team and, later, the entire Delaware Valley that these Phillies were not at all like the incarnations that had passed through town before. A new identity had been created, one that broke with the past and allowed both city and suburban residents to see something new and kindred whereas before they had seen only something old and disparate, something that bore no connection with them. And once on board, the Phillies were at last the beneficiaries of all the good feelings people were experiencing with regard to all aspects of "their" rehabilitated city. As such, it made perfect sense for fans so quick to boo the team in the past to now look for reasons to cheer them — people favor "us" over "them" even in nonsensical situations.[46] Even though the 1974 season would turn out much like the ones that came before it (the team struggled after Luzinski tore up his right knee in early June — losing 16 of its next 25 games — falling out of the divisional race and then finishing the season at 80-82, eight games out of first), 1974 *was* different in that a connection between the team and its fans had finally been made. Whereas before, the Phillies were the unwelcome face of a city gone bad — a city full of "thems" as branded by the hordes of frightened and disgusted people streaming out into the suburbs and looking to sever their ties with what they considered an urban disaster — now they were brought into the fold by people returning to the city either physically or in spirit, people who took pride in what their city had become. They had become the face of the new Philadelphia — the face of a city reborn.

8

Breaking from the Past

Black Friday: Eighth Inning

Garber was as untouchable in the eighth as he had been in the seventh. Once again he proved that he was on his game. Nobody was able lift any of his pitches off the ground. Garber mixed a slider and a fastball that would have been delectably hittable were it not in such sharp contrast with his leaden change-up. That change kept the LA hitters off-balance in the box and heading back to the dugout almost as soon as they dug in. Reggie Smith beat the first pitch he saw into the ground and watched the ball trickle to Sizemore for the first out. Ron Cey at least hit his ball a bit harder but still only a few feet from Schmidt, who was guarding the line and had no trouble fielding it and taking care of him; Garvey topped a sinking change to Bowa who threw high but still got him in plenty of time. Seven pitches, three outs. If only the Phils could put something on the board in the bottom of the inning, they looked likely to take a 2–1 lead in the series. And with Carlton on tap for game four, that would be all as far as the Dodgers were concerned.

The Phillies' hopes grew stronger as they geared up for their at-bats in the eighth when Lasorda finally ran out of tricks and had to turn at last to his actual bullpen. Elias Sosa — the same Elias Sosa who imploded in the ninth inning of game one by giving up three successive hits and then balking in a run — was on the mound. There were no more Rhodens or Raus, converted starters, left to mask LA's Achilles' heel; they would now win or lose the game on the strength of their officially designated bullpen. The Phils, and the faithful, smelled blood.

Hebner led off and got so far ahead of Sosa's first pitch — a floating, hanging slider — that in his haste hooked it foul down the first base line. No matter, two pitches later he adjusted and this time ripped the ball deep to right, where it barely missed clearing the fence and, instead, bounced off it. He hit it so hard, in fact, that it reached Reggie Smith in such a hurry that, had he played it well, he might have had Hebner at second. However, although

171

Smith played the ball perfectly off the wall, he overthrew his cutoff man Lopes—portent of things to come—allowing Hebner to make it without a play.

With Maddox due to bat, Dodger pitching coach Red Adams trotted to the mound, hoping to settle his pitcher down and avoid a repeat of game one. Whatever he said, it was quickly evident that it didn't work and that, moreover, by this point Sosa was not his only concern. Maddox stung his first pitch into right for a single and Smith charged, setting up yet another play at the plate, the fourth of the game. With the slow-footed Hebner, a grave digger in the off-season, rounding third (indeed, his uneven, muscular gait made it look as if he had one foot in a ditch even as he ran) Smith appeared to have a shot at redemption for his earlier poor throw. However, his throw this time made that one seem like a bulls-eye in comparison; he tossed it off-line and all the way into the Dodger dugout. Hebner scored, giving the Phils a 4–3 lead, and Maddox, who was on his way to second at the time of the throw, took third on the error.

The usually reliable Smith's consecutive errant throws, along with the presence of Sosa on the mound, hinted at the problems on the horizon for the Dodgers; after doing a remarkable job of keeping themselves together and righting their listing ship after the second inning, they appeared to be coming unglued once again and at the absolute worst possible time. With Boone now at the plate and the speedy Maddox a mere 90 feet away, Yeager was thinking suicide squeeze, so he called for a first pitch pitchout. Sosa, however, either missed the sign or the ensuing target because he threw a fastball on the outside corner of the plate, which just missed being called a strike. This forced Yeager to stab at it from the standing position he was now in given his anticipation of the called pitchout. He caught it but no one among the nearly 64,000 in attendance missed the significance of the play: LA was now officially vulnerable once more. As Yeager called time and trotted to the mound to straighten things out, the decibel level climbed with each step.

With his next pitch, at least Sosa redeemed himself, although he would be the only one. He fooled Boone, causing him to nearly topple over as he swung, hitting a weak dribbler to Cey, who was in at third in the hope of cutting off a fifth run. He fielded it and, given that the normally slow Boone was even slower still in getting out of the box, had plenty of time to check Maddox back to the bag before throwing over to first. After making sure that Maddox stayed put, he threw off his back foot, tossing the ball into the heavens, at least 10 feet over Garvey's head, the third consecutive bad throw in the inning. Maddox scored and Boone reached second while Garvey chased the ball up the rightfield foul line where it rolled after bouncing off the fence behind first base. The score now stood at 5–3, Philadelphia.

As Sizemore strolled to the plate, Ozark had a decision to make. With nobody out, he could bunt Boone to third and try to pick up a sixth run; however, if he did that, he'd necessarily have to hit for Garber who was on-deck, taking a pitcher who was not only one of his most effective all season but nearly unhittable this afternoon out of the game. Instead, he decided to do the next best thing: get McGraw up in the bullpen as a decoy and have Sizemore fake a couple of bunt attempts in an effort to get Sosa to throw him a fat fastball that he could drive. It didn't work, as he eventually grounded to Cey, who this time had no trouble holding Boone at second and throwing him out. With that, McGraw sat back down and Garber came to the plate.

Although not a bad hitter, at least for a relief pitcher who typically only experienced about a dozen at-bats per season at best, Garber was hitless for 1977, having gone 0 for 10. In any event, the often cited, but never seen, baseball "book" would undoubtedly call for him to take his chances and swing away; with two outs it would make little sense to sacrifice Boone to third for McBride as he likely would score from second on anything but the most sharply hit single. However, given how rattled the Dodgers appeared to have become, and with the stadium practically shaking on every pitch, Ozark decided to close the book on this occasion. Realizing that Garber was far more likely to put the ball in play with a bunt than with a swing, he called for it anyway, perhaps figuring that if only Garber could put the ball in play, there was at least a decent chance that the Dodgers would fumble it somehow; the "book" did not take into account the screaming multitudes surrounding the Veterans Stadium plastic grass who had once again managed to worm themselves inside the heads of the players on the field. This necessitated a recalculation of baseball's time-honored "percentages." On his second attempt, Garber did indeed bunt the ball in fair territory, although this time Sosa fielded it cleanly and threw him out at first.

With that, Sosa was gone. Lasorda replaced him with left-hander Lance Rautzhan to face the left-handed McBride (he would eventually retire him to finally end the inning). As he made his way to the Dodger dugout, Sosa was greeted with a loud, derisive cheer — clearly directed toward him — which was the crowd's way of letting him know that they had claimed another victim, although in this instance, it was Cey and Smith who technically were more deserving of their attention. Regardless, these two weren't the ones leaving the field at the moment and the bloodthirsty fans did not appear to be in a mood to be particular. If ever anyone had wondered just what it might have sounded like in the Roman Colosseum, this perhaps was something of an approximation. Another Christian down and out. Three outs to go and the lions could all but officially claim the series for themselves.

Ghosts

It should not have been at all surprising that a city as embedded in its past as deeply as Philadelphia would be haunted by ghosts even as it reoriented itself toward the future. Still, when the ghosts appeared, they were chilling nonetheless, casting doubt as to the extent of the true transformation of the city. Once they were finally exorcised in 1975 and '76, however, they departed a city that felt stronger for having turned them back and confident that whatever ropes may have held it down before had finally been untethered, leaving the city to soar as it never had before.

The first of these ghosts made its presence known on September 14, 1974. On that date, Dick Allen "retired" from the Chicago White Sox. However, as with all things concerning Allen, things were not nearly as simple as they appeared in the "Transactions" column in newspapers across the country the following morning. Allen, the 1972 American League MVP, was at the time the league's home run leader (a position he'd retain at year's end despite missing the final weeks of the season) and the most vital cog on a White Sox team that was at least on the periphery of the American League West pennant race (they'd finish the season nine games behind the Oakland A's). In typical Allen fashion, the announcement was slathered in contradictions: he arrived at the ballpark that morning, suited up for the game, took batting practice, called his teammates together, told them that he'd "never been happier anywhere than here," and then promptly retired.[1] The move was consistent with Allen's résumé in one respect in that despite his long-standing complaint that all he wanted in life was to be left alone, he seemed to have gone out of his way once again to act so outrageously as to draw every eye in the sporting nation in his direction.

It was a technique he had honed during his initial stint in Philadelphia. In 1969, after returning from yet another suspension and reciting his mantra, he moved his locker out of the team's locker room and relocated to what had been a storage area at Connie Mack Stadium, thereby ensuring that the media's attention would be focused squarely on him for the foreseeable future.[2] In August of that season — one in which he'd complain bitterly about the fans' treatment of him — he antagonized the crowd by scratching "Oct. 2" into the infield dirt, his putative last day on the field for a team he desperately wanted to be traded from once the season ended.[3] A few days later he scratched "Boo" into the dirt instead, drawing the expected response.[4] All the while, he claimed to be hurt by the increasing savagery of the fans and pinned their reaction to him on racism.[5] While there obviously was a racist tinge among some, who particularly relished hurling derogatory insults in his direction, Allen was blind to the fact that it was he who antagonized the majority of his detractors.

It was largely Allen who made race an issue, causing people to react to the front he carefully (or carelessly, depending on the viewpoint) cultivated and presented to the public. As the 1960s progressed, the once budding superstar became notorious for one incident after another in which he either arrived at the stadium drunk, refused to take batting practice or missed team flights or games altogether. These events were covered in the media on a daily basis and soon played out much like a serialized soap opera with fans opening their sports sections every morning in anticipation of what the next chapter in the Allen saga held in store for them. For a man who claimed to want nothing as much as his privacy, he had a peculiar way of seeking it out. Because of his polarizing ways, baseball writer Bill James would later remark that he "did more to *keep* his teams from winning than anybody else who ever played major league baseball."[6] Still, in Allen's mind, it was racism that was the cause of his troubles; he believed he was only a passive victim.

By the time he left Philadelphia after the 1969 season, he had managed to make himself the personification of the myriad problems the city found itself struggling to free itself from: racism, anger, disgust, hopelessness. Upon his departure, *Evening Bulletin* writer Sandy Grady anointed Cardinals general manager Bing Devine (who took Allen off of the Phillies' hands) the biggest hero in Philadelphia and playfully suggested that the Phils name their new stadium after him.[7] Of course, because this was a trade involving Allen, even his departure was not without controversy: Curt Flood, who was to have been one of the players shipped to Philadelphia in exchange for Allen, refused to report, choosing instead to challenge Major League Baseball's reserve clause, eventually fighting his case all the way to the Supreme Court (where he would lose, although he would never report to the Phillies).[8]

Allen's troubles, meanwhile, continued to follow him wherever he went. In St. Louis, he celebrated the clean slate he had been given by initially refusing to report and missed much of spring training.[9] Still, when he returned he played well, making the All-Star team. However, the team was struggling and had little use for a highly paid slugger — particularly one who refused to speak to anybody he "didn't know real well" — and they traded him to the Dodgers prior to the 1971 season. In Los Angeles he played well once again but still showed up late for two games during a season in which the team was in the thick of a pennant race. Moreover, he refused team owner Walter O'Malley's repeated requests to make public appearances and was shipped to the White Sox the following season. In Chicago he seemed to have finally found a home; by all accounts he enjoyed playing for easygoing manager Chuck Tanner and responded immediately to the trade by having his MVP season in 1972. He continued to play well in 1973 but then suffered a hairline fracture of his left leg in June and was shut down for much of the rest of that season. Then came

1974, a year in which the now 31-year-old slugger, in the prime of his career, returned to form, hitting .301 with 32 home runs and 88 RBIs. Then promptly and without notice, she retired. So, when he announced after the season had ended that he in fact had not retired and that he was "gonna play somewhere next year — even if it's Jenkintown,"[10] apparitions of the troubled star began to appear with increasing frequency in the city's newspapers.

For here were the Phillies, the "Yes We Can" Phillies that could until Greg Luzinski went down with a leg injury in June. That injury, upon reflection, turned their 1974 season into yet another hopeless one. If only they had an additional bat in the lineup, someone to protect both of their young sluggers, Schmidt and Luzinski, as well as providing insurance should they suffer another devastating injury during the 1975 season, they could legitimately shoot for the division title that year. With all of the good will built up throughout the 1974 season, the temptation was strong to protect themselves in order to keep the momentum, which had been absent for so many years before now, going. Speculation in the media — much of it fueled by Richie Ashburn, who repeatedly used his *Evening Bulletin* columns to lobby for the return of Allen[11]— led to discussions in the front office. The talks resulted in a clandestine February visit by Ashburn, Schmidt and Cash to Allen's Bucks County farm during which the three tried to convince him to suit up in 1975 for the Phils.[12] By this time Allen's rights had been purchased by the Atlanta Braves, who subsequently put him on the voluntarily retired list after he said he would never play for them. Despite this, Cash came away impressed with Allen and announced that he did not believe that he would disrupt the club.[13] By this point, the organization's philosophy, when it came to team chemistry, was essentially "In Cash We Trust." If Cash believed he could handle him, that was good enough for the front office. Just like it had with Ollie Brown in '74, the team was willing to turn over yet another troubled head to Cash and his power of positive thinking. This time it would be the ultimate test.

As spring training approached, however, Allen remained on his farm. And with each passing day, the number of potential suitors dwindled as team after team publicly passed on the opportunity to add a potential Hall of Famer to their roster. The Cardinals were not willing to revisit their relationship with him, with third baseman Joe Torre stating that he thought that the Cardinals' reluctance to sign him had something to do with team owner Gussie Busch sensing that Allen's presence might "affect the team over a long period of time."[14] Mets manager Yogi Berra was more explicit, stating that he would not add Allen to his club even if he didn't have to give anybody up to get him.[15] Regardless, the Phils continued their quest.

In Philadelphia, the feeling was that, this time, things would be different.

Anger, hostility and resentment had all dissipated in the years since Allen left, both on the team and in the city. They could handle him now, in part because the stigma of racism had largely been scrubbed from the city's conscience (particularly given the relocation of the Phillies' home out of North Philadelphia). Dick Allen would return to a city much different from the one he departed six years earlier. Once Allen was able to experience the revitalized, rehabilitated city, he would relax and just play ball. Race would not be on everyone's lips (particularly Allen's) the moment he took the field. Accordingly, most of the players on the team were vociferous in their support of the team's quest to sign him. Even the player most directly affected, first baseman Willie Montanez (who coincidentally was the player shipped to the Phils from St. Louis after Flood refused to report in 1970) announced that he'd gladly move to the outfield in order to accommodate Allen at first base. To a man, the team wanted Allen, even if he never took batting practice again.[16] This time, it would not be a problem.

Still, spring training progressed and Allen remained at home. Notwithstanding the uncertainty regarding his future in Philadelphia, the mood this spring was a far cry from what it had been in 1974, before "Yes We Can" took hold. This time, there was no sniping, this time there was nothing but harmony.[17] In 12 short months, the team had been transformed into one that believed that it could do anything — even change someone as stubborn as Dick Allen. Schmidt could only envision Allen helping the team win the division; he could not imagine a scenario where he could hurt the club.[18] Cash believed the same even though Allen's work habits contradicted Cash's every step of the way (one of Cash's mantras preached the value of pre-game preparation: "the more you sweat in peace, the less you bleed in war,"[19] a philosophy that resided in a galaxy far, far away from Allen). Only Luzinski professed some reservations about pursuing him, although his voice was largely drowned out by the "We Want Allen" brigade.[20]

By the midpoint of spring training, the Phils "officially" ended their pursuit of Allen when they were unable to work out a deal with Atlanta for his rights. Although he refused to comment on the record, Ozark was obviously pleased by this development. Now, *Inquirer* columnist Frank Dolson remarked, he finally would have a realistic shot at completing the new two-year contract extension he signed the previous summer.[21] At least for the time being, his fate was no longer destined to sink into the same abyss as the two previous managers who tried to handle Allen in Philadelphia, Gene Mauch and Bob Skinner.[22] Mauch managed him the longest and, at least for a while, had the most success with him. Still, once Allen's actions became more outrageous in the mid to late 1960s, Mauch's attempts to discipline him proved futile as owner Bob Carpenter repeatedly overruled him and refused to enforce the myriad fines Mauch imposed on him. Finally, in 1968, fed up with both Allen and Carpenter, Mauch issued an ultimatum to his owner: he had to choose between him or Allen. Carpenter chose Allen and Mauch was dismissed. Bob Skinner was hired to replace Mauch and he tried to discipline Allen as well. Skinner quit after Carpenter repeatedly refused to collect on Allen's fines. (One time Carpenter asked Allen to select a charity to receive the money from his fines. Allen refused to do this, and, in response, Carpenter chose the Police Athletic League and then donated $10,000 to it in Allen's name.) Ozark no doubt saw himself heading down the same road should Allen join the club.

Once the Phils ended their quest, however, Allen, who initially dismissed the possibility of returning to Philadelphia because of his concerns over how he would be treated by the media, changed his mind. Speaking publicly before members of the same media at, appropriately enough, Keystone Race Track, Allen announced that he was "available and I want to play baseball."[23] He stated that he was in "great shape" and that he "could be ready to play in five days to a week." In a remark that would be deemed curious for any player other than Allen, who had just quit on his former team, he insisted that "they can't deny a man a right to earn a living." In addition, Allen contended that the White Sox traded him to Atlanta "without consulting me" (as if that mattered given that he had just quit on Chicago months earlier) and then attempted to clarify things by stating that he did not want to play in Atlanta because he did not want to be "another (Henry) Aaron, a drawing card." For any team wondering if the events over the winter of 1974-75 had led to a more contrite Allen, he answered this emphatically by stating that while he wanted to play, "I'm not going to beg for a job." Finally, he admitted that he was "confused" by the sequence of recent events and did not understand why Chicago traded him. However, as it turned out, he was apparently confused, but not very curious to find out why. He had previously requested a meeting with White Sox general manager Roland Hemond to clarify his situation and when the request was granted he failed to show up for the scheduled meeting.

Although several red flags should have gone up as a result of these statements, the Phillies ignored them. Behind the scenes, they continued to pursue Allen and, in April, they put in a claim for him when Atlanta attempted to sneak him through waivers. This forced Atlanta to withdraw him from the waiver wire, putting pressure on them to deal with the Phillies for the rights to Allen's services. Finally, on May 7, after owner Ruly Carpenter (Bob's son) met with Allen at his farm and was reassured by Allen that he "could live with the situation" in Philadelphia, he signed him.[24] In keeping with his role as team leader, Cash issued the first challenge to the Philadelphia public, exhorting them that "when Allen comes, [to] give him a chance."[25] As would become apparent very soon, they were willing to do this and then some. However, Allen, in his jubilation over the signing, provided a glimpse of what was to come over the next year and a half when he initially said that he was so eager to play baseball, he would have played anywhere, even "in Alaska, if the snow stopped long enough."[26] Of course, it rarely snowed at all in Atlanta and it never snowed in Chicago during the summer but he adamantly refused to suit up with either the Braves or the White Sox. When asked why he refused to play for Atlanta, he replied to a white reporter that he would have played there "if you would let me borrow your skin."[27]

Regardless, things started off well for Allen. He was greeted by cheering fans during warm-ups before his first game at the Vet and then, during the announcement of the starting lineups for that evening's game, PA announcer Dan Baker could get only so far as "Batting fifth, number 15..." before he was drowned out by the roaring crowd. The cheers lasted so long that Baker was unable to finish announcing the Phillies' starters for that evening.[28] After that game, and despite being removed from it after the sixth inning, Allen made a point of running down the clubhouse runway in an effort to congratulate his new teammates after the team's 4–0 victory over the Reds. He beamed to the press that the cheers affected him deeply. "You don't know what it means to me. It's a different situation altogether." He vowed that this time, playing in Philadelphia would be fun. Very quickly however, it proved to be anything but.

At the plate, it was apparent that his once magical stroke had abandoned him and was not about to return anytime soon. In July, two months into his second tenure with the team, he was hitting all of .233 with four home runs in 50 games. Luzinski generously claimed that despite his average Allen was effective in protecting him in the lineup[29] but it was difficult to see why any pitcher would give the Bull anything decent to hit with the feeble Allen waiting on deck. By August his July numbers would actually look robust by comparison as he was now hitting in the .220s and had hit all of one home run in the previous two months. Defensively, he was an even greater liability at first base as his lack of range and inability to dig throws out of the dirt contributed to shortstop Bowa's worst statistical season ever: by early September he had been charged with 22 errors, twice as many as in each of his previous five seasons in the majors. Although reluctant to directly criticize Allen, Bowa couldn't help but vent his frustration to the media eventually: "I'm not going to sound off," he said. "Knowledgeable people know what's going on."[30]

By season's end, Allen was hitting .233 with 12 home runs, 62 RBIs and more than one strikeout for every four at-bats—clearly not the numbers the

Phillies expected from the reigning American League home run champ when they signed him. While the team expressed ambivalence about resigning him for 1976,[31] Allen wanted to play. The team had improved on 1974 — they finished second, only 6.5 games behind the division winning Pirates and with 86 wins had completed their first winning season in eight years— and so it was decided to give Allen the benefit of a full spring training to see if his skills would return. The Phillies would come to regret this decision. In 1976, just as they had back in the 1960s, Allen's troubles would spill off of the playing field and into the locker room, threatening to undo all of the progress the team had made since Cash's arrival, stretching the bond that had been forged both among the players and between the team and the city nearly to the point of breaking. In Allen, the city had come face to face with a formidable spirit indeed.

Everyone is all smiles at the May 7, 1975, press conference announcing the resigning of Dick Allen. From left: Allen; general manager Paul Owens; manager Danny Ozark (Temple University Libraries, Urban Archives, Philadelphia, PA).

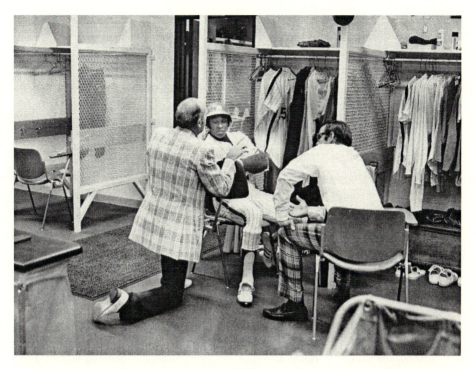

May 12, 1975: Before his first official workout as a member of the team, Allen appears to be in a less-than-receptive mood to the advice being given by Owens, left, and owner Ruly Carpenter, right (Temple University Libraries, Urban Archives, Philadelphia, PA).

The first indication of trouble off the field came during the course of the 1975 season, when Allen and Schmidt formed a bond in which Allen took the young slugger under his wing.[32] In Schmidt, Allen saw a lot of his younger self: a powerful, graceful athlete with unlimited potential but with a sensitive ego, one which bruised with every critical comment made in the media or boo from the stands. However, that Schmidt was white but also seemingly received the same harsh treatment that Allen had earlier — treatment that, in light of such similarities clearly had more to do with a city's frustrated expectations of a superstar than with race — did not resonate with Allen. The shared experience did not cause him to reevaluate his own opinion as to the root cause of his tortured career in Philadelphia during the '60s. Instead, he carried his baggage into what would become for him an increasingly frustrating 1976 season, now with Schmidt's ear as a willing receptacle for his opinions to boot. As a pupil, Schmidt was, in the words of his wife Donna (who reflected upon this era in a 1979 profile of her husband), "easily led."[33] His first true friend on the team had been Cash and his eagerness to follow him gave him the confidence he needed to become the best third baseman in base-ball.[34] His next was Allen, who had been his boyhood idol back in Dayton, Ohio, where he would spend his days attempting to mimic Allen's batting stance.[35] His influence on Schmidt would lead to far less positive results. According to his wife, "Dick Allen, Dave Cash, they led him around.... Poor Michael is always so strongly for the underdog. He doesn't always see what is happening to him."[36] Early in the '76 season, Schmidt credited Allen with helping him learn to relax and enjoy himself.[37] The 1976 season, however, would turn out to be anything but relaxing in a number of different ways.

The 1976 season started off for Allen much the way 1975 ended. He was unable to find his stroke, which by now appeared to have abandoned him for good. By the 11th game of the season, Allen was deemed a liability by Ozark and was replaced in the lineup by Tommy Hutton. Later, when called on to pinch hit in the ninth inning of a game in which the Phils trailed his much-despised Atlanta Braves 3–2, he refused. Ozark sent up Jerry Martin instead. After the game, Ozark experienced precisely how Mauch and Skinner must have felt all those years ago. The press stormed the clubhouse, wondering where Allen was, to which Ozark could reply only that he was "unable to play."[38] A few questions later, nerves obviously frayed, Ozark attempted to clear the clubhouse of the press. After exiting his office, slamming the door behind him and then kicking the wall and a waste paper basket as he left, he threatened to punch a reporter who questioned Ozark's authority to do so. A few minutes later, owner Ruly Carpenter cursed out the same writer and then issued a more general epithet to the entire press corps as he entered his elevator. Things would only go downhill from there.

A few weeks later, Allen, who was by now being platooned with Bobby Tolan and who was hitting all of .250 with a lone double serving as his only extra-base hit of the season, expressed dismay that he had been dropped to seventh in the batting order. "If I'm going to slow 'em up that much," he said, "I'd rather not be in there at all."[39] Still, the fans remained firmly behind him, offering encouragement whenever the opportunity arose. In June, they stopped a game with a rousing ovation after Allen recalled past glories by hit-ting two home runs in a 12–4 rout of the Cardinals.[40] Although he was touched by the show of support, adding that that the fans' backing in Philadelphia meant more to him than anywhere else "because of what went on before," he continued on his downward slide both on the field and in the locker room. By August, with the Phils in first place and ready for a stretch run they hoped would bring them into the postseason for the first time in over a quarter of a century, Allen caused everyone on the team and in the city to revisit the 1960s all over again. On July 25, he was injured during a collision on the basepaths with Pirate pitcher John Candelaria. The next day he telephoned

Ozark complaining of soreness and dizziness and requested the night off.[41]
The following day he neither phoned nor arrived at the stadium. The day after
that he showed up at the game, stayed for three innings and then departed
without telling anyone. This was followed by another day in which he failed
to either show up to the stadium or explain his absence. This resulted in a
team meeting at which Ozark classified Allen as being AWOL. At a press conference the team announced that he would be fined for his absences—a threat
that this time seemed to have some teeth in it because Ruly Carpenter was
not his father and, as the bearer of this news, appeared determined to follow
through on his words. However, when Allen showed up unexpectedly the
next night in New York, Ozark rescinded the fines, remarked that Allen could
not play due to his injuries and placed him on the disabled list even though
he had never been examined by a physician.

On August 10, he was eligible to come off the disabled list. He called the
team instead, insisting that he was still hurt, having visited a doctor for the
first time the day before he was due to return. Nearly a month later, on September 3 and six weeks after the collision with Candelaria, he pronounced
himself fit to play once more. By late September, with the division title up
for grabs and with Luzinski's now chronically sore knee acting up again,
Allen—who was signed precisely to protect the team in such situations—
was of little use to anybody. He had gone 3 for 40 since his return and his
fielding had become even worse than before. Moreover, his availability from
game to game was never assured; he showed up to a key game against the
second-place Pirates less than 30 minutes before game time and his erratic
behavior caused him to be benched in other games in which he otherwise
might have played.[42]

However, his locker room behavior was even worse. By early August he
announced that Ozark's outfield platoon system (which had no direct bearing on him in any event) was racially motivated. He questioned why black
players such as Ollie Brown and Bobby Tolan were not getting as much playing time as their white counterparts and he suggested that the Phillies were
"working a quota system."[43] As the Phillies chugged toward the postseason,
Allen continued to simmer and stew, amping up his venom as the season
grew longer. By the time the team finally clinched the division title in late
September, what should have been the culmination of "Yes We Can" togetherness was instead soured by a divisiveness spurred by Allen, who had
managed to split the team along racial lines. As the team celebrated its championship in the bowels of Montreal's Jarry Park, Allen sat alone on the frigid
bench, refusing to join the celebration.[44] Eventually, he would enter the clubhouse but his presence would only cement the division that was already present: Allen, Cash, Maddox and Schmidt removed themselves from their

teammates and continued their celebration privately, in a clubhouse broom closet.[45] The "Broom Closet Incident," as it would come to be known, brought all of the simmering hostility to the surface. In little less than a year and a half, Allen had managed to sink the Phillies back into the muck they had worked so desperately to climb out of over the last several years.

After the Montreal series, Allen skipped the team flight to St. Louis and announced that he would not participate in the playoffs unless Tony Taylor (who was at the tail end of a long career, had all of 26 at-bats during the season and was by now more of an unofficial coach than player) was placed on the active roster.[46] This would have required the Phils to deactivate a pitcher in order to make room for him, something they were not willing to do. Allen's words and deeds required quick action in order to fend off an impending insurrection. Left with no choice, Ozark granted Allen "permission" to go home even though he already had.[47] Then, in yet another team meeting, Ozark made it clear that no one was going to tell him what players to include on the postseason roster. With that, talk of boycotting the playoffs spread throughout the team as it now split openly along racial lines.[48] Several black players questioned Ozark, echoing Allen in wondering why the white Jerry Martin rather than the black Ollie Brown played in the second game of the doubleheader in Montreal, after the Phils clinched the division. Ozark's response, that "Ollie hasn't been hitting for the past month," did little to soothe them.[49] Other players, such as Larry Bowa, were upset with Allen for having absented himself from the St. Louis series and with the other participants for having gone off by themselves in the broom closet incident.[50] Tug McGraw remarked at a team meeting that "some of us white guys" looked around during the second game of the Montreal doubleheader and "wondered where all the black guys were."[51] This comment angered Garry Maddox, who later questioned the motivation of some of his teammates: "Either we had great unity on this team all year or it's been a great acting job by the players keeping their feelings inside.... Now when all the racial stuff starts coming out, when guys start to say how they actually feel, then you know how it is ... I signed a five-year contract with this team. I hope I didn't make a mistake."[52] Race, once again, had become an issue.

With the playoffs only days away, Ozark found himself captaining a leaky boat miles from shore. He had come close to abandoning his post back in July, when Allen first went AWOL, but changed his mind at the last minute, determined to stay on because, despite Allen, his team seemed destined to win the division anyway.[53] Now that it had, it hardly seemed worth it. Despite the success, Ozark was reliving Mauch's nightmare.

An agreement was reached in the Allen/Taylor fiasco on the eve of game one of the League Championship Series against Cincinnati's "Big Red

Machine"— one of the greatest teams in baseball history with names such as Rose, Morgan, Bench and Perez that were legendary even at the time and one that would have presented a seemingly overwhelming challenge for even a focused Phillies team. Under the agreement, Taylor would be in uniform for the postseason but as a coach, not as a player. Allen then backtracked and said that his main concern was that Taylor be in uniform, not on the active roster and that he was pleased with the outcome.[54] Whatever the reason, Allen also agreed to suit up again for the club, talk of a boycott diminished and the Phils finally began to prepare for the Reds.

However, any hope that the brokered deal between the club and Allen would mark the end of hostilities was quickly dashed during the playoffs (a tidy, three game sweep by Cincinnati). During the series, Allen refused to take batting practice, an act that his broom closet compatriots Cash and Schmidt rightly figured would become yet another controversy given what had gone on beforehand. Therefore, in a questionable show of solidarity and in an effort to deflect some of the heat from Allen, both Cash and Schmidt refused to take infield practice before each game.[55] While this most likely did not cause the sweep, it surely did not help the Phillies' cause in what would have been a difficult series in any event. In these acts, Bill James's conclusion regarding Allen was borne out: because of him, those around him stooped to his level to the detriment of the team.

By the end of the 1976 season, even his staunchest supporters within the organization could not disagree with the conclusion that bringing back Allen had been a mistake.[56] By seeing race wherever he looked, Allen brought back all of the cynicism and negativity that so many thought had been abandoned along with Connie Mack Stadium years before. In Allen, the city was compelled to confront a ghost it had thought long scared away.

Allen's was not the only ghost visiting the Phillies during the '70s. His manager for much of his first stint in Philadelphia, Gene Mauch, likewise continued to haunt the city for years after he left it, although, unlike Allen, Mauch would never officially return to the team — in the flesh. At first, on his departure in 1968, it seemed as if there literally was a ghost haunting Connie Mack Stadium. On the day after he was fired, the scoreboard malfunctioned such that for the entire game the next day, only Mauch's uniform number "4" glowed where the batters' numbers should have been.[57] Later, when he became the first manager for the expansion Montreal Expos in 1969, he continued to haunt the Phils, disturbing even the increasing multitude of players who had never played for him.

With the exception of the 1971 season, the Phils continually struggled against the talent-deprived Expos throughout Mauch's term there as manager. Between 1969 and 1974 they lost substantially more games than they won against him, losing five season series out of six and going 43–63 against the Expos overall in those five years. As for why this happened, those involved could only guess, although, to a man, they all agreed that for some reason, everyone in the clubhouse became so tense whenever Mauch was on the schedule that they were unable to concentrate and play their best baseball. Luzinski admitted to becoming distracted: "I think that everybody tries to accept the fact we're playing Montreal (and not Mauch), but there's something about him."[58] Bob Boone claimed that for some reason Mauch made him uptight, and he would try so hard to beat him that he wound up beating himself instead. Bowa recognized that while he should have focused on the team on the field, he couldn't help but fixate on the little general in the dugout instead. Years after Mauch's departure from the organization, his hold on it was mystifying.

Perhaps it was mere coincidence. Perhaps Mauch was just "an agitator," as one player referred to him, grating to many teams, with the Phillies being no different. Except that for some reason it felt different in Philadelphia. The reason it felt different in Philadelphia was because, here, Mauch had a past. His past, like that of Allen, was inexorably tied to the city's; every time he returned to the city, he brought with him a reminder of the ugliness that once was and what everyone was trying to put behind them once and for all. Like an ever-present child from a failed first marriage, Mauch's mere presence set everyone on edge because to look at him was to invariably see beyond him and to recall the shortcomings, misdeeds and regrets from before. The city felt it and so, therefore, the players felt it as well, honing in on the vibe until no one could concentrate on anything other than the little man with the big shadow.

While Mauch's ghost may have been implicit, a more explicit derivation of it spooked the city during the late summer of 1976. In the midst of that season, despite the daily machinations of the Allen saga, a season in which the Phils caught fire in May and ran away from the rest of the Eastern Division in June, the ghost of their infamous 1964 collapse rose up. By July, the team had put together three consecutive months of blistering baseball such that for all practical purposes, the division race was over. On August 24, after pounding the Braves 14–3, they stood at 82–41, an astounding 15 and a half games ahead of the Pirates. It seemed as if nothing stood between them and the playoffs other than five perfunctory weeks of baseball — until the losing began.

At first it was not much of a concern. The Phils lost the series finale against the Braves, snapping their latest of several winning streaks that season, this one of four games. Next they lost three out of four to the Reds, which again was certainly not cause for alarm given the size of their lead and the quality of their opponent. And, after all, the pedestrian Astros and Mets were next on the schedule; a few wins in those series were all but assured.

June 26, 1972: During a bench clearing brawl in Montreal, Phillies pitcher Jim Nash (42) prepares to unload a right hook on Expos manager Mauch (see arrow) (Temple University Libraries, Urban Archives, Philadelphia, PA).

However, they never came. The Astros swept the Phils and the Mets took two out of three. The Phils had now lost nine of their last 11 games, which even then would not have been significant if the Pirates had not chosen this precise time to go on a tear. While the Phils were losing, the Pirates were winning — 10 straight to significantly cut into the Phils seemingly insurmountable lead. It was now down to seven games with the Phils headed to Pittsburgh for what was now a surprisingly crucial series.

In Pittsburgh, the ghost of 1964, which during the early part of the team's collapse was merely a whisper, rose audibly with each passing game.[59] The Pirates not only swept the Phils but handled them with ease in all three games, outscoring them 17–4 in the series. The lead was now down to four. The team returned to Philadelphia, battered and bruised psychologically, and dropped two out of three to the woeful Cubs. They rebounded temporarily against the Expos (who, for purposes of karma, were thankfully now managed by Charlie Fox, with Mauch having been fired after the 1975 season), taking two straight. But then they faced the Pirates once again, albeit this time at the Vet where up to now they had been nearly unbeatable, playing .658 baseball throughout the 1976 season. No matter, they were swept again. After following that with yet another loss to the Cubs, their lead stood at a mere three games with 16 left to play.

Although even a three-game lead should be safe with but 16 games remaining on the schedule, the Phillies certainly did not feel secure. And given that only a dozen years earlier, their predecessors blew a six-and-a-half game lead in only 12, they were justified in their unease. By this point, "1964" was the dirtiest word in the city, although one that residents could not purge from their lips. With each passing loss, the similarities with the earlier collapse were analyzed in the media.[60] Fans who lived through that season recalled it both with horror in its own right as well as with dismay because incredibly, it was occurring all over again. Some even went so far as to blame the schedule maker, contending that the mere fact that such an epic Phillies' collapse was happening twice in their lifetime was proof that the season was far too long. If only the season were three weeks shorter, they believed, the Phillies would have been champions twice over by now.[61] As the panic escalated, the players tried to convince themselves that things were different this time; that this was 1976, not 1964.[62] The ending did not have to be the same. Regardless, the '64 question was put to them after every game, every loss, every botched double play or man left on base.[63] Finally, Bobby Wine, a shortstop on the 1964 club and a coach on the '76 one, asked Ozark for permission to address the club.[64] He pointed out the similarities but then noted the many important differences: the 1976 club was a legitimate contender, the 1964 one was not. The 1976 club was deeper, more talented and deserving of postseason play. The 1964 club played well until their deficiencies caught up with them. Most importantly, the 1976 club still had plenty of tomorrows. The 1964 club ran out of them before they had the chance to turn things around. This was all well and good except for one thing: with each loss, the '76 Phils had one fewer tomorrow than before.

Exorcism

Ultimately, Wine proved to be prophetic. With 16 tomorrows remaining on the schedule and a team that clearly was the most talented in the division ready to play them, the Phils were able to right themselves before it was too late. Proving that, despite their collapse, they deserved the Eastern Division championship, the team won 12 of those final 16 games to pull away from the Pirates in the end, winning a franchise record 101 games and finishing nine games ahead of them. The Pirates, for their part, cooled off, losing eight of their final 15 games, not that it mattered. The Phillies' blazing finish would have assured them the division title regardless of how well Pittsburgh played. On the cold, rainy day in Montreal when the Phillies officially clinched the division, the '64 question was answered once and for all: that was then, this is now (although the broom closet incident that afternoon would muddy the distinction somewhat). In the end, the connection between the two was superficial at best. The team eventually won not merely because another team collapsed but on its own merits. Unlike the 1964 team, the '76 one deserved to win and ultimately did, at least at the divisional level. With the move by Mauch to Minnesota of the American League, where he would remain for the rest of his career and where he could no longer haunt his former team,[65] along with the resurrection of the '76 team during the last few weeks of the season, the ghost of 1964 could be put to rest once and for all. The past was past. It was time to look to the future.

At the conclusion of the '76 season, the team as well as the city's entanglement with Dick Allen would also be resolved. Although he was able to splinter the team along racial lines for a while, the division did not last. After the season, he was released, but a much different reaction accompanied his departure from the city this time around. Rather than being greeted with a firestorm, this time his exit elicited little response at all. He was officially released in November, a move that did not even garner enough interest to merit a story on the front page of the *Inquirer*'s sports section. No analysis, no regrets, no taking sides, no questioning of either the team or the city's role in his treatment and behavior accompanied the short, dry, perfunctory announcement.[66] This time everyone agreed: despite a city and media that bent over backward to accommodate him and give him every benefit of the doubt, his failures were all of his own making.[67]

As for the divergence in reaction between his first and second exits from the city, there are several possible explanations. Perhaps it was a case of the adage: "fool me once shame on you, fool me twice shame on me." Perhaps it was the insight that came with the city witnessing the continuation of Allen's troubles in St. Louis, Los Angeles and Chicago and realizing that despite how it may have appeared at the time, the problems surrounding Allen in Philadelphia during the 1960s had more to do with Allen than the city. And perhaps it was the realization that Allen's statements during his second stint in Philadelphia simply did not jibe with what people now knew to be true with regard to both the team and the city, namely, that, regardless of what went on in the past, the Phillies of 1976 were not the Phillies of old and neither was the city. Although certainly neither was perfect, both were working to get beyond the mind-set of the past, the mind-set that fogged Allen's perception wherever he looked. This time around, rather than stick a dagger into both the team and the city, Allen ultimately succeeded in demonstrating just how out of touch he was. As Allen departed, wondering where he would end up next, Ozark prepared for the 1977 season. Much to his surprise, he not only survived Allen but also emerged from the ordeal more secure in his position than before, triumphing largely on the strength of a rejuvenated team and city that helped carry him through. The past, as it were, truly was past.

9

History's Ultimate Triumph

Black Friday: Ninth Inning

Hanging from a thin, silver chain in Gene Garber's Vet Stadium locker was a medallion that defiantly displayed its years of service.[1] Nicked and bruised, it had seen its share of battles through the years when, time after time, it had shown Garber the light where before, without it, he had only seen darkness. On it was the image of St. Anthony, the patron saint of lost and found. Three years earlier, in the course of fighting his way up to the majors, Garber had lost something he realized he couldn't afford to be without: his slider. Side sessions didn't work, ignoring it didn't work. His slider had disappeared and with it went his chances of staying in the big leagues — a change-up pitcher without a second pitch quickly becomes a pitcher with a very slow fastball. One day, unannounced, St. Anthony arrived in his mail along with crossed fingers and encouraging words from a fan, and Garber figured it was worth a shot. Although not a superstitious man otherwise and, heck, not even a Catholic, he hung him in his locker and hoped for the best. That evening he went out and, without warning, threw the nastiest sliders of his life. And Gene Garber then emerged from the wilderness, finding, first, a secure position in the Phillies bullpen and, then, in 1977, the spotlight as the team's most trustworthy reliever — a man so valued that the team would trade the potential for additional insurance runs in the eighth inning of their most important game in over a quarter century for the security of having him out there to close out the ninth. And St. Anthony had been with him every step of the way.

Top of the Ninth: First Two Outs

On this afternoon, under St. Anthony's watchful eye, Garber appeared to be in secure possession of everything he would need to polish off the Dodgers. Dusty Baker stood in first and Garber started him with a change-up that fooled Baker completely, causing him to lunge desperately at the ball.

He followed that with his reclaimed slider that Baker could manage only to cue foul, dribbling it toward the Phillies dugout on the first base side. After yet another bouncing foul, this one into the Dodgers' executive box on the third base line, an act that seemed to be a plea from Baker to the suits looking on in dismay, saying, "Here, you try it if you think you can do any better," he straightened one out just enough to bounce harmlessly to Schmidt who short-hopped the ball as he charged in from deep third and got him easily at first. One out.

Monday was next in what felt like a perfunctory at-bat; despite his earlier single ripped into right field, he was digging in as the eighth batter faced by a pitcher who had induced the previous seven into innocuous infield bounce outs. There seemed little chance that he would do anything else. After taking the first pitch inside for a ball, he made it eight for eight with a ground ball to second. Before Sizemore's throw even smacked the leather of Hebner's glove for the second out, the postgame scurrying had already begun. As Monday returned to the dugout and Lasorda contemplated his final chance of the game, uniformed security guards rushed from the exits, down the aisles in the 200 level and against the many gates that separated the paying from the paid participants that afternoon. If they possibly could, stadium officials would attempt to prevent a crowd that had asserted itself vocally into the game from surging onto the field once it was over. However, as the guards surveyed the masses that now rose in anticipation of the inevitable, they could only know what the Dodgers knew all day long: that once unleashed, there would be no harnessing them afterward. As Vic Davalillo strode to the plate, a 40-year-old fossil who had been out of baseball for three years before being signed by LA six weeks earlier in a desperate attempt to shore up a weak bench, they surely must have sympathized with Burt Hooton. At their posts, staring down the thrumming city, they had to know that they didn't stand a chance.

The Summer of '77:
Philadelphia Highs and New York Lows

Along with Allen, Cash would also leave the team after the 1976 season. While a blow to the team, his departure signified something larger: the Phillies had finally matured to the point where they no longer needed their spiritual leader. As pitcher Wayne Twitchell put it shortly after his departure: "From the Phillies position maybe you can say Dave served his purpose. Now we can carry on without him."[2] Having been taught so well, the students no longer had much use for the teacher. In fact, Cash had been so effective in getting the organization to think like winners that, ultimately, he succeeded in working himself out of a job; by the end of the 1976 season, the team believed that it could win no matter what, with or without him.[3] Going into 1977, then, the Phillies had demonstrated their maturity in two ways: by surviving Allen and outgrowing Cash. Although it may have been difficult to believe when compared with a team that just won 101 games, the 1977 Phils were, if anything, going to be an even stronger group; solid from top to bottom both in talent and in perspective. It appeared that nothing was going to stop the Phillies this time, especially with the city now firmly behind them and in full bloom, particularly when compared with the continued descent of New York.

The mid–'70s were not kind to Gotham. Teetering on the brink of bankruptcy, victimized by an avalanche of bad press and mocking late night monologues, the city welcomed 1977 not so much for itself as for the simple fact that it could at least turn the page on what had been another rough year. By July of '77, however, a city that believed that it had already hit rock bottom managed to burrow a little deeper into the ground.

On July 13, the city experienced a citywide blackout that, ironically, shone a spotlight on just how desperate its problems had become.[4] The chaos, looting and violence that erupted in response resulted in what became the largest civil disturbance in the nation's history at the time. During the 25 hours of blackout, 1,037 fires erupted, 1,616 stores were either damaged or looted, 3,776 people were arrested and 426 policemen were injured, 18 of them seriously.[5] And the end of the blackout did not even mark the end of the crisis. A few weeks later, on August 3, two bombs exploded in midtown Manhattan office buildings.[6] These were followed by numerous additional bomb threats, requiring the evacuation of over 100,000 people from over a dozen other office buildings. The scope of the lawlessness from the blackout alone dwarfed any previous disturbances in the city's history: a 1964 race riot in Brooklyn and Harlem resulted in a mere 373 arrests, and the rioting that took place after the assassination of the Reverend Dr. Martin Luther King, Jr., led to only 465. A comparison with the last major blackout in the city's history — in 1965 — showed only how much things had apparently deteriorated in the ensuing 12 years: during that blackout, crime actually decreased. Whereas at that time the loss of electricity brought the city together, now it tore it apart. The message this conveyed about the city was, to many people, distressing.

Some pointed their fingers at the city itself, contending that rising unemployment, the loss of city services, low wages and high inflation had combined to create a seething underclass, boiling with resentment and waiting for any opportunity to lash out. The '77 blackout was merely one such opportunity. Others scoffed at the notion that the lawlessness was a form of social protest. In their minds, it was simply an instance of the growing criminal element in the city having, in the dark, their moment in the sun. President Jimmy Carter perhaps came closest to pinpointing the root cause of the uprising in a subsequent radio address when he indirectly chided the spectacular failure of urban renewal in New York by stating that "deteriorating urban areas have been neglected too long."[7] However forthcoming Carter was with his opinions, he was less generous with federal aid: he refused to classify New York City as a disaster area, on the theory that the blackout was not a natural disaster, thereby depriving it of these funds. In doing so, he became the second president to essentially tell the city to drop dead.

Through the many analyses regarding the cause of the events of that summer, Carter's conclusion emerged as the one that everybody could agree on. As such, if it accomplished nothing else, the blackout clearly focused the nation's attention on the failures of the urban renewal efforts of Robert Moses. New York may have been given a glimmering Lincoln Center, numerous luxury apartments, bridges and parkways, but it had been given them at an enormous price, namely, the disaffection of hundreds of thousands of people who had been pushed to the side and ignored in order to make these physical achievements possible. Throughout July and August of 1977, very few people were marveling at the accomplishments of Moses now. Instead, they were frightened about all he had wrought in the process.

By contrast, Philadelphia's 1977 summer demonstrated the other end of the urban spectrum. While chronicling the horror of New York from afar (and comparing the city's residents to earthquake survivors left to fend for themselves),[8] the *Inquirer* followed another emerging story throughout that summer: the final step in the revitalization of Center City Philadelphia. Just a few weeks after New Yorkers tore much of their city to the ground, Philadelphians welcomed to their city the Gallery, the first attempt in the nation's history to bring a suburban mall to an urban downtown location.[9] Moreover, in the Gallery's flagship store, Gimbels, the city was bearing witness to the first new department store built in an eastern U.S. downtown in half a century.[10] In many ways, the Gallery was the culmination of over 30 years of efforts to remake the city. First, local government was overhauled, next came housing, followed by office space, and now, finally, shopping. Through all of this reform and reconstruction, the goal was always the same: to lure people back to the city.

The idea for the Gallery actually emerged, like so many other things, in Ed Bacon's City Planning Commission in 1960.[11] In proposing the redevelopment of the city's deteriorated Market Street East area as a way to link the redeveloped Society Hill area with the Penn Center complex west of City Hall, the CPC first came up with a comprehensive plan in 1958 that focused mainly on transportation improvements: a new bus terminal and enormous parking garage in the area. Two years later, the project was expanded to include a subterranean shopping mall. In 1964, it was expanded again, this time to include an above-ground shopping mall as well. Finally, in 1966, federal funds were secured for the project and the Gallery was on its way. Eventually, most of Market Street East was included in the plan, with a new 20-story office building adjacent to the historic Wanamakers department store being erected as well. In 1974 the official plans for the layout of the Gallery were agreed on and, on August 7, 1977, four days after bombs exploded in Manhattan, the country's grandest and most idealistic urban shopping experiment was officially launched. The symbolic import of the Gallery's opening, coming as it did on the heels of the chaos in New York, could not have been missed by anyone paying attention; by the summer of 1977, while people could not escape New York fast enough, they were seemingly lining up to live, work and shop in Philadelphia.

The Phillies provided yet another vehicle for the city to showcase before the nation. Hopes ran high for the '77 team and, very quickly, those hopes were realized as the team ripped through the National League, dominating it in every possible way. Rival managers could not help but admire their conquerors whenever the Phils tore into their troops, leaving little more than bones behind once they were through with them. Sparky Anderson, manager of the Big Red Machine that itself had its way with the '76 squad, remarked that the '77 team was far superior, noting that from the first player on their roster to the last, these Phils were the best in baseball.[12] Chuck Tanner, who by now was managing the Phils' biggest rivals, the Pirates, concurred, adding that, in his opinion, they were as good as any team he'd ever seen, including the legendary Oakland A's teams of the early '70s, which won three consecutive World Series championships with players such as Reggie Jackson, Catfish Hunter, Rollie Fingers and Vida Blue on the marquee.[13] Although Tanner was often given to hyperbole, here the numbers suggest that this time he was not. At season's end, the Phils would lead the league in batting, slugging and runs scored on offense. On the mound Steve Carlton would win his second Cy Young award, Larry Christenson would win 19 games and the bullpen would lead the league in saves and boast of four relievers with sub 3.00 earned run averages, giving the team, in effect, four closers to choose from on any given day. They hit more home runs at home (101) than any Phillies team before them and set an all-time Major League record for come-from-behind victories with 57.[14] Maddox, Schmidt and Jim Kaat would win Gold Glove awards at season's end and they, along with Bob Boone and Larry Bowa, would form the stingiest defense in all of baseball. In short, the Phils could beat anybody in a myriad of ways and at any juncture of any game. The Big Red Machine may have had more superstars but no team in baseball proved as deep and as versatile as the 1977 Phillies, not that year and, arguably, not ever.

Their bench made them even stronger. Depending on who was in the starting lineup on any given day, Danny Ozark had an embarrassment of riches to choose from when things got tight later on. Of course, Jerry Martin would spell Luzinski in the late innings (entering most games, like clockwork, whenever the Phils were ahead and The Bull had had his presumptive last at-bat for the game[15]), but he was only one of a number of options available to Ozark when considering outfielders alone. Jay Johnstone and Ollie Brown were also on call, depending on whether the situation called for a right-handed or left-handed bat. In the infield, Tommy Hutton (who hit .309 and was one of the best defensive first baseman in baseball) and Davey Johnson (who had previously hit 43 home runs with the 1973 Atlanta Braves and who hit .321 in '77) were the *two* options at first should Ozark decide to give Hebner a rest. And Steve Carlton had his own personal catcher in Tim McCarver, who hit .320 seemingly just for good measure. The team was so good that it did not require the clarity of hindsight to recognize its greatness: as the Phils marched through their opponents, the writers following the team were in agreement that they were watching the best team in Phillies history.[16] Although, given the sorry history of the franchise, this might seem like damning with faint praise, a few years later, after the 1980 incarnation won the World Series, these same writers would nevertheless come to the same conclusion: the 1977 team was flat-out better.[17]

Perhaps not surprisingly, a team this good and this versatile did not lack for confidence and this shared strength gave them a cohesion that the '76 team lacked.[18] This time, there was no Dick Allen to divide them; instead, they were all pulling in the same direction, heading for a summit they all knew they would reach. Because of this, they were able to stay loose, stay relaxed, stay focused; in the end, things were going to go their way no matter what.[19]

Before long, the city began to feed off of this feeling and welcome the team into its heart more so than ever before. Season ticket sales went through the roof, setting an all-time record. Everybody, it seemed, wanted to be part of the new face of their city. In fact, there were many reasons for locals to feel good about their city whenever they opened their sports pages during 1977: the NHL's Flyers, which had won back-to-back Stanley Cups in 1974 and '75, were still a top team, having gone to the finals again in '76 (losing to Montreal) and winners of their division once again in '77; and the NBA's Sixers returned from the depths of a 9-73 season in 1972–73 to the NBA Finals in the Spring of '77, boasting in Julius Erving the unquestioned best basketball player on the planet. Even the NFL's Eagles were ascending at long last, having hired the top college coach in the nation, Dick Vermeil, and heading to respectability for the first time since the early 1960s. In the words of *Inquirer* columnist Bill Lyon in an early April 1977 column: "The City of Losers, at long last, has shed that dreadful image. We are in the midst of full-blooming Jock Renaissance."[20] And the Phillies were leading the way.

As the season progressed, the fans became increasingly willing to demonstrate the power behind their commitment to the Phils, turning the Vet into an ear-splitting horror show for opposing teams game after game. The raucous crowds made players on teams such as Pittsburgh and Cincinnati envious of the reception reserved for their home town heroes. Despite numerous trophies on their teams' mantels, players in those towns remarked that nothing matched the excitement and noise generated at the Vet. Other players were not so much envious as intimidated. The once mighty Reds, who dominated the Phils in Cincinnati, struggled at the Vet, losing four of six games and admitting to falling under the "spell of the Vet."[21] Pirates players complained that they were not able to hear each other out on the field, something they hadn't experienced anywhere else. Therefore, balls that normally would be caught in other places fell in for unexpected hits at the Vet. "The crowd got 'em that run," Dave Parker lamented after letting in an important one in a crucial September loss to the Phils. And, he continued, "[i]t's not the first time it happened. The Phillies really got to be proud of their fans."[22] Left fielder Al Oliver added that "at one stage they roared so loud I thought I was having an inner ear problem again. That crowd could wake up a dead man." Pitchers, stoic and impervious as they often were, were nevertheless occasional fodder for the crowd (typically whenever the scent of blood wafted through the stands), losing concentration at inopportune times, throwing balls in places they never intended, sometimes with disastrous results.[23] As such, it was no surprise that the Phils played .750 baseball at the Vet. By themselves, the 1977 Phillies were very difficult to beat. Together with their fans, they seemed to be practically invincible.

Black Friday: The Ten-Minute Collapse

Before being signed by LA in August, Vic Davalillo hadn't played Major League Baseball since May of 1974 when he was released by the Oakland A's after getting all of four hits during the entire month of April. In the interim, he bounced around the Mexican League, playing most recently for Aguascalientes, on a team as obscure as he had now become. He was a baseball "lifer" as the term implies, however, as despite his advanced age (he was generously listed as 40 years old although few people, including himself, took that number seriously) he was determined to keep playing, suiting up for whatever team in whichever league would have him. In the Mexican League, he regularly took 36 hour bus rides from game to game with no meal breaks to speak of. "You ate where you could," he once said. "Cookies, milk, then back on the bus. The regulars plus the starting pitchers rode the back of the bus. Room to lay down. The other players sat up."[24] As for air conditioning during these marathon trips during the suffocating Mexican summers, it existed if one chose to look at things optimistically. "You opened the windows. That was the air-conditioning."[25] All the while, he worked on what he did best, spraying the ball all over the field, using his legs, which, no matter his age, were still amazingly quick, hoping to return to the Majors where he had had a solid 11-year career (over 1,000 big league hits; a career average around .280) before his release.

As the Dodgers headed toward the postseason, they realized that they contrasted sharply with their likely playoff opponents, the Phillies, in many areas but most notably in their bullpen and woefully short bench. Although they could hope to whitewash their bullpen deficit by pitching some of their starters out of the 'pen during the playoffs, they would need some outside help if they were going to have anyone of talent on their bench at all come the postseason. So they literally began beating the bushes, hoping to scare up whatever they could find. One day, while scouring the statistics in *The Sporting News,* general manager Al Campanis noticed that Davalillo was hitting .392 for Aguascalientes.[26] Figuring that it was worth a shot, he sent scout Charlie Metro south of the border to check him out. In the five games Metro attended, Davalillo went 9 for 20. Even more impressive, however, was his speed. Metro timed him at four seconds flat from batter's box to first, an impressive time for players half his age. All of this was good enough for Metro and Campanis, who were having no luck anywhere else, so they signed him for 62,500 pesos—all of $2,500. Soon, Davalillo was on a flight back to the United States, where he would sit next to Manny Mota (another Latin ballplayer generously listed as 39 years of age) on what now might have been the oldest bench in baseball ("Old?" Tommy Lasorda once said, "Mota was a waiter at the Last Supper and Davalillo cleared the dishes"[27]). Regardless, and for whatever it was worth, the Dodgers at least had some warm bodies with big league experience on their bench.

And now, down to their last out in a game that would likely decide the series, they had no choice but to use it. With catcher Steve Yeager due to bat, Lasorda sent up Davalillo instead, hoping that Davalillo's speed would come in handy given all of the ground balls Garber was inducing. At least with Davalillo at the plate, a bouncer, which by this point was a foregone conclusion, could become interesting if it was bobbled or softly hit or at least not hit directly at one of the Phillies infielders. None of this was cause for much optimism given the circumstances but at least it was something and something was better than the nothing Yeager offered. And so it was Davalillo and not Yeager who strode to the plate with the Veterans Staduim crowd on its feet once again, in anticipation of the final out of the game.

Since being signed by the Dodgers, Davalillo had been a pleasant surprise, hitting .312 in 48 at-bats along with four pinch hits, something he had become proficient at in his later years (in 1970, he set a league record for most pinch hits in a season while playing with St. Louis, although that mark had since been eclipsed). Digging in, surveying the landscape, he was eminently comfortable despite the gravity of the situation. There were two reasons why. First, in Garber, Davalillo faced a pitcher he felt he knew even though he had never faced him before; the Mexican League was full of Gene Garbers. "Lot of pitchers like Garber," he would say after the game, "throw junk balls, sinkers and sliders."[28] Second, in the Phillies' defensive positioning, Davalillo recognized that he was being given a gift. On the right side of the infield, Hebner and Sizemore were playing deep, a strategy that might normally make sense but here it surely did not. No one had hit the ball hard all day off of Garber; playing back here was not only unnecessary but also might make it difficult for either of them to catch up to yet another of the slow bouncers Garber had been throwing all afternoon. Moreover, with the left-handed Davalillo an expert bunter, somebody, at a minimum Hebner, needed to play at least even with the bag in order to discourage such a tactic. After taking a big swing at Garber's first pitch and missing badly on a change-up, Davalillo decided to take what was being given him.[29] On the second pitch, he dragged a perfect bunt past the mound and toward second. Sizemore charged but by the time he caught up with the trickling roller it was too late. He tried to flip the ball with his glove to first but Davalillo easily beat the throw. The Dodgers had life.

With the pitcher Rautzhan due up, Lasorda then went to the second of his "Last Supper" employees. Like Davalillo, Manny Mota was an expert pinch hitter; at the time, his 120 lifetime pinch hits ranked second all time behind Smokey Burgess's 144. More impressively, in an era dominated by pitching, Mota, whose career stretched all the way back to 1962, was at the time one of only five active players with a lifetime average above .300.[30] In his very limited role off of the Dodger bench, he hit .395 during the regular season, managing somehow to stay sharp despite going long stretches without getting to the plate. In justifying his decision to bat arguably his better hitter after Davallilo, when only one out would end the game and presumably the series, Lasorda remarked afterward that "Manny is more of a line-drive hitter. I wanted him hitting behind Vic, hoping he might find a gap and score the run."[31] In fact, his motivation for the move came five days earlier, when Mota homered off of Houston's J.R. Richard during the Dodgers' final game of the season. Lasorda was reminded of it by pitching coach Red Adams during the inning and decided on the spot to organize his pinch hitters in the hope that history might repeat itself. "Red said, 'no reason why he can't do it again,'"[32] Lasorda recalled after the game. In reality, however, there were many reasons. Mota's home run that afternoon was not merely his only of the year and 31st in 15 seasons, it was his first in five years. In fact, in what would be Mota's last decade in the majors (1973–82), that home run off of Richard would be the only one he would hit. Still, left without anything better, he held Mota back and let Davalillo hit in front of him, hoping against hope that Mota would tie the game with one swing of the bat should Davalillo somehow reach base. A few miles north of the stadium, at the New LaFayette Grill in Center City, nearly 100 Phillies fans packed the tiny, 24-seat bar, anxious for the final out to be recorded. As Mota strode to the plate, some grabbed their coats, others made plans for the World Series, others still laughed and joked, watching the old man dig in. "Hurry up," somebody shouted as he waited for the at-bat to begin. "Get it over, Garber."[33]

Garber's first pitch was the one Lasorda was hoping Mota would get. A floater that hung right over the plate, it was the kind of pitch that ends pitchers' afternoons more often than not. This time, however, Mota did not lift the bat off his shoulder and the count was 0–1. Garber then quick-pitched him, feigning his usual 180 degree spin but stopping short after no more than a quarter turn. He then slung his blessed slider toward the plate, catching Mota offguard. This time, Mota swung but it was a bad swing, out of rhythm, big and looping, with little chance of making meaningful contact. He missed the ball completely and it was now 0–2. The Dodgers were down to their final strike.

With the crowd once again on its feet, chanting "Dee-fence, Dee-fence," Garber wound up for what he hoped to be the final time. Going with his slider once again, he placed it perfectly, down and in a location that made it difficult to hit, at least with any authority. Mota, by this point in the count a defensive hitter, went after it anyway, lifting a high fly ball surprisingly deep to left field. As the ball carried and carried, all the way to the warning track, another surprise was in store for the 63,719 in the stands that afternoon. Rampaging back to catch the ball was not Jerry Martin but Greg Luzinski. The absence of the expected public address announcement prior to the inning indicating the rote substitution most likely went unnoticed by many in the stands, as the noise between the bottom of the eighth and top of the ninth was such that one probably would have gone unheard in any event. Instead, such a routine replacement had simply been assumed and the recognition that it had not occurred this time was taking place for most of the crowd right now, with the ball in flight and with the confluence of the ball, the left fielder and the left field wall rapidly approaching. In the dugout,

Martin was watching the play as well, experiencing the helpless feeling one gets after peering a split-second into the future, unable to prevent the inevitable from happening.[34]

Watching the play from nearly 400 feet away, Martin could only despair as he followed the path the Bull took toward the ball. Rather than doing what a more accomplished outfielder like Martin would do in such a situation, that is, spotting the ball, then choosing a spot on the field, then running toward the spot where the ball would most likely land and picking up the ball once again before catching it, Luzinski played the ball as would a Little League outfielder, keeping his eye on the ball the entire time, running blindly and hoping for the best. As he approached the wall with his back facing home plate, he stopped and lunged in the air toward the wall in an attempt to stab at the ball before it rocketed past him. If only he had measured his path beforehand, he would have realized that he had at least two more steps before he ran out of room; he could have reached his spot, pivoted and then caught the ball with his back against the wall. Instead, at the moment of truth, he was hopelessly twisted around and facing the wrong way. To his credit, he was able to snag the ball in his glove momentarily; however, his momentum toward the wall, combined with the force of his arm going forward as he ran toward it, caused his body, arm and glove to smack into the Plexiglas all at once. The ball had no chance. It dislodged on impact, bouncing off of the wall and back into Luzinski's body as he ricocheted off the wall. He managed to corral it before it hit the ground but by this point it was of no matter, the third out of the inning was nullified the moment the ball touched the wall. Davilillo was racing toward third and Mota on his way to second.

At this point, the Phils had reason to be concerned but they were still in control. They still led by two runs and, despite the hits by Davalillo and Mota, were one out away from victory. However, they would begin to lose control even before the completion of the play on Mota's hit, which was scored a double. Luzinski's throw in to Sizemore at second was on target but somehow it skidded right through the second baseman's legs, rolling out into shallow right field. As Sizemore ran back to catch up to it, Davalillo scored and Mota took third. Sizemore's error made it a one-run game with the tying run now only 90 feet away.

As Lopes now strode to the plate, the frenzy on the field matched the intensity of the one in the stands. Everyone was loud, unsettled and anxious. Garber's first pitch would only set everything in motion once again. Lopes jumped on it, keeping with the pattern of grounders that had only been broken by Mota, but breaking another pattern in that, this time, the grounder was a smash. It rocketed toward Schmidt at third who, with Davalillo on third, was playing in, despite the fact that there were two outs (perhaps in an attempt to discourage another drag bunt by a hitter who was adept at such things). Schmidt was unable to get his glove on the ball so it hit his knee instead, bouncing sharply towards shortstop Larry Bowa. Bowa barehanded it on one hop and fired to first, where the stretching Hebner caught it a fraction of a second before Lopes reached the bag. Behind the bag, first base umpire Bruce Froemming scampered into position and played the call precisely the way he had been taught in umpiring school, keeping his eyes on the bag and his ears alert for the sound of the ball popping into the mitt. Only somehow, he called Lopes safe.

Like a petulant child, Hebner, who had initially begun to pump his fist in the air in celebration, balled his fists, stomped up and down, and kicked dirt in the general direction of Froemming as soon as his call registered. Quickly, Sizemore ran over to his first baseman and grabbed him, hoping to prevent a physical confrontation with the umpire. Ozark trudged out of the dugout (even when incensed, Ozark still managed to trudge) to register his protest as well. Hebner continued his rant even as he disengaged from Froemming, yelling at full throat to no one in particular. All of this was to no avail. On an afternoon when the Veterans Stadium crowd had been so loud as to intimidate a pitcher off the mound, so loud that, afterward, catcher Steve Yeager would remark that he was unable to even hear the ball hit his glove despite the fact that his ears were only inches away, the noise drowned out the sound of the ball hitting Hebner's mitt as well, and at the worst possible time.[35] As a result, although Froemming saw Lopes's foot hit the bag, he never heard anything other than the thundering crowd. He could do nothing other than call him safe. At the time of Lopes's hit, the crowd was still buzzing over Mota's hit and it only amped up louder and louder as the ball kicked off of Schmidt's knee, into Bowa's hand and over to Hebner, in anticipation of the final out of the game. By the time the ball smacked into Hebner's mitt, the crowd was in full roar. Meanwhile, a few feet behind Hebner, Froemming was helpless.

On the play, Mota crossed the plate, tying the game at five. Although it seemed as if things could not get any worse for the Phils, they quickly would. With two outs and the Dodgers hoping to get the go-ahead run into scoring position, Garber knew that he had to keep an eye on the swift Lopes, who had led the league in steals in 1975 and '76 and who had 47 during the 1977 season. After getting his signal from Boone, Garber adjusted his grip on the ball. He would start the next hitter, Bill Russell, with St. Anthony's slider, a pitch that Dodger batters had done nothing but beat into the ground all afternoon. First, however, he checked Lopes. Suddenly, he stepped off the mound and, forgetting to first change his grip, fired to Hebner, catching Lopes off guard. Lopes dove back into the bag head first, kicking up a veritable dustbowl as he did so; the play was going to be close. Hebner positioned

Black Friday, ninth inning: Richie Hebner and Ted Sizemore react with incredulity after Lopes is called safe at first (Temple University Libraries, Urban Archives, Philadelphia, PA).

his glove where the ball was headed and then, at the final instant, the ball dove into the ground — a perfect slider — and into the dust and disappeared.[36] When it emerged, it was bouncing far away, in foul territory. Lopes advanced to second, and the stench of fetid inevitability permeated the stadium. Russell singled a few pitches later, scoring Lopes, and the Dodgers had a 6–5 lead.

By the time Reggie Smith came to the plate, the Vet had been completely drained of all the energy that had electrified it all afternoon. Lone claps could be heard above the silence, a few cheers cascaded like tumbleweeds down the aisles and onto the field. Smith grounded out to Garber to finally put an end to the inning but by then the atmosphere in the stadium had become funereal. As Bill Conlin of the *Philadelphia Daily News* would write the following morning, "[d]eath had come to the executioners. The Phillies had met the enemy and it was them."[37]

Aftermath

After the game, when asked why he left Luzinski in the game for the ninth inning, Ozark replied: "He's the third batter up in the ninth. I wanted him in there in case the game was tied."[38] What was left unsaid was that the only way there was even going to be a bottom of the ninth was if a monumental collapse preceded it, the type of collapse that only occurs when those in charge of the chess pieces stop thinking, stop playing, and leave themselves exposed and vulnerable to the unimaginable. In fact, Ozark proved tragically prophetic: there was a bottom of the ninth after all, although it only occurred after he had done everything in his power to make it so.[39] After Bowa and Schmidt were retired easily, Luzinski stepped up in precisely the situation Ozark somehow conjured up in his imagination when the Phillies took the field for the top of the inning. Here he was, at bat in the bottom of the ninth with the game on the line. However, contrary to Ozark's plan, he would not get a chance to be a hero. Mike Garman, who was now on the mound for the Dodgers, hit him with his first pitch, demonstrating that Ozark's foolishness in keeping him in the game for a possible game changing at-bat in the ninth would not be equaled by LA's decision to give him the opportunity to do so. Instead, they would take their chances with Richie Hebner. Once Luzinski reached first, Ozark poured salt on the city's open wound by replacing him with, at last, Jerry Martin. The few in the crowd with the energy to do so whipped up a sarcastic cheer as Martin ran on to the field, too late to make a difference. The rest just sat on their hands, in stunned silence as the reality of what had occurred in just the last ten minutes sank in. Garman needed all of one pitch to put the city out of its misery; Hebner grounded to Garvey who stamped on the bag as if squashing a cockroach, and the game was over.

At the New LaFayette Grill, the bar cleared out quickly after the top of the ninth and was empty for the bottom of it. "When it happened," a bartender remarked after the game, "it was like a vacuum. I mean nobody stayed. Two minutes and they were gone and this is Friday night. Nobody's here."[40] Almost immediately, questions were raised, questions with an impact that would eventually resonate far beyond the game itself. This was more than simply a bad loss. Bad losses occur regardless of the circumstances; those can be dealt with. Instead, because of the specifics of this particular loss, many of the assumptions people had formed about the revived Phillies and, ultimately, the revitalized city of Philadelphia itself, were thrown into doubt. People were left to wonder how it was that a team that so successfully and publicly disengaged itself from its hard-luck and defeatist past could be taken down once again so easily by negativity and at the worst possible moment.[41] Was it possible that the "Yes We Can" Phillies, who chose to see nothing but the sunshine on a partly cloudy day, were the same Phillies who assumed that only the worst would occur in the top of the ninth inning of the biggest game in over a quarter century? Beyond the slogans and the proud talk of the previous few years, was there really any difference between the 1977 Phillies and the 1964 Phillies other than the fact that what occurred over a two-week span

Phils owner Ruly Carpenter, left, commiserates with Tim McCarver, seated, and Tug McGraw, on floor, in the locker room after the Black Friday defeat (Temple University Libraries, Urban Archives, Philadelphia, PA).

then took all of ten minutes now? Had things changed? Or were there more similarities than many had been led to believe? Rather than becoming a show-case for the "new" Phillies, Black Friday (as it quickly came to be called) wound up "encapsulat[ing] a century of Phillies misery."[42] More than any other single event in Phillies history, Black Friday demonstrated to a stunned city that things existed on a continuum more than anyone had previously assumed. Escape from the past was not as easy as had been thought. History was ever present, hovering over the events of the day, injecting itself into everything it touched. Like a virus, it was in the bloodstream, not to be ignored in the naïve hope that it would simply go away.

Very quickly, the loss that afternoon ran deeper than merely a lost playoff game; instead, it permeated the community.[43] Just as sport has the ability to lift a city up on its shoulders, to make it feel better about itself than perhaps it otherwise should, it can drag it down as well. As he wandered out of the New LaFayette Grill after the game, one fan, a middle-aged city employee who had spent his lifetime working for a city that had taken more than its share of punches and was just starting to deliver some of its own, recognized the connection between the team and the city and the blow the Phils had just delivered to his home town. "It hurt," he said, reflecting upon the collapse. "People have taken to this team very seriously. They have taken great pride in it. It means a lot to a lot of people. Maybe it's our vicarious way of succeeding, through this team.... What happened today was just awful."[44] Even before the Phils had cleared their locker room, the cynicism of the past had returned. The middle-aged man, by now shaking his head slowly in recognition of a shift in perspective, continued: "I think that this is a great Phillies team, but I think there will always be a little doubt now." "Yes We Can" was officially dead.

In Black Friday, Philadelphians were forced to confront the uncomfortable truth that their link to the past was not only unbroken but also unbreakable. Catchy slogans, choosing to see the proverbial glass as half-full only goes so far; at the end of the day, the glass remains half-empty regardless. With that recognition, a familiar sense of futility began to settle in, initially, merely as things pertained to the Phillies but, later on, with regard to the city overall. Baseball-wise, many fans simply disengaged from the team after that loss, unwilling to once again stick their necks out for a franchise that was so proficient in seeing to it that they would be cut off.[45] Beyond the negativity that permeated Ozark's decision to keep Luzinski in the game, the events that followed that decision in rapid succession — the skipped throw through Sizemore's legs, the blown call at first, Garber's plunging slider to Hebner — only crystallized the suspicion that despite the giddiness of the previous few years, the Phils were, above all, a cursed franchise. Despite their talent, the 1977 Phils were unable to outrun the legacy of all those teams that came before them. What was worse was the recognition that if this group could not, then nobody could. Over time, and on a larger scale, the prevailing mood of the city would change as well. Only two years later, despite recognizing the strides made by the city since World War II, sociologist E. Digby Baltzell, famously classified Philadelphia as a city comprised of "detractors and losers."[46] The intervening two years would be anything but kind to the city and its reputation.

More immediately, however, the effects of Black Friday were on full display the very next night. In game four, a game played in a constant downpour, the Phillies were "glassy-eyed," walking around in a manner that called to mind someone who had "just been informed they were suffering from a terminal illness."[47] For a time, the fans tried to ratchet up the excitement much as they did on Black Friday, hoping to shake Dodgers pitcher Tommy John much they way they had Burt Hooton, but this time he was ready. Prepared for the onslaught, John simply outwaited the boos and taunts and jeers, stepping off of the mound during a tense moment in, coincidentally, the second inning once again. With the bases loaded and, in yet another coincidence, a Phillies pitcher at the plate — this time Steve Carlton — John missed on his first two pitches. With visions of Hooton and his public dressing down during the Christenson at-bat during Black Friday on its collective mind, the crowd stood and offered a reprisal of the day before. John, however, stepped off the mound in an effort to test its endurance. Eventually, he succeeded in wearing out the fans because on this night, without the unshattered confidence of the previous afternoon, the crowd lost enthusiasm much more quickly. John then struck Carlton out, ending the inning as well as the fans' participation in the evening's affairs. They were not a factor for the remainder of the dreary game. The Dodgers would go on to win the game 4–1 and move on to the World Series. The Phillies had nowhere to go but home.

In the end, although the previous few years taught both the Phillies and their fans the power of belief in themselves, in confidence, in optimism, none

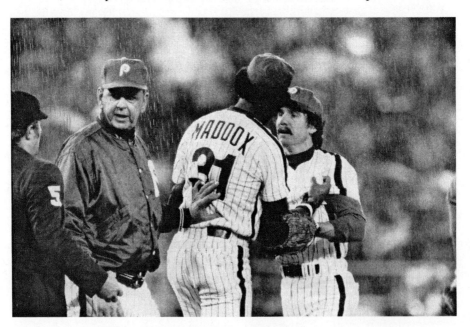

Game four: Ozark and Maddox try to calm an angry Larry Bowa (right) as rain pours down on the game and the Phillies' 1977 season (Temple University Libraries, Urban Archives, Philadelphia, PA).

of this altered the outcome of events. Ultimately, "Yes We Can" didn't matter. The Phils believed that they could not lose at home, believed that they were the most talented team in baseball, believed that they were destined for greatness, yet they still lost.[48] The fans too believed in their collective power to alter the current of history; yet, the team not only came up short on Black Friday, the very next night they were visibly shone up by a pitcher who managed to quell them simply by stepping off of the pitcher's mound. On Black Friday, a lethal mix of the old with the new came together to doom Philadelphia. New-era overconfidence combined with a dash of old-time negativity at the most combustible moment possible to cause the Phillies' season to explode, leaving the city wondering what, if anything, the previous few years were all about.

The sense of failure, the sense of doom, the sense that things were closer to an end than to a beginning, was inescapable. After game four, the front office held a cocktail party to celebrate a season, which, despite the playoff loss, was historic in many aspects. However, the drinks and hors d'oeuvres that were set out were packed away a short time later; nobody showed up for the party.[49] Instead, many players preferred to replay the events of Black Friday in their heads, trying to make sense of what happened. Gene Garber tried several times, without success, to put the inning into words to Ozark in the locker room after game four before giving up and heading home for the winter.[50] Other players quietly packed their belongings away and dispersed once and for all. Rather than relive the good moments together, they chose to rehash the torment on their own, in what would be, in the words of *Inquirer* columnist Bruce Keidan, "the winter of their discontent."[51]

As the weather turned cold, Philadelphia watched as others moved on. Burt Hooton's next start would be in game two of the World Series against the Yankees at Yankee Stadium, where he dominated them, striking out eight while walking only one in a 6–1 victory. Although the Yankees tried to force a repeat of Hooton's Black Friday experience by taking an inordinate number of pitches early in the game in the hope of unnerving him once again through the possibility of a bad call (in fact, six of his strikeouts occurred in the first three innings when the Yanks were exceedingly patient), this time he, like John before him, was ready.[52] Claiming that he had "re-learned" how to keep his composure, Hooton added that "[a]fter the Vet, anything had to be a piece of cake."[53] In Philadelphia, however, things did not move forward quite as smoothly after the game.

Just as the repudiation and ultimate failure of Nicholas Biddle's Second National Bank would shake the city's confidence and cause it to lose much of its swagger, so too would the Black Friday defeat portend, at least in retrospect, the start of a descent. Philadelphia was a city historically comfortable with an attitude of negativity and cynicism, and not much was needed to push it back in this direction once again, despite the strides made over the previous years. In some respects, things simply came to light after Black Friday that were hidden beforehand while in others, a new gloss was provided to events that previously had been seen through what now were considered rose-colored glasses. In either case, in the months following the game, a string of events would take place in the city that, when combined with the accumulating snowball of episodes that had already occurred over the previous few years but which, at the time, were not considered particularly telling as to the state of the city, would cause Delaware Valley residents to see Philadelphia in a different, harsher, light. To be sure, there would still be strong support for both the Phillies as well as the city after that game but the wide-eyed optimism of the previous few years was gone; in the glare of this bright, unsympathetic light, the enthusiastic cheerleading that went on before would be seen as childish and naïve.

As with so many things, the Phillies would feel the wrath of this collective change of temperament first. On opening day 1978, the two-time defending National League Eastern Division champions were greeted by the Veterans Stadium crowd with extended boos before the first pitch of the season was even thrown; the doubt that crept back in during Black Friday was now firmly entrenched within the city's collective consciousness once again.[54] The thunderous ovations, the roaring crowds of 1977 were gone, tempered by the melancholy realization that failure was, if not imminent, eventual and unavoidable. In this act, one that would set the tone for the 1978 season as well as the seasons that would follow it, the Phillies' return to their role as the "other" was confirmed. No longer part of the collective "us"— a group that would soon likewise splinter once again between city dwellers and suburbanites just as it had during the 1950s— they had become one of "them." Like the Sixers, who also crushed the spirit of the city by losing the 1977 NBA finals to the Portland Trailblazers after seemingly taking control of the series,[55] "they" owed "us" one.[56]

10

Results, Repercussions and Reassessments

The opening day boos were merely one indication of things to come for the Phillies of the late 1970s. Before the first pitch of the season, it was clear that the unity, the cohesion, the warmth of 1977 was a thing of the past. In spring training, the tight locker room was torn apart, literally as well as figuratively, by Greg Luzinski who became enraged when forced by team officials to travel to the Dominican Republic for a series of meaningless exhibition games. Making matters worse, Steve Carlton, Ted Sizemore and reserve infielder Jose Cardenal were permitted to stay back in Florida. In full view of his teammates—and, in fact, egged on by some of them — the Bull smashed Carlton's nameplate with the lead baseball Carlton used as a conditioning device, denting his locker. Next, he proceeded to smash the three players' helmets to pieces, toss their jerseys into the shower, pile garbage cans and mounds of towels on top of them and then douse them in water along with the equipment man's console radio.[1] The Bull's mood remained grim throughout the 1978 season. Even after this incident passed, he was provided with daily reminders of his Black Friday failure; Ozark, now with an itchy trigger finger and to the Bull's visible agitation, pulled him routinely in the seventh inning or even earlier, regardless of whether the outcome of the game was in doubt and despite the fact that he was likely to come to the plate once more in the late innings.[2] For Ozark, as well as Luzinski, there would be no getting over the fateful ninth inning of the previous October.

Schmidt, too, would have his problems in 1978. From the outset, his offensive disappearance against the Dodgers grated many fans, who in any event interpreted his relaxed affect as one of simply not caring.[3] As the season progressed the booing got worse, with every strikeout vivid proof of his worthlessness. Schmidt and his demons carried each other into a valley so dark and deep that they would not be able to escape it all year; he would hit only 21 home runs and drive in all of 78 runs in what would turn out to be the least productive season of his career, other than his rookie year. By season's end, Schmidt would admit publicly what many had assumed for a long while: that he preferred to play on the road, away from the Philadelphia fans who needled him unrelentingly, hacking away at his confidence until there was nothing left.[4]

Despite the tenor at the Vet, the Phils managed to win their third consecutive division title in 1978. This time, however, unlike in 1977, there was a feeling that they had done so on their own, despite the fans rather than because of them. During the 1978 League Championship Series, once again against the Dodgers, the Phils heard it from their fans throughout the first two games of the series, both of which they lost. Boos thundered down on them as they left the field for what would turn out to be the final time of the season, after losing game two of the series. Afterward, the players' frustration with their fans was obvious. "For the city to get down on us ... I dunno," said pitcher Dick Ruthven. "They can get down on us if they want to. They can even come to the conclusion we choked. I think that's wrong."[5] *Inquirer* sports editor Frank Dolson came the closest to summing up the rift between the city and the Phils during the 1978 season when he wrote during the playoff series: "There were those huge, red banners strung up outside City Hall this week. 'Philadelphia Salutes the Phillies,' they said. I wonder how many people looked up at those words ... and muttered something under their breath, or saluted this town's baseball team with a Bronx cheer or a good, old-fashioned Philadelphia jeer."[6] That quickly, after all that was seemingly accomplished during the "Yes We Can" era, the anger had returned. And with a vengeance.

As the tension increased, the hostility spilled over from all sides. With the city no longer as supportive of the team as it had been, stories more critical of the Phillies began to appear with increasingly regularity in the city's newspapers. Unable to confront the fans who remained physically apart from them, confined as they were in the stands or in their living rooms, players and team officials began to lash out at the media instead, the people who confronted them in their locker room after every game, demanding comment on the issues their readers were most concerned about. Determined to kill the messengers, some players became confrontational with the media to an unprecedented degree. Soon, an adversarial relationship developed between the team and the media that mimicked the one that now existed between the team and the city. In August, Larry Bowa and a writer got into a skirmish that resulted, the writer alleged, in Bowa's hitting him in the face.[7] Very quickly thereafter, and without bothering to learn any of the facts behind the allegation, the battle lines were drawn with many members of the media lined up behind the writer while the Phillies lined up behind Bowa.[8] Ruly

Carpenter even got into the fray himself. He blamed it all on the media for instigating things by routinely blowing events "out of proportion."[9]

Even when they weren't physically attacking each other, the team and the media went for the kill on a daily basis in other ways. As Schmidt would later describe the local press corps, "Philadelphia is the only city where you can experience the thrill of victory and the agony of reading about it the next day."[10] After the Bowa incident, many members of the team stopped talking to the media altogether.[11] In the opinion of many veteran Phillies beat writers, the 1978 team was the most uncooperative they had ever covered up to that point.[12] However, things would only get worse.

In 1979, the anger, the animosity, the sheer nastiness, increased despite the addition of Pete Rose to the team. Once again, the boos commenced even before the first pitch of the season was thrown and, when the team fell out of the pennant race due to a rash of injuries, grew even louder and more constant. By July, with the Phils in fifth place, some fans were coming to the Vet for the sole purpose of booing them from the moment they took the field to the moment they trudged off of it.[13] Worse, as the team fell off the chase, the atmosphere turned dangerous. By now, Luzinski was responding to the boos by doffing his cap to the fans and waving his arms in mock appreciation; objects such as batteries were being hurled onto the field on occasion. Ozark, who by now could rouse the city's anger by simply stepping out of the dugout, even challenged one screaming fan to address him personally and to his face rather than from the comfort of his box seat several yards away.[14]

Each night a baseball game was played at the Vet, the hostility was palpable. The city was out for blood. As Schmidt would describe the atmosphere emanating from the stands a few years later, "No one can imagine the feeling. You feel the hatred. If any one of them had a weapon, I'd be dead."[15] Finally, on the last day of August 1979, the fans registered a kill: Ozark was finally, mercifully fired. The news was received predictably; one Center City bar owner said, "I think there should be 30 minutes of mourning followed by three days of intense drinking."[16] By the end of 1980, with the tables turned and the Phils on top and, for a change, their fans vulnerable, the team would exact its revenge. After clinching the divisional title, the players erupted in a violent locker room celebration, smashing champagne bottles with such force as to cause their teammates to duck in order to avoid the flying shards of glass. Later, outfielder Lonnie Smith climbed atop the lockers in Montreal's Olympic Stadium and led an obscene chant against the fans and the local media. According to Thomas Boswell of the *Washington Post*, "[o]bservers had never seen so much unfocused, intense anger where, presumably, only delight ought to be expected."[17] The sweet harmony of 1977 seemed so long ago and so far away.

The city too, experienced a shift in perception and emotion as the 1970s drew to a close. Part of it stemmed from the utter success of Bacon's safe zone plan; a plan that, if anything, worked too well. Because the spotlight of rehabilitation throughout the 1950s and '60s remained focused on Center City and because of the barriers placed between it and the rest of the city, Philadelphia basked in what was soon revealed to be the artificial glow of reform. In reality, North and West Philadelphia seethed and buckled under the weight of continued neglect and deterioration, and, by the end of the decade, when it was no longer possible to continue to ignore the problems that by now had reached the crisis stage, and when the accumulating weight of other problems afflicting the city had reached the tipping point, the mood of the city as a whole would spike downward for the first time in several years.

The Disappearing Poor

For a time, it was possible for those who did not live in the depressed areas to believe that the problems that plagued other large, northeastern cities such as New York did not exist, at least to the same extent, in Philadelphia. After all, with the concentration of business, culture and entertainment in Center City and the sports complex in South Philadelphia, these people no longer had any reason to travel through North and West Philly. And so these areas fell victim to the maxim of out of sight out of mind. The invisibility of North and West Philadelphia throughout the 1950s and '60s served to disguise the despair and hopelessness of these sections. But the problems did not go away. Instead, they only got worse as they were continually ignored until they finally exploded in the late 1970s.

Just as it had in other cities, urban renewal exacted a harsh, visceral cost to those most directly affected. Black and ethnic Polish, Ukrainian and Italian residents were pushed out of their homes and neighborhoods in order to make room for the affluent white citizens the city was courting and who were counted on to serve as the foundation for the rehabilitation of various parts of the city.[18] Of all these groups, black residents were hit the hardest and in the largest numbers. As a result, in a city that was more integrated than others its size by the early 1950s, and one which was praised as recently as 1954 by the federal Housing and Home Finance Administration as "a city with a distinctly favorable level of readiness for racially unrestricted housing development"[19] and, therefore, one in which integrated, interracial housing could thrive, precisely the opposite occurred over the next two decades as black citizens were repeatedly pushed out of one safe zone neighborhood after another. As the displacement increased, the city was forced to deal with the mounting problem of what to do with the displaced. Soon, the city that prided itself on low-rise housing capitulated to the quick relief offered by high-rise, low-income housing projects.[20] However, unlike the ones being erected amid protest and controversy in New York, the ones in Philadelphia were built in relatively out of the way places—out of the way at least for the affluent whites who did not have to confront them on a daily basis. As a result, at least for a time they went up with far less fanfare and protest as a sizeable segment of the city's population was washed out of the safe zone and relocated to parts of the city that were anonymous and invisible to many.

The effect of urban renewal on large swaths of North and West Philadelphia was devastating. The housing problem, which had spurred the initial interest in urban renewal in the 1930s, only worsened as a result of the urban renewal policies of the 1950s and '60s. Just as they were in New York, ghettos were expanding as more and more poor residents were funneled into areas that had insufficient and substandard housing to begin with.[21] By 1960, according to one study that tracked the relocation moves of people displaced by renewal in Philadelphia between 1955 and 1960, only 10 percent of all displaced people (80 percent of whom were black) were able to find satisfactory replacement housing.[22] Black residents from integrated, established neighborhoods were more often uprooted and left to fend for themselves, often finding shelter only in segregated ghettos, living in substandard housing. Even the high rises, scourge that they were (indeed, all of the public housing projects planned and built between 1956 and 1967 were located in either ghetto or "transitional areas"[23]), were not an option for many of the displaced. Due to the admission standards in place in much of government housing at the time, many people who were otherwise eligible to relocate to this form of public housing were turned away because they were either "single persons or 'unrelated individuals.'"[24] In 1955 alone, 638 out of 888 otherwise qualified applicants were denied public housing for these reasons.

To be sure, the ghettoization of black Philadelphians was not something that evolved without protest. Black community leaders repeatedly criticized the practice throughout the 1960s and denounced the tactic, accusing the city of "warehousing and ghettoizing the black poor."[25] However, city leaders had other things on their minds, namely, the restoration of Society Hill and the Center City business district. To a large degree, these complaints went, if not unheard, unacted upon. Instead, the city went ahead with its safe zone beautification and restoration plan. In 1962, in an act that spoke louder than any official response to the concerns of his black residents, James Tate, on taking office as mayor from Richardson Dilworth, appointed Gustav Amsterdam as chairman of the city's Redevelopment Authority. Amsterdam focused precisely on those areas favored by Dilworth and the Young Turks: Society Hill, Center City and University City (along with the redevelopment of

Temple University).[26] Amsterdam believed that the key to transforming Philadelphia into "a city reborn" lay in the restoration of the areas. The rest of the city was just going to have to be someone else's problem.

The Lessons Learned from Eastwick

Even on those occasions when city officials were paying attention to the plight of their poor, mainly black, residents, the manner in which they did so caused many of these people to question whether those in power who claimed to be acting on their behalf really had their best interests at heart. Nowhere was this more plainly illustrated than in the utopian jewel of the Young Turks' reform crown: the Eastwick renewal and redevelopment project. The suspicions that were raised and the conflicts that ensued through the multidecade development of Eastwick contributed greatly to the feelings that underlay the eventual explosion of racial hostility in the late 1970s.

Before the Young Turks set their sights on it, Eastwick had been a sparsely populated, dilapidated (spotted with "auto junkyards and burning garbage dumps") but integrated section of Philadelphia.[27] Although the northwest portion of Eastwick was largely white, the majority of the section was fully integrated, with 2,188 white families living alongside 1,127 nonwhite families. These families sent their children to integrated schools, called on doctors without regard to race and generally formed a community described, albeit bureaucratically, by one federal housing official as "considerable racial interspersion of residence." In seeking to remake Eastwick as a large-scale, integrated community, the Young Turks would not only tear apart a community that was already integrated but also they would attempt to artificially re-create it on a grand scale. In doing so, they — and, more specifically, the New Eastwick Corporation (NEC), a company formed and charged by the city to develop Eastwick on an integrated basis— would undertake methods that called into question their utopian goals and left many black citizens wondering who in Philadelphia, if anyone, was looking out for them.

The overarching challenge confronting the Young Turks was to ensure integration in the newly built neighborhoods. Although certainly a utopian goal, there were more practical reasons for the need to achieve a racial balance in Eastwick, namely, the profitability of the project depended on it. In order to pay for itself, houses in the area had to sell for at least $10,000 and, at that price, a study conducted by the University of Pennsylvania concluded that there was insufficient demand from black buyers alone to support a project of Eastwick's size. Thus, in order to attract a sufficient number of blue-collar families, Eastwick would have to draw from as large a pool as possible.

If the balance should tip and Eastwick became predominantly nonwhite, the Penn study warned that the project would fail.

With both the practical and the utopian goals in mind, city officials decided that a delicate and, ultimately illegally maintained, racial balance needed to be struck in order to ensure Eastwick's success. They set about achieving this in numerous ways. First, they decided that while they wanted to attract black families, they didn't want to attract too many of them for fear that they would upset the racial balance they were looking for (an NEC official later admitted that the NEC had determined that the black presence in East-wick could not exceed 20 percent "if we are to make this thing a go"). In order to keep the number of black residents within this range, the NEC quickly real-ized that it was going to have to raise the price of the homes to $12,000 in order to reduce the number of black families who could afford to move into the area. When this proved ineffective (indeed, white interest in Eastwick diminished by as much as two-thirds by 1962 when it was learned that East-wick was to be integrated to any degree), the city and NEC became more aggressive in controlling the racial makeup of Eastwick as new homes started to come onto the market. In April 1962, a system of "racial management" was adopted by NEC, with its goal to steer potential black customers away from Eastwick. Pursuant to this plan, potential black buyers were encouraged to consider other new housing developments outside of Eastwick in order to make Eastwick appear less unique and attractive to them. More insidious, however, was the city's agreement to "acquiesce to slightly dilatory tactics in the acceptance of Negro buyers." Initially, this consisted in the NEC's real-tors' asking interested black buyers to hold off on their purchases for one year in order to allow enough white families to move in and so therefore to assure an integrated community. This led the NAACP to file a complaint with the Pennsylvania Human Relations Commission that same month, and as a result, the NEC pronounced that it would abandon its restrictive practices imme-diately. However, rather than doing so, it merely attempted to make its prac-tices more difficult to discern.

With the NAACP now alert to the growing problem in Eastwick, the NEC changed tactics. Now, rather than overtly discussing the racial balance with potential nonwhite buyers, it sought to maintain its preferred racial bal-ance covertly. This time, it made its realtors inaccessible to blacks looking in the area but available to whites. Once potential black buyers were able to locate a realtor, they were given short, unhelpful answers to their questions or told flatly that no homes were available. Potential white buyers, on the other hand, were aggressively pursued by the NEC's realtors and encouraged to purchase homes immediately. These practices were uncovered in 1963 and, once again, the NEC pledged to change. A year later, however, the NEC again admitted that it was still attempting to control the black presence in East-wick. A pattern of behavior was thus established, resulting in repeated protests by civil rights groups, numerous discrimination complaints filed against the NEC and a pall of mistrust that fell over the entire project as well as the city's handling of it. By 1970, things had barely improved. A total of 19 discrimination complaints were filed in that year alone.

Ultimately, on its completion several decades later, Eastwick succeeded, at least on the surface, in fulfilling the utopian vision of the Young Turks back in the 1950s. Between 1970 and 1990, Eastwick not only was one of only three sections of Philadelphia to experience population growth, it was also an established, integrated community. By 1975, the black population stood almost exactly at the percentage the NEC had set more than a decade earlier: 20.8 percent. Twenty years later, it remained stable and integrated with the *Philadelphia Daily News* characterizing it as an exception to the segregated nature of the rest of the city. "Color-Blind, and Happy: In Eastwick, Black, White Amity Rules," ran the paper's 1994 headline trumpeting its success.[28]

To the many black citizens who endured the pain that accompanied the clearing and redevelopment of Eastwick from the early 1950s through the early 1970s, however, success was not so glibly assumed. To them, the message of Eastwick was not one of racial harmony but rather one of discrimination — of embracing abstract, utopian ideals over the people who got in the way of them. The Young Turks, who stormed City Hall in the 1940s and early '50s, taking control of it and setting out on their agenda of reform, proved to be, at least to them, no different from the machine Republicans they replaced. Although seemingly acting in their interest, these reform Democrats either engaged in, encouraged, or at least did very little to prevent, the very sort of discrimination that left many black and other poor residents without a voice for so long before they arrived. Despite the integrated community that emerged or perhaps because of it, the Eastwick project vividly demonstrated to many black residents that city government, whether controlled by Republicans or Democrats, was not to be trusted. Their faith in the city's power structure shattered, many would soon look to people and groups outside of the political establishment for support and for solutions to their fears and concerns. Their inclination to do so was heightened after 1972, when whatever remnants of faith in their city leaders that remained after Eastwick were dislodged by James Tate's mayoral successor: Frank Rizzo.

Rizzo Means Business

Idealistic and high-minded as the Young Turks were, when they left power they ceded to their successors a structure of city government and a set of policies that threatened to undermine all they had done to change the mood of the city. In 1962, when Dilworth resigned the mayoralty to launch a failed run for governor, he turned the office over to Tate, who had previously been City Council president and who was described by an *Evening Bulletin* editorial writer as being, in contrast to his predecessor, "old-fashioned and non-elitist, shaped by personal loyalties and deals rather than ideas or ideals."[29] With the change of helmsman, the reform movement, at least so far as the mayor's office was concerned, was over, and the party politics of the machine system now returned. A decade later, this shift would be cemented when Rizzo was elected.

With the safe zone firmly in place and with Philadelphia now more heavily and clearly segregated than ever, Rizzo played upon white fears of crime and violence by pledging to his base (white Philadelphia) that he, the former chief of police, would protect them against any encroaching threat (black Philadelphia). His 1971 mayoral campaign slogan was "Rizzo Means Business" and, in the words of the *Philadelphia Inquirer,* in its summary of the Rizzo years:

> there was never a scintilla of confusion in anybody's mind over just what business he meant to be about. It was the business of safety and security ... White middle class Philadelphia was ... not just a little bit frightened. Rizzo would protect them. He would protect their neighborhoods. And if all that meant that he would keep the blacks in their place, then so be it.[30]

Given the absolute success of Bacon's safe zone plan, the relevant battle lines were now clearly demarcated. Rizzo vowed to uphold these lines along with the multitude of others that now clearly marked the divisions between white and nonwhite Philadelphia.[31]

One of his earliest fights involved his resistance to the proposed construction of a public housing project in the white Whitman Park section of South Philadelphia.[32] Time and again, Rizzo defied the federal government's orders to commence work on the project by blocking any and all progress at the site. In time, the Whitman Park standoff served to symbolize the battle between predominantly black public housing tenants and Rizzo-supported white residents who, with each battle, became more resolute in their defiance of the law and their opposition to enforced racial integration. Finally, in 1976, Rizzo was defeated when a federal court ruled that the city had violated the Fifth, Thirteenth and Fourteenth Amendments to the Constitution by its refusal to build the project. The project was subsequently built and public housing residents moved in, but the damage had already been done. Through the Whitman Park standoff, black Philadelphians received the very clear message that, while Rizzo may in fact be the mayor of Philadelphia, he was most certainly not *their* mayor.

Under Rizzo's watch, the most insidious by-products of machine politics once again became entrenched. Like Tate and unlike Clark and Dilworth, Rizzo was not a visionary; there was no grand plan for the continued development of the city beyond that which was already in place on his arrival. Worse, he ruled in typical city machine style, rewarding friends and punishing enemies.[33] Both of these aspects of his style came to the public's attention in 1973 when it became known that Rizzo had sealed a deal in a hotel men's room by which he agreed to allow the city's Democratic chairman to select the architects to be used in city projects if the chairman would endorse Rizzo's candidate for district attorney. At the same time, Rizzo's secretly commissioned, 33-man special police unit was exposed as an agency used to spy on and harass his political enemies. After steadfastly denying both charges and agreeing to take a polygraph test to clear his name, Rizzo failed the test.[34] Although he still maintained his innocence with regard to the men's room deal, claiming that the police unit was being used to unearth "official corruption," the revelation of the existence of such a police unit could not have been good news either for those who opposed the mayor or for those he simply viewed as obstacles in his way. To all of those on the wrong side of the ledger, although Philadelphia was now technically controlled by Democrats rather than Republicans, there was little discernable difference between the two. During Rizzo's two terms as mayor, the Democratic machine was revved up and operating on all cylinders.

Throughout the 1970s, much of the city continued to deteriorate. However, as was the case during Dilworth and Tate's mayoral terms, because so much of the deterioration occurred beyond the scope of white Philadelphia's vision, much of it went unnoticed. Instead, the larger successes of the city, namely, those that occurred within the safe zone in Center City, were celebrated. And Rizzo garnered more than his share of the credit for the city's renaissance: a December 1977 *Philadelphia Inquirer* op-ed piece concluded that it was only fair to concede to him a place on the congratulatory stage otherwise occupied by Clark and Dilworth.[35] However, as the decade waned, the problems became more and more difficult to ignore. And Rizzo's role in these problems became more apparent as well.

By the fall of 1977, a gathering storm began to accumulate over the city. Its approach became evident only three weeks prior to Black Friday when Rizzo's manipulation of the city's crime statistics throughout the decade was uncovered. In order to make good on his pledge to keep Philadelphians safe, the former police chief vowed to reduce crime in the city. For several years, according to the city's plummeting crime rate, it appeared as if Rizzo had kept his word on this count. However, in late 1977, a secret 1972 pact between then president Richard Nixon and Rizzo was unearthed in which a phony

August 1973: Mayor Frank Rizzo leaves the Bellevue-Stratford hotel after failing his lie detector test (Temple University Libraries, Urban Archives, Philadelphia, PA).

drug-prevention program was exchanged for Rizzo's endorsement of Nixon in the 1972 presidential election.[36] As it would be revealed, Nixon, who desperately sought Rizzo's endorsement in his effort to carry Pennsylvania in the national election, inquired of Rizzo as to what his endorsement would cost. Rizzo responded that he wanted immediate help in lowering the city's crime statistics. A pact therefore was cemented by which, in exchange for Rizzo's endorsement, Nixon designated Philadelphia a pilot city in the White House's "Treatment Alternative to Street Crime" (TASC) program, funneling a substantial sum of discretionary money to the city in order to run a program designed to divert heroin addicts arrested for certain crimes into the TASC treatment program rather than sending them to jail. Through this program, which, in addition, led to the waste of several hundreds of thousands of dollars because it was not properly staffed or executed, scores of crimes were reclassified as drug offenses, thereby lowering the city's crime rate.[37] Satisfied with the deal, Rizzo, technically a Democrat, publicly pledged his support to Nixon in the spring of '72. Two days later, one million dollars of TASC money arrived in Philadelphia. Rizzo was so pleased with the arrangement that he repeated his endorsement several times, calling Nixon "the greatest president in U.S. history" on one occasion. Even after the extent of the fallout from Watergate became known, Rizzo would hedge his enthusiasm for the former president only slightly, calling him thereafter simply "one of the greatest presidents."[38] Through the exposure of the city's TASC program, Philadelphians received yet another glimpse of the backroom deals and fudging of statistics that were occurring in the name of a supposedly reborn city.

Throughout his tenure as mayor, further evidence of his misdeeds came to light on occasion, which, as one piled on top of another, cast an even darker pall over the city by the time he left office in 1979. Quick to ride the coattails of an energized city, Rizzo proudly insisted throughout his mayoral tenure that the economic woes that were stifling other northeastern cities at the time, most notably New York, were absent in his Philadelphia. During his campaign for reelection in 1975, Rizzo trumpeted the fiscal condition of the city, repeating more than once that Philadelphia was "not going to be another New York."[39] A few days after his inauguration, however, Rizzo was forced to admit that things were not as rosy as they seemed. The city was facing a monumental budget deficit that could be addressed only through the same drastic measures—measures such as instituting massive tax hikes, slashing city services and closing a publicly funded hospital—he had assured the electorate would never be needed given the supposed economic stability of the revitalized city.[40] A few years later, as his second term was drawing to a close and his thoughts turned to cementing his legacy, Rizzo bragged that once again, the city was in solid financial shape, that he had helped it to turn the corner and that he was leaving a stabilized city to his mayoral successor. Once that successor, Bill Green, was able to examine the city's financial ledger for himself, however, Philadelphians learned that, once again, they had been hoodwinked. At this point, Philadelphians had no choice but to confront the sobering truth: Philadelphia was in desperate straits. The city's deficit was not, as Rizzo claimed, a manageable $9.8 million but a staggering $72 to $134 million, depending on which projection one wanted to believe.[41] Moreover, this estimate did not even include the city's crumbling school system, which was, in Green's words, in "worse than its usual shape," and which would tack an additional $25 million onto the deficit in its current form, not including the expected and necessary teacher salary raises that were no doubt forthcoming upon the expiration of their union contract in the fall of 1980.[42] Just as in the 1940s when the city could not afford to change the light bulbs on city streets, the Philadelphia of the late '70s and early '80s seemingly could not provide many basic civic services to its residents. The past, as Faulkner once wrote, was not dead after all. It was, as he alleged and to the great shock of many Philadelphians who believed in Rizzo's reassurances despite being burned before, not even past.

Beyond the numbing statistics, which, as they were revealed number by number during the late 1970s led Philadelphians to soberly reassess the state of their city, the quirky persona of their leader further eroded much of the good feeling that had enveloped the region during the early and middle years of the decade. Rizzo was clearly a man of some of the people but not all. Worse, even to many of those who worshipped or even tolerated him, he began to reveal himself as a paranoid figure who was damaging to the national image of a city that had worked so hard to overcome the negative one it had become branded with for so long. The polygraph fiasco and the discovery of Rizzo's secret police squad, which made headlines across the nation in 1973, were early indicators of what was to come in much larger doses later on. Another came during the preparation of what should by all rights have been Philadelphia's finest hour, the celebration of the nation's 1976 bicentennial.

With the eyes of not only the nation but also the world focused on the city, the opportunity presented itself to catapult Philadelphia once again, much as it had been 200 years earlier, into the international spotlight. An estimated 20 to 40 million people were predicted to make pilgrimages to the city during the bicentennial year, all of whom would come to view not only the historic landmarks of Independence Hall and the Liberty Bell but also a revitalized, modern Philadelphia. They would come to sample the distinctly Philadelphia cuisine offered in the many flowerpot restaurants that had sprouted up across the city, to tour Society Hill, to experience the revitalized Center City business district and to enjoy the nightlife in a city that no longer closed at 5 P.M. and on weekends. Rizzo, however, saw not opportunity but a threat to the constituents to whom he pledged security and safety. He saw chaos, he saw looting, he saw crime. In order to combat these potentialities, regardless of how remote they may have been, he called out the National Guard, requesting 15,000 federal troops to police the city on the day that could have been the biggest day in the city's modern history: July 4, 1976.[43] Although the nation's weakening economy surely played a role in the diminished numbers who eventually showed up (7 to 8 million), Rizzo's tough talk — his predictions of violence and mayhem in his city — also undoubtedly helped to keep many potential visitors away.

Later, in December 1977, Rizzo's paranoia reared its head once again when he alleged that there was a far-ranging federal, "liberal-leftist conspiracy" to frame the Philadelphia police and "embarrass" his city.[44] In response to growing criticism of the tactics used by Rizzo's police force, the Department of Justice (DOJ) considered stepping into the fray in order to rein in rogue police conduct and protect the civil rights of victims— the overwhelming number of whom were black — who were at the mercy of such tactics and without recourse to fighting them at the local level. Investigations into such allegations revealed a systematic practice of coerced confessions, leaders within the police department routinely denying certain individuals (again, many of them black) their civil and constitutional rights and substantial evidence of racial discrimination in police tactics.[45] Those victims who were bold enough to complain about their treatment at the hands of the police were unlikely to have their complaints heard; the DOJ's investigation revealed that, in 1976 alone, only one out of 69 complainants alleging police brutality was ever asked to testify in any police proceeding stemming from these allegations. As a result, the DOJ reported that many people in certain communities reported a "sense of helplessness" when it came to citizen-police relationships. Rizzo, however, saw not the failings of his police department — failings some alleged were caused by his encouragement and leadership — but a plot carefully orchestrated against him. In a bizarre press conference in December 1977, Rizzo attempted to outline the plot to the media, hoping to demonstrate instances wherein federal officials had attempted to "manufacture evidence" and "frame the police."[46] The result, when combined with the bicentennial fiasco of the previous year, was yet another public black eye for the city courtesy of Rizzo; the unveiling of a conspiracy theorist of the first order with, at least in the eyes of some, a disturbing worldview.

The upshot of both Rizzo's press conference and the publication in the *Inquirer* of the actual text of the DOJ's letter outlining its findings and recommendations which so enraged the mayor, proved more significant. From now on, the racial unease that for so long had been pushed aside and driven underground within the city would be out in the open. No one could deny any longer that Philadelphia was somehow inherently different from the New York that exploded during its blackout the previous July. Instead, it appeared now that Philadelphia had just been luckier than its neighbor to the north for the simple reason that, to date, its lights had remained on. Philadelphia, like so many other large northeastern cities, had significant racial problems and it now had no other choice but to confront them and deal with them.

By now, many black residents had completely lost faith in the ability of the city's power structure to help them. Much as in New York, urban renewal was now a dirty word in many predominantly black and Hispanic neighborhoods, where some residents now committed themselves to preventing the gentrification of their neighborhoods, which they knew would lead to their eventual eviction from them. In April 1977, a Puerto Rican resident of a Spring Garden neighborhood in the early throes of renewal firebombed a white neighbor's house that was in the process of being rehabilitated. "This isn't just a vandal fire or a prank," said a fire marshal investigating the incident. "Some people want this to be a new Society Hill and they are meeting with resistance."[47] The plans for urban renewal duplicated the feelings of helplessness many of these citizens felt with regard to the police. The city, they believed, considered them to be obstacles to overcome or to be pushed aside rather than residents whose needs deserved an ear. If the city wasn't going to help them, they would have no choice but to seek out other, alternative avenues to secure power and a voice. Some people, such as the Spring Garden resident, turned inward, vowing to fight the city on their own. Other residents teamed up with neighbors to resist demolition of any kind within their neighborhood, regardless of the stated cause, believing instead that the city's underlying motive was to clear the land for new housing geared toward the white middle class.[48] Tensions in gentrifying neighborhoods grew as black and Hispanic residents became wary of their new, white neighbors, seeing in them visible signs that soon they would be forced out of their homes.[49] Over time, more and more long-time neighborhood residents became determined to dig in their heels, refusing to leave their homes, distrustful of the city government's intent as well as what it could offer them as an alternative. Out of this environment, with a large swath of the city's population overcome with feelings of abandonment and mistrust, left to their own devices to fend for themselves, sprang MOVE.

MOVE

MOVE was the creation of one man, Vincent Lopez Leaphart, a black man with a 79 IQ who had been classified as a child as "orthogenetically backward"— mildly retarded.[50] After enrolling in a school for students with learning disabilities in 1946 at age 15, he dropped out after only one year, was arrested for armed robbery and automobile theft, and then later was drafted into the army, serving two years in Korea. Upon his return, he married, found work arranging shop displays and fancied himself an "interior designer." By

1965, his wife had become involved in a religious sect, the "Kingdom of Yahweh" that preached the "principles of natural law."[51] Two years later, he separated from his wife and, a few years after that, moved into the Powelton Village section of West Philadelphia, a neighborhood that bordered Drexel University and the University of Pennsylvania, the hubs of Bacon's envisioned intellectual metropolis, "University City." At the time, University City was in the throes of renewal: entire blocks were being razed, decaying houses were being torn down and hippies; young professionals and academics were moving in, living alongside and threatening to squeeze out the predominantly black residents who had lived in the area for several years beforehand.

Although he could barely read or write, Leaphart could talk, and he was not shy about rhapsodizing over his "philosophy," some of which he gleaned from his wife's "back to nature" experience with the Kingdom of Yahweh, some of which he developed through a succession of conversations he engaged in with the local intelligentsia, whom he chatted up while earning money as a neighborhood handyman and dog walker. Eventually, one of these new-found friends, a young, white middle-class idealist who had just received his master's degree in social work at Penn and who himself was fond of engaging in philosophical dialogues, offered to assist him in putting his thoughts down on paper. When they were through, they had produced a 300-page manifesto, which would later be known as the "Teachings of John Africa" (as he now preferred to be called). Soon, the American Christian Movement for Life, or MOVE, as it came to be called, was born.

Despite his limited intellectual capacities, Leaphart's sermons, which he now frequently gave, resonated with many of his Powelton Village neighbors. He focused in his talks on what many of his growing army of followers called "the absolute truth;" giving voice to what he believed to be the rationale behind the deplorable treatment of certain segments of society by those in power. As one follower described it, "we were being taught about the system, the corruption of this system, the corruption in politics. We were being taught family. We were being taught health. We were being taught how to sustain ourselves physically, mentally, but mainly it was just the absolute truth."[52] To those pushed aside in the name of the development of Center City, Society Hill, University City and elsewhere, to those harassed and beaten by the police, to those whose voices were silenced within the confines of City Hall, his words resonated. Soon, MOVE acted as a de facto government within the Powelton Village neighborhood, providing services to assist citizens ignored by those officially in charge. It helped alcoholics and drug addicts deal with and overcome their addictions and straighten out their lives, and it attempted to curb gang violence. By following the "Teachings of John Africa," community problems were addressed and resolved. MOVE provided a structure, as skewed as it would turn out to be, where previously there had been none.

Leaphart, as well as his growing band of followers, offered explanations for the ills plaguing many in his Powelton Village neighborhood. According to Leaphart, "the hierarchy" was responsible for everything that was wrong with society: drugs, dirty water, dirty air, the corruption of industry. Although, according to MOVE, everyone was ultimately victimized by the system, black people bore the brunt of it as they were the most oppressed. Again, to those on the wrong side of the ledger in Rizzo's Philadelphia, these explanations were not so easily dismissed. One such person was Ramona Johnson. Johnson, who was working as a paralegal and planning to attend Temple Law School, kept one eye on MOVE while the other was attending to business in Rizzo's City Hall. While performing her duties there, she saw evidence of what MOVE was preaching: a predominantly white system processing a predominantly black population of criminal defendants; white cops intimidating witnesses; courtrooms being run like sideshows rather than serious, impartial, legal proceedings; evidence ignored; delays abundant; jails filling up with young black men. Soon, she came to believe that MOVE was right: that the city's government was not her government and that by going to law school, she was only submitting to a system that, at its core, was designed to keep her down, keep her in her place. What was needed, she believed, was what MOVE had been advocating, namely, people willing to oppose the system, people willing to bring it down instead. Soon she abandoned her plans to attend Temple, changed her name to Ramona Africa and became a full-fledged member of MOVE.[53]

As the '70s progressed, despite its increasingly bizarre behavior, MOVE attracted a growing band of citizens who, although not affiliated with it such as Ramona Africa (and who, on a point-by-point basis, would probably disagree with most if not all of the "Teachings of John Africa"), at least sympathized with it as a counterpoint to the increasing menace of Rizzo's Philadelphia. Watching on television or reading in the newspapers, these people witnessed the police beatings of MOVE members, the arrests and trials of various MOVE members that seemed to come one right after another, the general harassment of a group that, over time, began to appear out of all proportion to whatever damage they had done. In March of '76, yet another confrontation ensued, one in which an infant living within the MOVE compound was killed. The confrontation began when a bus pulled up to MOVE headquarters to drop off seven MOVE members who had just been released from jail. A very long and very noisy celebration followed, to which the Philadelphia police were ultimately summoned. After yelling at the police to "leave us the fuck alone," MOVE members began hurling bricks at the police. The police retaliated and a bloody battle was underway. Neighbors watched in horror as the police beat whomever they could get their hands on. "It was the worst thing I ever saw," said one neighbor. "I think they [the police] were really provoked, but I think they were overreacting. I've never seen such brutality."[54] Through its response to MOVE, the city unwittingly bestowed legitimacy on what was, at its core, an illegitimate group.

Soon, MOVE became a springboard for discussion of the larger racial issues present in the city. In the relationship between MOVE and the city, people began to see a microcosm of the city's overall treatment of blacks and other minorities. In MOVE, the city confronted a predominantly black group that it could not shut away and relocate out of view of white Philadelphia as MOVE's central mission was to be heard and confronted. Whatever racial issues that had been present but suppressed for the past several decades were now debated almost daily. As time went on, more and more people were willing to look beyond the absurdities of MOVE itself and focus on its symbolic role instead. And what they saw jarred them, causing them to see their city much differently from how they had previously seen it.

Rizzo and his police force did themselves no favors time and time again. After the March confrontation, the police alleged that MOVE was attempting to either make or acquire an atomic bomb, and the department requested the assistance of a National Guard atomic weapons specialist. The specialist refused to consider this ridiculous request and Delaware Valley residents were given yet another glimpse into the workings of the Philadelphia government. To many, this incident confirmed their suspicion that, although MOVE might be unreasonable and far fetched in its actions, the Philadelphia police were no different.

As the decade waned, MOVE may have been unsuccessful in changing many outsiders' opinion of itself but it was more successful in changing many of these same people's opinion of a city they had just started to feel so good about. As both MOVE and the city dug in their heels, tensions increased and the inevitability of yet another bloody clash was a given. By the late '70s, MOVE turned increasingly violent, claiming that "evil justifies evil." In its view, "if Rizzo is a racist, then it's okay for MOVE to break its commitments. If our legal system treats black people unfairly, then it's okay for MOVE to do whatever it wants."[55] In August 1978, another showdown ensued. In full view of the newspaper and television stations that had assembled outside of the MOVE compound in anticipation of the battle, police officers assembled in full riot gear. They exchanged bullets with MOVE members. This time, a police officer was killed and a MOVE member was dragged to the ground and beaten repeatedly by several officers as cameras clicked away. Afterward, with the media's attention not only on the downed officer but the beaten MOVE

A crying child stands in front of the MOVE compound during the August 1978 shootout in Powelton Village as a police sharpshooter takes aim. Although the child was eventually rescued unharmed, photographs such as this caused many people to see the MOVE issue within a broader social context (Temple University Libraries, Urban Archives, Philadelphia, PA).

member, Rizzo blamed the media for its misdirected focus. To many in the Delaware Valley, however, the confrontation only highlighted what they were now beginning to believe: that when it came to the city versus MOVE, it was becoming increasingly more difficult to tell the good guys from the bad ones.

This dilemma was highlighted even more plainly a few years later, when, in 1981, a black activist, Mumia Abu-Jamal, was arrested in the shooting death of a Philadelphia police officer. Despite overwhelming evidence indicating that Abu-Jamal did indeed pull the trigger, many within the city and throughout the world were willing to give credence to Abu-Jamal's defense that his was just another case of the Philadelphia police intimidating and framing an innocent black citizen.[56] The lessons of MOVE had indeed resonated and far beyond Powelton Village at that. In just a few years, the city's image had undergone a transformation both nationally and internationally from a progressive, forward-thinking metropolis to a racially hostile backwater awash in corruption. By 1981, it was clear that the anger and rage that had spilled

Nine days after the Powelton Village shootout, a demonstration takes place outside of City Hall. Police look on in riot gear (Temple University Libraries, Urban
Archives, Philadelphia, PA).

over in New York back in July of 1977 was just as present in Philadelphia. The
only difference between the two cities was that in Philadelphia, the emotions
bubbled up in a steady stream over time whereas, in New York, they exploded
all in a matter of 25 hours. If that fact made Philadelphia any better than New
York, fewer and fewer Philadelphians were now willing to say so than they
were just a few years earlier.

A Reassessment of Bacon's Vision

Beyond the enveloping racial tension within the city, the late 1970s and
early 1980s also highlighted the shortcomings of Bacon's grand plan to remake
the city. Although never one to run from criticism, Bacon received an increasingly larger share of it as the '70s waned. Even though he had been out of
office for nearly a decade by 1979, he had served as the face of the city's renewal
and rehabilitation efforts for decades and the results of his handiwork and
influence were everywhere, encased in brick and steel and concrete and
asphalt. In pointing out all that was right with the city, people couldn't help
but talk about Bacon. Conversely, when the conversation turned negative, as

it frequently did during the closing days of the decade, Bacon's name was frequently uttered as well.

In Center City, despite high hopes for the Gallery, the realities of a downtown shopping complex in a large northeastern city in the midst of an economic crisis soon became apparent. Even before its second birthday in 1979, warning signs were everywhere. Revenue from the mall's 125 stores failed to keep up with inflation and the possibility of tenants either relocating to the suburbs or shuttering their businesses altogether was real.[57] Despite these ominous signs, plans for an expansion of the Gallery proceeded. However, by 1984 the recently christened Gallery II, which, together with the original Gallery formed the largest urban mall in the nation, was declared a colossal bust.[58] The people behind the concept and construction of the new building made sure to include in it everything anyone could want from a mall with one exception: "they forgot the customers," according to one suffering merchant.[59] By this point, the original Gallery had rebounded to some degree, with revenue increasing to a level above the national mall average, but this success rang hollow given the desperate straits of the new addition. In order to entice merchants to stay, rents were lowered, further reducing the revenue stream for the struggling building.

Aesthetically speaking, both the Gallery and Gallery II — the latter the brainchild of developer Willard Rouse — were magnificent buildings and, along with Society Hill, Penn Center and the several other office buildings that went up during the decade, embodied Bacon's quest to remake the look of the city. To stroll through Center City in 1979 was to experience architecture, sculpture and physical beauty on a scale never before seen in the city. The new structures stood in sharp contrast to the aura of decay that permeated the area only a few decades earlier, before Bacon assumed control of the City Planning Commission. Yet, despite its updated appearance nothing could stop the stream of people and jobs fleeing the city, leaving it in desperate shape. During the '70s, Philadelphia lost 140,000 jobs and nearly 14 percent of its population, the steepest decline in the city's history.[60] Jane Jacobs's insistence, in her *Death and Life of Great American Cities* nearly two decades earlier, that the revival of cities depended on functionality rather than aesthetics and her admonition about Bacon's devotion to the physical rather than the interpersonal in his approach to development now appeared prescient. "A city cannot be a work of art," she wrote.[61] Bacon's Philadelphia was unquestionably beautiful, but to what end?

Beyond Center City, Bacon's vision did not even have aesthetics in its favor. By late 1978, University City had seen a plethora of buildings come down but very few go up in their stead. Instead of an intellectual mecca, the area was known more for the "desert-like vacant lots" that replaced the row homes that lined the streets for years. An *Inquirer* report on the area at the time painted a grim picture:

> University City lacks any sense of place. Virtually all the commercial areas have been torn down and replaced by fast-food establishments, movie theaters and shops that cater to students. For a major university community, it is, as many of its supporters will agree, barren.[62]

About the only thing the area had produced within the last decade was MOVE and neither Bacon nor anybody currently in power within the city were about to stand up and take credit for that.

The Death of Philadelphia's Baseball and Urban Renaissance

If the winds regarding the popular perception of the state of the city began to shift during the late 1970s, at the confluence of Rizzo's paranoid rant, Black Friday, and the growing realization that things were not quite what they had seemed, they blew with their greatest force on May 13, 1985, the day Mayor W. Wilson Goode and the Philadelphia police engaged in what would become the ultimate showdown with MOVE, which by now had relocated to Osage Avenue in West Philadelphia. On that day, city officials authorized the bombing of MOVE headquarters and then let the fire rage, hoping to smoke the stubborn MOVE members out of their compound. By the time the fire department was permitted to step in and contain the fire it was out of control. One after another, well-kept row homes— 61 in all, occupied by black and white citizens alike — burned to the ground, leaving 11 people dead and dozens more homeless and essentially destitute, all at the hands of the city. Before the smoldering remains had even gone out, it was clear that whatever renaissance the city had been experiencing was now over. The editor of the *Inquirer's* editorial page noted that the months following the bombing were no better for the city. "In the nine years I've been here," he remarked, "I have never encountered so many public officials and business and labor leaders who are disheartened about the city's immediate future."[63]

The next year, Goode attempted to revive both his reputation as well as the city's by trumpeting the construction of One Liberty Place, an office tower that would at last break through the city's unofficial ban on buildings higher than the top of William Penn's hat situated atop City Hall (491 feet). During the prolonged debate over the merits of altering the city's skyline, gentlemanly Philadelphia asserted itself once again, this time in the person of Bacon himself. The restriction, he recounted in a letter to the *Inquirer*, was never set in stone or parchment but was, rather, in the form of a gentleman's agreement. Accordingly, he directed a barb at Mayor Goode and to those who sought to break that agreement, in stating that, they would have "to answer the age-old question, 'Are you a gentleman?'"[64] The building was built despite the sting from Bacon's pen, so apparently they were not, at least in his eyes. Although Goode characterized the groundbreaking of the historic building as a moment that "says we have arrived," many both within the city and nationwide believed that to have been the case over a decade earlier.[65] If anything, the ceremony could optimistically be viewed as the end of a decline that began in the late '70s and picked up steam in each successive year.

By the morning of the Liberty Place groundbreaking, it was difficult to look back on the previous two decades in the life of the city with anything approaching the optimism that existed for much of that time. By now, through the kaleidoscope of perspective, that time looked much like it did in 1986, full of racial tension and violence, official incompetence and corruption, economic crisis and potential collapse. To someone looking back at the 1970s in Philadelphia, it would be the negatives that would be most apparent: Rizzo, MOVE, the corruption and decline of a once great city. At the time, however, to those living in the moment, the perspective was quite different: given all of the good things going on all around them — the revival of Center City and Society Hill, the restaurant renaissance and, perhaps most importantly, the young, exciting Phillies who put a face on the city's good mood — the bad things were recognized but they were considered isolated events. They were troubling to be sure but not representative of anything beyond themselves. However, the accumulated weight of the negatives eventually overtook everything else until the positives became obliterated. In retrospect, Black Friday marked the day the scales tipped, the day all of the bad seemed more relevant and telling than all of the good. After that day, the good things about the city would not be representative of anything. Philadelphia would become a cold, cynical place once again.

That it would be a baseball game and not the release of employment statistics or the cold, hard news of the city's economic woes that would tip the balance and fuel the city's downward spiral seems absurd only in the abstract. For the perception of reality is driven more by feelings than by facts.[66] Once that perception is changed, facts are sought retrospectively in an effort to justify the feeling.[67] Rizzo's antics, Eastwick, MOVE, none of these were perceived to be representative of anything larger so long as the feeling of rebirth and renewal persisted. Once that feeling disappeared, however, they became all-telling. As such, it is not surprising that it would be baseball that would be responsible for the shift in perception; nothing else stirs the passions and emotions of so many people, particularly when the games count for as much as the one played on Black Friday did. And Black Friday was hardly the first time baseball played such a role. Bobby Thomson's 1951 "shot heard 'round

the world" occurred the same afternoon the Soviet Union successfully deto-
nated its second atomic bomb test, ushering in the nuclear age and officially
launching the cold war. Although the explosion hardly went unnoticed
(indeed, it shared top billing with Thomson's home run in the following
morning's New York Times[68]), it would be Thomson's blast that would resonate more deeply, at least in New York. Jubilation or despair in the days and
weeks afterward depended more on whether one was a fan of the Giants or
Dodgers than on the realization that the world as every American knew it had
changed forever.[69] Don Delillo, in his novel Underworld, would write about
it afterward: "[i]sn't it possible that this mid-century moment enters the skin
more lastingly than the vast shaping strategies of eminent leaders, generals
steely in their sunglasses— the mapped visions that pierce our dreams?"[70]
Emotional events bring on emotional responses. And when they resonate
deeply, they color the perception of other, seemingly unrelated events.

As the 1980s progressed, the city continued to deteriorate in the eyes of
many. By 1986, despite Goode's attempt to deflect attention through the construction of Liberty Place, the mismanagement of the city and its agencies
dominated newspaper headlines.[71] Payoffs, waste, misdirection of funds, criminal investigations were now not only commonplace but also seen as indicative of the state of the city. In 1988 Mayor Goode won reelection but admitted
in his inaugural speech that by now, it had become commonplace in city government "to allow influence to be bought with favors."[72] He vowed to change
the culture. Given the onslaught of public corruption to which locals had
been exposed, however, this appeared to be a tall order and left many disheartened over both who was running the city as well what its prospects were
for the future. At this time, much of the city's symbolic heart, the City Hall
tower and the William Penn statue atop it, had been encased in scaffolding
for nearly three years in what seemed to be an endless renovation project,
full of frustrating and inexplicable starts and stops that served for some as a
fitting symbol for their feelings regarding modern-day Philadelphia.[73] Imprisoned indefinitely in a cage, the founder of the Quaker city still stood, although
it was difficult to discern either Penn or his "greene countrie towne" behind
the well-entrenched matrix that now obscured the both of them.

By 1990, whatever spirit of renewal and rebirth that trickled through the
'80s was gone. Now the city was concerned merely with survival. Although
most older cities in the Northeast and Midwest dealt with the same sorts of
problems afflicting Philadelphia, nowhere else were so many of them seemingly so prevalent. "Sadly enough," said a Rutgers professor of urban planning, "Philadelphia is showing the way."[74] Philadelphia was a leader once
again, although now, it led in a race no one wanted to win.

Of course, doom was not pervasive. Just as all things were not as rosy as they were portrayed during the '70s, the late '80s and '90s did not constitute an uninterrupted downward spiral into the abyss. Once again, the area's culinary scene blossomed and yet another "restaurant renaissance" was soon declared. This rebirth, however, would be far different in scope and in tone from the one that preceded it. Unlike the restaurant revival in the '70s, this one was largely bereft of the concept of food and restaurants serving as vehicles for social change. This time, there were no Young Turks to energize the populace and provide the foundation for the spirit of renewal and rehabilitation that had previously overtaken the city. With the notion of the city as a vital, vibrant force now either largely forgotten or discarded, the new restaurateurs focused on entertainment rather than on the revival and sustenance of the neighborhoods in which they operated. Although there were dozens of people who fueled this new restaurant resurgence, one of the most successful and influential individuals was also the one who provided the sharpest counterpoint to his predecessors: Stephen Starr.

Unlike Steve Poses and Jay Guben, Starr came to the restaurant world not from an urban reform background but from an entertainment one — he was a comedy club owner and a rock concert promoter before turning to restaurants.[75] He brought the same sensibilities from these endeavors to his restaurants. "I always wanted to produce television or movies, and didn't do it," he once said. Restaurants are "a production — music, food, lighting. It's like a show."[76] He was the first to admit that he did not possess a sophisticated palate. However, he claimed, "I know what sophisticated people like."[77] He, along with the dozens who tried to emulate him and copy his success, catered to these "sophisticates," the overwhelming majority of whom were suburbanites (70 to 80 percent on weekends at his most popular restaurants[78]), providing them with a carefully orchestrated theatrical experience that, although it took place technically within the city, was not of the city. Without the larger social goals that motivated establishment of many restaurants back in the '70s, Starr's restaurants were in many respects true to the relationship many suburbanites in the 1990s and 2000s now had with regard to the large, decaying cities located within driving distance of their homes, a relationship based purely on entertainment. Each of Starr's restaurants — one of which sported a giant golden Buddha as a centerpiece while others trafficked in various other themes — was merely a plaything, like the city itself, to be experienced at the convenience of these out-of-town residents.[79] Some of them even offered valet parking, providing their customers the opportunity to whisk in to the city, enjoy the show and whisk out without experiencing any aspect of the city beyond the sidewalk in front of the restaurant. There existed no connection between these restaurants and the city that housed them, and they offered no opportunity to reinvigorate the neighborhoods in which they were located; if it was not for the fact that many people still enjoyed the gimmick of dining in the city, they could just as well have been located in the suburbs, nestled alongside the homes of the clientele to which they catered.

In this respect, the restaurant "renaissance" of the 1990s and 2000s more appropriately resembled a depressing urban death march as more and more restaurateurs applied their version of Starr's business plan to their establishments. They provided quick, easily accessible entertainment to folks who preferred to zip in and out of the city within a couple of hours, leaving its larger problems behind — problems that by now, many suburbanites assumed were virtually unsolvable. Beginning in the 1980s, perhaps because of the decay of so many large cities in the Northeast and Midwest and the conclusion drawn by many that the nation's massive urban renewal policies of the 1950s were a disastrous failure, perhaps because of the commercial growth of so many suburban areas to the extent that they became economic forces in and of themselves, or perhaps because of the combined effect of all of this, the concept of regionalism in gauging the health of a geographic area became prevalent. Consequently, the realization took hold that no longer did the decline or collapse of a particular city in itself portend doom for those living in its suburbs if the surrounding region was vibrant. Atlanta and Detroit proved as much. The era of cities as bellwethers for the regions that encompassed them was over. During the '70s, the shrinking population and economic base of Philadelphia were causes for alarm; by the 2000s, the possibility that Phoenix might surpass it as the nation's fifth-largest city proved to be little more than an interesting sidelight, a blow to the civic ego perhaps but little more than that. In just 30 years, cities became less relevant than they ever had been before.

Accordingly, through the course of this change in mind-set, the health of cities became less and less important to more and more people, and that fact explains the fundamental difference between Philadelphia's restaurant booms of the 1970s and the 1990s. Steve Poses and Jay Guben could rightly believe in their day that they were not merely opening up restaurants, they were also taking up arms, engaging in a vital, urgent social cause. However, Stephen Starr could just as rightly believe that his obligation was merely to put as many smiles on as many faces as possible. All that really mattered to the vast majority of people who now resided and worked in suburban communities was the opportunity to spend an evening every once in a while in a place that conveyed a romanticized *idea* of a city. Therefore, his role was merely to make sure that he provided the entertainment his clientele expected, and so his obligations extended no further than the façade of his restaurants or the walk between his patrons' cars and his front door. The infrastructure of the city could crumble to the ground but so long as his customers were able to come away from his restaurants believing that they had "experienced" an evening in the city, this was all that mattered. As such, and perhaps drawing lessons from the failures that came before them, Starr and others aimed at creating illusion and spectacle — tackling the reality of a city was more than they were prepared to handle.

The city declined steadily throughout the '80s and '90s and so too did the Phillies and Veterans Stadium, to such a degree that, by the end of the century, attending a Phillies game provided a depressing, telling microcosm of the city itself. Aside from their fortuitous, out-of-nowhere pennants in 1983 and '93, the Phils spent the rest of these decades mired in mediocrity or far worse. Player after forgotten player — Sil Campusano, Chris James, Ron Stone, Rick Schu — or forgettable players — Von Hayes, Joe Cowley, Gregg Jeffries, Kevin Millwood — drifted on and off the team, contributing to one losing season after another. All the while, as the city and the team fought over its upkeep, the Vet decayed, providing fans yet another symbol, like the imprisoned William Penn statue several blocks up Broad Street, of urban disarray and corruption, specifically, within the Phillies themselves. By the late 1990s, a trip to the Vet recalled the disquieting feelings that accompanied excursions to Connie Mack Stadium decades earlier. The experience provided an instant cue as to the troubles surrounding it. Decay and neglect were everywhere anyone chose to look: in the bathrooms, on the field, in the concession stands, in the front office. As both the Phils and the Vet deteriorated, each became the butt of so many jokes and so much derision that, at times, it was difficult to separate criticism of one from criticism of the other. In such a mocking atmosphere, the cynicism and negativity that lifted briefly during the mid '70s fell heavily over the franchise once more.

Although the Phils would leave the Vet after the 2003 season and move into clean, beautiful Citizens Bank Park, the aura of negativity traveled across the parking lot and settled in comfortably at the new stadium. Fans scoffed at the team's pledge to put a winner on the field and even though the team began to play respectable baseball consistently from one season to the next (they finished above .500 five out of six years between 2001 and 2006 after finishing below .500 for 13 of the previous 14 seasons), few were placated. Boos rained down on many players, and near-miss playoff seasons were considered failures rather than successes although at least in comparison to previous teams, they were anything but. The legal entanglements of one frustrated fan provided an extreme, although illustrative example of the relationship between the Phils and their fans during this time. In January 2005, an extensive FBI investigation led to the conviction of the fan on 79 counts of fraud, identity theft and computer hacking. According to the FBI, the fan collected email addresses, hacked into computers in several states and then fired off rants that were supposedly sent from local sportswriters. "In court, the fan's lawyer said his client was obsessive, perhaps even psychotic, but not an intentional lawbreaker. He meant only to say that the Phillies stunk."[80] Just as before, the passion of the city's baseball fans was never in question. And now, once again, neither was their hatred of the Phillies. As always, the Phillies have remained the symbol of the city in which they play. And that symbol is now, much as it has been for decades, one of doubt, negativity and cynicism.

Today, the sanguine feelings during what was then perceived to be the glory days— both of the city as well as of the Phillies— seem long ago and of a different time. In one sense, both the team and the city are back where they had been for years before the glory time, although, in another, things are, if anything, worse; the optimism so brutally crushed then only weighs more heavily now. Every so often, however, such as throughout the Phillies' improbable late season march to the 2007 division title, glimpses of that earlier age peek through, sending one back in time if only for a moment and giving hope that, perhaps one day, those feelings will return in full. Another such glimpse occurred in 1998 when, 41 years after its creation, Ellsworth Kelly's "Sculpture for a Large Wall" was put on display in what was hailed by the *New York Times* as the "best architectural show of the year."[81] Kelly's piece was commissioned by the city back in 1957. It served as a precursor to works commissioned under the city's Beautification Ordinance as part of the construction of Penn Center's Transportation Building, itself a vital element in Bacon's utopian vision for the future of Philadelphia. Decades later, the Transportation Building sat abandoned and boarded up, but the sculpture remained, although now displayed against a background of deflated dreams rather than buoyant ones. It was subsequently removed, although "even wrenched loose from its architectural setting," the *Times* noted, "the sculpture retains Kelly's optimistic view of the power of abstract art." So too, of the power of ideas, the power of hope, the power of rebirth. If nothing else resonated from Kelly's sculpture, it was this idea: that what once had been could be again.

Chapter Notes

Prologue

1. Frank Fitzpatrick, *You Can't Lose 'Em All* (Lanham, Md.: Taylor Trade Publishing, 2004), 232.
2. Ibid., 157.
3. Thomas Boswell, "Failure Shadows Second-Place Phillies," *Washington Post*, September 29, 1980, C1.
4. Fitzpatrick, *You Can't Lose 'Em All*, 176.
5. Ibid., 199.
6. Frank Dolson, "Soured: Writers Tarnish a Great Year for Schmidt," *Philadelphia Inquirer*, December 5, 1980, C1,7.

Chapter 1

1. Jane Shoemaker, "Knowing a Winner When You See One," *Philadelphia Inquirer*, October 7, 1977, A1.
2. Allan Lewis, "Happiness for Hooton Is 7th Game," *Philadelphia Inquirer*, October 18, 1977, C1.
3. Shoemaker, *Knowing a Winner*, A1. The local Philadelphia media made much about the difference between the 1977 Phillies and their unfortunate ancestors in the weeks leading up to the 1977 NLCS. Much of the difference was attributed to their uncharacteristically optimistic fans (*see* Frank Dolson, "For Phillies, Boo-Birds Are Gone as Fans Make a Winning Racket," *Philadelphia Inquirer*, September 13, 1977, D2), and the supremely confident, loose team (*see* Skip Myslenski, "Keeping Loose: It's What Phils Do Best of All," *Philadelphia Inquirer*, October 2, 1977, E1). By the start of the playoff series against LA, the Phils were convinced that they not only could not lose but also that they would have little trouble dispatching the Dodgers. Greg Luzinski said: "I've got a feeling this thing could go three in a row. I don't know why, but I feel it." Frank Dolson, "The Grand Slam's Band Didn't Scare the Phils," *Philadelphia Inquirer*, October 5, 1977, C1. *See also* Tug McGraw, "The Phillies in 4 Games....," *Philadelphia Daily News*, October 4, 1977, back page. At least McGraw allowed LA one win.
4. E. Digby Baltzell, *Puritan Boston and Quaker Philadelphia* (Boston: Beacon Press, 1982), 4.
5. Peter L. Bernstein, *Wedding of the Waters: The Erie Canal and the Making of a Great Nation* (New York: W.W. Norton, 2005), 366.

6. Robert E. Wright, *The First Wall Street: Chestnut Street, Philadelphia, and the Birth of American Finance* (Chicago: University of Chicago Press, 2005), 16. For a detailed history of the Quaker influence on Philadelphia, *see* Steven Conn, *Metropolitan Philadelphia: Living with the Presence of the Past* (Philadelphia: University of Pennsylvania Press, 2006).
7. Wright, *The First Wall Street*, 16.
8. Bernstein, *Wedding of the Waters*, 366.
9. Ibid.
10. The city was captured in September 1777 and under British control for nine months, until June 1778 when the British withdrew.
11. Baltzell, *Puritan Boston*, 193.
12. Wright, *The First Wall Street*, 11.
13. Ibid.
14. Baltzell, *Puritan Boston*, 192.
15. Wright, *The First Wall Street*, 21–24.
16. Baltzell, *Puritan Boston*, 192.
17. Ibid., 192. Noting that, as stated by Henry Adams, "Boston was our Bristol, New York our Liverpool, and Philadelphia our London."
18. *Philadelphia: The Capital City*, http://www. nps.gof/inde/phila.html. Accessed 9/29/05.
19. Bernstein, *Wedding of the Waters*, 136.
20. Wright, *The First Wall Street*, 14–15.
21. Ibid.
22. Bernstein, *Wedding of the Waters*, 137.
23. Ibid., 22–23. Bernstein's text provides much of the source material contained herein for the discussion of the Erie Canal's impact on both New York and the nation.
24. Ibid., 349, 368.
25. Wright, *The First Wall Street*, 125. Wright's text is an invaluable resource for the impact of the Erie Canal on Philadelphia as well as the much less known story surrounding Philadelphia's haphazard and ultimately belated attempts to catch up. The discussion of the Erie Canal's impact on Philadelphia draws heavily from this material. See Ibid., 123–29.
26. This is not to suggest that Philadelphia suddenly or even eventually became devoid of intellectual attractions. Among other things, the American Philosophical Society, the myriad world-class universities led by, but by no means limited to, the University of Pennsylvania, and perhaps the nation's

greatest collection of medical institutions remained. However, due to the influx of immigrants and the explosion of factories during the nineteenth century, the city embraced its blue-collar character rather than its intellectual one. The dichotomy of these two faces of Philadelphia remains to this day, with the blue collar one still predominant.

27. Baltzell, *Puritan Boston*, 230.

28. *See* Bernstein, *Wedding of the Waters*.

29. Wright, *The First Wall Street*, 72. This section is based on Wright's discussion of the battles over the First and Second Banks. *See also* 148–62.

30. Baltzell, *Puritan Boston*, 232.

31. Ibid., 43–44.

32. Wright, *The First Wall Street*, 125.

33. *See* Baltzell, *Puritan Boston*. Baltzell's book focused on the withdrawal of Philadelphia's upper classes from public life during the postcolonial period as well as the historical inability of Philadelphia to regularly produce either regional or national public leaders in politics, the arts or education, a seemingly unlikely result given the centralized role Philadelphia played in all of these areas, among others. Although the conclusions he draws regarding the reasons for this have been the focus of much scholarly discussion and debate (in his opinion, Philadelphia's Quaker origins are largely to blame), his study nevertheless provides worthwhile information and documentation regarding the city's temperament in comparison to other, more progressive cities such as Boston.

34. Ibid., 43.

35. Ibid., 304–05.

36. Conn, *Metropolitan Philadelphia*.

37. Leslie Bennetts, "The Philadelphia Story, Updated," *New York Times*, May 10, 1981, SM 15.

38. *See* Conn, *Metropolitan Philadelphia*. Conn notes that given the deluge of history confronting residents on a daily basis, Philadelphians are unique in this regard.

Chapter 2

1. Red Smith, "East Is East and West Is Ahead," *New York Times*, October, 8, 1977, 35.

2. Allen Lewis, "Some Guys Never Give Up," *Philadelphia Inquirer*, September 24, 1975, D1.

3. Allan Lewis, "Happiness for Hooton Is 7th Game," *Philadelphia Inquirer*, October 18, 1977, C1. "To look at him, you'd never imagine that his nickname is 'Happy.' Pitcher Burt Hooton has a solemn, deadpan expression reminiscent of the late character actor Ned Sparks." *See also* Stan Hochman, "LA.'s Burt Hooton Hypnotizes Yankees," *Philadelphia Daily News*, October 13, 1977, 67, noting that Hooton "looks like a guy wearing underwear that is two sizes too small." Hochman recounted Hooton's physical and emotional struggles throughout his career, starting in Chicago, where, along with a weight problem there existed another, in Hochman's language, "above the eyebrows." Hooton claimed that pitching for the Cubs ruined his confidence and that he started seeing Dr. Arthur Ellen, a California hypnotherapist, who helped him erase negative thoughts.

4. Smith, "East Is East," *New York Times*, October, 8, 1977, 35.

5. *See* note 3.

6. Allen Lewis, "Hooton Turns Unsettling Experience to His Benefit," *Philadelphia Inquirer*, October 13, 1977, D1. On reflection, Hooton admitted that he "overkeyed" himself for the game in Philadelphia, remarking: "I lost my cool. I had let my team down ... I lost confidence in myself and lost my head, so to speak." Although Hooton refused to allow for the possibility that the fans played a role in his unraveling, his teammates thought otherwise. *See* note 9.

7. Stan Hochman, "LA.'s Burt Hooton Hypnotizes Yankees," *Philadelphia Daily News*, October 13, 1977, 67, quoting Hooton reflecting on the game in saying that he "let my emotions [get] away from me." Lopes recalled his mound visit in the second and said, "I went out there and I tried to calm him down. There's not much you can do for a guy. You just try to break the tempo." Yeager added, "I went out to say, hey forget about it. But I was helpless, absolutely helpless."

8. Smith, "East Is East," *New York Times*, October, 8, 1977, 35.

9. Tom Cushman, "Lasorda Looks for Divine Guidance," *Philadelphia Daily News*, October 8, 1977, 39. According to Ron Cey, "Burt lost his composure for a moment, and after that, I think he became a little unnerved because of the fans." *See also* Dave Kindred, "The Umpire Couldn't Hear the Out," *Washington Post*, October 8, 1977, D1, quoting Davey Lopes, who added that, because of this, Hooton: "was crying about everything." But *see* Stan Hochman, "LA.'s Burt Hooton Hypnotizes Yankees," *Philadelphia Daily News*, October 13, 1977, 67, wherein Lasorda claimed that Hooton's angst was directed primarily at Wendlestadt: "He felt the umpire missed a call when he was pitching to Larry Christenson. That got to him." According to both Cushman and Hochman, however, along with many in the press who covered the game, it was the fans who ultimately unnerved Hooton to the point where he became unable to find the strike zone. *See also* Joseph Durso, "Pinch Hits in Ninth Key 3-Run Rally with 2 Outs," *New York Times*, October 8, 1977, 35; Smith, "East Is East," *New York Times*, October, 8, 1977, 35; Bruce Keidan, "Dodgers Score 3 in 9th for 6–5 Win," *Philadelphia Inquirer*, October 8, 1977, 4C.

10. Again, although he later denied it, several of his teammates concluded that the crowd unnerved him. *See* Tom Cushman, "Lasorda Looks for Divine Guidance," *Philadelphia Daily News*, October 8, 1977, 39. According to Yeager: "One pitch doesn't make a game ... and I think Burt let it affect him for the rest of the time he was out there. I'm sure he was nervous. It was his first playoff start. And the crowd had to have an effect. Hell, I think all the fans here have megaphones."

11. Ibid.

12. Durso, "Pinch Hits in Ninth," 19. Durso noted that as the inning progressed, Hooton appeared to become increasingly more bewildered about the turn of events, noting that, at one point, after throwing a ball to McBride, "he held his arms out to ask: 'Why?'" By the time he was removed

from the game, Durso noted that Hooton was "stalking off, flapping both arms at the umpire and flinging his glove into the dugout."

13. *See* notes 6–12.

14. Cushman, "Lasorda Looks for Divine Guidance," 39.

15. Harold Seymour, *Baseball: The Early Years* (New York: Oxford University Press, 1989), 42. The discussion of early baseball in Philadelphia draws from this text. *See also* pp. 159, 349–50.

16. Neil Lanctot, *Negro League Baseball: The Rise and Ruin of a Black Institution* (Philadelphia: University of Pennsylvania Press, 2004), 52.

17. Steven A. Riess, *Touching Base: Professional Baseball and American Culture in the Progressive Era* (Urbana: University of Illinois Press, 1999), 8–9. The discussion of the role of civic pride draws from this text. *See also* pp. 20, 22.

18. Ibid.

19. Henry Fetter, *Taking on the Yankees: Winning and Losing in the Business of Baseball* (New York: W.W. Norton, 2003), 388.

20. Harold Seymour, *Baseball: The Golden Age* (New York: Oxford University Press, 1989), 95.

21. Riess, *Touching Base*, 7.

22. David M. Jordan, *The Athletics of Philadelphia: Connie Mack's White Elephants, 1901–1954* (Jefferson, N.C.: McFarland & Co., 1999), 14. Jordan's account of the birth of the Philadelphia Athletics remains perhaps the most authoritative source for this information and, hence, much of the discussion on this topic draws from it.

23. David M. Jordan, *Occasional Glory: The History of the Philadelphia Phillies* (Jefferson, N.C.: McFarland & Co., 2002), 14–16. Jordan's account of the early years of the Phillies is the source for this paragraph. *See also* p. 19.

24. Harold Kaese, *The Boston Braves, 1871–1953* (Boston: Northeastern University Press, 2004), 99–100.

25. *See* Jordan, *The Athletics*, 14–29, for his discussion of the birth of the Athletics and their early relationship with the Phillies.

26. In 1918, the white elephant first appeared on the left sleeve of the players' uniforms and, in 1920, it replaced the familiar "A" on the player's left breast. It disappeared in 1928 and would return from time to time throughout the Athletics' existence and travels. Today, it appears once again on the left sleeve of both the home and the road uniforms of the Oakland A's. *See* "Dressed to the Nines: A History of the Baseball Uniform," *http://www. baseballhalloffame.org/exhibits/online_exhibits/ dressed_to_the_nines/introduction.htm.*

27. Jordan, *The Athletics*, 26.

28. Bruce Kuklick, *To Everything a Season: Shibe Park and Urban Philadelphia 1909–1976* (Princeton, N.J.: Princeton University Press, 1991), 14–15, 36. Kuklick's book provides the source material for the discussion of Mack's appeal to Philadelphians.

29. Jordan, *The Athletics*, 40, 50–61, 92, 105. Jordan's book provided the basis for the discussion of the Athletics' success through the early 1930s.

30. The contrasting moods of New York and Philadelphia extended (and still does to this day) to their preferred vacation destinations. As noted by Steven Conn, because the Poconos have evolved as a Delaware Valley mountain range, its resorts are "more staid, reserved, [and] perhaps stiffer and duller than the more boisterous Catskills, which belong entirely to New York." Conn, *Metropolitan Philadelphia*, 153.

31. Proof that the Yankees of the 1920s had not declined by the early 1930s comes from the fact that, in 1932, with the Athletics on the decline (although still winners of 94 games) and with a team led by the same players as before, the Yankees won 107 games and the World Series, picking up right were they left off in 1929 when the Athletics rose to prominence.

32. Jordan, *The Athletics*, 114; Seymour, *Baseball: The Golden Age*, 441.

33. Kuklick, *To Everything a Season*, 53.

34. Fitzpatrick, *You Can't Lose 'Em All*, 28.

35. "Judge Frees Boy Held for Stealing Foul in Phillies' Ball Park," *Chicago Daily Tribune*, July 20, 1923, 16; "In the Press Box with Baxter," *Washington Post*, July 21, 1923, 10.

36. Seymour, *Baseball: The Early Years*, 194.

37. Jordan, *The Athletics*, 42; Kuklick, *To Everything a Season*, 18.

38. Seymour, *Baseball: The Golden Age*, 41–42. Seymour noted that between 1900 and 1920, the urban population rose from 40 percent of the U.S. population to 50 percent.

39. Kuklick, *To Everything a Season*, 28.

40. Ibid.

41. Ibid.

42. Kuklick, *To Everything a Season*, 19.

43. Ibid., 34.

44. Ibid., 34.

45. Fetter, *Taking on the Yankees*, 101.

46. Seymour, *Baseball: The Golden Age*, 137–38.

47. Ibid., 125.

48. Kuklick, *To Everything a Season*, 90–91.

49. Ibid., 47, 89–91, 145. This section, discussing the "sins" of the Phillies, draws from Kuklick's book as a resource.

50. Gerald R. Curtis, "Factors That Affect the Attendance of a Major League Baseball Club" (master's thesis, University of Pennsylvania, 1951).

51. Ibid.

52. Jordan, *The Athletics*, 146.

53. Kuklick, *To Everything a Season*, 147.

54. Lanctot, *Negro League Baseball*, 236.

55. Kuklick, *To Everything a Season*, 146.

Chapter 3

1. Bill Conlin, "Maddox Out — Barring Miracle," *Philadelphia Daily News*, October 4, 1977, back page.

2. Bill Lyon, "Bake Will Surely Heat Things Up in Phils Clubhouse," *Philadelphia Inquirer*, June 17, 1977, C1.

3. Bruce Keidan, "Ozark: '77 Phils Are Improved Club," *Philadelphia Inquirer*, March 4, 1977, C2.

4. Seymour, *Baseball: The Early Years*, 98; Kuklick, *To Everything a Season*, 13.

5. Riess, *Touching Base*, 98.

6. Seymour, *Baseball: The Early Years*, 24–25, 31. Seymour's work provides the source material for much of the discussion of professional baseball during the nineteenth century contained herein.

7. Ibid., 75.

8. Ibid., 81.

9. Ibid., 91. *See also,* Riess, *Touching Base*, 33, 135.

10. *See* "Schoolboy of 16 Inherits $20,000,000," *New York Times*, March 18, 1919, 6, in which it is noted that, on the death of his uncle, oil and timber magnate (as well as half owner of the Detroit Tigers) William H. Yawkey, the adopted, 16-year-old Thomas Austin received half of his $40 million estate, making him, "one of the wealthiest boys in the country," according to the Times. *See also* "Powel Crosley Jr. Is Dead at 74; Owner of the Cincinnati Reds," *New York Times*, March 29, 1961, 33. In the obituary, Crosley, the son of a lawyer, is remembered for once saying, "I was born with a silver spoon in my mouth but it was jerked out before I could distinguish its taste from that of the common dime-store variety." Accordingly, he was known as the "baron in homespun." However, he was apparently far less a baron than was Yawkey.

11. Riess, *Touching Base*, 76; Fetter, *Taking on the Yankees*, 63–66. Stoneham was, according to Fetter, "hardly a pillar of the financial establishment," and was accused of running a "'bucket shop,' enticing the gullible with an 'offer unparalleled' to 'buy an income' through investments that would 'yield an annual income of one-half the sum invested." He was also involved in, according to Riess, ticket scalping, book making and rum running.

12. Riess, *Touching Base*, 7–8, 17. Riess's book is the source for much of the discussion in this chapter of the baseball creed.

13. Ibid., 17.

14. Ibid., 7.

15. Ibid.

16. Ibid., 12.

17. Ibid., 54.

18. Ibid., 54–55.

19. Jordan, *The Athletics*, 15.

20. Ibid., 58–59.

21. Peter Golenbock, *The Spirit of St. Louis: A History of the St. Louis Cardinals and Browns* (New York: HarperEntertainment, 2001), 9, 56.

22. Ibid., 56.

23. Riess, *Touching Base*, 22, quoting *Atlanta Constitution*, April 14, 1913.

24. Ibid., 29, quoting *Atlanta Constitution*, July 18, 1919.

25. Kuklick, *To Everything a Season*, 92–93.

26. John Helyar, *Lords of the Realm: The Real History of Baseball* (New York: Villard Books, 1994), 23.

27. Ibid., 13. This quote was attributed to E. R. "Salty" Saltwell, the Cubs business manager for a time.

28. Seymour, *Baseball: The Golden Age*, 64.

29. Michael Shapiro, *The Last Good Season: Brooklyn, the Dodgers and Their Final Pennant Race Together* (New York: Broadway Books, 2004), 95. Frank Graham, Jr., who handled the press for the Brooklyn Dodgers, believed that O'Malley's occa-

sional attempts to "affect a bond with the common man" came off as transparent. Graham's wife noted once that O'Malley made her "shiver."

30. Seymour, *Baseball: The Golden Age*, 344 (noting that in the 1920s ticket revenue accounted for approximately 87 percent of total revenue); Fetter, *Taking on the Yankees*, 268 (noting that the 1946 Giants realized 80 percent of their revenue from ticket sales); Helyar, *Lords of the Realm*, 51 (discussing the simplicity of the baseball economics of the time).

31. *See* "Shibe Park and the Seed of the Athletics Demise" in chapter 2, and accompanying notes.

32. Jordan, *The Athletics*, 115–16; Kuklick, *To Everything a Season*, 62.

33. Kuklick, *To Everything a Season*, 90–91. From 1913 to 1942, through the regimes of William Baker (1913–1930) and Gerry Nugent (1930–1942), the Phillies managed to remain profitable through the sale of players despite their perpetual second-division status.

34. Seymour, *Baseball: The Golden Age*, 24.

35. Fetter, *Taking on the Yankees*, 302 (citing Roger G. Noll, "Major League Team Sports," in *The Structure of American Industry*, edited by Walter Adams, 5th ed. [New York, New York: MacMillan, 1977], 365).

36. Seymour, *Baseball: The Golden Age*, 71.

37. John Rossi, "The Nugent Era: Phillies Phlounder in Phutility," *The National Pastime* 25 (2005): 15, 17.

38. Arthur Daley, "Those Two-Team Cities," *New York Times*, February 24, 1953, 28. In discussing the plight of the struggling Athletics, Browns and Braves, Daley noted that the days of the sustainable team drawing 250,000 fans per season had ended. However, it is important to note that despite his comments, teams were still drawing fans at approximately this rate during this time and somehow they remained solvent.

39. Riess, *Touching Base*, 181–82, 184. Here, Riess reports the result of a study he conducted on the locales of origin of Major League players playing during the Progressive era (1900–1919). In it, he found that the ten leading cities as birthplaces of Major League players active during this era were as follows: (1) New York; (2) Chicago; (3) Philadelphia; (4) Brooklyn; (5) St. Louis; (6) Boston; (7) Baltimore; (8) San Francisco; (9) Cincinnati; (10) Cleveland. In all, although these cities comprised only 11.7 percent of the U.S. population in 1890, they produced 16.8 percent of all Major League players. Of course, eight of these cities were home to 11 of the 16 teams with Baltimore a short distance from Washington, D.C. Moreover, when viewed by state and not city, the preference for local talent is even more evident. Riess noted that in the early 1900s, Pennsylvania (14 percent), Ohio (10.6 percent), Illinois (8.5 percent) and New York (7.6 percent) produced 40.7 percent of all Major League players. These four states were home to nine teams. In the 1920s and 1930s, this practice continued to a degree, with cities such as St. Louis, Cincinnati and Pittsburgh all producing players at 2–3 times their expected rate given their populations. One explanation for this statistical anomaly would be the most simple one, namely, that team owners in these cities

were content to pluck players from their backyards, not focusing their resources on the larger pool of talent that existed farther away.

40. *See* Fetter, *Taking on the Yankees,* 106, for a detailed discussion on the formation and workings of the Cardinals' system.

41. Jordan, *The Athletics,* 145.

42. Ibid., 141–42. Jordan details Mack's spend-thrift nature over the years, noting that, at one point, a player refused to sign with the A's, con-tending that he could "make more than that by pitching on weekends near my home."

43. Seymour, *Baseball: The Golden Age,* 197; Paul Zingg and Mark D. Medeiros, *Runs, Hits and an Era: The Pacific Coast League, 1903–58* (Urbana: Univer-sity of Illinois Press, 1994), 34–35.

44. Riess, *Touching Base,* 172. Heilman returned to the Tigers in 1916 on his way to the Hall of Fame.

45. Zingg and Medeiros, *Runs, Hits and an Era,* 106. *See also* Larry Stone, "Those Were the Most Wonderful Days I Believe I Ever Had," in *Rain Check: Baseball in the Pacific Northwest,* edited by Mark Armour (Cleveland, Ohio: Society for Amer-ican Baseball Research, 2006), 99. In Stone's article, several former PCL players reminisce and discuss their brushes with Major League Baseball. Some, such as Eddie Basinski, a shortstop who briefly played for the Brooklyn Dodgers in the mid–1940s, turned down contract offers from Major League teams (Basinski spurned a contract from the Yan-kees) because the money was better in the PCL. Basinski was not unusual in refusing such overtures. Although the Majors would offer enough money to entice the top PCL talent to sign on, lesser players (but no doubt Major League caliber players) were not offered enough to cause them to uproot their families, particularly given the fact that they would be taking a pay cut to move up to the "Majors."

46. Seymour, *Baseball: The Golden Age,* 406–09. Seymour's text provides the basis for the discussion of the draft rule vagaries discussed herein.

47. New York, Chicago and Pittsburgh.

48. Philadelphia, Boston and Chicago.

49. Golenbock, *Spirit of St. Louis,* 293–94.

50. "Snapshots" of attendance figures through-out this period confirms this. According to "official" attendance figures, in 1909, American League teams averaged 6,032 fans per game and National League teams 5,639. In 1919, AL teams averaged 6,525; NL teams 5,158. In 1929, AL teams averaged 7,606; NL teams 7,996. In 1939, AL teams averaged 6,944; NL teams 7,642. In 1944, AL teams averaged 7,751; NL teams 6,380. Moreover, although attendance rose somewhat during this time, in 1944, five American League and four National League teams averaged less than 7,000 fans per game.

51. A comparison of attendance figures for both Philadelphia teams with the growth in population within the city of Philadelphia provides a useful ex-ample. In 1910, the combined attendance at Athlet-ics and Phillies games was 885,502. The population of Philadelphia at this time was 1,549,008. In 1953 (the year before the relocation of the Athletics), the combined attendance at Athletics and Phillies games was 1,215,757 compared to Philadelphia's population (as of the 1950 census) of 2,071,605.

Thus, during this time, baseball attendance rose 37 percent against a 34 percent rise in the city's pop-ulation. The year 1953 was used as a comparative figure rather than 1950 in order to gauge typical Philadelphia attendance. In 1950, there was an atyp-ical spike in attendance due to the excitement gen-erated by the pennant-winning "Whiz Kids" of that season. The 1953 season was a more typical year in terms of overall attendance. Likewise, 1954 (the final year of two Philadelphia baseball teams) was not used because, given the apathy over the Athlet-ics and their rumored departure, total attendance that season was atypically low (1,043,065) and not representative of the city's interest in its profes-sional baseball teams.

52. Frank Hobbs and Nicole Stoops, U.S. Census Bureau, Census 2000 Special Reports, Series CENSR-4, *Demographic Trends in the 20th Century* (Washington, D.C.: U.S. Government Printing Office, 2002), 33. This report notes that, in 1910, less than one-third (28 percent) of the total popu-lation lived in metropolitan areas (defined as cen-tral cities and suburbs). By 1950, 56.1 percent did. Moreover, while the percentage of citizens residing in central cities remained relatively steady after 1930 (hovering around 30 percent), the percentage of cit-izens residing in suburban communities soared, ris-ing from 7.1 percent in 1910 to 23.3 percent in 1950. Contrary to popular assumption, which pinpoints suburban growth as a phenomenon of the 1950s, this migration began in earnest during the 1920s when the suburbs grew by a then unprecedented 50 percent. Hence, it may be somewhat inaccurate to gauge a metropolitan area's interest in its baseball team merely by comparing attendance to the cen-tral city's population. Certainly by 1930, teams had the ability to draw from a significantly larger base than that. As a result, in Philadelphia, for example, although Philadelphia baseball attendance roughly matched the city's population growth, it lagged far behind the increase in population in the Delaware Valley during that time.

53. Seymour, *Baseball: The Golden Age,* 68.

54. Golenbock, *The Spirit of St. Louis,* 226.

55. Jeffrey Stuart, *Twilight Teams* (Gaithersburg, Md.: Sark Publishing, 2000), 81, in noting that the 1953 St. Louis Browns drew 980 paid fans for their game against Detroit on Thursday, August 13.

56. *See* "Brush's Death Blow to Baseball World," *New York Times,* November 27, 1927, 11; "C. H. Ebbets Dies of Heart Disease," *New York Times,* April 19, 1925, 26; "Chas. A. Stoneham, Giants' Owner, Dies," *New York Times,* January 7, 1936, 21; "Charles A. Comiskey Dead," *Chicago Daily Tri-bune,* October 26, 1931, 1; "Wrigley Rites Tomor-row in Pasadena Home," *Chicago Daily Tribune,* January 27, 1932, 1; "Tiger Owner Walter Briggs Dies Suddenly," *New York Times,* January 18, 1952, C3; "Clark C. Griffith of Senators Dies," *New York Times,* October 29, 1955, 25; "Powel Crosley Jr. Is Dead at 74; Owner of the Cincinnati Reds," *New York Times,* March 29, 1961, 33; "Walter F. O'Mal-ley, Leader of Dodgers' Move to Los Angeles, Dies at 75," *New York Times,* August 10, 1979, A-1; Re-gardless of where these men started in life, they were, on the whole, self-made, as these obituaries

make clear. Brush was an orphan who found work as a clerk in a clothing store, eventually opening his own and making his fortune; Ebbets was a vendor selling scorecards at Brooklyn games during their inaugural year; Stoneham was a "board boy" in a brokerage office before branching out on his own, if ethically dubious, financial career; Comiskey was a first-generation American, his father having immigrated from Ireland to a Chicago slum; Wrigley was the son of a prosperous soap manufacturer in Philadelphia but ran away from home at age 11 to work in a newsstand in New York, sleeping in the street. Eventually he returned home where he worked as a traveling soap salesman for his father's company; Briggs began his professional career as a $20/week railroad car checker. He would then work as a body trimmer in an automobile plant and then open up his own body company, which would eventually become one of the largest in the country; Griffith was a mascot for his local Vernon, Missouri, team; Crosley peddled novelties — vending buttons, stickers, advertising caps and aprons, and window displays — in Cincinnati before working for a mail order firm, which he eventually bought and made millions; O'Malley was legal counsel for the Dodgers before taking over the team.

57. Zingg and Medeiros, *Runs, Hits and an Era,* 69–70.

58. "Night Ball 'Fad,' Says Mack," *New York Times,* February 16, 1935, 17.

59. Zingg and Medeiros, *Runs, Hits and an Era,* 69.

60. Lanctot, *Negro League Baseball,* 22, 23, 38, 41, 279, 280–81, 288. Lanctot's discussion of Rickey's involvement with Robinson and the purchase of his contract form the basis of the discussion of this topic herein. Moreover, Lanctot's book, more generally, served as the source for the discussion of the talent level of the Negro Leagues as well as the frequent interaction between players of the Major and Negro leagues through the years and playing venues of various Negro League teams contained herein.

61. William C. Kashatus, *September Swoon: Richie Allen, the '64 Phillies, and Racial Integration* (University Park: Pennsylvania State Press, 2004), 11–12. For a time, Connie Mack himself agreed to pit his Athletics against the Negro League Hilldales of Philadelphia and suffered a number of losses during the 1920s. In one instance, Judy Johnson and the Hilldales defeated Lefty Grove 6–1. In later years, Grove would deny ever playing against the Hilldales, let alone losing to them.

62. Fetter, *Taking on the Yankees,* 70–71.

63. The 1952 Braves, for example, nearly doubled their average attendance (3,629) on Sundays (6,538); the 1953 Browns averaged 3,860 fans overall but 6,783 on Sundays; and the 1954 Athletics averaged 3,906 overall but 7,131 on Sundays.

64. The Browns drew 133,086 of their total of 297,328 fans during games either played on Sundays or against the Yankees.

65. The Athletics drew 114,116 of their 304,666 fans on games played either on Sundays or against the Yankees.

66. Helyar, *Lords of the Realm,* 65, 523.

67. Fetter, *Taking on the Yankees,* 8.

68. Shapiro, *The Last Good Season,* 73, noting that, during the 1950s, approximately half of the Giants' total attendance came from their games against the Dodgers; Fetter, *Taking on the Yankees,* 263, noting that in 1954, one-third of the Giants' total attendance came from games against the Dodgers; Jules Tygel, *Past Time: Baseball as History* (New York: Oxford University Press, 2001), 178, noting that in 1956, one-third of the Giants' total attendance came once again from games against the Dodgers.

69. John Drebinger, "Night Baseball on Limited Scale Adopted Unanimously by National League," *New York Times,* December 13, 1934, 31.

70. The generally acknowledged horridness of many Major League teams is summed up nicely in a humorous quote attributed to Doc Prothro, manager of the Phillies between 1939 and 1941. During his stewardship, the Phils compiled a winning percentage of .302 (138–320–2). At one point, a Phils pitcher approached him to ask if the Phils indeed were in the big leagues. "Son," Prothro replied, "we might not be in the big leagues, but the teams we play are." Frank Fitzpatrick, "Morning Bytes: Sorry, Phillies Fans, but It Could Be Worse," *Philadelphia Inquirer,* May 13, 2005, D2.

71. Seymour, *Baseball: The Golden Age,* 434. The discussion of the relationship between Frazee and Ruppert, as well as the relationship between the Yankees and Red Sox, is based on Seymour's text.

72. Fetter, *Taking on the Yankees,* 317.

73. Ibid., 48–49.

Chapter 4

1. *See* Kaese, *The Boston Braves,* 262–77, for a detailed discussion of the improvements made by the Braves during the 1940s to update their image and modernize their organization, including their minor league operations.

2. Joshua Prager, *The Echoing Green: The Untold Story of Bobby Thomson, Ralph Branca and the Shot Heard Round the World* (New York: Pantheon Books, 2006), 42.

3. Golenbock, *The Spirit of St. Louis,* 68.

4. Seymour, *Baseball: The Golden Age,* 400.

5. Jordan, *The Athletics,* 145.

6. Kuklick, *To Everything a Season,* 36–37, 40. Kuklick's book provides the source material for the discussion of Mack's system of player selection.

7. *See* Jordan, *The Athletics,* 69–77, 85, for his analysis of Mack's player movements between 1914 and 1922 as well as his decision regarding the possibility of signing Babe Ruth.

8. Seymour, *Baseball: The Golden Age,* 137–38.

9. *See* Jordan, *The Athletics,* 85, 116–20, for his discussion of the causes behind Mack's dismantling of his second dynasty of the late 1920s and early 1930s.

10. Kuklick, *To Everything a Season,* 63.

11. Ibid.

12. Fetter, *Taking on the Yankees,* 170.

13. Ibid.

14. Kuklick, *To Everything a Season,* 95.

15. Ibid., 112; Jordan, *The Athletics,* 124. Ben Shibe died in 1922, bequeathing his shares in the

Athletics to his four children. However, his sons Tom and Jack took over the day-to-day responsibilities of overseeing the club. Tom became president of the club on Ben's death and remained in that position until his death on February 16, 1936. Thereafter, Jack assumed the presidency but relinquished the post to Connie Mack shortly before Jack's death on July 11, 1937. On Jack's death, his shares in the Athletics passed to his widow, who then sold them to Mack, giving Mack a controlling share in the club for the first time.

16. Kuklick, *To Everything a Season,* 114. Kuklick's book, along with Jordan's, *The Athletics of Philadelphia,* both detail the specifics of the fall of the House of Mack during the 1940s and '50s described herein.

17. Jordan, *The Athletics,* 152. Jordan's book details the specifics of the A's brief dalliance with Hank Aaron.

18. Ibid., 143.

19. Kuklick, *To Everything a Season,* 115.

20. Ibid.

21. Both Kuklick and Jordan discuss the intricacies of Mack's personal life, including the relationship between Mack and the children from both of his marriages, and both authors serve as excellent references on the specifics of this issue.

22. Kuklick, *To Everything a Season,* 113–14.

23. Sources vary on the exact amount of the Macks' annual mortgage payment to Connecticut General. Kuklick states that it was $250,000 whereas Jordan states that it was $200,000.

24. Kuklick, *To Everything a Season,* 92; Jordan, *The Athletics of Philadelphia,* 134, 176; Jordan, *Occasional Glory,* 93–108; and Fitzpatrick, *You Can't Lose 'Em All,* 34–36, for a discussion of R.R.M. Carpenter, Jr. along with the rise of the Phillies after his purchase of the team. These books all served as sources for the discussion of the topics contained herein.

25. Golenbock, *The Spirit of St. Louis,* 353. Parts of the discussion of the impact of the PCL on the relocation of the Braves, Browns and Athletics originally appeared, in slightly different form, in Nathanson, "The Irrelevance of Major League Baseball's Antitrust Exemption: A Historical Review," *Rutgers Law Review* 58, 1 (2005).

26. *See* Golenbock, *The Spirit of St. Louis;* Kaese, *The Boston Braves;* and Jordan, *The Athletics of Philadelphia.*

27. Jordan, *The Athletics.* Jordan notes that for the majority of the time that both the Athletics and the Phillies shared the same city, Philadelphia was clearly an "A's" town, with the Phillies struggling by comparison. It was only in the late 1940s and early 1950s, with the combination of the Phillies' "Whiz Kids" and the deterioration of both Connie Mack's health and his Athletics, that the city's allegiances shifted toward the Phillies for the first sustained period ever.

28. Golenbock, *The Spirit of St. Louis,* 280–81. According to Golenbock, the move to Los Angeles had been all but finalized, with the Browns scheduled to play their 1942 opener at LA's Wrigley Field. All that remained was official recognition of the move, which to that point was kept secret from even

some of the Browns' directors, that was expected to be granted during the Major League winter meeting to be held on December 8, 1941, in Chicago. After the bombing of Pearl Harbor the day before, the meeting went on as scheduled but the proposed relocation was taken off the table. It is important to note that despite the cancellation of the move, the Browns did not in fact dissolve. They survived in St. Louis for another 12 seasons. Apparently, the revenue provided by the Yankees and Sunday baseball was sufficient to support even the most hopeless of causes.

29. Zingg and Medeiros, *Runs, Hits, and an Era,* 17. Zingg and Medeiros's text provides a useful overview of the origins and history of the PCL during this time, when more than a few people considered the overall level of play to be more comparable to the Majors than many within Major League Baseball would have liked to believe.

30. Ibid., 107–08.

31. "Coast Major League Baseball Debated by Heads of Clubs," *Los Angeles Times,* March 19, 1946, A7.

32. Al Wolf, "Chandler Ducks Talk of Third Big League Here," *Los Angeles Times,* July 21, 1946, A5, wherein Chandler is quoted as saying that "the Pacific Coast League's desire to go major is entitled to every consideration; nobody recognizes the importance of this part of the country more than I."

33. "PCL to Give Majors One More Chance," *Los Angeles Times,* June 23, 1951, B2.

34. Ibid.

35. "Coast League Outlaw Plan Fails to Carry," *Los Angeles Times,* July 28, 1951, B1.

36. "Frick Says Major Status Up to Coast," *Los Angeles Times,* August 1, 1951, C1.

37. Ibid.

38. Ibid. Celler is quoted as saying, "If we exempt you, you'll have to reorient your thinking. You can't keep this complete hold on major league status. Stop saying there will be major leagues only east of the Mississippi."

39. Ibid.

40. "Major Coast Ball Asked by Hillings," *Los Angeles Times,* October 15, 1951, C4.

41. "Wrigley Sees Pacific Coast Major League," *Los Angeles Times,* October 18, 1951, C1.

42. "Major League Plan Would Assist PCL," *Los Angeles Times,* November 15, 1951, C1.

43. "Coast League Nabobs Laud Recommendations," *Los Angeles Times,* November 15, 1951) C33.

44. "New Proposal Dims PCL's Major Hopes," *Los Angeles Times,* November 29, 1951, C1.

45. "Congressmen Rap Majors' Monopoly," *Los Angeles Times,* May 23, 1952, C1.

46. Ibid. The *Times* noted that the report pointed out "that several clubs in the presently-operated circuits have been losing money in large amounts and over continued periods *and rais[ed] the question whether Boston, St. Louis and Philadelphia are two-team cities*" (emphasis added).

47. Golenbock, *The Spirit of St. Louis,* 353. *See also* "Braves Block Bid to Shift Browns," *New York Times,* May 4, 1953.

48. Ibid.

49. Ibid.

50. *See* "New Milwaukee Park Is Really Big League," *New York Times*, March 22, 1953. The new Milwaukee stadium was designed to Major League specifications and would initially seat 28,111 with plans for 12,000 additional seats.

51. Ibid. (noting that Perini was on the "hot spot" for keeping Milwaukee out of the Major Leagues after stating that he would never stand in its way.) *See also* Kaese, *The Boston Braves*, 282, stating that after the completion of the 1952 season, Perini promised Milwaukee fans that he would help them obtain a Major League franchise.

52. Ibid. Accounts regarding the exact figure offered by Veeck to Perini vary, with the *New York Times* stating that it was $500,000 and Golenbock claiming that it was $750,000. *See* Golenbock, *The Spirit of St. Louis*, 353.

53. Louis Effrat, "Braves Move to Milwaukee; Majors' First Shift since '03," *New York Times*, March 19, 1953, 1.

54. Golenbock, *The Spirit of St. Louis*, 326–54; Helyar, *Lords of the Realm*, 9, 234–35. Golenbock's and Helyar's books provide much detail on the life of Veeck, particularly as owner of the Browns along with his penchant for picking fights with the commissioner, the American League president and his fellow owners, most notably, Topping and Webb of the Yankees.

55. Seymour, *Baseball: The Golden Years*, 288.

56. Helyar, *Lords of the Realm*, 235.

57. Ibid., 234.

58. Golenbock, *The Spirit of St. Louis*, 352–53.

59. Golenbock's book, along with Jeffrey Stuart's *Twilight Team*, 51–94, detail the Browns' frantic, final season in St. Louis along with the machinations of Veeck and his American League brethren throughout that year as Veeck frantically fought, to no avail, for permission to relocate.

60. "AL to Study Brownie Shift," *Los Angeles Times*, September 10, 1953, C1. The committee gave no reason for its failure to attend the scheduled meeting but promised to reconvene "as soon as possible." Chuck Comiskey, another committee member, warned, however, that the relocation of the Browns was by no means a sure thing. He said, "There are so many other factors, such as minor league territorial rights to consider. This would not be as simple as was the Boston Braves' shift to Milwaukee this year." Comiskey did not elaborate or explain why the territorial rights issue was any more complicated with the Browns than it had been with the Braves.

61. Golenbock, *The Spirit of St. Louis*, 357.

62. Ibid. Allegedly, one of Webb's "friends" was Howard Hughes and, according to Golenbock, Webb dangled a signed $1million check from Hughes in front of his fellow owners as incentive for the move.

63. Jordan, *The Athletics*, 181–83. For the 1954 season, the Athletics modernized their look, replacing their traditional "A" on the left chest with a script "Athletics." In addition, red was added to their traditional white and blue uniforms. Unfortunately, many of the same players who donned the old uniforms in 1953 were issued the new ones in 1954 and another miserable season ensued regardless.

64. Stuart, *Twilight Teams*, 121–22.

65. "Johnson to Compensate Yankees if Athletics Go to Kansas City," *New York Times*, October 8, 1954, 29.

66. Jordan, *The Athletics*, 181–84.

67. Kuklick, *To Every Thing a Season*, 120. Although Roy wanted to remain as owner of the team and keep the team in Philadelphia, his brother Earle wanted out.

68. Jordan, *The Athletics of Philadelphia*, 184.

69. Shirley Povich, "This Morning: To Whom It May Concern," *Washington Post and Times Herald*, November 21, 1954, C1. Povich noted the curious coincidence of the Yankees' backing of the relocation of the Athletics and Webb's construction company emerging shortly thereafter to win the Kansas City stadium project.

70. Kuklick, *To Everything a Season*, 120–26, and Jordan, *The Athletics of Philadelphia*, 181–86, both provide similar accounts of the last days of the Philadelphia Athletics and the specifics regarding their relocation.

71. Both Kuklick and Jordan also note that Connie, Sr. vehemently opposed the relocation of his Athletics, even traveling in his infirmed condition up to New York to attend one league meeting in which he personally pled with his fellow owners to approve the sale to the local syndicate. His pleas went unanswered.

72. *See* "Shift of Athletics to Kansas City Is Authorized by the American League," *New York Times*, October 13, 1954, 34. One of the offers came from Tommy Richardson, a director of the Athletics under Mack and president of the Eastern League while the other came from a group headed by Jack Rensel whose goal was to buy out the Macks and keep the team in Philadelphia.

73. Ibid.

74. Stuart, *Twilight Teams*, 131.

75. Arthur Mann, "How to Buy a Ball Club for Peanuts," *Saturday Evening Post*, 25 (April 9, 1955). Mann's article provides a detailed breakdown of the origin of virtually every penny of the $3.5 million used by Johnson to purchase the Athletics.

76. Stuart, *Twilight Teams*, 135.

77. Mann, "How to Buy a Ball Club for Peanuts," 74. Johnson became involved, at least professionally, with Topping and Webb in 1951 when Johnson was elected vice chairman of the Automatic Canteen Company, a Kansas City investment group. Webb and Topping backed his promotion to this position, providing a portion of the $1.5 million necessary for Johnson to buy out the current vice chairman who was stepping down and looking to sell his shares. After Johnson's election, Johnson, Webb and Topping worked together to purchase both Kansas City and New York real estate, along with both Kansas City's minor league ball park and Yankee Stadium. In many of these deals, Webb and Topping sold their holdings to Johnson, lending him the money to make the purchase, who then rented them right back to them. The three men worked so closely together in this fashion that worries of favoritism crept into the proposed sale of the Athletics to Johnson once it was announced, worries that would be borne out after the sale and relocation were completed.

78. Fetter, *Taking on the Yankees*, 317; Helyar, *Lords of the Realm*, 73.

79. Effrat, "Braves Move to Milwaukee," 38.

80. Shapiro, *The Last Good Season*, 251.

81. Tygel, *Past Time*, 174.

82. Ibid., 175.

Chapter 5

1. Fitzpatrick, *You Can't Lose 'Em All*, 16, 228.

2. See A. Joseph Newman, Jr., "Philadelphia Blues," *United States Banker* 98, no. 3 (March, 1989): 39. In discussing the Philadelphia banking community's history of failures and misfortunes, Newman blamed much of it on the city's geographical nexus with New York. Expanding on a theory proposed by a Wharton professor, Newman concluded that Philadelphia bankers run into trouble largely because they seek to compete and "outdo" New York, causing their institutions to crumble underneath them. "Philadelphia's northern suburbs are becoming New York's southern suburbs. That's why ... Philadelphians in business ... have a 'thing' about New York. It's a thing that often gets them in trouble." Under Newman's theory, it is not so much an inferiority complex but, rather, the sense that "Philadelphians do seem to have to justify the importance of Philadelphia in relation to New York. And to justify means to want to grow bigger." Newman's theory echoes sentiments that have driven Philadelphians for nearly two centuries.

3. H. Walton Cloke, "Philadelphia Sees Herself as Fitting World Capital," *New York Times*, April 29, 1945, E7.

4. "Phila. High on List for U.N. Capital Site; Decision Due Today," *Philadelphia Inquirer*, December 2, 1946, 1.

5. Henry C. Wolfe, "Evatt Carries Torch for World's Underdogs (Except Phillies and A's)," *Washington Post*, December 9, 1945, B2. Dr. Herbert Vere Evatt, referred to as the "wild man" of the 20 United Nations committees on which he served, also confessed to being a die-hard Brooklyn Dodger fan.

6. Ivan H. Peterman, "U.S. Favors Site in East for U.N.; San Francisco Eliminated by Austin," *Philadelphia Inquirer*, December 7, 1946, 5.

7. Ibid., 1, 5; "New York Skyscraper Home Now Possible as U.N. Center," *New York Times*, December 8, 1946, 1, 11. The *Times* noted that, despite New York's late push, "Philadelphia has the best theoretical standing of any city, with New York now perhaps a rapidly-closing second placer."

8. Cloke, "Philadelphia Sees Herself as a Fitting World Capital," E7.

9. "Phila. High on List for U.N. Capital Site," 1.

10. Ivan H. Peterman, "N.Y. Offer Hurts Phila. Bid for Site," *Philadelphia Inquirer*, December 12, 1946, 2. The article noted that, on consideration of New York's late offer to place the world capital in America's most congested city, a member of the UN's secretariat reminded his colleagues that if they chose the site, they would be choosing a site "without any of the open air countryside or distinction it so desired."

11. Ivan H. Peterman, "New York Selected as World Capital by U.N. Committee Dominated by U.S.," *Philadelphia Inquirer*, December 13, 1946, 1.

12. Robert Caro, *The Power Broker: Robert Moses and the Fall of New York* (New York: Vintage Books, 1975), 771.

13. Ibid.

14. "U.N. May Select Phila. Site Today, Delegates Assert," *Philadelphia Inquirer*, December 11, 1946, 2. The article noted that after the committee's finding, Philadelphia was left with "no organization opposition from any bloc."

15. Caro, *The Power Broker*, 771–72.

16. Ibid., 772.

17. George Barrett, "Decision Is Final: Skyscraper Parliament of World to Rise on Mid–Island Tract," *New York Times*, December 15, 1946, 1, 5.

18. Caro, *The Power Broker*, 773–74.

19. Barrett, "Decision Is Final," 1.

20. Ibid. "Through all the long site search in San Francisco, Boston , Philadelphia and New York, it was never any secret that the United Nations delegates were generally agreed that New York was the best place to establish a permanent world capital." Peterman, "New York Selected as World Capital," 1. Peterman noted that in the choice of New York to be the UN's new home, Philadelphia was "deserted by friends" such as the British, South Americans and Arab leaders who previously voiced their support for the Philadelphia location.

21. Barrett, "Decision Is Final," 5.

22. "This City Is Still the Best U.N. Site," *Philadelphia Inquirer*, December 13, 1946, 20.

23. Riess, *Touching Base*, 20.

24. See Paul Taylor, "Phila's Decade: Progress, Strife and Frank Rizzo," *Philadelphia Inquirer*, December 30, 1979, C4, in remarking how the city's resurgent sports teams, particularly the Flyers' two Stanley Cups, helped to bring respectability back to the city during the 1970s.

25. The stadium was so renamed in 1953.

26. Kuklick, *To Everything a Season*, 92–93. Kuklick remarked that Carpenter was a "decent, pleasant man of ordinary abilities."

27. Jordan, *Occasional Glory*, 118.

28. See Kuklick, *To Everything a Season*, 92–93. Besides opening his wallet, Carpenter's main role while the Whiz Kids were being assembled during the 1940s was that of an "uncritical fan" who himself admitted that his favorite pastime was sitting "in my box seats and talking to great old players." He was hardly of the mind-set to make the cold, tough decisions needed to put a winner on the field. Rather, these decisions were left to Pennock.

29. William C. Kashatus, *September Swoon: Richie Allen, the '64 Phillies, and Racial Integration* (University Park: Penn State Press, 2004), 37.

30. William C. Kashatus, "Dick Allen, the Phillies, and Racism," *NINE: A Journal of Baseball History and Culture* 9, no. 2 (spring 2001): 151, 155.

31. Jordan, *Occasional Glory*, 122.

32. Kuklick, *To Everything a Season*, 32. As recounted by Kuklick, the *Sporting News* noted that unruly fan behavior was not limited to "foreigners" given that it was so common in Philadelphia, "a bastion of 100 percent Americanism."

33. Ibid., 109.

34. Jordan, *Occasional Glory*, 123–26.

35. Ibid., 127. Jordan notes that the Phils of the late '50s had "no spark, no personality, to arouse the fans."

36. Ibid., 79.

37. For recollections of Chuck Klein's career, *see* Red Smith, "Chuck Klein's Cooperstown," *New York Times*, March 16, 1980, S3; Red Smith, "Chuck Klein of Baker Bowl," *New York Times*, August 6, 1980, B7; "Hall Inducts Snider, Kaline, Yawkey, Klein," *Washington Post*, August 4, 1980, D2.

38. *See* Smith, "Chuck Klein's Cooperstown," S3. F. Dane Buck, a professor of law at Franklin Pierce Law Center, campaigned hard for Klein for many years throughout the 1970s, compiling and comparing his statistics with his contemporaries and sending his conclusions to members of the Hall's Veterans Committee, along with members of the media such as Smith.

39. Roscoe McGowen, "Mayor Says His Baseball Aide Talked to Phils about Shift Here," *New York Times*, April 16, 1959, 41.

40. Ibid.

41. Ibid.

42. Ibid. A few years later, in 1964, Carpenter attempted to turn up the heat again, this time by actually purchasing 100 acres of land in Camden. Later, his son Ruly would admit that his father never had any real intention of building a ballpark there and moving the Phillies. "It was really just a ploy to put pressure on the city to get its act together and build a new stadium. I don't think he would've moved to New Jersey." Rich Westcott, *Veterans Stadium: Field of Memories* (Philadelphia: Temple University Press, 2005), 4.

43. John Drebinger, "Sports of the Times: What Now?" *New York Times*, July 18, 1960, 19. The struggling Cincinnati Reds were likewise rumored to be possibly relocating to New York. Both of these possibilities were preferable to expansion in solving New York's National League void because, through relocation, the owners could keep their sacred club closed to outsiders.

44. Jordan, *Occasional Glory*, 128.

45. John F. Bauman, *Public Housing, Race and Renewal: Urban Planning in Philadelphia, 1920–1974* (Philadelphia: Temple University Press, 1987), 83.

46. Ibid.

47. Ibid., 80.

48. *See* Taylor, "Phila's Decade: Progress, Strife and Frank Rizzo," 4C.

49. Bauman, *Public Housing*, 80.

50. Ibid., 79.

51. Cloke, "Philadelphia Sees Herself as Fitting World Capital," E7.

52. Taylor, "Phila's Decade: Progress, Strife and Frank Rizzo," 4C. The marketing slogan was initiated during the early 1970s and addressed the city's self-image problem that dated back for decades to the days surrounding the fall of Nicholas Biddle and the Second National Bank and reinforced during the particularly gloomy 1940s and '50s.

53. U.S. Bureau of the Census, "Population of the 100 Largest Urban Places," *http://www.census. gov/population/documentation/twps0027/tab15.txt.*

Between 1950 and 1960, the city's population decreased from 2,071,605 to 2,002,512.

54. Hobbs and Stoops, U.S. Census Bureau, Census 2000 Special Reports, Series CENSR-4, *Demographic Trends in the 20th Century*, 33.

55. Ibid. 32.3 percent of the population resided in cities versus 30.9 percent in suburban areas.

56. Ibid. During this time frame, urban population jumped from 21.2 percent to 32.3 percent, an increase of 52 percent, whereas suburban population jumped from 7.1 percent to 30.9 percent, an increase of 335 percent.

57. Ibid., 37, Table 1.3: "Ten Most Populous Metropolitan Areas: 1950–2000."

58. Jennifer L. Eberhardt and Susan T. Fiske, "Motivating Individuals to Change: What Is a Target to Do?" in *Stereotypes and Stereotyping* (New York: The Guilford Press, 1996), 369, 383–84. Other sources consulted in the discussion herein regarding the nature of groups include: Wolfgang Stroebe and Chester A. Insko, "Stereotype, Prejudice, and Discrimination: Changing Conceptions in Theory and Research," in *Stereotype and Prejudice: Changing Conceptions*, edited by Daniel Bar-Tal, Carl F. Graumann, Arie W. Kruglanski and Wolfgang Stroebe, 3 (New York: Springer-Verlag, 1989); David J. Schneider, "Modern Stereotype Research: Unfinished Business," in *Stereotypes and Stereotyping*, 419; Henri Taijfel, "Experiments in Intergroup Discrimination," *Scientific American* 223, no. 96 (1970); John A. Bargh and Tanya L. Chartrand, "The Unbearable Automaticity of Being," *American Psychologist* 54, no. 462 (1999); Brian Lickel, David L. Hamilton, et al., "Varieties of Groups and the Perception of Group Entitavity," *Journal of Personality and Social Psychology* 78, no. 223 (February 2000).

59. David Berreby, *Us and Them: Understanding Your Tribal Mind* (New York: Little, Brown, 2005), 16. Berreby's book summarizes much of the recent social science on the research of groups and concludes that one of the things unique to the human race is the desire to divide itself up into "tribes" consisting of "us" and "them." Because breaking the world into groups comprised of "us" and "them" is how humans make sense of the world around them (for at the end of the day, any particular person is ultimately perceived, and judged, as being one of "us" or one of "them"), the delineation of groupings ultimately dictates the perception of the people believed to be members within or outside of these groups. And because humans also have a natural urge to maintain a positive social identity (everyone likes to feel good about themselves and, therefore, believes deep down that they are a "good" person), it is likewise only natural for individuals to value "their" perceived groups (as well as the people within them) more highly than those they do not feel they belong to. After all, it would be quite difficult to think highly of ourselves if we did not think highly of those with whom we kept company or with whom we consider ourselves to be aligned. As social psychology has discovered, however, this requires individuals, unfortunately, to feel a natural urge to denigrate those groups to which they do not belong, for it is difficult to value "our" group highly if there is nothing to which to compare it — some-

thing that can be looked down on. As more and more people switched groups during the 1950s and '60s, Philadelphia paid the price.

60. Berreby, *Us and Them*, 124.

61. Miles Hewstone, "Contact and Categorization: Social Psychological Interventions to Change Intergroup Relations," in *Stereotypes and Stereotyping*, 323, 324.

62. Of course, to use a sociological term, "decategorizing"—seeing the individual rather than the group—can always occur but this requires constant interaction between group members. Given the trend at the time toward fewer, not greater, contact between suburbanites and city dwellers, this was not likely to occur. *See* Eberhardt and Fiske, "Motivating Individuals to Change," 383–84.

63. Kuklick, *To Everything a Season*, 153–54.

64. Bauman, *Public Housing, Race and Renewal*, 183.

65. Kuklick, *To Everything a Season*, 139.

66. Bauman, *Public Housing, Race and Renewal*, 188. Much of the source material for the August 1964 riot in North Philadelphia comes from Bauman's text.

67. Kashatus, *September Swoon*, 112–13; Kuklick, *To Everything a Season*, 143.

68. With expansion in 1962 (the National League added the New York Mets and Houston Colt .45's (who would later be renamed the Astros) came an extended schedule, from 154 games to 162, resulting in 81 home games instead of the traditional 77.

69. Bauman, *Public Housing, Race and Renewal*, 86. Bauman's book provides the source for the discussion herein on the racial makeup of Philadelphia during the 1940s and early 1950s.

70. Lanctot, *Negro League Baseball*, 49, 52, 139.

71. Jordan, *Occasional Glory*, 100–01.

72. Ibid., 101.

73. Kashatus, "Dick Allen, the Phillies and Racism," 154. For a concise history of the treatment of the Phillies toward Robinson in 1947, *see* John Rossi, "Jackie Robinson in the City of Brotherly Love," *Elysian Fields Quarterly* 2, no. 15 (1998): 25.

74. Jordan, *Occasional Glory*, 101. Kashatus casts doubt on whether Pennock ever uttered those words, believing the statement to have been insufficiently documented in order to be confirmed. He notes that Rachel Robinson, Jackie's widow, refuses to take a position on this alleged statement based on this ground. *See* Kashatus, *September Swoon*, 28.

75. This is not to suggest that Philadelphia was a bastion of tolerance; indeed, when the Dodgers tried to check in to the Benjamin Franklin Hotel for that first series in Philadelphia, they were told that there were no rooms available to them "while you have any nigras with you." *See* Kashatus, *September Swoon*, 29. However, the point is that Philadelphia was no different than any other metropolitan area at the time; perhaps no better but certainly no worse.

76. Kashatus, "Dick Allen, the Phillies and Racism," 155.

77. Ibid., 156–57.

78. Ibid.

79. Both Taylor (acquired from the Cubs) and

Amaro (acquired from the Cardinals) were acquired via trade although Amaro did spend some time in the Phillies farm system after he arrived.

80. Kuklick, *To Everything a Season*, 159–60.

81. Ibid.

82. Ibid., 160.

83. Ibid.

84. Ibid.

85. Kashatus, *September Swoon*, 170–71. Allen recalled that, by 1967, he would head to the bars on his way to the ballpark and would occasionally show up at the stadium drunk. On July 8, 1967, he was so drunk that he could not walk a straight line nor speak without slurring his words. He was told to go home but stayed instead. Manager Gene Mauch fined him for being late to the ballpark and benched him although he did come up in the eighth inning to pinch hit, striking out in a 6–4 Phils loss. After the game, Mauch covered up for Allen before the media, insisting that he benched Allen merely to give him a rest.

86. Ibid., 177. Kashatus's book provides a detailed analysis of the role of the Philadelphia media in the disintegration of the Phillies clubhouse in the late 1960s.

87. Kuklick, *To Everything a Season*, 160.

88. Fitzpatrick, *You Can't Lose 'Em All*, 40; Kashatus, *September Swoon*.

89. Fitzpatrick, *You Can't Lose 'Em All*, 40.

90. Kashatus, *September Swoon*, 67.

91. The 1993 Phils were coming off of a last place season in 1992 but rode an unexpected hot start to the division title (they spent only one day all season out of first place). After defeating the Braves in the NL LCS, the surprising Phils took the defending world champion Toronto Blue Jays to the sixth game of the 1993 World Series and appeared to have the game won, taking a lead into the bottom of the ninth. However, closer Mitch Williams, erratic but ultimately effective all season, blew the save, giving up a series-ending home run to Joe Carter—only the second time a World Series had ended on a home run (Bill Mazeroski's homer in the 1960 Series being the first). After it was over, few could argue that the Phils were robbed of the title; the way they lost was heartbreaking but, much like the 1964 team, few expected them to even be there in the first place. Although the 1993 collapse lasted all but a few minutes whereas the 1964 collapse evolved over a period of two weeks, they were similar in that they were crushing baseball events that meant little beyond the field.

Chapter 6

1. Christopher Klemek, "Aesthetic Reform–Social Analysis and Design in Philadelphia Planning," in "Urbanism as Reform: Modernist Planning and the Crisis of Urban Liberalism in Europe and North America, 1945–1975" (PhD diss., University of Pennsylvania, 2004). Available at *www.history.upenn.edu/~klemek/docs/klemekchapter5.pdf*, 205.

2. "The City: Under the Knife, or All for Their Own Good," *Time*, November 16, 1964, 69.

3. Robin Pobrebin, "Edmund Bacon, 95, Urban

Planner of Philadelphia, Dies," *New York Times*, October 18, 2005.

4. Robert A. Caro, *The Power Broker: Robert Moses and the Fall of New York* (New York: Vintage Books, 1975), 52–53. Caro's book serves as the primary source of reference for the analysis of Robert Moses and the reshaping of New York during the twentieth century contained herein. *See also* the following pages: 33–34, 65–67, 161–67, 545, 896–97, 1133.

5. Ellen Karasilk, "Suburbs? Foo! Some Are Returning to City's Stoops," *Philadelphia Inquirer*, September 4, 1977, A17, discussing the transformation of Center City and quoting Caroline Golab, an urban historian from the University of Pennsylvania, who said: "It's almost a return to the colonial city ... In the 1700s, the rich lived in the center city and the working people lived on the outskirts ... Now the well-to-do have come back to center city."

6. "Under the Knife," 69–70; William G. Weart, "Skyscrapers Due in Philadelphia," *New York Times*, December 11, 1960, R1.

7. *See* Thomas Hine, "University City: Will It Prove That Renewal Works?" *Philadelphia Inquirer*, December 21, 1978, B1.

8. Bauman, *Public Housing, Race and Renewal*, 100. The "bright, clean city" campaign was championed by the Citizens' Council on City Planning (CCCP), which worked closely with Bacon in reshaping the central city.

9. Klemek, "Urbanism as Reform," 210. Klemek notes that the Independence Hall demolition plan was championed by Philadelphia Common Pleas Court judge Edwin O. Lewis, who not only considered the idea an effective measure to counter bombing threats but an attractive one as well given his personal disdain for the city's Victorian architecture, which he hoped to reduce through his plan.

10. Ibid., 210–11. Klemek's dissertation was a valuable source for the discussion of the genesis of Bacon's vision contained herein.

11. Bauman, *Public Housing, Race and Renewal*, 107–08. Chapter 5 of Bauman's book, "Race, Redevelopment, and Renewal" (pp. 79–117) provides a detailed analysis of the rise of the Young Turks and the process by which they were able to wrest control of the city and remake it pursuant to their vision. As such, it was a source for the discussion of these topics contained herein.

12. Klemek, "Urbanism as Reform," 202–03; Bauman, *Public Housing, Race and Renewal*, 119–20.

13. Bauman, *Public Housing, Race and Renewal*, 97.

14. For an analysis of the "Better Philadelphia Exhibit," see Bauman, *Public Housing, Race and Renewal*, 100, and "Under the Knife," 69.

15. The exact attendance at the exhibit is unclear. Bauman states that it was over 400,000; the *Time* article puts the total at 385,000.

16. "Under the Knife," 69.

17. Bauman, *Public Housing, Race and Renewal*, 102.

18. Klemek, "Urbanism as Reform," 204.

19. Bauman, *Public Housing, Race and Renewal*, 118–19. Bauman's book provides much of the source material for the discussion of Philadelphia's mid-century political reform contained herein.

20. Ibid., 103.

21. William G. Weart, "Urban Renewal Housing Goes Up in Philadelphia," *New York Times*, October 1, 1961, R15.

22. *See* chapter 1. Klemek's dissertation (pp. 201–02) likewise discusses the decay of the city due to the cultural elite's abandonment of it to the Main Line.

23. Bauman, *Public Housing, Race and Renewal*, 107–08. Bauman's book provides the source material for the discussion of the East Poplar and Yardville urban reform experiments.

24. Ibid., 94.

25. The city purchased the area for $257,552 and then resold it to the newly created nonprofit Mutual Housing Corporation for $78,400. *See Public Housing, Race and Renewal*, 108.

26. According to Bauman, the East Poplar plan, "create[d] harmonious order out of the unplanned chaos of the urban past." This was in keeping with the teachings of Bacon's mentor, Eliel Saarinen, the world-famous architect who granted Bacon a fellowship at his Cranbrook Academy of Art in Michigan and who became, in Bacon's words, "my great master and teacher." *See also* "Under the Knife," 69.

27. Indeed, Bauman notes (pp. 110–11) that the rehabilitated East Poplar neighborhood resulted in housing costs beyond the means of most of its former residents, with the result that many of them were left with little choice but to relocate to either the public housing projects or in rapidly overcrowding surrounding neighborhoods that suffered accordingly. These local problems, Bauman notes, were overshadowed by the overwhelmingly positive national response to the project. Chapter 10 discusses the ramifications of this situation, many of which came to light during the 1970s.

28. Ibid., 111–13.

29. Ibid., 111.

30. "Under the Knife," 70.

31. Bauman, *Public Housing, Race and Renewal*, 181–82.

32. Klemek, "Urbanism as Reform," 209–16. Klemek's analysis of the method and practices involved in the restoration of Society Hill provided much of the source for the discussion of this topic herein.

33. Ibid., 206.

34. Bauman, *Public Housing, Race and Renewal*, 139–40.

35. Ibid., 144.

36. "Under the Knife," 70.

37. Klemek, "Urbanism as Reform," 206. Klemek contrasted Bacon with his predecessor at the CPC, Robert Mitchell, by noting that "Mitchell had wanted to examine urban processes, such as traffic, while Bacon was focused primarily on the beautification and aesthetic modernization of his hometown. This design emphasis was evident already from the time of Bacon's 1932 Cornell senior thesis ... Bacon was convinced that he could provide 'visible (and understandable) solutions to complex urban problems ... [thereby demonstrating] the power of urban design to serve as the key element in an overall strategy for the city's physical and economic recovery'" (quoting Madeline L. Cohen, "Postwar City Planning in Philadelphia: Edmund

N. Bacon and the Design of Washington Square East," PhD diss., University of Pennsylvania, 1991).

38. Ibid., 207.

39. His approach would achieve some level of vindication many years later when the city's Liberty Two tower, which was originally designed to be a clone of the sleek and graceful Liberty One, was widened at the top at the request of the building's main tenant at the time, CIGNA, who wanted more office space on the upper floors. In 2005, when ACE USA (the successor to CIGNA) moved out of the building, the city was left with a bloated remnant of that decision made less than two decades earlier. Several months later, the ugly building remained vacant.

40. *See* "Philadelphia Hails Mrs. Johnson as She Views Its Urban Renewal," *New York Times*, June 11, 1966, 17, noting the First Lady's approval of the ordinance.

41. Conn, *Metropolitan Philadelphia*, 185.

42. "Under the Knife," 70. Influential New York architect Robert W. Dowling criticized Bacon's plan, concluding that Bacon's design, which called for the towers covering 30 percent of the ground space, was not sufficient to make the complex profitable. He contended that they needed to cover 45 percent of the ground space. Bacon fought this assessment but Dowling eventually won out.

43. Ibid., 70.

44. Klemek, "Urbanism as Reform," 228–35. Klemek's discussion of the ring of highways is the source for the analysis of the topic contained herein.

45. Hine, "University City," B3.

46. Weart, "Urban Renewal Housing Goes Up in Philadelphia," R15.

47. Guian A. McKee, "Liberal Ends through Illiberal Means: Race, Urban Renewal, and Community in the Eastwick Section of Philadelphia, 1949–1990," *Journal of American History* 27, no. 5 (July 2001): 547–83. McKee's article is the source for the discussion of the Eastwick renewal project contained herein.

48. Caro, *The Power Broker*, 1006–07. Caro's book provides the source material for the discussion of the criticism of Moses and New York's Title I projects contained herein. *See also* pp. 1007–08, 1014, 1024–25.

49. Jane Jacobs, *The Death and Life of Great American Cities* (New York: Random House, 1992), 358.

50. Carl Bridenbaugh "The Home of Biddles and Scrapple," *New York Times*, October 13, 1963, 338; Weart, "Urban Renewal Housing Goes Up in Philadelphia"; Weart, "Plaza Projected for Philadelphia," *New York Times*, October 15, 1961, R1.

51. Caspar W. Weinberger, "Philadelphia Might Have Lesson for Us," *Los Angeles Times*, September 29, 1965, A5.

52. Wolf Von Echardt, "A 'Vision' Inspired Philly's Center," *Washington Post-Times Herald*, November 28, 1965, G6.

53. "Philadelphia Hails Mrs. Johnson," *New York Times*, June 11, 1966, 17.

54. Paul Taylor, "Moved Out: The Society Hill Suit," *Philadelphia Inquirer*, June 19, 1977, A1.

55. Karasilk, "Suburbs? Foo!" *Philadelphia Inquirer*, September 4, 1977, A1.

56. "The City: Under the Knife, or All for Their Own Good," *Time*, November 16, 1964, 60.

57. Ibid., publisher's note.

58. Rich Westcott, *Veterans Stadium: Field of Memories* (Philadelphia: Temple University Press, 2005), 2. Westcott's book provides the source for the discussion of the location of Veterans Stadium contained herein. *See also* pp. 4–7, 168.

59. Ibid., 6.

60. Sandy Grady, "Carpenter Has His Say in the Great Phillies 'Great Debate,'" *Evening Bulletin*, August 25, 1969.

61. Westcott, *Veterans Stadium*, 15–16, 27.

62. Indeed, Phillies infielder John Vukovich said as much. "We knew we were moving into a palace. We were all very excited about it." Ibid., 19.

63. Pitcher Rick Wise denigrated it as such, noting that the new stadium "didn't have the character of Connie Mack Stadium." Ibid, 20.

64. Kuklick, *To Everything a Season*, 143–44.

65. Dick Allen, of all people, considered it such. Westcott, *Veterans Stadium*, 28.

66. *See* Kuklick, *To Everything a Season*, 163.

Chapter 7

1. Murray Dubin, "Moving In: Tension in the City," *Philadelphia Inquirer*, June 19, 1977, A9.

2. Mary Walton, "The New City Dwellers Turn Rush Hour Around," *Philadelphia Inquirer*, June 20, 1977, A1.

3. Taylor, "Moved Out," *Philadelphia Inquirer*, June 19, 1977, A1. The article cited an incident in which a school crossing guard was evicted from her $49-a-month apartment in Society Hill as it was being rehabilitated and brought up to the new standards of the area. In 1977, the apartment was renting for $460 a month.

4. Georges Perrier, *Le Bec-Fin Recipes* (Philadelphia: Running Press, 1997), 10–17. The introduction to Perrier's cookbook provides a brief autobiography of the chef and details his journey to Philadelphia as well as his culinary struggles in attempting to open a world-class restaurant in a city that knew of no such thing before his arrival.

5. Marian Burros, "A Restaurant Revival in the City of Brotherly Love," *Washington Post*, June 14, 1979, E1. This remark was credited to Steve Poses, the owner of Frog and The Commissary.

6. Steven Poses, Anne Clark, and Becky Roller, *The Frog, Commissary Cookbook* (Garden City, N.Y.: Doubleday, 1985), vii–xiii. Just as with Perrier's cookbook, the introduction to Poses's provides much insight as to the progression of Philadelphia's 1970s restaurant renaissance. Due to the dearth of scholarly analysis of this cultural phenomenon, relevant cookbooks provide the most detailed and comprehensive insight with regard to the process to date and serve as primary sources for the discussion provided herein. Unless otherwise noted, Poses's book is the source for the discussion of his restaurants and their impact on the Philadelphia restaurant renaissance contained herein.

7. *See* Jacobs, *Death and Life*.

8. Phyllis Richman, "The New American Cui-

sine," *Washington Post Magazine*, December 31, 1978, 16, 19.

9. Ibid., 21.

10. Ibid., 20–21. Richman's article provides a helpful sketch of the Restaurant School's brief but radical history up to that point.

11. Ibid.

12. Ibid., Leslie Bennetts, "The Philadelphia Story, Updated," *New York Times Magazine*, May 10, 1981, 15.

13. Richman, "New American Cuisine."

14. Bill Collins, "Black Banana Rates High, Takes a Bunch of Money," *Philadelphia Inquirer*, March 19, 1976, C3. Although Collins gave the Black Banana a mixed review, he concluded that, "[i]f nothing else, the proprietors of the Black Banana (nee Banane Noire) must be respected for their pioneering spirit. Twice now they have gone where no other reputable restaurant has gone before." He noted that the Black Banana's success on South Street "helped change the neighborhood. At least a half-dozen other little restaurants have followed it into the locale, which today is one of the more bustling, though still bohemian sections of Southeast Philadelphia."

15. Ibid. Collins advised "less open-minded guests" to use the other washroom instead.

16. Richman, "New American Cuisine."

17. Craig Claiborne, "The Chef Could Only Beam and Tell His Class, 'Une Merveille!'" *New York Times*, March 21, 1974, 48.

18. Burros, *A Restaurant Revival*. Poses, with his architectural and city planning roots, recognized this and stated as well that "Philadelphia is a very attractive city." Of course, he was most likely not talking about North Philadelphia or anyplace else outside of the safe zone.

19. James T. Wooten, "Rebirth of Night Life Jolts Old Philadelphia," *New York Times*, June 28, 1974, 16.

20. Desmond Ryan, "Intelligent Films Fill His Screens but Not His Seats," *Philadelphia Inquirer*, October 2, 1977, F1. The article focused on the early struggles of Posel's Ritz Three Theater, which was not the instant success some had thought it would be (although in the article, Posel stressed that the first several months exceeded his expectations). In time, however, business improved, which necessitated an expansion of the Ritz Three to the Ritz Five and then, later, expansion first into Philadelphia's historic Bourse building, next onto Second Street and then finally, in the 1990s, to Voorhees, New Jersey, providing Delaware Valley residents 28 screens on which to watch foreign, independent or lower budgeted movies where previously they had none.

21. Michael Carlton, "The Philadelphia Story: City May Have Last Laugh on the Comeback Trail," *Washington Post*, May 11, 1980, E4; Bennetts, "The Philadelphia Story, Updated."

22. Jonathan Mahler, *Ladies and Gentlemen, the Bronx Is Burning: 1977, Baseball, Politics and the Battle for the Soul of a City* (New York: Farrar, Straus & Giroux, 2005), 7–9, 224, 256. Mahler's book provides an interesting counterpoint to *The Fall of the 1977 Phillies* in that it examines the 1970s (particularly 1977) from New York's perspective. He con-

cludes that, unlike the Philadelphia profiled herein that seemingly was thriving but which was rotting underneath the surface, New York was the opposite: down for the count in most estimations but stronger at its core than many people realized. Taken together, the two books provide case studies of two cities headed in different directions, although not in the directions predicted for either at the time. Mahler's research on New York's various crises during the 1970s provides the source material for the discussion contained herein.

23. Ibid., 8.

24. Frank Dolson, "What a Difference Four Floors Make," *Philadelphia Inquirer*, January 24, 1974, D1.

25. Ibid., D4.

26. Bruce Keidan, "Luzinski: Aaron Should Get Mark at Home," *Philadelphia Inquirer*, March 5, 1974, D3.

27. Bruce Keidan, "Phillies Hit Stride, Lose Opener, 5–2." *Philadelphia Inquirer*, March 10, 1974, E1.

28. Bruce Keidan, "Luzinski Ignites Phils Win, Then Goes into Seclusion," *Philadelphia Inquirer*, March 21, 1974, C1. In the article, Larry Bowa remarked that Luzinski was "ticked off" about the televised report, to which Danny Ozark responded with "a stream of expletives. 'Bleeping negativism,' he explained. 'The bleeping Philadelphia press.'"

29. Frank Dolson, "Phils Hot on Scent of Something Big," *Philadelphia Inquirer*, April 7, 1974, G1.

30. Bruce Keidan, "Phils Rip Cards for 5th in Row," *Philadelphia Inquirer*, April 17, 1974, D1.

31. Ibid. Surprisingly, the Phils energized the city after such a moribund spring training. Bowa recognized the cause of all the excitement: "It's Cash," he said. "That guy's crazy!"

32. John Dell, "Lonborg, Phils Tip Dodgers," *Philadelphia Inquirer*, May 5, 1974, E1.

33. Bill Lyon, "'Yes We Can' Man More Than a Player," *Philadelphia Inquirer*, August 28, 1974, C1. Lyon noted that when the Phillies traded popular pitcher Kenny Brett to Pittsburgh for Cash in what was then an unpopular trade in Philadelphia, they received not only a second baseman but "a locker room shrink, a father confessor, ego massager and a creator of — pesto! — instant slogans. Yes We Can. 'Jeez,' Danny Ozark sighed, 'Dave Cash has given us class, motivation and positive thinking.'"

34. Bruce Keidan, "Being a Sitting Duck Isn't for Dave Cash," *Philadelphia Inquirer*, April 23, 1974, D2.

35. Frank Dolson, "Is This Any Way to Run a Contender?" *Philadelphia Inquirer*, June 24, 1974, C1.

36. Bruce Keidan, "'Yes We Can' Just Might Do It," *Philadelphia Inquirer*, July 21, 1974.

37. Bruce Keidan, "Phils Win on HR by Taylor," *Philadelphia Inquirer*, June 18, 1974, D1. Keidan wrote: "It is becoming a lyric thing, this charmed time that is the Phillies' 1974 baseball season. When it is done, they may have to hire a novelist instead of an historian to chronicle it."

38. Bruce Keidan, "Phils Trip Dodgers on Cash Hit in 9th," *Philadelphia Inquirer*, July 11, 1974, D1.

39. Eddie Olsen, "Even High Schools Play 'Yes We Can,'" *Philadelphia Inquirer*, June 4, 1974.

40. Bruce Keidan, "Dick Allen Back in Phil Uniform?" *Philadelphia Inquirer*, November 13, 1974. In contemplating whether Dick Allen could thrive, let alone survive, another stint in Philadelphia, Keidan remarked that both the city as well as the team had changed significantly since he departed in 1969. Testament to these changes was the impact of Cash, a black man who was, only five years later, the leader and most popular player in Philadelphia.

41. Ibid.

42. *See* Berreby, *Us and Them. See also* Anne Maass and Luciano Arcuri, "Language and Stereotyping," in *Stereotypes and Stereotyping*, edited by Charles Stangor and Miles Hewstone (New York: The Guilford Press, 1996), 193. Maass's and Arcuri's article stresses the importance of language in the creation of groups and stereotypes.

43. Maas and Arcuri, "Language and Stereotyping," 198. Maas and Arcuri cite a study in which in-group or out-group designators (such as "ours" or "theirs") were presented to subjects and then masked by positive or negative trait adjectives. The study found that "as hypothesized, the priming of in-group pronouns strongly facilitated the recognition and categorization of positive traits ... whereas negative traits were more accessible after the priming of out-group pronouns. Thus, in-group or out-group-related words such as 'us' or 'them' seem to carry an evaluative connotation that is activated automatically when such words are primed."

44. Ibid. This would explain fans' enthusiasm for the 1974 Phils, a team that was, in reality, little more than a .500 club for most of the season.

45. Berreby, *Us and Them*, 31, 181.

46. Ibid., 207. Berreby notes that in one experiment, subjects found that the syllables "exh" and "yof" (which are meaningless in English and were deliberately chosen by the researchers to test the limits of nonsensical allegiance) to be more pleasant when they were paired with words such as "we," "us" and "ours" than with the words "they," "them" and "theirs." Another study by the same researchers found that subjects were "quicker to associate positive adjectives like *skillful, competent, careful*, and *courteous* with 'us' words and quicker to associate unpleasant adjectives like *sloppy, irritable, wasteful*, and *gullible* with 'they' words." As such, Phillies fans subconsciously felt more hesitant to boo a team they now felt was connected with them because to boo them would be to cast aspersions on themselves in a way.

Chapter 8

1. "Tearful Dick Allen Announces Retirement," *Philadelphia Inquirer*, September 15, 1974, F4.

2. Kashatus, *September Swoon*, 195. Although he initially told the press that he moved out of the locker room to keep them away, he later told manager Bob Skinner that he moved because he "just wanted to be left alone."

3. Ibid., 198.

4. Ibid.

5. Ibid., 191. Howie Bedell of the Milwaukee Braves recalled one instance in which Allen asked him to shag balls in the outfield with him before a game at Connie Mack Stadium. "C'mon Howie," he said, "let's go shag some flies. You're a white guy. If you go out there, they won't throw anything at me!"

6. Bill James, *The Politics of Glory: How Baseball's Hall of Fame Really Works* (New York: Macmillan, 1994), 322–25.

7. Sandy Grady, "So Far Everyone Concerned Thinks the Trade Is Super," *Evening Bulletin*, October 9, 1969.

8. For an in-depth analysis of Flood's reasons for challenging baseball's reserve clause as well as his perceptions of the Phillies and Philadelphia at the time of the trade, *see* Brad Snyder, *A Well-Paid Slave: Curt Flood's Fight for Free Agency in Professional Sports* (New York: Viking Press, 2006).

9. For a discussion of Allen's stints in St. Louis, Los Angeles and Chicago, *see* Skip Myslenski, "The Allen Years Anything but Boring," *Philadelphia Inquirer*, May 8, 1975, C1.

10. Bruce Keidan, "Dick Allen Back in Phil Uniform?" *Philadelphia Inquirer*, November 13, 1974.

11. Frank Dolson, "Richie Allen: Phillies Could Go to Top — Or to Pieces — With Him," *Philadelphia Inquirer*, March 2, 1975, F1, 8. According to Luzinski, "I think Richie Ashburn the guy who's really making the push as far as whether Richie Allen comes here. His articles and his persuasion have maybe prompted the Phillies to do a little something."

12. Allen Lewis, "Phils Secretly Trying to Lure Dick Allen Off the Farm," *Philadelphia Inquirer*, February 4, 1975, C1. Because of tampering rules, the Phils had hoped to keep the visit to Allen (who was at the time the property of the Atlanta Braves) secret. However, news of the visit leaked quickly, forcing the Phils to respond to tampering allegations by the Braves.

13. Bill Lyon, "Phils Believe They Can Win It All ... With Dick Allen," *Philadelphia Inquirer*, February 11, 1975, D1, 2.

14. Frank Dolson, "Mets Tune Out Richie Allen, Fear Lack of Harmony," *Philadelphia Inquirer*, March 4, 1975, D1, 2.

15. Ibid.

16. Allen Lewis, "Montanez Ready to Vacate First for Allen," *Philadelphia Inquirer*, March 3, 1975, C4.

17. Dolson, "Richie Allen: Phillies Could Go to Top," F8. Said Luzinski, who only one year earlier announced that he found playing in Philadelphia depressing, "I've never been on a team as close as we are right now. I think it's great."

18. Ibid.

19. Allen Lewis, "The Cash Theme Song — He's Only Just Begun," *Philadelphia Inquirer*, March 7, 1975.

20. Dolson, "Richie Allen: Phillies Could Go to Top," F8.

21. Frank Dolson, "That Was a Smile on Ozark's Face...," *Philadelphia Inquirer*, March 14, 1975, E1, 6.

22. For a discussion of the Mauch and Skinner tenures in Philadelphia, *see* Kuklick, *To Every Thing a Season*, 161–62.

23. Russ Harris, "Allen Set to Play but 'Won't Beg,'" *Philadelphia Inquirer*, March 26, 1975.

24. Frank Dolson, "Deal for Allen All but Finalized," *Philadelphia Inquirer*, May 7, 1975, C1, 2.

25. Frank Dolson, "Phils New Slogan: Give Him a Chance," *Philadelphia Inquirer*, May 8, 1975, C1.

26. Ibid.

27. Ibid.

28. Frank Dolson, "The Boos Turn to Cheers for Richie Allen," *Philadelphia Inquirer*, May 15, 1975, D1.

29. Frank Dolson, "The Man Behind Greg Luzinski," *Philadelphia Inquirer*, July 7, 1975, C1.

30. Ralph Bernstein, "Bowa: Stiff Arm, Failure to Adjust to Allen Blamed for the Errors of His Ways," *Philadelphia Inquirer*, September 5, 1975, C1.

31. Allen Lewis, "Allen's Future? 'I Gotta Play,'" *Philadelphia Inquirer*, September 13, 1975, C1.

32. Kashatus, "Dick Allen, the Phillies, and Racism," 181.

33. Tony Kornheiser, "Body and Soul," *Inside Sports* 1 (October 1979): 24, 29.

34. Bruce Buschel, "Even Superstars Get the Blues," *PhillySport* 1, no.1 (June/July 1988): 38, 86.

35. Ibid.

36. Kornheiser, "Body and Soul," 29.

37. Allen Lewis, "The Anticipated Explosion," *Philadelphia Inquirer*, April 20, 1976, C1.

38. Frank Dolson, "Ozark's Composure Shatters Noisily...," *Philadelphia Inquirer*, April 26, 1976, C1.

39. Allen Lewis, "Allen's Pride Is Hurt: Bats 7th," *Philadelphia Inquirer*, May 19, 1976, D1.

40. Allen Lewis, "Allen Clouts 2; Phils Win, 12–4," *Philadelphia Inquirer*, June 26, 1976, C1.

41. For a summary of the incidents involving Allen during July and early August 1976, *see* Bruce Keidan, "Today's the BIG Day That Allen Comes Back," *Philadelphia Inquirer*, August 10, 1976, C2.

42. Frank Dolson, "Allen Now a Rich Spectator," *Philadelphia Inquirer*, September 20, 1976, C1,3.

43. Kashatus, "Dick Allen, the Phillies, and Racism," 183. This quote originated in Allen's autobiography (co-written with Tim Whitaker), *Crash: The Life and Times of Dick Allen* (New York: Ticknor & Fields, 1989), 163.

44. Bruce Keidan, "Allen Declines to Join in Phils' Fun," *Philadelphia Inquirer*, September 27, 1976, C1.

45. Kashatus, "Dick Allen, the Phillies, and Racism," 184; Kornheiser, "Body and Soul," 30.

46. Keidan, "Allen Declines to Join in Phils' Fun."

47. Bruce Keidan, "Phils Are Resting Uneasily as Ozark Hides Hurt and Anger," *Philadelphia Inquirer*, September 30, 1976, C1.

48. Bruce Keidan, "Phils Get Warning, Then Win," *Philadelphia Inquirer*, September 30, 1976, C1.

49. Ibid.

50. Frank Dolson, "Phillies Bewildered in a Tower of Babel," *Philadelphia Inquirer*, October 1, 1976, D1.

51. Ibid.

52. Ibid.

53. Keidan, "Phillies Are Resting Uneasily."

54. Bruce Keidan, "Allen to Play, Taylor to Coach: Owner Settles Dispute," *Philadelphia Inquirer*, October 1, 1976, D1.

55. Bruce Keidan, "'They Grew Up in a Few Days,' Ozark Declares," *Philadelphia Inquirer*, October 14, 1976, C1. Once again, Ozark bore the brunt of the blame for Schmidt's and Cash's decision, although there was not much he could do about it. The story was leaked to Keidan by "an impeccable clubhouse source" according to the reporter.

56. Dolson, "Allen Now a Rich Spectator." When asked if Allen could possibly be resigned for the 1977 season, general manager Paul Owens said, "I can't afford to pay a man that much if he (the manager) won't play him. I'm not going to dictate the lineup."

57. Frank Dolson, "Phillies Spellbound by Mauch Mystique," *Philadelphia Inquirer*, May 14, 1974, D1.

58. Ibid. Dolson's article chronicled the history of the Phillies' problems against Mauch in the preceding five seasons.

59. Murray Dubin, "Fans Keeping Their Faith in Phils," *Philadelphia Inquirer*, September 10, 1976, D1.

60. Frank Dolson, "Phils Answer '64 Question," *Philadelphia Inquirer*, September 19, 1976, E1.

61. Dubin, "Fans Keeping Their Faith in Phils."

62. Dolson, "Phils Answer '64 Question."

63. Ibid.

64. Ibid. Prior to Wine's talk, a group of players, including Allen (who was a member of the '64 team), Maddox, McGraw (whose "ya gotta believe" slogan helped to carry the 1973 Mets to the National League pennant), Jim Kaat and Cash, addressed them. The talk proved effective temporarily: the Phils won their next three games. However, they then lost three more in a row, including two straight to the Pirates, prompting Wine to suggest to Ozark that he give it a go.

65. After Minnesota, Mauch would resurface in California where he would miss out on the World Series once again after suffering another last minute collapse with the 1986 Angels in their league Championship Series against the Boston Red Sox. After California, he would not manage again.

66. "Allen's Exit from Phils Finally Becomes Official," *Philadelphia Inquirer*, November 9, 1976, D2.

67. Frank Dolson, "Phillies Album: Dick Allen," *Philadelphia Inquirer*, September 12, 1976, D10. In assessing Allen's treatment during his second stint in Philadelphia, Dolson remarked: "The Phillies, their fans, even the press, have gone out of their way to make him feel like a human being this time around." At the time, Dolson held out hope that Allen would repay these acts of kindness with a key role in the Phils' stretch drive. However, as things turned out, he would not.

Chapter 9

1. Bill Lyon, "Garber's Edge Becomes Dull," *Philadelphia Inquirer*, June 1, 1975, E1.

2. Frank Dolson, "Loss of Cash Saddens Phils," *Philadelphia Inquirer*, October 31, 1976, E1.

3. Frank Dolson, "Value of Cash Divides Phils," *Philadelphia Inquirer*, March 14, 1977, C1.

4. For a detailed analysis of New York's 1977

blackout, *see* Mahler, *Ladies and Gentlemen, the Bronx Is Burning,* 218–29, from which the discussion herein draws its facts.

5. Ibid. *See also* "A Battered New York Returning to Normal," *Philadelphia Inquirer,* July 16, 1977, A1, 2.

6. Mahler, *Ladies and Gentlemen, the Bronx Is Burning,* 255.

7. Ibid., 229. Carter made this remark in an interview with the National Black Radio Network.

8. "A Battered New York Returning to Normal," A2.

9. Andrea Knox, "The Gallery: A Test of City and Its Stores," *Philadelphia Inquirer,* July 17, 1977, E1.

10. Ibid.

11. "Market Street East Renewal It All Began 20 Years Ago," *Philadelphia Inquirer,* August 7, 1977 (advertising supplement). This article traces the development of the Market East restoration project from its inception in 1958 to its completion in 1977.

12. Frank Dolson, "Reds Fall under Spell of the Vet," *Philadelphia Inquirer,* September 4, 1977, G6.

13. Frank Dolson, "The Sound of Silence? Not at the Vet," *Philadelphia Inquirer,* September 13, 1977, D2.

14. This record would stand until 2004 when the Yankees broke it with 61 such victories.

15. Don McKee, "Jerry Martin's Credo: 'You've Got to Be Ready,'" *Philadelphia Inquirer,* May 7, 1976, C2. Martin was admittedly "not crazy about what I do" but "I'd rather do that job here than play every day in AAA ball." Ozark attempted to clarify Martin's role to him by telling him that "he was gonna use me almost every day."

16. Sandy Grady, "Phils Were on Noah's Ark, but It Sank in Rainstorm," *Evening Bulletin,* October 10, 1977, D3. Grady noted that among the accolades routinely heaped upon the 1977 Phils were, "[b]est team in Phillies history, deepest talent in baseball, fattest payroll in the game."

17. Bill Conlin, "The Worst of Times," *Philadelphia Daily News,* September 2, 2004. In reviewing the Phils' sorry history, Conlin, a beat writer for the team since 1965, stopped at the 1977 team, calling their performance that season "the best all-around baseball ever played by a Phillies team."

18. Frank Dolson, "Invisible Weapon in Phils' Arsenal—Togetherness," *Philadelphia Inquirer,* September 29, 1977, C3.

19. Skip Myslenski, "Keeping Loose: It's What Phils Do Best of All," *Philadelphia Inquirer,* October 2, 1977, E1.

20. Bill Lyon, "Winning with a Free Press," *Philadelphia Inquirer,* April 2, 1977, C1.

21. Dolson, "Reds Fall under Spell of the Vet."

22. Dolson, "The Sound of Silence? Not at the Vet."

23. Ibid. During one September game against Pittsburgh, in a game that would foreshadow Black Friday's second inning, Pirate pitcher Jerry Reuss became unnerved when, with the bases loaded, the roar of the crowd caused him to lose concentration and walk in a run.

24. Stan Hochman, "Davalillo Takes Care of Himself and Dodgers," *Philadelphia Daily News,* October 11, 1977, 67.

25. Ibid.

26. Ibid.

27. Sandy Grady, "Lasorda's Prayers Louder Than Fans," *Evening Bulletin,* October 8, 1977, 13.

28. Ray Didinger, "A Little Bit of Gray Doesn't Matter," *Evening Bulletin,* October 8, 1977, 13.

29. Tom Cushman, "Latin Connection Puts Dodgers over the Hill," *Philadelphia Daily News,* October 8, 1977, 38. Davalillo's bunt was not called beforehand. After the game, he said, "I don't go up there thinking to bunt, but when they give me a chance, I'll take my shots. They were playing back at first and second. It's a decision I make instantly."

30. Didinger, "A Little Bit of Gray Doesn't Matter."

31. Ibid.

32. Ibid.

33. "The Scene: The Bartender: 'Nobody Stayed ... Nobody's Here,'" *Philadelphia Inquirer,* October 8, 1977, C8.

34. Frank Dolson, "For the Phils, 'Tomorrow Is Another Day,'" *Philadelphia Inquirer,* October 8, 1977, C4. After the game as he watched the ball drift on Luzinski in the ninth, Martin said, "I was going crazy, man. When you're not playing you feel kinda helpless. I don't know what to say. It's just so hard sitting there watching. You wish you could do something."

35. Dave Kindred, "The Umpire Couldn't Hear the Out," *Washington Post,* October 8, 1977, D1. Froemming would not admit as much but, as Kindred highlighted in his article, nobody could hear anything on the field. Therefore, it was very likely that Froemming, relying on his ears to make the call, was only able to register half of the play: the half with his eyes where he saw Lopes' foot hit the bag. Nearly 30 years later, upon reflection, Froemming remained steadfast that he got the call right despite video and photographic evidence to the contrary. "I had one shot at it, and he was safe," he said. "I got it right." *See* Claire Smith, "Ump's Fingerprints Were on Phils' 'Black Friday' Playoff Mess," *Philadelphia Inquirer,* July 18, 2006, E5.

36. Although Hebner would refer to the pitch after the game as "a sinker that exploded" (Bill Conlin, "Phillies Can't Dodge Disaster," *Philadelphia Daily News,* October 8, 1977, 40), it should be noted that Garber did not have a sinker pitch, or at least one that he used that afternoon. Instead, his entire Black Friday repertoire consisted of a fastball, slider and a changeup, with his slider the only pitch that broke down precisely as his pickoff attempt did.

37. Conlin, "Phillies Can't Dodge Disaster." Conlin is likewise generally credited with having coined the phrase, "The 10 Minute Collapse" to describe the Phils' fateful ninth.

38. Ibid.

39. Frank Dolson, "They Lost as a Team," *Philadelphia Inquirer,* October 10, 1977, C6. In Dolson's words, "That classic example of negative thinking backfired."

40. "The Scene: The Bartender: 'Nobody Stayed ... Nobody's Here.'"

41. *See* Dolson, "They Lost as a Team"; Ray Kelly, "Ghastly Ending Lifts LA," *Evening Bulletin,* October 8, 1977, 13.

42. Fitzpatrick, "You Can't Lose 'Em All," 51.

43. Skip Myslenski, "The Legendary Philadelphia Fan," *Philadelphia Inquirer*, October 30, 1977, E13. Jim Murray, then the general manager of the Eagles, reflected on Black Friday and remarked that the loss was more than simply a loss; it affected the community deeply.

44. "The Scene: The Fan: What Happened Was Just Awful," *Philadelphia Inquirer*, October 8, 1977, C5.

45. Buschel, "Even Superstars Get the Blues," 84. Buschel remarked that after Black Friday, "a lot of people shut down. They just couldn't take it. They watched the Phillies with half a heart. They found other things to cry about."

46. Baltzell, *Puritan Boston and Quaker Philadelphia*, xi. Baltzell, a professor at the University of Pennsylvania, couldn't help but see the negatives and not the positives at the time he was writing his book. However, he was encouraged by the renaissance he had seen take place within the city over the previous few years and held out hope that one day, he and "citizens of all classes" would "eventually become boosters and winners." From his perspective in the late 1970s, however, that was not presently the case.

47. Bruce Keidan, "Phils Drift into Sunset Lugging Their Memories," *Philadelphia Inquirer*, October 10, 1977, C1.

48. Ray Didinger, "Phillies Derailed by Dodgers' 'Blue Grit,'" *Evening Bulletin*, October 9, 1977.

49. "Deep Throat at the Playoffs," *Philadelphia Inquirer*, October 9, 1977, D6.

50. Keidan, "Phils Drift into Sunset Lugging Their Memories."

51. Ibid.

52. Ray Kelly, "Hooton Cools Yanks, Dodgers Even Series," *Evening Bulletin*, October 13, 1977.

53. Ibid.

54. Frank Dolson, "Phillies Justify Fans' Lukewarm Greeting," *Philadelphia Inquirer*, April 8, 1978, C1.

55. Dick Weiss, "Fans Expect 76ers to Pay Off Their IOU," *Philadelphia Daily News*, October 13, 1977, B-3. After the Sixers lost the '77 Finals in six games after winning the first two, the team's 1978 rallying cry was "We Owe You One," a misguided, disastrous slogan that succeeded only in driving a wedge between the organization and its fans who now felt justified in taking every loss as a personal affront to them, inflicted by the team. The slogan would remain as a noose around the team's neck for several years, until they finally won the title in 1983.

56. Larry Eichel, "The '78 Phillies Owe Us One, Too: Play Ball!" *Philadelphia Inquirer*, April 5, 1978.

Chapter 10

1. Larry Eichel, "Bum Trip Sent Bull on Rampage," *Philadelphia Inquirer*, March 22, 1978, E1.

2. Frank Dolson, "Ozark Is Making Bull a Vanishing Act," *Philadelphia Inquirer*, May 22, 1978, C1.

3. Larry Eichel, "Schmidt: Down in a Valley," *Philadelphia Inquirer*, August 15, 1978, C1. According to Eichel, "[i]n the eyes of many, Schmidt has come to personify the frustrations of a ballclub that has ... failed to live up to its obvious potential."

4. Frank Dolson, "Far from the Booing Vet Crowd, Mike Schmidt Plays His Best Ball," *Philadelphia Inquirer*, September 21, 1978, C4. Said Schmidt, "It's a little more relaxing (on the road) ... When I put that (home) uniform on and go on the field it's real test for me to control my inner emotions and play good baseball. Could you write a story if you had 15 editors standing behind you, looking over your shoulder? Could you write a story every time you chose a wrong word they all booed?"

5. Frank Dolson, "Now, They Owe Us One," *Philadelphia Inquirer*, October 6, 1978, C4.

6. Ibid.

7. Allen Lewis, "Writer Says Bowa Hit Him; Bowa Denies It," *Philadelphia Inquirer*, August 11, 1978, C1.

8. Frank Dolson, "Both Sides Share Blame," *Philadelphia Inquirer*, August 13, 1978, E1.

9. Lewis, "Writer Says Bowa Hit Him."

10. Fitzpatrick, "You Can't Lose 'Em All," 6.

11. Dolson, "Both Sides Share Blame."

12. Ibid.

13. Al Morganti, "How the Phillies Sit with Fans...," *Philadelphia Inquirer*, July 3, 1979, D1. One fan attempted to draw a curious distinction between himself and other Phillies fans as he explained his reasons for attending Phillies games during the 1979 season: "I didn't come here to boo, I came to hear the boos. I don't know if it will do any good but I know they're (the Phillies) gonna hear it."

14. Frank Dolson, "Ugly Fans Have Ozark Fuming," *Philadelphia Inquirer*, August 31, 1979, C1. After the game, Ozark said, "Buying a ticket does not give a person the right to act the way some of those 'great Philadelphia fans' have been acting at the Vet. How can people go home and look at themselves in the mirror after they do some of the things they do? ... I thought it changed here in '75 and '76 but now it's back to where it was. Everybody in the United States knows about it and it's a disgrace to the city."

15. Buschel, "Even Superstars Get the Blues," 41.

16. Maida Odom, "Whoops and Sighs as Fans Hear of Coup," *Philadelphia Inquirer*, September 1, 1979, A1.

17. Thomas Boswell, "Strange Series, Strange Champ: Love and Hate Win Out for Philadelphia," *Washington Post*, October 23, 1980, F1.

18. Leslie Bennetts, "The Philadelphia Story, Updated," *New York Times Magazine*, May 10, 1981, 15.

19. Bauman, *Public Housing, Race and Renewal*, 124.

20. Ibid., 130.

21. Ibid., 149–50.

22. Ibid., 150.

23. Ibid., 151. "Transitional areas" were defined as those areas abandoned by fleeing white residents.

24. Ibid.

25. Ibid., 170. At one point, in 1968, the militant North City Congress appealed to Washington, D.C., protesting the Philadelphia Housing Authority's public housing plans in North Philadelphia, hoping to get results there after pleading to deaf ears on the

local level. By then, however, it was too late; the ghettoization of North Philadelphia was complete.

26. Ibid., 186–87.

27. McKee, *Liberal Ends through Illiberal Means*; Bauman, *Public Housing, Race and Renewal*, 124. Unless otherwise noted, McKee's longitudinal study of the Eastwick renewal project serves as the basis for the discussion of this topic herein.

28. Yvonne Latty, "Color-Blind, and Happy: In Eastwick, Black, White Amity Rules," *Philadelphia Daily News*, April 1, 1984, 1.

29. Michelle Osborn, "The Crosstown Is Dead Long Live the Crosstown?" *Architectural Forum* (October 1971): 39.

30. Paul Taylor, "Phila.'s Decade: Progress, Strife and Frank Rizzo," *Philadelphia Inquirer*, December 30, 1979, C1.

31. Bauman, *Public Housing, Race and Renewal*, 202.

32. Ibid.

33. Taylor, "Phila.'s Decade." According to Taylor, writing on the final day of the Rizzo administration, Rizzo "was not, after all, either a master planner or a master builder. His whole approach to government leaned instead toward the reward of friends and the punishment of enemies. And even now, with the last few hours of his mayoral tenure ticking away, it is already difficult to identify any substantial legacy he has left behind."

34. "Mayor Rizzo Flunks Lie Test," *Los Angeles Times*, August 14, 1973, 1; "Rizzo Is 'Baffled' at Lie Test Result," *New York Times*, August 15, 1973; "Philadelphia Newspaper Battle Results in a Setback for Rizzo," *New York Times*, August 19, 1973, 38.

35. George Wilson, "All the Gains Weren't Clark-Dilworth Gains," *Philadelphia Inquirer*, December 2, 1977, A9.

36. Aaron Epstein, "The Odd Couple: A Nixon-Rizzo Book Report," *Philadelphia Inquirer*, September 11, 1977, A1.

37. Ibid. According to the probe into the Philadelphia TASC project, it was "grossly overbudgeted and underused," with approximately 50 percent of its budget dedicated to establishing expensive treatment facilities on the false assumption that there existed a demand for these centers. Moreover, TASC staff members were often poorly trained if they were trained at all. According to one former city probation officer, "TASC was forced on Philadelphia for political publicity." In subsequent years, TASC was reformed and was more effective, although "its impact on crime statistics [was] negligible."

38. Ibid.

39. James T. Wooten, "Philadelphia Also Facing Crisis of Funds Shortage," *New York Times*, May 20, 1976, 1, 44.

40. Ibid.

41. Bennetts, "The Philadelphia Story, Updated"; William K. Marrimow, "City Budget Gap: At Least $72 Million," *Philadelphia Inquirer*, November 15, 1979, A1.

42. Ibid.

43. Creed Black, "Farewell to the Bicentennial — But Not Its Memories," *Philadelphia Inquirer*, December 26, 1976, E7.

44. "Rizzo Detects a Plot in City," *Philadelphia Inquirer*, December 25, 1977, E1.

45. "The U.S. Letter That Enraged a Silent Mayor," *Philadelphia Inquirer*, December 25, 1977, E1. The DOJ's findings and concerns, discussed herein, are taken from the text of a letter written by Frank E. Schwelb of the DOJ to Peter Hearn, a Philadelphia attorney, after a meeting took place in the city to discuss the tactics and methods employed by the Philadelphia police.

46. "Rizzo Detects a Plot in the City."

47. Murray Dubin, "Moving In: Tension in the City," *Philadelphia Inquirer*, June 19, 1977, A1, 9.

48. Ibid.

49. Ibid.

50. John Anderson and Hilary Hevenor, *Burning Down the House: MOVE and the Tragedy of Philadelphia* (New York: W.W. Norton, 1987), 1. Unless otherwise noted, Anderson's and Hevenor's book forms the basis for the discussion of MOVE contained herein.

51. Ibid., 2. Pursuant to the Kingdom of Yahweh's teachings, all members were required to maintain a strict vegetarian diet, which was one of the "principles of natural law." Later, Leaphart (who now referred to himself as "John Africa") would develop his own "naturalist" philosophy, which prohibited, among other things, the use of insecticides on the theory that roaches were no different from human beings. As a result, an infestation of roaches overwhelmed Leaphart's home as well as the homes of several of his neighbors. In addition, his philosophy resulted in his keeping numerous dogs and cats (at least 30 at any given time) within the house, resulting in numerous other health and safety code violations.

52. Ibid., 5.

53. Ibid., 191–92.

54. Ibid., 12.

55. Ibid., 26.

56. There are numerous articles that detail not only the facts surrounding the case but also the international response to it. *See* Wikipedia.org for some of the most accessed links to the case: *http://en.wikipedia.org/wiki/Mumia_Abu-Jamal*.

57. Ewart Rouse, "Almost 2, the Gallery Feels a Little Blue," *Philadelphia Inquirer*, July 19, 1979, C7.

58. Bill Steig, "They Gave a Mall and Nobody Came," *Washington Post*, October 13, 1984, E36.

59. Ibid.

60. Bennetts, "The Philadelphia Story, Updated."

61. Jacobs, *The Death and Life of Great American Cities*, 372–73. She writes: "When we deal with cities we are dealing with life at its most complex and intense. Because this is so, there is a basic esthetic limitation on what can be done with cities: *A city cannot be a work of art* (emphasis in original).... To approach a city ... as if it were a larger architectural problem, capable of being given order by converting it into a disciplined work of art, is to make the mistake of attempting to substitute art for life."

62. Thomas Hine, "University City: Will It Prove That Renewal Works?" *Philadelphia Inquirer*, December 21, 1978, B1, 3.

63. William K. Stevens, "Despite Bombing's

Scars, Many Say Philadelphia Resurgence Is Going On," *New York Times*, March 16, 1986, 51.

64. "In Memoriam of Edmund Bacon," Philadelphia Planning Association, *http://www.planningpa.org/news_memoriam101905.shtm*. accessed October 4, 2006.

65. William K. Stevens, "Philadelphia Hopes Rise by 60 Stories," *New York Times*, December 14, 1986, 40.

66. Berreby, *Us and Them*, 213–15. Berreby notes that the brain unconsciously processes the myriad information hurled in its direction and produces feelings. These feelings, however, are not the result of calculations made by the rational mind. Rather, they precede the calculations. Our feelings, therefore, are the product of subconscious processes rather than rationally deduced observation. *See also* Bargh and Chartrand, "The Unbearable Automaticity of Being," *American Psychologist* 54 (1999): 462, 463, 465, 475–76.

67. Berreby, *Us and Them*, 169. The brain works both ways: Sometimes the rational perception precedes the feeling but other times, the feeling precedes the perception and causes the rational brain to search for facts in order to justify the unconscious feeling. A sobering example is provided in Berreby's study: "For example, hundreds of thousands of people ... were killed, supposedly for being Communists or Communist sympathizers, during Indonesia's 1965 coup d'etat and its aftermath. Many of these people ... weren't leftists. But they were dead. An explanation was needed. They were not killed because they were deemed Communists; they were deemed Communists because they had been killed." *See also* David Berreby, *All about Us and Them* (2005) at *http://www.davidberreby.com/work3.htm*, in which he notes that this "feelings first, facts later" process likewise occurs in the formation of stereotypes. Oftentimes, we feel a difference between ourselves first and thereafter search for facts to justify our feelings. Although we believe that our feelings of differences are based upon objective, solid information, in truth we have merely justified our unconscious feelings to our rational selves.

68. The October 4, 1951, edition of the *New York Times* had two headlines of equal billing. On the top left of the front page ran the headline referring to the baseball game: "Giants Capture Pennant, Beating Dodgers 5–4 in 9th on Thomson's 3-Run Homer," while on the top right ran the headline referring to the Soviet test: "Soviet's Second Atom Blast in 2 Years Revealed by U.S.; Details Are Kept a Secret."

69. Prager, *The Echoing Green*.

70. Don Delillo, *Underworld* (New York: Scrib-

ner/Simon & Schuster, 1997), 59–60, quoted in Prager, *The Echoing Green*, 304. Prager also quotes anthropologist Marshall Sahlins: "So is it truly chutzpah to put 'the shot heard 'round the world' on the same place as the Peloponnesian War or the 2000 presidential election?"

71. Lindsey Gruson, "Project Hurts Philadelphia's Mayor," *New York Times*, September 7, 1986, 52. The article noted that in the recent past, "several ... articles in The Philadelphia Inquirer and The Philadelphia Daily News have ... detailed incidents of loose management at the (city's) Parking Authority and the city motor pool ... 'It's probably too much to expect city government to run without glitches,' The Daily News concluded this week in an editorial. 'But when embarrassing — sometimes criminal — activities become daily occurrences, the cost of government begins to exceed its worth, and serious top-to-bottom overhaul is in order.'"

72. William K. Stevens, "A Call for Honesty in Philadelphia," *New York Times*, January 5, 1988, A14.

73. Debbie M. Price, "Philadelphians Choosing Sides over City Hall," *New York Times*, February 14, 1988, 52.

74. Michael deCourcy Hinds, "After Renaissance of the 70s and 80s, Philadelphia Is Struggling to Survive," *New York Times*, June 21, 1990, A16.

75. Wendy Tanaka, "Mastermind Behind High-Concept Eateries since '95, Stephen Starr Has Built a Restaurant Empire," *Philadelphia Inquirer*, May 26, 2002.

76. Ibid.

77. Ibid.

78. Ibid.

79. *See* Conn, *Metropolitan Philadelphia*, 3–5. The nature and demographics of the city's restaurant boom of the '90s was consistent with Conn's analysis of the treatment of the city by those who live outside of it. "Suburbanites in great numbers," he wrote, "from both Pennsylvania and New Jersey treat the city as their playground, using it for everything from art and high culture to drugs and prostitution, while simultaneously, often angrily, disavowing the notion that they share any responsibility for the city's considerable problems." This lack of responsibility allows large cities like Philadelphia to crumble with nary a protest from those who live nearby.

80. Jere Longman, "The Phillies' Wild Idea Has Fans Believing," *New York Times*, September 27, 2006, D1, 2.

81. Herbert Muschamp, "Public Space, Private Space and Anti-Space," *New York Times*, December 27, 1998, AR38.

Bibliography

Periodicals

American Psychologist
Architectural Forum
Atlanta Constitution
Baseball Research Journal
Chicago Tribune
Elysian Fields Quarterly
Inside Sports
Journal of American History
Journal of Personality and Social Psychology
Los Angeles Times
New York Times
NINE: A Journal of Baseball History and Culture
Philadelphia Daily News
Philadelphia Evening Bulletin
Philadelphia Inquirer
PhillySport
Psychological Review
Saturday Evening Post
Scientific American
The National Pastime
Time
United States Banker
Wall Street Journal
Washington Post

Books and Articles

Allen, Dick, and Tim Whitaker. *Crash: The Life and Times of Dick Allen.* New York: Ticknor & Fields, 1989.

Anderson, John, and Hilary Hevenor. *Burning Down the House: MOVE and the Tragedy of Philadelphia.* New York: W.W. Norton, 1987.

Assefa, Hizkias, and Paul Wahrhaftig. *The MOVE Crisis in Philadelphia: Extremist Groups and Conflict Resolution.* Pittsburgh: University of Pittsburgh Press, 1990.

Bacon, Edmund N. *The Design of Cities.* New York: Viking Penguin, 1967.

Baltzell, E. Digby. *Puritan Boston and Quaker Philadelphia.* Boston: Beacon Press, 1982.

Bargh, John A., and Tanya L. Chartrand. "The Unbearable Automaticity of Being." *American Psychologist* 54, no. 462 (1999).

Bauman, John F. *Public Housing, Race and Renewal: Urban Planning in Philadelphia, 1920–1974.* Philadelphia: Temple University Press, 1987.

Bernstein, Peter L. *Wedding of the Waters: The Erie Canal and the Making of a Great Nation.* New York: W.W. Norton, 2005.

Berreby, David. *All About Us and Them.* 2005. http://www.davidberreby.com/work3.htm.

_____. *Us and Them: Understanding Your Tribal Mind.* New York: Little, Brown, 2005.

Caro, Robert. *The Power Broker: Robert Moses and the Fall of New York.* New York: Vintage Books, 1975.

Cohen, Madeline L. "Postwar City Planning in Philadelphia: Edmund N. Bacon and the Design of Washington Square East." PhD diss., University of Pennsylvania, 1991.

Conn, Steven. *Metropolitan Philadelphia: Living with the Presence of the Past.* Philadelphia: University of Pennsylvania Press, 2006.

Curtis, Gerald R. "Factors That Affect the Attendance of a Major League Baseball Club." Master's thesis, University of Pennsylvania, 1951.

Delillo, Don. *Underworld.* New York: Scribner/Simon & Schuster, 1997.

Dressed to the Nines: A History of the Baseball Uniform, http://www.baseballhalloffame.org/exhibits/online_exhibits/dressed_to_the_nines/introduction.htm.

Eberhardt, Jennifer L., and Susan T. Fiske. "Motivating Individuals to Change: What Is a Target to Do?" In *Stereotypes and Stereotyping,* edited by Charles Stangor and Miles Hewstone. New York: The Guilford Press, 1996.

Fetter, Henry. *Taking on the Yankees: Winning and Losing in the Business of Baseball.* New York: W.W. Norton, 2003.

Fitzpatrick, Frank. *You Can't Lose 'Em All.* Lanham, Md.: Taylor Trade Publishing, 2004.

Golenbock, Peter. *The Spirit of St. Louis: A History of the St. Louis Cardinals and Browns.* New York: HarperEntertainment, 2001.

Haidt, Jonathan. "The Emotional Dog and Its Rational Tail: A Social Intuitionist Approach to Moral Judgment." *Psychological Review* 108, no. 814 (2001).

Helyar, John. *Lords of the Realm: The Real History of Baseball.* New York: Villard Books, 1994.

Hewstone, Miles. "Contact and Categorization: Social Psychological Interventions to Change Intergroup Relations." In *Stereotypes and Stereotyping,* edited by Charles Stangor and Miles Hewstone. New York: The Guilford Press, 1996.

Hobbs, Frank, and Nicole Stoops. U.S. Census Bureau, Census 2000 Special Reports, Series CENSR-4, *Demographic Trends in the 20th Century.* Washington, D.C.: U.S. Government Printing Office, 2002.

"In Memoriam of Edmund Bacon." Philadelphia Planning Association, http://www.planningpa.org/news_memoriam101905.shtm.

Jacobs, Jane. *The Death and Life of Great American Cities.* New York: Random House, 1992.

James, Bill. *The Politics of Glory: How Baseball's Hall of Fame Really Works.* New York: Macmillan, 1994.

Jordan, David M. *The Athletics of Philadelphia: Connie Mack's White Elephants, 1901–1954.* Jefferson, N.C.: McFarland & Co., 1999.

_____. *Occasional Glory: The History of the Philadelphia Phillies.* Jefferson, N.C.: McFarland & Co., 2002.

_____, Larry R. Gerlach, and John P. Rossi. "The Truth about Bill Veeck and the '43 Phillies." *The National Pastime* 6, no. 3 (1995).

Kaese, Harold. *The Boston Braves, 1871–1953.* Boston: Northeastern University Press, 2004.

Kashatus, William C. "Dick Allen, the Phillies, and Racism." *NINE: A Journal of Baseball History and Culture* 9, no 2 (spring 2001): 151.

_____. *September Swoon: Richie Allen, the '64 Phillies, and Racial Integration.* University Park: Pennsylvania State Press, 2004.

Klemek, Christopher. "Aesthetic Reform-Social Analysis and Design in Philadelphia Planning." In "Urbanism as Reform: Modernist Planning and the Crisis of Urban Liberalism in Europe and North America, 1945–1975." PhD diss., University of Pennsylvania, 2004. (*www.history.upenn.edu/~klemek/docs/klemekchapter5.pdf*).

Kuklick, Bruce. *To Everything a Season: Shibe Park and Urban Philadelphia 1909–1976.* Princeton, N.J.: Princeton University Press, 1991.

Lanctot, Neil. *Negro League Baseball: The Rise and Ruin of a Black Institution.* Philadelphia: University of Pennsylvania Press, 2004.

Lickel, Brian, David L. Hamilton, et al. "Varieties of Groups and the Perception of Group Entitavity." *Journal of Personality and Social Psychology* 78, no. 223 (February 2000).

Maass, Anne, and Luciano Arcuri. "Language and Stereotyping." In *Stereotypes and Stereotyping,* edited by Charles Stangor and Miles Hewstone. New York: The Guilford Press, 1996.

Mahler, Jonathan. *Ladies and Gentlemen, the Bronx Is Burning: 1977, Baseball, Politics and the Battle for the Soul of a City.* New York: Farrar, Straus & Giroux, 2005.

McKee, Guian A. "Liberal Ends through Illiberal Means: Race, Urban Renewal, and Community in the Eastwick Section of Philadelphia, 1949–1990." *Journal of American History* 27, no. 5 (July 2001): 547.

Nathanson, Mitchell. "Gatekeepers of Americana: Ownership's Never-ending Quest for Control of the Baseball Creed." *NINE: A Journal of Baseball History and Culture* 15, no. 1, 68 (September 2006).

_____. "The Irrelevance of Major League Baseball's Antitrust Exemption: A Historical Review." *Rutgers Law Review* 58, 1 (2005).

Newman, A. Joseph, Jr. "Philadelphia Blues." *United States Banker* 98, no. 3 (March 1989).

Noll, Roger G. "Major League Team Sports." In *The Structure of American Industry,* edited by Walter Adams. 5th ed. New York: MacMillan, 1977.

Orodenker, Richard, ed. *The Phillies Reader.* Philadelphia: Temple University Press, 1996.

Osborn, Michelle. "The Crosstown Is Dead. Long Live the Crosstown?" *Architectural Forum* (October 1971).

Perrier, Georges. *Le Bec-Fin Recipes.* Philadelphia: Running Press, 1997.

Poses, Steven, Anne Clark, and Becky Roller. *The Frog, Commissary Cookbook.* Garden City, N.Y.: Doubleday, 1985.

Prager, Joshua. *The Echoing Green: The Untold Story of Bobby Thomson, Ralph Branca and the Shot Heard Round the World.* New York: Pantheon Books, 2006.

Philadelphia: The Capital City, http://www.nps.gof/inde/phila.html.

Riess, Steven A. *Touching Base: Professional Baseball and American Culture in the Progressive Era.* Urbana: University of Illinois Press, 1999.

Rossi, John. "Jackie Robinson in the City of Brotherly Love." *Elysian Fields Quarterly* 2, no. 15 (1998).

_____. *The 1964 Phillies: The Story of Baseball's Most Memorable Collapse.* Jefferson, N.C.: McFarland & Co., 2005.

Schneider, David J. "Modern Stereotype Research: Unfinished Business." In *Stereotypes and Stereotyping*, edited by Charles Stangor and Miles Hewstone. New York: The Guilford Press, 1996.

Seymour, Harold. *Baseball: The Early Years.* New York: Oxford University Press, 1989.

_____. *Baseball: The Golden Age.* New York: Oxford University Press, 1989.

Shapiro, Michael. *The Last Good Season: Brooklyn, the Dodgers and Their Final Pennant Race Together.* New York: Broadway Books, 2004.

Snyder, Brad. *A Well-Paid Slave: Curt Flood's Fight for Free Agency in Professional Sports.* New York: Viking Press, 2006.

Stone, Larry. "Those Were the Most Wonderful Days I Believe I Ever Had." In *Rain Check: Baseball in the Pacific Northwest*, edited by Mark Armour. Cleveland, Ohio: Society for American Baseball Research, 2006.

Stroebe, Wolfgang, and Chester A. Insko. "Stereotype, Prejudice, and Discrimination: Changing Conceptions in Theory and Research." In *Stereotype and Prejudice: Changing Conceptions*, edited by Daniel Bar-Tal, Carl F. Graumann, Arie W. Kruglanski, and Wolfgang Stroebe. New York: Springer-Verlag, 1989.

Stuart, Jeffrey. *Twilight Teams.* Gaithersburg, Md.: Sark Publishing, 2000.

Taijfel, Henry. "Experiments in Intergroup Discrimination." *Scientific American* 223, no. 96 (1970).

Tygel, Jules. *Past Time: Baseball as History.* New York: Oxford University Press, 2001.

U.S. Bureau of the Census. "Population of the 100 Largest Urban Places." *http://www.census.gov/population/documentation/twps0027/tab15.txt*

Wagner-Pacifici, Robin. *Discourse and Destruction: The City of Philadelphia versus MOVE.* Chicago: University of Chicago Press, 1994.

Westcott, Rich. *Veterans Stadium: Field of Memories.* Philadelphia: Temple University Press, 2005.

Wright, Robert E. *The First Wall Street: Chestnut Street, Philadelphia, and the Birth of American Finance.* Chicago: University of Chicago Press, 2005.

Zingg, Paul, and Mark D. Medeiros. *Runs, Hits and an Era: The Pacific Coast League, 1903–58.* Urbana: University of Illinois Press, 1994.

Index

Aaron, Hank 51, 83, 178
Abu-Jamal, Mumia 227
Adams, Red 172, 198, 199
Africa, John (aka Vincent Lopez Leaphart) 223–225
Africa, Ramona (aka Ramona Johnson) 225
Alexander, Grover Cleveland 44
Allen, Dick (Richie) 5, 124–125, 167, 174–185, 186, 189, 191, 192, 195
Amaro, Ruben 124
Amsterdam, Gustav 213–214
Anderson, Sparky 194
Ashburn, Richie 88, 176

Bacon, Edmund 5, 131–147, 148, 150, 156, 157, 158, 159, 162, 166, 212, 227–230, 231, 236
Baker, Dan 179
Baker, Dusty 9, 10, 11, 25, 27, 74, 75, 76, 128, 190, 191
Baker, Frank "Home Run" 42, 49, 72, 79, 83, 88
Baker, William (Phillies owner) 44–45
Baker Bowl 112–113
Baltzell, E. Digby 205
Banks, Ernie 113
"baseball creed" 36–37, 60–62
Beame, Abe (New York City mayor) 164
Beautification Ordinance (1959 enactment) 144, 236
Bench, Johnny 185
Bender, Chief 49, 79
Bernard, Bill 39
Berra, Yogi 176
"Better Philadelphia" exhibit 137, 138, 140, 157, 166
Biddle, Nicholas 20, 207
The Black Banana 161–162
Blue, Vida 194
Bolen, Stew 40
Boone, Bob 10, 25, 26, 28, 30, 32, 54, 57, 74, 76, 105, 128, 129–130, 131, 172, 173, 186, 194, 201
Boswell, Thomas 211
Bowa, Larry 9, 10, 11, 25, 33, 34, 105, 106, 153, 155, 166, 167, 171, 179, 184, 186, 194, 201, 203, 210, 211
Boyer, Clete 73, 102
Breadon, Sam (Cardinals owner) 49
Brecheen, Harry 95
Broad Street Railroad Station 134, 144
"Broom Closet Incident" 183–184, 188

Brown, Ollie 167, 176, 183, 184, 195
Brusstar, Warren 8, 74, 75, 76
Burgess, Smoky 198
Busch, Gussie (Cardinals owner) 96, 176

Campanella, Roy 51
Campanis, Al 197
Campusano, Sil 235
Candelaria, John 182, 183
Cardenal, Jose 209
Carlton, Steve 2, 8, 9, 10, 25, 28, 29, 31, 165, 171, 194, 195, 206, 209
Caro, Robert 132
Carpenter, Robert "Bob" R.M., Jr. (Phillies owner) 51, 60, 61, 87, 88, 111, 112, 113, 114, 123, 124, 151, 177–178; and role in the 1954 sale of the Athletics 101
Carpenter, Robert "Ruly" R.M., III (Phillies owner) 178, 182, 183, 210–211
Carson, Johnny 164
Carter, President Jimmy 193
Cash, Dave 54, 166–169, 176, 177, 178, 180, 181, 182, 183, 185, 191–192
Celler, Emanuel 90
Cey, Ron 8, 10, 11, 25, 33, 57, 74, 75, 105, 106, 130, 155, 171, 172, 173
Chamberlain, Wilt 36
Chandler, Happy 90, 122
Chapman, Ben 122, 123
Christenson, Larry 9, 10, 11, 25, 27, 30, 31, 52, 74, 75, 194, 206
Citizens Bank Park 235
Citizens Council on City Planning (CCCP) 137
City Policy Committee 136, 137
Claiborne, Craig 162
Clark, Joseph (Philadelphia mayor) 136, 138, 156, 218
Clinton, DeWitt 19, 108, 132
Cobb, Ty 43
Cochrane, Mickey 43, 49, 80, 81, 85, 88, 111
Collins, Eddie 42, 44, 49, 79
Columbia Park 46
Comiskey, Charlie 46, 62, 94
Conlin, Bill 202
Connie Mack Stadium 174, 185; deterioration of stadium and surrounding neighborhood 113–114, 118–121, 122, 125, 146, 151, 152, 153, 235; renaming of 111

Coombs, Jack 79
Covington, Wes 124
Cowley, Joe 235
Cox, William (Phillies owner) 87
Cranbrook Academy of Art 132
Cravath, Gavvy 44
Crosley, Powel (Reds owner) 60

Davilillo, Vic 191, 196–198
Dean, Dizzy 95
Delahanty, Ed 37
DeLillo, Don 232
DeMars, Billy 106
Devine, Bing 175
DeWitt, Bill (Browns owner) 94
Dilworth, Richardson 114, 136, 138, 141, 142, 144, 151, 156, 166, 213, 217, 218
DiMaggio, Joe 65, 70, 71, 95
Doby, Larry 50–51
Dolson, Frank 177, 210
Drebinger, John 114
Duggleby, Bill 39
Duren, Ryne 73, 102
Dykes, Jimmie 85

Eastwick (development of) 146–147, 150, 214–216, 231
Ebbets, Charles 46, 64
Egan, Wish 82–83
Ennis, Del 88, 112, 125, 167
Erie Canal 16–18, 19, 21
Erving, Julius 195
Evans, Rowland 164

Feller, Bob 69
Fingers, Rollie 194
First National Bank of the United States 15, 18
Flick, Elmer 39
Flood, Curt 175, 177
"flowerpot" restaurants 161
Ford, President Gerald 164
Foster, George 29
Fox, Charlie 187
Fox, Nellie 83
Foxx, Jimmy 43, 49, 80, 83, 88, 111
Fraser, Chick 39
Frazee, Harry (Red Sox owner) 72
Freed, Roger 54
Frick, Ford 90–91, 95
Froemming, Bruce 57, 201

Garber, Gene 8, 130, 154, 155, 171, 173, 190, 197–202, 205, 207
Garman, Mike 131, 203
Garvey, Steve 8, 10, 11, 25, 26, 74, 76, 128, 130, 171, 172, 203
Gehrig, Lou 43, 71
Gibson, Josh 51
Goode, W. Wilson (Philadelphia mayor) 230, 231, 232
Goodson, Ed 154
Grabarkowitz, Billy 54
Grady, Sandy 175
Grant, M. Donald (Mets owner) 62
Greater Philadelphia Movement (GPM) 138, 141
Green, Bill (Philadelphia mayor) 220–221

Greenfield, Albert M. 141
Grote, Jerry 8
Grove, Lefty 43, 69, 81
Guben, Jay 159, 163, 166, 233, 234

Haines, Richard 124
Haines, Robert 124
Hamey, H. Roy 112
Hamilton, "Sliding" Billy 37
Hamner, Granny 88
Harridge, Will 101
Hayes, Von 235
Hebner, Richie 9, 10, 29, 30, 52, 54, 55, 57, 75, 105, 106, 129, 155, 171, 172, 191, 195, 198, 201, 203, 205
Heilman, Harry 65
Hemingway, Ernest 47, 70
Hemond, Roland 178
Hillings, Patrick 91
Hisle, Larry 124
Hoerner, Joe 54
Hooton, Burt (Happy) 9, 10, 11, 27–35, 52, 54, 55, 129, 191, 206, 207
Hornsby, Roger 95
Hough, Charlie 9, 130
Hourning, Paul 36
Hoyt, Waite 44, 72
Hunter, Jim (Catfish) 10, 194
Hussenot, Xavier 161, 163
Hutton, Tommy 76, 182, 195

Independence Hall/Mall 135, 137

Jackson, President Andrew 20
Jackson, Reggie 10, 194
Jacobs, Jane 158–159, 161, 163, 229
James, Bill 175, 185
James, Chris 235
Jeffries, Gregg 235
John, Tommy 8, 206, 207
Johnson, Arnold (and purchase of the Athletics) 99–103, 110
Johnson, Ban 37, 38, 61
Johnson, Davey 8, 9, 195
Johnson, Judy 50, 83
Johnson, Lady Bird 148–149
Johnson, Robert L. 107
Johnstone, Jay 11, 56, 195
Joint Committee on City Planning 136
Jones Beach 133

Kaat, Jim 194
Kahn, Louis 137
Keidan, Bruce 165–166, 167, 168, 207
Kell, George 82
Kelly, Ellsworth 236
Kennedy, John (first black Phillies player) 51
Klein, Chuck 113

Lajoie, Napolean "Larry" 37, 38,
Lamberton, Robert (Philadelphia mayor) 137
Landis, Kenesaw Mountain 87, 95
Lardner, Ring 48
Larsen, Don 73
Lasorda, Tommy 28, 30, 31, 32, 34, 55, 130, 131, 155, 171, 173, 191, 197, 198, 199

Lazzeri, Tony 43
Lincoln Center (construction of) 148, 193
Lis, Joe 124
Lopes, Davey 8, 10, 11, 12, 28, 29, 31, 52, 57, 76, 104, 131, 155, 172, 200, 201, 202
Lopez, Hector 73
Luzinski, Greg 8, 10, 11, 27, 29, 52, 54, 55, 56, 57, 105, 106, 153, 155, 165, 166, 170, 176, 177, 179, 183, 186, 195, 199, 200, 202, 203, 205, 209, 211
Lyon, Bill 195

Mack, Connie 2, 38, 39, 40, 41, 42, 43, 44, 45, 46, 47, 48, 49, 50, 51, 61, 63, 65, 66, 69, 72, 78–86, 87, 88, 89, 94, 97, 101
Mack, Connie, Jr. 84–86
Mack, Earle 84–86, 88, 99, 101
Mack, Roy 84–86, 88, 99, 101
Maddox, Garry 9, 10, 11, 25, 27, 30, 54, 55, 56, 57, 74, 128, 129, 172, 183, 184, 194
Marion, Marty 68, 95
Maris, Roger 73, 102
Market Street East 145–146, 193–194, 229
Marone, Phillip 55, 56
Martin, Billy 10
Martin, Edward (Pennsylvania governor) 107
Martin, Jerry 56, 57, 105, 182, 184, 195, 199–200, 203
Mauch, Gene 124, 177, 178, 182, 184, 185–186, 187, 189
Mays, Carl 72
Mays, Willie 36
McBride, Bake 9, 10, 11, 32, 33, 56, 75, 76, 131, 173
McCarver, Tim 130, 131, 195
McCoskey, Barney 82
McGraw, John 39, 41, 47, 82, 104
McGraw, Tug 1, 2, 8, 29, 173, 184
Metro, Charlie 197
Miles, Clarence W. (Orioles owner) 97
Millwood, Kevin 235
Minoso, Minnie 51
Mize, Johnny 73
Monday, Rick 10, 26, 55, 75, 128, 129, 130, 191
Montanez, Willie 177
Morgan, Joe 185
Moses, Robert 108, 109, 132–133, 135, 147–148, 150, 159, 193
Mota, Manny 197–200, 201
MOVE 223–227, 230, 231

New Eastwick Corporation (NEC) 214–216
1964 riot in North Philadelphia 118–120, 124
Nixon, President Richard 218–220
Novak, Robert 164
Nugent, Gerry (Phillies owner) 51, 64

O'Doul, Lefty 66
Oliver, Al 196
O'Malley, Walter (Dodgers owner) 62, 94, 175
"$100,000 infield" (Stuffy McInnis, Eddie Collins, Jack Barry, Frank "Home Run" Baker) 42, 79
One Liberty Place 230–231, 232
Owens, Paul 126, 165, 167
Ozark, Danny 26, 27, 28, 30, 55, 56, 57, 74, 75, 105, 130, 131, 154, 167, 173, 177, 178, 182, 183, 184, 188, 189, 195, 201, 202, 203, 205, 207, 209, 211

Pacific Coast League (PCL) 65–66, 68–69, 90–93
Paige, Satchel 51
Parker, Dave 196
Parkside Field 122
Penn Center 193, 229, 236; construction 144–147, 148
Pennock, Herb 79, 87, 111, 123
Perez, Tony 185
Perini, Lou (Boston/Milwaukee Braves owner) 93
Perrier, Georges 157, 158, 162, 163
Philadelphia City Planning Commission (CPC) 5, 135, 137, 138, 141, 144, 146, 156, 193, 229
Philadelphia Housing Authority (PHA) 115, 137
Phillips, Walter 136, 138, 141, 147, 156, 157, 166
Pipp, Wally 72–73
Plank, Eddie 49, 79, 88, 111
Polo Grounds 77
Posel, Ramon 162
Poses, Steve 158–159, 161, 163, 166, 233, 234
Potter, Nelson 84

Quinn, John 124

Rafsky, William 144
Rau, Doug 130, 131, 155, 171
Rautzhan, Lance 173, 198
Reach, Al 38
Reed, Ron 8, 30, 76, 104, 105, 128, 129, 130, 154
The Restaurant School 159–161
Rhoden, Rick 34, 52, 54, 55, 57, 75, 76, 105, 106, 129, 130, 131, 155, 171
Richard, J.R. 198, 199
Rickey, Branch 65, 69, 78, 122, 123
Rizzo, Frank (Philadelphia mayor) 5, 216–222, 225, 226, 227, 230, 231
Roberts, Robin 88, 111, 124
Robinson, Jackie 50, 69, 121–122
Rockefeller, John D. 108–109
Rogers, Steve 55
Rose, Pete 2, 185, 211
Rouse, Willard 229
Rowland, Clarence 91
Ruppert, Jacob (Yankees owner) 72
Russell, Bill (Celtics Center) 36
Russell, Bill (Dodgers Shortstop) 10, 11, 29, 30, 52, 76, 105, 106, 131, 155, 201, 202
Ruth, Babe 43, 71, 72, 79–80
Ruthven, Dick 210

"Safe Zone" (Center City) 146, 152, 156, 162, 212, 213, 217, 218
"Safety Fund" 19–21
Sain, Johnny 73
Samuel, Bernard (Philadelphia mayor) 107, 137
Sawyer, Eddie 114
Schmidt, Donna 181–182
Schmidt, Mike 2, 9, 10, 11, 12, 25, 27, 34, 52, 54, 55, 106, 128, 129, 130, 155, 166–167, 171, 176, 177, 181, 182, 183, 185, 191, 194, 200, 201, 203, 209, 210, 211
Schu, Rick 235
Second Bank of the United States 18–21, 107, 136, 164, 207
Selma, Dick 54
Seymour, Harold (baseball historian) 36
Shantz, Bobby 73, 102

Shea, Bill 113
Shibe, Benjamin 38, 39, 45–47, 61, 80, 83
Shibe Park: creation 45–47; mortgage 86; Phils
    relocation 49; renovation 80, 85
Simmons, Al 43, 49, 80, 88, 111
Simmons, Curt 88, 111, 124
Sizemore, Ted 10, 30, 31, 34, 75, 76, 129, 130, 131,
    154, 171, 173, 191, 198, 200, 201, 205, 209
Skinner, Bob 177, 178, 182
Slaughter, Enos 73
Smith, Lonnie 211
Smith, Reggie 8, 10, 11, 52, 105, 106, 131, 171, 172,
    173, 202
Society Hill 140–143, 146, 147, 148, 150, 156, 162–
    163, 193, 213, 221, 224, 229, 231
Somers, Charles W. 37, 38
Sosa, Elias 9, 130, 171, 172
Speaker, Tris 43
Spink, Al 61
Starr, Stephen 233–235
Stone, Ron 235
Stoneham, Charles (Giants owner) 60
Stonorov, Oscar 137, 140
Suzuki, Ichiro 113

Tanner, Chuck 175, 194
Tate, James (Philadelphia mayor) 156, 213, 216,
    217, 218
Taylor, Tony 124, 167, 184, 185
Terry, Ralph 73, 102
Thomas, Frank 124, 125
Thompson, "Big" Sam 37
Thomson, Bobby 231–232
Tipton, Joe 83
"Title I" (Housing Act of 1949) 139–140, 144, 147–
    148
Tolan, Bobby 182, 183
Topping, Dan (Yankees co-owner) 96, 97, 100,
    102, 110
Torre, Joe 176
"Treatment Alternative to Street Crime" program
    (TASC) 220

Treaty of Paris 13
Turley, Bob 73
Twain, Mark 23
Twitchell, Wayne 191

Unitas, Johnny 36
United Nations 107–110, 115
University City 146, 213, 224, 229–230

Van Buren, Martin 19–21, 107, 108, 165
Veeck, Bill (Browns owner) 92–97, 103
Vermeil, Dick 195
Veterans Stadium 1, 2, 4, 25, 151–153, 202, 207,
    211, 235
Von Starck, Peter 157, 163, 166

Waddell, Rube 49
Wagner, Robert (New York City mayor) 113
Water Works (Philadelphia) 144–145
Webb, Del (Yankees co-owner) 96, 97, 100, 102,
    110
Weinberger, Casper 148
Weiss, George 95
Wendlestadt, Harry 26, 28, 31, 32, 33, 34, 105
Wheat, Zack 43–44
Whitman Park (standoff over) 217
Whiz Kids (1950 pennant winners) 2, 86, 103, 111–
    112, 123
Williams, Ted 65, 113
Wilson, Willie 1
Winchell, Walter 122
Wine, Bobby 188
Wise, Rick 124
"Workshop of the World" (Philadelphia as) 17,
    18, 22, 115
Wrigley, Phil (Cubs owner) 62
Wrigley, William, Jr. (Cubs owner) 69, 94

Yawkey, Tom (Red Sox owner) 60
Yeager, Steve 10, 27, 28, 32, 34, 75, 76, 106, 129,
    172, 197, 198, 201